'A blow-by-blow account of the fateful day. I couldn't put it down.' *Independent*

'Gripping ... The hour-by-hour account is packed with fascinating and often poignant vignettes.' *Daily Express*

'Shows us the battle at its grittiest and bloodiest, but through it all manages to maintain a grip on the bigger picture.' *Scotsman*

'Kershaw writes well and makes sense of the battle ... a clear and straightforward military view.' *Literary Review*

'So where does this leave Robert Kershaw's *24 Hours at Waterloo*? Very simply, in a class of its own ... brings the events to life with judiciously chosen first-hand accounts ... there could be no better companion to the battlefield than Kershaw's.' *Spectator*

24 HOURS AT
WATERLOO
18 JUNE 1815

Robert Kershaw

WH
ALLEN

3 5 7 9 10 8 6 4 2

WH Allen, an imprint of Ebury Publishing,
20 Vauxhall Bridge Road,
London SW1V 2SA

WH Allen is part of the Penguin Random House group of companies
whose addresses can be found at global.penguinrandomhouse.com

Penguin
Random House
UK

First published by WH Allen in 2014
This edition published by WH Allen in 2015

www.eburypublishing.co.uk

A CIP catalogue record for this book is available from the British Library

ISBN 9780753541449

Maps by Tim Mitchell, Matt Stokes and Andy Screen
Typeset by e-type

Printed and bound in Great Britain by Clays Ltd, St Ives plc

For my wife, Lynn

Contents

10. The Road to Genappe
8.30 pm to Midnight

Waterloo Time-Line

1814	Napoleon is exiled to Elba, while the Allied Congress of Vienna decides the future of Europe after French Imperial rule.
8 JANUARY 1815	In North America, US forces under Andrew Jackson defeat a British advance on New Orleans despite the war ending a month earlier.
15 JANUARY	Lord Nelson's mistress, Emma, Lady Hamilton dies in Calais, France, where she fled to avoid her debts.
16 FEBRUARY	Napoleon escapes exile in Elba and arrives at Cannes, southern France, with a force of 1,500 men on 1 March. The '100 Days Campaign' clock begins.
6 MARCH	Corn Bill riots in London are put down by the army.
13 MARCH	The Allies declare Napoleon an outlaw.
19 MARCH	Louis XVIII, France's Bourbon king, flees to Ghent, Belgium.
20 MARCH	Napoleon enters Paris in triumph, after marching through France with a gathering force, averaging 23 miles and facing down opposition each day. French re-armament begins.

23 MARCH   Parliament passes the Corn Bill to protect grain farmers. The army fires upon further riots.

25 MARCH   The Allies declare war on Napoleon. Recruiting and mobilisations begin in Britain, Prussia, Austria and Russia. Napoleon raises 300,000 men within eight weeks.

28 MARCH   The *Thames* paddle steamer is the first steam ship to carry passengers and cargo from Dublin to London.

5 APRIL   Wellington assumes command of the multi-national (seven nations in all) Allied army in Belgium.

29 APRIL   Napoleon announces the re-establishment of Imperial control in France.

MAY–JUNE   The Allied and Prussian armies deploy south and east of Brussels near the French border.

9 JUNE   Belgium and Holland are united by the Treaty of Vienna to form the Kingdom of the Netherlands under the Prince of Orange.

15 JUNE   Napoleon's Armeé du Nord invades Belgium at Charleroi and unexpectedly emerges between Wellington and Blücher's Prussian army. Both Blücher and Wellington, the latter attending the Duchess of Richmond's ball in Brussels, are completely surprised.

16 JUNE   The Prussians are pushed back from the French border and badly mauled at Ligny before Blücher's army can fully assemble. Wellington's army arrives too late to support the Prussians and barely manages to hold the line at Quatre-Bras.

17/18 JUNE	Wellington's army falls back on Waterloo ten miles south of Brussels during a violent summer storm as the Prussian army retreats north to Wavre, roughly parallel to the east. Only Wellington's army blocks Napoleon's entry to Brussels.
MIDNIGHT 17 JUNE	The Allied and French armies deploy on the opposing ridges of Mont St Jean and La Belle Alliance.
03.30	Wellington receives confirmation that the Prussians will come to his aid.
04.45	Sunrise. The vanguard formation of the Prussian army, von Bülow's IV Corps, moves through Wavre en route to Waterloo.
06.00–10.00	The two opposing armies at Waterloo breakfast and deploy.
10.30	Napoleon stages a precise French military review as they deploy to intimidate the opposing army.
11.20	The French Grande Batterie opens fire and the first French feint attacks by Reille's II Corps are mounted against the Hougoumont farm complex.
13.30	Napoleon's main effort of the day, the massed infantry attacks by d'Erlon's I Corps, are mounted against the centre of the Mont St Jean ridge. They are repelled and routed by British heavy cavalry. Napoleon sees the Prussians approaching from the east.
16.00	Marshal Ney directs massed French cavalry charges between La Haye Sainte in the east and Hougoumont farm to the west, thinking Wellington's army is in retreat. The Allied infantry squares hold and are pounded all afternoon.

16.30 The Prussians emerge to the east of the battle-field and attack Plancenoit, which is bitterly held by the French.

18.30 La Haye Sainte farm falls to the French, and Wellington's line is visibly teetering in the centre.

19.30 Napoleon commits the Imperial Guard reserve as his last ditch effort to break Wellington's line. Never defeated before, they are repelled.

20.00 Von Ziethen's Prussian I Corps links up with the left of Wellington's line. The French army is broken and in full retreat, as the Prussians flood the battlefield from the east. Plancenoit finally falls to the Prussians.

20.30 Wellington orders a general advance by the Allied army.

20.55 Sunset. The French are in full retreat.

21.00 Wellington meets Blücher near the Belle Alliance inn and the pursuit is handed over to the Prussians.

MIDNIGHT The French retreat has become a rout, log-jammed around the small bridge at Genappe.

19 JUNE Grouchy breaks off his battle with the Prussian rearguard at Wavre and retreats into France.

21 JUNE Napoleon arrives back in Paris and abdicates the following day.

29 JUNE Viscount Castlereagh, the British Foreign Secretary, proposes a public monument be erected to commemorate the Battle of Waterloo.

3 JULY	The Allied army occupies Paris.
8 JULY	Louis XVIII returns to Paris.
15 JULY	Napoleon surrenders aboard HMS *Bellerophon* and is exiled to St Helena, where he dies six years later.

Waterloo Campaign Map

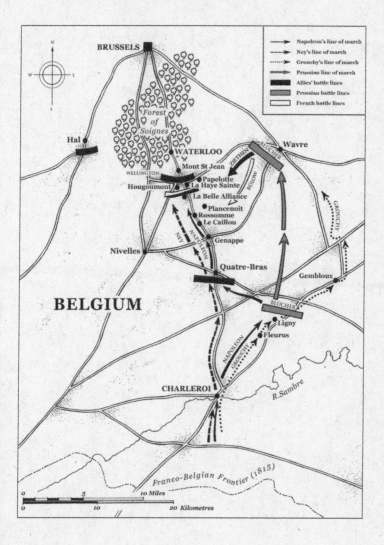

Introduction

When Napoleon stepped ashore at Cannes in the south of France on 1 March 1815, the clock was running against him. He had been becalmed for much of the tense three-day voyage following his narrowly achieved escape from British exile at Elba. There was barely time to paint his small brigantine the *Inconstant* to resemble a British navy ship during the brief period his minder, Colonel Sir Neil Campbell, had sailed to Italy to visit his doctor. Campbell had taken HMS *Partridge*, the only Royal Navy ship picketing the harbour at Portoferraio, Elba's capital. Napoleon was still becalmed and in sight of Elba when HMS *Partridge* returned.

Campbell observed 'three sail' to the southwest, but chose not to investigate. French Royalist sloops encountering Napoleon's miniature fleet of six ships merely waved them by with a benign eye. Tension was high on landing, the voyage having taken 60 hours instead of the anticipated 15. Time was of the essence as Napoleon set off to Paris, 800 kilometres to the northwest, with just over 1,000 men. Campbell was carpeted by British Foreign Secretary Castlereagh once the news was out. The rumour was that he was visiting Italy to see his mistress rather than the doctor.

The headlines of the French newspaper and official broadsheet *Le Moniteur Universel* charted Napoleon's emotional re-conquest of France. He transitioned from the 'Corsican Ogre' and 'Monster' to the Emperor. In two weeks the tone of the reportage changed from 'The Cannibal has left his den' to 'His Majesty the Emperor today made his public entry' to Paris on 20 March and 'nothing can exceed the universal joy'. One week earlier the Allies had declared Napoleon an outlaw, and five days after his entry to Paris, they declared war on him.[1]

Napoleon's 1,000 men had burgeoned into two divisions on arrival in Paris and France rearmed. British cavalry regiments policing the Corn Bill riots in London that March were immediately diverted to the south coast and embarked for Ostend in Belgium. By April, Wellington was in command of the multi-national Allied army deployed to the southwest of Brussels alongside von Blücher's Prussian army to the southeast.

Two and a half months later, Napoleon invaded Belgium, and the *24 Hours at Waterloo* clock began running as, during the early hours of 18 June 1815, more than 150,000 mud-splattered, disgruntled soldiers filed into makeshift bivouacs and open fields beneath teeming rain. The armies gathered in an area five kilometres wide by four deep, separated by a valley with two gentle ridges in between. Any chances of repositioning or even posturing for tactical advantage were over. Seventy-two hours of exhausting marching and counter-marching after the Emperor Napoleon had 'humbugged' the Duke of Wellington's Allied army had taken their toll. The French had suddenly appeared at Charleroi between the two Allied armies of Wellington and Blücher on 15 June, coming as if from nowhere.

Blücher's Prussian army, caught off balance, was badly mauled the following day at Ligny, before they could even form up with just three of their four corps. Painfully they fell back northwards, shedding disgruntled deserters all the way, to Wavre some 13 miles away. Wellington's forces, arriving too late to support, had to fight a piecemeal engagement at

Quatre-Bras, to Blücher's northwest. It was a tense and costly affair and they only just managed to hold their ground. Once the Prussians retreated on his left, Wellington had no option except to backtrack nine miles north towards Brussels, to maintain linkage and cohesion with his worsted ally. Napoleon, as intended, had snatched the initiative, by placing himself undetected between the two armies on invading Belgium 48 hours before. Now, it was the unexpected appearance of a brutal summer storm that was dictating events.

All three armies moved laboriously, as best they could. They saw each other only fleetingly if at all. Off-road movement was impossible in knee-deep mud, and conditions worsened by the hour. The French snapped at Wellington's heels because only one road led to Brussels. Blücher's army had disappeared in the gloom. Some of it was spotted by the French heading north to Wavre, but the bulk of his force, evidenced by the large numbers of Prussian stragglers and deserters they came across, appeared to be heading east, as expected, towards Namur and home. Wellington's men, filing along the Mont St Jean ridge, knew they would be going no further, instinctively recognising that they would fight on this ground at daybreak.

There was no battle-winning intelligence available to provide an opportunity for anything other than a stand-up fight. Waterlogged open fields bordered by undulating woodland both to the left and to the right towards Brussels offered little chance of creative manoeuvre. Time was limited for Napoleon. Somewhere to the east was a badly mauled Prussian army. Its arrival was unpredictable. All that remained for the French to do, they assumed, was lever aside this final rearguard screening Brussels. Lunch inside the city beckoned. But their opponents were going nowhere. This was to be a one-on-one, bare-knuckle prize fight, the sort of all-out contest familiar to soldiers in an age of endemic violence.

The only unknown was whether the Prussians would arrive late. Commanders had little idea; line soldiers had none. Over the next 24 hours another 48,000 soldiers would join the 150,000 crammed into this same constricted area with 60,000 horses and 537 artillery pieces. Europe would never see its like again, so many men and animals fighting a major battle in such a small space. The horde of soldiers arriving at the beginning of the 24-hour cycle would be gone by its close. At the finish one in four men would be dead or maimed, falling at the rate of 5,400 men per hour or one or two per second.[2] Room was so limited that bodies would be piled on top of each other. A war was lost and won during these 24 hours, the outcome reshaping imperial Europe into something more like today's form.

Waterloo was the last mass battle of the pre-industrial age to be fought in Europe. War would never again be fought in such splendid uniforms. Robust, healthy-looking soldiers from peasant stock would be superseded by pale, slightly-built men coming from the undernourished urban poor of post-industrial Europe. At Waterloo, despite the density and lethality of flying missiles, there was still a good chance of being slashed by a sabre or pierced by bayonet and sword. The next large-scale European conflict would be fought with ant-like armies dressed in drab khaki serge or grey in 1914. Millions of soldiers would face weapons of mass destruction, the machine-gun, gas and huge railway-mounted artillery pieces.

When the armies lined up facing each other from opposing ridge lines at Waterloo, nobody could predict the outcome. Communication was by word of mouth, the beat of the drum, bugle call or dispatch-rider. Events were influenced and constrained by what individuals could see or hear. Almost by definition the vast majority of participants had little clue about what was going on, but because the battlefield was such a small arena they could see a lot, and later write about it.

The prime attraction of the battle of Waterloo is that it is such a human tale, best told from a roving correspondent's eye view. Recently published sources have unearthed more stories from the ranks. These provide a more earthy contrast to the officer accounts famously harvested by H L Siborne in his *Waterloo Letters*, to support his famous battlefield model. Sergeants were only appointed if they could write, as they maintained many of the mundane company rolls. *24 Hours at Waterloo* draws upon much of this previously unseen material.

The outcome of the battle was, in Wellington's words, 'the nearest run thing you ever saw in your life'. The two days leading up to the battle had been an unmitigated disaster for the Anglo-Allies, outmanoeuvred, separated and badly mauled during Napoleon's deft opening moves. Wellington's staunchest ally, the Prussian general Blücher, had 'got so damnably licked', the Duke declared, 'I could not find him on Saturday morning'. Now it was Sunday and he was still not sure where Blücher was. Wellington had his back against Brussels walls, only ten kilometres to his rear. Napoleon was on the cusp of claiming his deserved prize. His carriage was prepared for the ceremonial entry and the Brussels proclamations were already written.

This is not a story about the commanders' deliberations, so often handled in previous Waterloo accounts; it is rather the impact that their command decisions had upon their men. The soldiers' day began with four hours of fitful sleep in the pouring rain. Exhausted by 72 hours of fighting and counter-marching, they slumped, crouched or simply lay in the mud. Drizzly daybreak merged into watery sunlight, enabling soaked soldiers five to six hours of watchful contemplation to ponder their chances of survival as corps and brigades formed up. The opposing sides were never more than 1,200 yards apart and sometimes as close as 300. There was plenty of time for nervous reflection amid the flag-waving, band-playing reviews that preceded the battle as they recovered from their night-time chills. A gentle breeze began to evaporate some of the moisture from the field. The format of the next nine and a half hours of savage fighting across this mud-splattered landscape was simple. The British and Allied troops stubbornly clung to the higher Mont St Jean ridge, desperately seeking a delayed Prussian arrival, while the French attacked tenaciously from the ridge line of La Belle Alliance opposite, to get them off.

People have written about the battle of Waterloo for 200 years. The wealth of first-hand accounts, diaries and letters offer the type of grainy authenticity and immediacy commonly used in TV war reports. Extraordinary images of men and women emerge from these accounts, as colourful as any contemporary tabloid newspaper. Life was filtered through entirely different perspectives compared to today. Pain and risk was accepted. Physical suffering was the lot of the nineteenth-century soldier in a society where people laboured hard simply to sustain life.

Death and mutilation were everyday occurrences. Violence was hardly unusual in an age whose sport and pastimes included bear-baiting, ratting, cock-fighting, duels and bare-knuckle prize fighting. An agrarian existence could be harsh. If a farm labourer broke his leg he would probably end up severely disabled or even dead. He could lose his smallholding and starve, leaving his family destitute. Childbirth complications would lead to death, and children taken ill often died. Military life by contrast was not half so bad.

Soldiers were fed, clothed and sheltered. Despite all this, the Waterloo battlefield bordered on the extreme, even by the harsh standards of the day. Hardened campaigners who had seen Europe's worst were taken aback.

24 Hours at Waterloo monitors a battle fought between three armies. The nine national groups fighting represent an interesting microcosm of the future members of the present-day European Community. There were British, French, Prussians and Germans. Among the Germans there were Hanoverians, Nassauers and Brunswickers and alongside them were Poles, Danes, Swiss and Croats. Netherlands troops belonged to a barely formed national confederation, while the Dutch-Belgians had spent the previous few decades fighting with Napoleon. This lack of cohesion at the soldier level in Wellington's army has never really been explored. Napoleon's forces by contrast were nationally pure and veterans. As would be anticipated, the clock in *24 Hours at Waterloo* is the constant throughout, providing the thread linking personal accounts dimmed by memory or tinged with national prejudice. Timings are, however, not as accurate as suggested. No two time-pieces on the battlefield gave the same reading. Accuracy is to within a half-hour, sometimes an hour, dependent on the accepted historical interpretation.

Time for the soldiers was simply about the present. How long would they have to endure this awful weather? When would they fight the battle? When might they eat? Were their lives to be measured in hours? *24 Hours at Waterloo* is about the soldier's day. Days and hours tended to become subsumed by heart-stopping incidents that lasted minutes. Flashbacks permanently imprinted on subconscious thoughts in perpetuity, if they lived.

CHAPTER I

Summer Storm —•

Midnight to 2 am

00.10 am

Night and Driving Rain

It had been raining for almost ten hours when the village clocks at Waterloo and Plancenoit struck midnight, heralding the start of a day to remember: 18 June 1815. For five of those hours rain had lashed the retreating Anglo-Allied columns falling back nine miles from Quatre-Bras to the village of Mont St Jean, just short of Waterloo. Many had marched 30 to 40 miles and fought a bitter battle in torrid heat 48 hours before. Some on arrival had covered 65 miles. The majority had not eaten. Hard marching, stifling heat and an indecisive battle with no food after a comfortable period of waiting in Belgium had taxed minds and bodies. Tired and dispirited, they had no greatcoats and the rain was freezing. The veterans were philosophical, but instinctively knew their situation had to improve. The French were pursuing them hotly and were close behind.

Summers since 1810 had been consistently poor, with severe winters in between. The winter of 1812 had witnessed the destruction of Napoleon's Grande Armée in Russia. England was experiencing its coldest June for three centuries; it had not been as bad as this since the 1690s. The uncharacteristic heat wave that preceded Wellington's battle at Quatre-Bras two days before lasted until about 2 pm the following day. 'The first part of the day was sultry, not a breath of air to be felt,' recalled Sergeant Edward Cotton, with the

7th Hussars. Temperatures climbed to 21° centigrade and then sank by 4.5° when cold air swept in from the west. An especially deep low, preceded by the fresh winds of an emerging cold front, crept up on the retreating columns. Despite their weariness, soldiers stopped looking at the plodding heels in front of them and looked with trepidation at the ominous mushroom cloud bearing down on them. Captain Alexander Mercer commanding a British horse artillery battery saw that the sky, 'overcast since the morning', had transitioned to 'a most extraordinary appearance':

> *Large isolated masses of thundercloud, of the deepest, almost inky black, their lower edges hard and strongly defined, lagging down, as if momentarily about to burst, hung suspended over us.*

Diminishing light began to cloak the retreating columns in a 'deep and gloomy obscurity'. Huge cumulo-nimbus clouds rolled in with their distinctive light 'mamma' underside. The pursuing French remained momentarily bathed in a brilliant sunlight.[1]

This significant meteorological event dropped barometer mercury levels seven millibars over 12 hours. 'The first gun that was fired' at them, Mercer recalled:

> *... seemed to burst the clouds overhead, for its report was instantly followed by an awful clap of thunder, and lightning that almost blinded us, whilst the rain came down as if a waterspout had broken over us.*

Sergeant Thomas Morris, among the columns of the 73rd Foot, leaning into the ascent of a steep hill, was overtaken by a turbulent sky that seemed to come down and touch the ground. 'We appeared to be enveloped in clouds, densely charged with electric fluid,' he remembered. 'Heaven and earth was coming together,' claimed Private John Lewis, with the 2/95th Rifles. 'The rain fell on so hard that the oldest soldiers there never saw the like in their life.' Morris and his companions slithered down slopes, just managing to stay on their feet amid rain that 'descended literally in torrents'. Behind them they could hear the unsettling distant reports of French cannon mingling with clashes of thunder.[2]

Wellington's columns were occupying the Mont St Jean ridge, 11 miles south of Brussels in the eerie light produced by the pouring rain. The ridge line was the final significant tactical obstacle to be crossed before reaching the city, something he had identified the year before. The French could be checked here.

Rain continued to cascade in sheets. Wellington's men on the Mont St Jean ridge were blundering about in pitch-blackness in the absence of any ambient light. The moon was between its first and second quarter and nobody could see anything[3] as they fanned out east and west along the ridge line either side of the north–south Brussels road where it intersected at the centre with the Nivelles road, branching off to the southwest. Waterloo village lay one and a half miles beyond, half a mile short of the road entrance to the Forest of Soignes. Only 12 hours earlier this area covering six to eight square miles had been completely devoid of troops. Now the 2,500 inhabitants of Mont St Jean and 1,800 in Waterloo had fled. By midnight on 17 June, Wellington's army numbering some 73,000 were deployed along the ridge line, milling about in the darkness. Opposite them were about 40,000 Frenchmen slowly closing on the opposite Belle Alliance ridge, the vanguard of Napoleon's army of 77,500. The rest were strung out in the rain from Plancenoit village and the Belle Alliance inn back to Quatre-Bras and beyond. Count d'Erlon's I Corps was moving up first. Its 17,000 infantry, 1,500 cavalry and 48 guns with caissons and trains stretched across seven to eight miles of muddy, deeply rutted roads to the south, beyond Genappe and Quatre-Bras. D'Erlon's huge column snake was just one of six corps laboriously trying to move up.

Nine miles further east was another concentration of intense military activity. Around Wavre, with its 4,000 inhabitants, 100,000 Prussians were gathering. Six miles to the south were 30,000 Frenchmen from Grouchy's corps, blundering around in the dark looking for them. Another 8,000 Prussian deserters were straggling or sleeping rough off roads and tracks leading east towards Namur. By first light there would be 150,000 men packed into the small area Wellington had identified as his battlefield. The numbers would expand to 200,000 before nightfall. Then, after eight hours of slaughter, it would empty again.

Few of Wellington's men forming up on the high ground in the wind and rain had the wit to appreciate they had been here just 48 hours before. 'We halted in a corn field for the night,' wrote Sergeant William Wheeler, with the 51st Regiment. 'As the storm continued, without any signs of abatement, and the night was setting in, orders were given to pile arms,' remembered Sergeant Thomas Morris, with the 73rd Regiment, 'but no man was on any account to quit his position.' Conditions were appalling; they stood knee-deep in mud and shivered. 'Under such circumstances our prospect of a night's lodging was anything but cheering.' Lieutenant William Hay recalled riding in late with the last 12th Light Dragoon rearguards:

> *The country around was covered with growing crops of wheat and rye in full ear, and, from the rain that had fallen and the height of the corn, it was like riding through a pond.*[4]

The scene two days before had been entirely different. Lieutenant John Kincaid with the 1/95th Rifles had breakfasted in the small inn on the left side of Waterloo village, pausing in the welcome sun after the shady passage of the Forest of Soignes. Quatre-Bras lay ahead. He saw the Duke of Wellington appear. 'I have since been convinced,' he later wrote, 'that his lordship had thought it probable that the position of Waterloo might even that day have become the scene of the action.' Sergeant Edward Costello, also with Rifles, recalled the brief stopover, 'a beautiful summer morning – the sun slowly rising above the horizon and peeping through the trees, while our men were merry as crickets, laughing and joking with each other'. Kincaid had returned and this time it 'rained excessively hard the greater part of the night'.

The storm aided Wellington's retreat because French cavalry were unable to pursue off the roads. Lieutenant William Turner, with the 13th Light Dragoons, had previously observed: 'The cavalry have advanced here chiefly by cross-country roads through the fields as it is not enclosed as in England.' But on pulling back the French cavalry were unable to harass retreating infantry without crossing swords with British mounted rearguards, blocking the single road. Attempts to move across the fields resulted in sinking up to the horses' hocks and even bellies in glutinous mud. 'The country here is open, rich in corn, and having occasionally large and rather thick woods,' remembered Colonel Augustus Frazer, commanding Wellington's horse artillery. In contrast to pre-industrial England, where enclosed fields were the distinguishing rural feature, the Belgian countryside was 'undulating and deep, but without hedges or obstacles of any kind to the movements of all arms'. This was ideal campaigning country, but not after a summer storm.[5]

The events of the previous 24 hours had visibly affected the local civilians. The charged atmosphere that accompanied the optimistic Allied march out from Brussels, with a roadside breakfast in the sun outside Waterloo, was gone. One of Wellington's quartermaster staff noticed that 'among the inhabitants themselves there was little appearance of excitement'. Napoleon's escape from Elba created a fanfare three months ago, but:

> They had seen too much of armies during the early portion of the preceding year to think more of them as a passing storm, highly disagreeable in its effects – an avoidable evil, to be borne with patient resignation.

Now the eight square miles around Waterloo were filling with even more troops, so the locals abandoned their houses.

Europe had declared war on Napoleon and massed huge armies. The French were grossly outnumbered, and until June the Anglo-Allied and Prussian armies in Belgium thought *they* would be doing the attacking. It was the French, however, who first attacked, at Charleroi, to the south. Lieutenant Henry Dehnel, with the King's German Legion, recalled the impact of the precipitate retreat from Quatre-Bras on the locals. 'Crowds of country people, loaded with their possessions and driving their cattle ahead, fled with wives and children in all directions.' Hundreds of them trudged into the comparative safety of the Forest of Soignes and began to erect shelters in the pouring rain.

The long irregular street of whitewashed cottages in Waterloo was left empty. English advance parties arrived and began scrawling names on the wooden doors. Charlotte Eaton, on holiday in Belgium, saw the chalk marks with '"His Grace the Duke of Wellington", "His Royal Highness the Prince of Orange" and other pompous titles written on the doors of these little thatched cottages'. 'All the inhabitants of Mont St Jean had fled from this village,' observed Captain John Whale, with the 1st Life Guards. There was one solitary exception, a woman who shut herself up in a farmhouse garret at the end of the village. 'All she had in the world was there,' Whale recalled, 'poultry, cows, calves and pigs', and the woman insisted she was going nowhere. 'If she did not stay to take care of them they would all be destroyed or carried off.'

She was right, because this empty eight square miles of potential battlefield was rapidly filling with soaking wet and very hungry soldiers. Doors, window shutters and furniture were quickly ransacked from houses and used for firewood. Carts, ploughs, harrows, wheelbarrows and anything combustible followed. Enterprising soldiers were soon selling chairs to officers, recalled John Gordon Smith, an Assistant Surgeon with the 12th Light Dragoons, anything that stood clear of the mud. 'Officers were paying two francs for them,' he remembered, 'and the men seemed, at first, to be very well able to keep up the supply.' However, they were soon sold out and Smith himself had to buy a bundle of straw.[6]

Private Thomas Jeremiah, with the 23rd Regiment, had marched 24 miles that day. 'We began to feel the wolf biting,' he recalled, 'formed hard marching and little sleeping is none so pleasant without nourishment.' His parent unit the 4th Division had missed Quatre-Bras and needed to march 65 miles to reach the battlefield. 'We were greatly fatigued from the extreme inclemency of this day's weather,' he admitted, 'the greatest rain that ever I saw, the heavens seemed to have opened their sluices and the celestial floodgates bursted open.' They deployed on the ridge north of the Nivelles road. Having out-marched their baggage and stores they found 'not an ounce of bread could be obtained in all the place' and half a ration of spirits per man was scant compensation. 'Hunger bites harder than a wet shirt,' he complained, 'poor comfort after two days hard marching and not so much as a mouthful of anything except water.' Jeremiah wasted little time and soon 'myself and my comrade took two wooden cudgels each and our haversacks and went to seek something to eat', as did thousands of others. Four to five German soldiers were spotted brandishing knives and bayonets, chasing after a pig and a calf. Only armed with cudgels, they decided the Germans were unlikely to share. Nearby was a flour wagon, also being ransacked by their German allies. They joined the boisterous queue, and 'in the struggle to get at the casks of flour, in the scuffle, I tumbled into the flour cask,' Jeremiah recalled. The result was 'flour stuck to the wet coat and I was as wet if not white as a miller'. He would fight the coming battle appropriately cloaked as a ghostly white spectre.

'Although midsummer was near,' Private Thomas Playford, with the 2nd Life Guards cavalry, remembered, 'we passed an uncomfortable night exposed to a cold wind and to heavy rain.' All along the ridge, men willed and prayed for the succour of dawn to end this agony. As temperatures dropped further, bodies overheated from the intense march were chilled:

> There we stood on soaked ploughed ground, shivering wet, and hungry; for there was neither food for man nor horse. Some soldiers complained of the hardship, some jested at their sufferings, and others tried to guess at what would happen on the morrow; and some hinted at the probability that not many of us would see the 19th June. But no one believed in gloomy prognostications.

The cavalrymen pulled down a fence, started a fire and gathered round, a small disconsolate group, intermittently lit by its flickering flame. 'But we gained little good by standing round it,' Playford admitted, 'for while one side was warming the other was cold and wet.' They decided to forage for food at dawn, but that would not be for three or four hours.[7]

Among the last troops to march in were the 95th Rifles, who had formed part of the army's rearguard with the cavalry. Richard Eyre, a second lieutenant with the 2nd Battalion, remembered covering 51 miles before arrival, 'like so many half drowned and half starved rats'. 'Our boots were in a poor state almost falling apart,' recalled Private Thomas Knight, marching up with the 3rd Battalion, 'the straps of our gaiters had snapped from the suction of the mud, which left them flapping about our ankles'. There were no greatcoats; they had been abandoned in the heat and left with the baggage.

Typical campaign loads varied between 60 and 80 lbs, badly carried inside a rudimentary tarred cloth and leather knapsack. This had an uncomfortable wooden frame and inhibiting chest strap, which tended to constrict the lungs painfully while on the march. The Baker rifle carried by the Rifles was only a half pound lighter than the 9 lbs 11 oz standard issue 'Brown Bess' India Pattern smoothbore musket and bayonet issued to the rest of the infantry. The average height of the British infantry at Waterloo was about 5 ft 7 ins. The Rifles recruited under the regulation height but insisted on a larger chest measurement, making for shorter but stockier infantrymen. Rifleman Harris, who had served in the Peninsula, commented, 'On service it was always the taller men that felt the hardship of a forced march before their smaller comrades!'

The Rifles uniforms were green, but with poor dye and pouring rain they had turned virtually black. Issue uniforms fitted badly, being in the main too large, tending to hang limply on lightly built soldiers who never got enough to eat. Boots in 1815 were a single issue; there was no such thing as a right or left foot. New recruits suffered regularly with blistered feet. Ensign Thomas Wedgewood, with the 3rd Foot Guards, wrote to his father complaining that for the first three days of the campaign he could not take his boots off: 'They got wet several times and dried again on my feet, and when I got them off at last, I could not get them on again without cutting the leather half-way down my foot.' The result was that 'the insteps of my feet were made quite raw'.

The Rifle companies already based in the Netherlands had not been issued new uniforms for two years. Thomas Knight among them recalled:

My own trousers being unserviceable I purchased two pairs of civilian ones of which both pairs split on the first day I wore them, I was however able to make one good pair out of the two torn pairs.

Even then it was not permitted to patch red or white over green. Knight described the state of the 3/95th slithering about on the Mont St Jean ridge following the 'mud march', which had left them tired, soaked to the skin, cold, hungry and splattered with mud. Each man sported a few days' growth of greasy beard.

On arrival the soldiers bivouacked in the open with improvised shelters. Peninsula veteran Lieutenant George Simmons, with the 1/95th, shared his makeshift shelter with a fellow soldier utilising a soaking wet blanket 'plastered over with thick clay', of which there was no shortage. They settled down on a couple of knapsacks, which doubled as pillows. His companion:

... dragged the loamy one [blanket] carefully over all, we were now as comfortable as possible. We heard the rain pelting on the clay in an agreeable manner which soon lulled us to sleep.[8]

1 am

'Foreigners' and Bad Memories

For many of the inexperienced foreign units in Wellington's army, this was to be their first experience of hard campaigning. Second Lieutenant Heinrich von Gagern, with the Nassau regiment, admitted that Quatre-Bras was his first battle and the next day was 'the first night I ever spent in the open air'. Moreover, the retreat to Waterloo 'was the very first day on which I had to walk on foot for a day's march because I had to leave my little black horse with the regiment'. His misfortunes had cumulatively piled up:

I had nothing to eat but dry bread for two days, and, secondly, after, had a fit of nausea that very morning, and, thirdly, having to suffer through the fiercest heat until about three o'clock in the afternoon, which left me all wet [with perspiration]. At three o'clock we had a terrible downpour. Everything that had become wet from the heat was now totally soaked by the rain.

During the hot temperatures he had given his heavy coat to a soldier to carry, and now as he 'slogged on through the mud' he did not have one. All he ate that day was a piece of half raw pork with some bread, which was more than most. The night 'was awful', he remembered, achieving just three hours' sleep, soaked through, lying on wheat straw. 'By twelve o'clock I had had enough and started to stand by the fire to dry myself on all sides,' he recalled. There was no chance to change any clothes because 'my portmanteau had been left with the baggage'. A rather precocious young von Gagern was beginning to learn that inclement weather was no respecter of rank.

Sergeant Johann Heinrich Doring's mood had darkened when, with the 28th Nassau Regiment, he watched a troop of Scots Greys lay about reluctant Dutch soldiers with the flat of their swords. They were forcing them across a hip-deep water crossing during the 'mud march' from Quatre-Bras.

Under these circumstances and feeling that everything was lost, we eventually reached the Waterloo farm under continuous downpours, and with the fire of the pursuing French following us.

Doring's unit formed part of the 2nd Netherlands Division, which had acquitted itself well at Quatre-Bras. Despite orders to the contrary it hung on to the vital crossroads until help arrived, losing nearly one in four men in the process. The British had glossed over their achievement and, he felt, handled them unsympathetically during the retreat. British preconceived notions about the shortcomings of foreign units had been confirmed by the sort of incidents Doring saw on the line of retreat. There had been confusion on arrival at the Mont St Jean ridge, which was not helped by language difficulties. 'The entire army was then put in battle order on both sides of Waterloo,' Doring remembered, 'involving an unending marching back and forth.' His regiment was deployed to the east side of the ridge line. During all the toing and froing 'I lost one of my shoes, which remained stuck in the heavy mud.' Fortunately he had another in his backpack. Troops upended muskets and stuck them in the ground with their bayonets to keep the loaded cartridges dry.

Little sleep was had that night. False alarms abounded after everyone had thrown themselves down in the mud to gain a little rest. They were so tired that 'no thought was given to food and drink, even if available'. The sharp report of an accidental musket shot led to an outbreak of shouting. Momentary panic ensued among the inexperienced troops, spooked by the darkness and poor visibility into believing they were under attack. It was rumoured the French had broken through on the right 'and were upon us in full force', Doring recalled:

> *Within a short time, that news proved to be unfounded. But only someone who has been through all this, on a pitch-dark night with constant rain and even a thunderstorm, can have an idea of what that did to our spirits.*

His friend Sergeant Achenbach was one of the first to be woken up in the flurry of activity and 'broke out into a series of the most violent curses'. This was worse than anything he had experienced throughout all his campaigns, he complained, saying he 'was sorry that a ball had not made an end to his life during the past days'. They both settled down again, trying to achieve at least some fitful rest. 'Lying down,' Doring remembered, 'we both burrowed so deep into the mud that [it was] only with difficulty we could get up again'.[9]

Captain Carl Jacobi, with the Hanoverian Lüneburg Battalion, recalled the fatiguing mud march along 'almost bottomless tracks; only with great effort could one extract one's feet from the mud, and many a shoe remained stuck in it'. Arriving shortly before dusk they appreciated the large numbers of troops deployed to their sides and rear meant 'that the retreat was over at least for today'. They were at the centre of the Mont St Jean ridge line. Rifles were stacked and the troops allowed to rest. 'But what kind of rest was it that we now faced?' Jacobi complained. There was no food and 'our raging thirst could not be stilled; those sent off to obtain water returned with empty canteens'. Somebody had already snapped the rope on the well bucket at the farm. Thousands of troops were crowding the ridge and the few wells supplying the needs of the surrounding villages had already been virtually 'emptied to the last drop'.

Jacobi was separated from his coat, which had been taken by his orderly, missing somewhere to the rear. 'Here I was dressed only in the short uniform (dolman) and was so thoroughly soaking wet that the falling sheets of rain penetrated directly to my skin.' He was still wearing tight dress boots instead of more comfortable and practical ones. 'I had already noticed that on my feet, swollen from my exertions and from dampness, some sore spots had developed.' Trench foot was burgeoning, not helped by the fact that 'the heavy rain had turned the ground of the fields that served as a camping sites to sludge, into which the grain stalks had been trampled'. There was no chance of retrieving fresh boots from his portmanteau, which was on his horse, at the rear. One of the superior officers noticed his predicament and generously offered him a blanket – his orderly's, however, not his own. 'I accepted it like a gift from heaven,' Jacobi remembered. Morale in the Lüneburg Battalion was reflecting the dismal weather. With his feet hurting when he walked, Jacobi was reduced to listlessly standing around in the pouring rain, bleakly regarding the flickering flame that 'offered so little warmth' to the stiff limbs surrounding it. The fire looked as if it might go out at any moment.

I was reduced to complete indifference to being alive or not; my limbs collapsed from exhaustion and chill; my soul no

longer seemed to dwell in my body. My total exhaustion even-
tually overcame everything and, notwithstanding my stiffness,
I fell asleep.

The rank and file were accustomed to privation and hardier than some of the privileged officers. Like all practical soldiers, they made the best of poor conditions. Captain von Scriba was in the Bremen Battalion of the 1st Hanoverian Brigade, the same as Jacobi's. He acknowledged that 'the night of the 17/18 June was extremely uncomfortable'. Persistent rain, which lasted throughout the night, 'brought markedly low temperatures, which felt like late October', he remembered. There was not a dry spot to be found, so 'most of the men remained standing up during the terrible night'. Better to fight than endure such conditions, many thought, but as von Scriba thoughtfully regarded his men, he was reassured:

Although spirits were low under these conditions, I can never-
theless attest to the fact that our fine men good naturedly put up
with the inevitable and, at most, loudly expressed their displea-
sure with the terrible weather.[10]

Sergeant William Wheeler, with the 51st Regiment, was 5 ft 9 ins tall. His dark hair and swarthy complexion, from service in Spain, made him look like the wily veteran he was. The 30-year-old former labourer from Bath had experienced poor conditions in the Low Countries before, having participated in the ill-fated Walcheren expedition of 1809. Having liberated the purse of a fleeing Belgian cavalryman after Quatre-Bras, he and his comrades were making the best of a bad job. The purse had provided money to buy cheese, bread and 'Hollands' gin from one of the enterprising civilians who had remained in Waterloo village. 'Having plenty of liquor' was a distraction from the teeming rain. 'We were, to use an expression of one of my old comrades, "wet and comfortable",' he recalled. Peninsula veterans wryly reminded recruits that rain had preceded their successes at Fuentus d'Onor, Salamanca and Vittoria. 'Thunder and lightning,' Wheeler commented 'was always the prelude to a victory.'

Not far to his left Sergeant Thomas Morris, a 19-year-old Cockney with the 73rd Regiment, had already given up trying to light fires. He concentrated instead on improvising a rudimentary shelter. Bunches of standing corn were gathered by the armful and rolled up to create mats, where they placed their knapsacks. They then sat on these, 'each man holding his blanket over his head to keep off the rain'. Thoroughly drenched, they balefully regarded the French on the other side of the valley, who seemed quite active. Sleep was hardly an option, so like everyone else on the ridge line they stood or squatted in the mud and chatted:

We passed the time in discussing the occurrences of the last two days, and the probable issue of the next day's contest, which we had every reason to suspect would be a most desperate one.

Quatre-Bras, the main topic of conversation, had been a cathartic experience for the 30,000 soldiers in Wellington's army who had arrived in time to fight the day before last. The soldiers viewed it as a close-run, bitter and seemingly disorganised scrap. The small hamlet at the 'four arms' crossroads, about 23½ miles south of Brussels, was first briefly held by 8,000 Dutch against 20,000 French soldiers, led by Marshal Ney, forming the left wing of Napoleon's advance on Brussels. While Napoleon badly mauled Blücher's Prussian army at Ligny, Quatre-Bras developed into a form of 'come as you are' uncontrolled meeting engagement for both sides. Ney

17

had been on the verge of winning, having secured the Bois de Bossu by 2.30 pm. With it would have come the strategic hamlet and a springboard to advance on Brussels, but 30 minutes later Picton's 5th Division arrived in the nick of time. Two hours later Alten's 3rd Division came from Nivelles followed by the Brunswick and Nassau contingents from Brussels. If the luckless French I Corps under d'Erlon had not been misdirected away from Quatre-Bras to Ligny, reaching neither in time, Wellington might not have been able to shore up his crumbling line by inserting reinforcements piecemeal, as they arrived. The soldiers saw little evidence of a plan, merely a stop-start forced march from Brussels reacting to the sound of distant gunfire.

Sergeant Thomas Morris was insightful as well as possessing an impressive memory, his diary revealed. 'Though it is considered a sort of treason to speak against the Duke,' he pointed out, 'the extraordinary fact' was 'that we had neither artillery or cavalry in the field.' Wellington had clearly been caught napping by Napoleon's unexpected appearance at Charleroi, because Morris observed the cavalry and artillery 'were quartered at too great a distance to be brought up in time'. 'Should it have been so?' he provocatively asked. Lieutenant Emanuel Biedermann, serving with the King's German Legion, shared Morris's misgivings. 'There was no question but that Napoleon had surprised us,' he insisted. The cavalry had to hurry from the interior, arriving only on the evening of the 17th, and 'officers of some brigades appeared on the battlefield on the 16th in their ball dress', fresh from the Duchess of Richmond's soirée the night before, and 'had had no time to change'.

Wellington's defensive stance in Belgium stretched too far west and meant that, despite promising to support Blücher, he was unable to deliver on time. British staff predictions for their arrival proved wildly over-optimistic. The French were checked, but at a loss of 4,500 Allied casualties compared to their own 4,000. If d'Erlon had arrived with his expected 20,000 additional men, Wellington could well have been as badly mauled as Blücher at Ligny. 'Fortunately for the Duke, the result was successful,' Morris wrote, 'had it been otherwise, he would have been deeply censured.' Possession of the field of battle at the conclusion spelled victory, in nineteenth-century military parlance. Wellington briefly held it, but had to retreat rapidly the following day to conform with Blücher's withdrawal north to Wavre. Wellington's Anglo-Allied soldiers instinctively sensed that Napoleon had grabbed the initiative. Brussels, where many had been quartered, was threatened by their retreat. They trusted the 'Beau', as Wellington was popularly nicknamed, to get it right. They also accepted another battle would be fought the next day and the outcome was by no means certain.[11]

Morris and his companions dwelt on the dramatic events of the previous 48 hours. Their indignant stance about the non-arrival of cavalry was understandable. They had been severely handled by French cuirassiers and lancers and were not looking forward to a repeat performance, particularly as their company commander, Captain Alexander Robertson, had not measured up. He was 60 years old and, despite 30 years' service, had seen no action. Morris and his horrified companions had watched the 69th Regiment square cut to pieces by French cavalry and their colours snatched away. Captain B Pigot, with the 69th, thought his superior, Major Lindsay, had been slow-witted. The decision to form square from line had been left too late:

But for that we should have got into square, as it was those companies that were really cut down. Poor man, to the day of his death he regretted having done so, but at the time he did it for the best.

Two companies had been overrun and the rest partly broken, with 150 men lost. Morris and the 73rd had run into the woods and watched the debacle from there. When they reformed under Captain Robertson, they too were charged by cuirassiers. His company commander 'knew nothing of field movements, and when going through the ordinary evolutions of a parade, the sergeant was obliged to tell him what to say and do,' recalled Morris. With cavalry bearing down 'he was at his wit's end, and there is no doubt we should all have been sacrificed'. The regimental adjutant had to step in. 'Captain Robertson, what are you about?' he shouted as he rode up. 'Are you going to murder your men?' They formed square just in time and beat off the attack. So Morris and his men were hardly relishing this morning's encounter with Robertson in charge. Morris had some unsettling memories of his own, picturing 'a private of the 92nd Regiment, whose arm had been taken off close to the shoulder by a cannon ball'. 'Go on, 73rd, give them pepper!' he had exclaimed. 'I've got my Chelsea commission!' Little chance of that, Morris had realised – he would bleed to death before treatment could reach him.

Captain Robertson's performance did not instil confidence, but then a newly arrived young subaltern reported for duty that night. He might well be better. He exuded confidence and appeared anxious 'those French fellows will not give us the slip'. Things were looking up, but by morning they were in retreat. Private Jeremiah Bates's musket unfortunately went off, when his trigger guard became entangled in corn, and 'the ball entered the officer's back, and passed through his heart'. With the new officer down, they were stuck with Robertson.

The only pleasant aspect to the retreat had been discovering a cellar full of liquor, after the barrels had been smashed. Everyone filled a canteen. As they staggered up the Mont St Jean ridge, 'literally knee-deep in mud', there was a brief exchange of artillery fire with the French. Just as it was getting dark 'one of their large shot killed two of our light company,' Morris remembered. 'It struck one of them in the cheek, and the other was killed with the wind of the passing ball as effectually as if he had been struck by it.' Death stalked them again.[12]

Quatre-Bras was a vicious engagement, vivid in the minds of the soldiers that had fought it just 48 hours before. Mathew Clay, with the light company of the 3rd Foot Guards, had a very close call. He remembered the passage of a shell splinter 'passing between my head and that of the comrade next in the rank', an intimidating experience. 'Its force and tremulous sound causing an unconscious movement of the head, not to be forgotten in haste,' Clay recalled. Assistant Surgeon Donald Finlayson, with the 33rd Foot, remembered Captain Haigh 'close by and saw him fall and his bowels all gush out'. Haigh's younger brother saw it and cried out 'Oh, kill me with him!' in his anguish. 'I endeavoured to console him,' remembered Finlayson, 'and said it might soon be our own fate.' Someone would have to tell Haigh's mother, but it would not be his brother because within 48 hours Haigh junior himself was shot through the neck, Finlayson recalled, 'dying soon after'.[13]

Within a few hours of daybreak they would face another, equally if not more intensely fought battle. Haunting images lingered. 'It was with great regret that many of us left that field on which some of our men lay breathing their last,' admitted Private James Anton, a Highlander with the 42nd Regiment. A particular fear among soldiers was to die anonymously and disappear without trace. Comrades were reluctant to leave mortally wounded friends unless they had expired. 'Among this number,' Anton recalled at Quatre-Bras, 'was a young man whose wound was in his forehead, from which the brain protruded.' He was not yet dead and despite the general withdrawal going on all around them, his friends were reluctant to abandon him. They patiently waited for him to die.

He had lain on the field during the night; his eyes were open, with a death film over them; two of his comrades were watching the last throb of his expiring breath before they would consign his body to the grave, already opened to receive it.

However, as Anton remembered, 'the call to arms made us leave him on the field'; it was the beginning of the retreat. He would have to be buried by strangers after all.[14]

Those on picket duty past midnight were too pre-occupied to reminisce. Captain William Verner, with the 7th Hussars, had enormous problems pulling on his tight, wet, short cavalry jacket, which had shrunk in the rain. 'I thought I should have torn the sleeves out of it,' he complained. Looking for their outpost in the pitch black night was not going to be easy. 'It was extremely dark and very cloudy, and quite impossible to see two yards in any direction.' Recognising his limitations, Verner confessed to his colonel, 'I am ready to be led, but I will not lead.' His ever-resourceful regimental sergeant-major stepped in and led him to 'the exact spot', which was 'in the midst of a field of standing rye, so high it reached as high as our heads on our horses'. Looking back, Verner would wonder irritably what had been the point of:

... ordering a squadron of dragoons, which had been in action all day and suffered severely, to go about the country at night in the dark, when it was impossible to distinguish a man on horseback at a distance of five yards.

Shackled by what he considered an ignorant measure, they were left to their own thoughts. 'There we remained all night, the horses up to their knees in mud and the rain pouring and raining into our boots.'

Verner had lost his friend and fellow squadron commander Major Edward Hodge the day before. He was missing after the confused rearguard fighting around the choke point at Genappe village, on the line of retreat. 'I felt that there was nothing to be gained by covering the retreat except hard knocks,' Verner recalled. Indeed, his squadron had lost half its men. 'The road was one mass of liquid mud and when we were halted and fronted,' he remembered, 'the men were so covered with mud that it was impossible to distinguish a feature in their faces or the colour of the lace on the dress.' They were ordered to counter-attack pursuing French lancers, which 'at the time were an unknown in our army'. The Hussars were at a disadvantage. 'We might as well have charged a house,' Verner complained, 'as the enemy's line [was] presenting a *Chevaux de Frise* of lances', with thousands of cavalry supporting them behind. 'They kept poking at us with their lances, and our men were unable to reach them with their sabres.'

Correspondence about Hodge's fate was to be passed around for another two and half months, during which time his wife was to desperately scour the field of action. Verner had witnessed the fight, in which the adjutant had been killed and Captain Elphinstone, another friend, pierced in the breast by a lance. It ended with Lieutenant Peters being dragged along by his horse after the inconclusive mêlée, ensnared by his pouch belt. Hodge, according to a surviving private soldier, lived and was taken prisoner. However, when the British 1st Life Guards charged in, the prisoners were dispatched with lances.

Hodge was piked in two places, through the neck and back, and he expired instantly – the soldier who told me this was within two yards of Hodge the whole time and was wounded himself in three places, having two pike wounds in his side and one in his head.

It was not vindictive. Nobody took chances. Restraining prisoners on horseback in the midst of a cavalry fight was not a realistic option. Sergeant Edward Cotton, with the 7th Hussars, watched the Life Guards counter-attack. 'With their weight of men and horses, [they] literally rode the enemy down,' he recalled, 'cutting and thrusting at them as they were falling.'[15]

Private Thomas Playford was with the 2nd Life Guards charge that clashed with the French lancers in the narrow village streets of Genappe. 'The use of firearms on horseback had not attained much perfection,' he observed. 'I watched the mounted skirmishers of the French and English armies, firing at each other for more than 20 minutes, and not one man or horse fell on either side.' Pouring rain soaked everyone's gunpowder, reducing the cavalry fight to the status of a medieval mêlée. 'The heaviest showers of rain I can remember fell,' recalled Lieutenant O'Grady with the 7th Hussars, which 'rendered firearms useless, and though the French fired a few pistol shots, I don't think they did any damage; our engagement was therefore one of sabre and lance.' Lieutenant John Kincaid, with the 1/95th Rifles, saw many of the Life Guards slip and roll over. 'Everyone who got a roll in the mud,' he wryly observed, went 'off to the rear, according to their Hyde Park custom, as being no longer fit to appear on parade!' Established peacetime conventions died hard. Kincaid, a hard-bitten Peninsula veteran, found this obsession with etiquette rather amusing; 'the uglier the better soldier!' was his view, quoting an old military proverb.[16]

Verner's state of abject misery enduring pouring rain on picket duty was much the same as that of Sergeant William Wheeler, on the other side of the Nivelles road. 'It would be impossible for anyone to form an opinion of what we endured this night,' he recalled. Being so close to the enemy they could not get under their blankets. The ground was too wet to lie down, so they sat on their knapsacks with no fires, waiting for daylight and sipping their 'Hollands'. 'The water ran in streams from the cuffs of our jackets'; it was as bad, he said, as being immersed in a river. 'We had one consolation,' the Peninsula veteran wryly observed, 'we knew the enemy were in the same plight'.[17]

1.50 am

'Blind Man's Bluff': The French and Prussians

When the French arrived at the Belle Alliance ridge opposite, they assumed they were facing an English rearguard. The enemy appeared to be in precipitate retreat. 'The ardour of the troops was incredible,' recalled a French officer, just before the summer storm burst over them. 'We now promised ourselves that the labour of the war was over; that the English, the main and the best hope of the Allies, were on flight to their ships.' So far as they were concerned 'we were in triumphal march upon Brussels'. They were contemptuous of the Prussian effort at Ligny, where they had inflicted 19,000 casualties, but they had lost 13,700 themselves. With the momentum clearly in their favour, the French had almost languidly taken up the pursuit of the two armies rapidly retreating north. Expectations were high, as the advance got under way. The French officer observed the soldiers were 'jesting with each other, and anticipating the amusements of Brussels'. Once Napoleon had got moving he became increasingly anxious. Marshal Ney had let the British slip away and they were about two hours behind them. All this was retrievable if they could hit Wellington's army with their combined forces that day, but the elements intervened.[18]

'A storm, such as I had never seen the like of, suddenly unleashed itself on us and on the whole region,' recalled Lieutenant Jacques Martin, with the 45th Line Regiment, part of the leading French corps. The 21-year-old Martin was a veteran of the final 1813–14 campaign, before Napoleon's abdication. 'In a few minutes the road and the plain were no more than a swamp which became more intractable, for the storm persisted and lasted the rest of the day and the whole night.' Up ahead was Lieutenant Pierre Guillot, carrying the cased eagle or 'golden cuckoo' of the 45th. It was brand new, having been presented to Guillot at a ceremonial parade just ten days before. His predecessor, Thomasin, had been judged 'too royalist', so Guillot carried the new one. The furled banner was not as grand as the former with the old 1804 emblem, presented by the people of Paris, but the King of France had consigned that to the flames during Napoleon's interregnum. Once uncased it would fly for Napoleon in battle for the first time.

Rain slowed the impetus of the French advance. Only the cavalry could harass Wellington's army, and they could not leave the roads and take short cuts across the fields. 'Men and horses sank into the mud up to their knees,' Martin remembered. They had to use the main thoroughfare, already churned up and rutted by the passage of Wellington's army.

As 21-year-old Sergeant Hippolyte de Mauduit, marching to the rear with the 1st Grenadier Imperial Guard Regiment, recalled, 'The tracks were so deep in mud after the rain that we found it impossible to maintain any sort of order in our columns.' The cohesion of the advance was breaking up. 'In looking for easier paths a large number of men went astray, and not until daybreak did they all manage to rejoin the columns.' 'The growing darkness prevented the troops from seeing each other,' remembered Jacques Martin, with the vanguard; 'battalions mingled and each soldier marched as best he could and where he could.' Discipline and order within units was fragmenting. It was becoming increasingly obvious a battle was not now going to be fought that day. 'We no longer formed an army,' Martin remembered, 'but a real crowd.' Even the Imperial Guard, Napoleon's elite corps, well to the rear and out of contact with the enemy, was reduced to a state of 'helter-skelter', Sergeant de Mauduit observed. Regiments were exhausted and in the growing confusion 'regiments, battalions, even companies became muddled; and in complete darkness and drenching rain people hunted vainly for their generals or officers.'

D'Erlon's leading I Corps managed to establish a front line along the Belle Alliance ridge, between Monplaisir farm and Plancenoit village, both sides of the Brussels road. It was covered by cavalry to its front and flanks. The cavalry divisions of Doman and Subervie, Milhaud's cavalry corps and the light cavalry of the Guard were coming to a halt on the heights of the farm at Rossomme, further back on the Brussels chaussée. The infantry of the Imperial Guard and the VI Corps had to turn off the road before the tortuously narrow

Genappe village and attempt to move north along small by-roads, so as to clear the main road for the artillery and its logistic trains. By about midnight two regiments of Guard Grenadiers had reached Glabais and started to establish biv-ouacs north and then south of the village. The whole French army was transforming from an instrument of pursuit to an amorphous mass, visibly dissolving in the storm as it spread beyond the Brussels road to seek bivouacs and shelter. Units were still marching up throughout the night.[19]

With daylight fading, Napoleon had ridden up to the Belle Alliance inn to observe. Peering through the mist ahead he could make out Marbot's French Hussars skirmishing with the last of the British cavalry. Four horse artillery batteries were brought up to fire at various formed bodies of Allied troops that could be discerned ahead. Milhaud's IV Cavalry Corps began to deploy, to carry on the advance. Wellington appeared to be escaping to the coast in order to board ships of the Royal Navy, just as he had done in Portugal. Irritatingly, it appeared the British ships were at hand yet again providing a safety net. Brussels nevertheless beckoned and Napoleon wanted to get his cavalry in a position to attract British artillery fire. Once he had detected the numbers and positions of this rearguard, he would sweep it aside.

Mameluke Ali, the Emperor's servant, was alongside, and he recalled the view from the high ground that dominated the vast valley before them. The shadowy outline of the Forest of Soignes provided a curtain to the north. 'The grey horizon did not allow the naked eye to see clearly,' he remembered. 'We noticed only an English rearguard followed by some French troops on our left where from time to time some cannon shots were being fired.' Napoleon methodically scanned the plain with his telescope, pausing to note the positions of telltale smoke. Then:

There came the flash of an immense line of fire and almost imme-
diately afterwards the sound of guns. It was the English artillery,
which showed the vast front of their army drawn up in battle
order. There was only one salvo, then we heard no more.[20]

One or two cannon shots banged out from both sides as the French vanguard broke contact and separated from the English rearguard.

Napoleon was agitated. An opportunity was slipping from his grasp. He wanted to press home an attack, but his generals urged against, saying they had done enough that day. 'Sire, our soldiers are exhausted and dying of hunger, allow them to make their soup,' pleaded Donezelot, one of his division commanders. 'No,' Napoleon had responded. 'Forwards, forwards, it is a good opportunity.' Napoleon had spotted the potential obstacle the Forest of Soignes would pose to Wellington's troops should he retire. His enemy had chosen a position that limited manoeuvre, with woods and villages restricting movement on both sides. If Wellington did retreat, his troops would become snarled up in the constricted space where the Brussels road entered the forest, just beyond the village of Waterloo.

It was unusual for an army to accept battle with such an obstacle to its rear, and the French were puzzled by their decision to accept this risk. Napoleon suspected Wellington had run out of choices. He, Napoleon, should therefore strike before Wellington could stabilise his rearward movement. But the generals finally convinced him that the soldiers must have their soup. The late start from Quatre-Bras was now to haunt him. Count Labedyère, with the accompanying staff, saw Napoleon gesticulate at the failing light and comment with some feeling: 'What would I not give, to be this day possessed of the power of Joshua, and enabled to retard

[Wellington's] march for two hours!' It was a *fait accompli* but Napoleon still feared the English might slip away again. 'Never, it is fair to say, has a general displayed less science in his choice of battlefield,' he surmised. There was no Prussian support. Napoleon could now demolish the surviving Allied army. 'If the English army remains there tomorrow,' he confided to Foy's staff, 'it is mine.'[21]

With the decision made to bivouac for the night, the army began to fend for itself, if only to get out of the storm. Sergeant de Mauduit recalled how crowds of soldiers, driven to the limits of patience, 'dashed into any buildings they came across, seeking shelter from the dreadful ordeal'. Any ordered allocation of bivouacs was subsumed by a general dispersion by the whole army, seeking food and dry billets. 'Grumbles and curses were levelled on all sides against the generals, on whom was laid the blame,' de Mauduit commented, 'quite unjustly, for all this hardship.' Troops blundered about in the darkness and pouring rain. 'We had constantly to push our way through thick hedges or deep ravines,' he remembered. 'In fact, discontent rose to such a pitch that repeated shouts of 'à la trahison!' ['Treason!'] were heard.' Local coalmines made conditions even worse, commented Captain Duthilt, a veteran of the Revolutionary Wars since 1793, with the 45th Line Regiment. Coal dust coated the local roads and produced 'a black mud mixed like ink'. The appearance of marching troops was transformed, 'their clothing, men and horses were painted from head to foot in such a way as to present a black and muddy mass'. When de Mauduit's Grenadier Guard battalion reached its bivouac at midnight, 'our greatcoats and our trousers were caked with several pounds of mud,' he recalled. 'A great many of the soldiers had lost their shoes and reached the bivouac barefoot.'[22]

There was no shelter for these late arrivals, who simply lay down in the mud. 'At least it was not all bad; our bed was not hard, to the contrary,' joked the phlegmatic Jacques Martin.

As soon as we lay down, one felt oneself softly sink up to one's mid-body, and with the simple precaution of putting a shako by way of a pillow, a feather bed could not be softer.

Martin, not without a sense of humour, insisted he could wallow from one side to the other to wash the mud off each soiled flank. 'Having had a good grumble, they gave themselves up to sleep,' he remembered. Many soldiers went beyond the allocated bivouac areas to find shelter in houses. 'The villages were not big enough for all the generals,' Martin grouched, 'houses were full of these leeches' and servants turned the men away. 'It is the lodging of General such and such,' they were told. Houses were always for *Monsieur le Maréchal* or *Monsieur le Prince* etc. – which left the soldiers singularly unimpressed.

We were soaked to the bones, scattered to the four winds, manoeuvring in the mud up to our knees in order to be in an advantageous position to cover these 'sirs' and protect them in the dark.

There was not really any soup for the soldiers. The few rations that came forward did not find them until they had given up and gone to sleep. Jacques Duthilt complained that 'bread, rice and brandy destined for the soldiers had been pillaged or spoiled on the spot', lost in the turmoil of retreat and advance by two armies. 'The villages were deserted, the inhabitants for the most part fled; even wine and brandy continued to be lacking.' French soldiers, the children of the revolution, were more opinionated, less compliant than their traditionally led adversaries. 'In passing through the bivouacs, I heard complaints on the almost total lack of rations for beasts and men,' recalled Bourdon de Vatry, on the 60th Division staff. He spoke to his commander, Prince Jérôme, remarking that 'commanders were helpless to repress them'. Gold was given over to buy food, an unusual measure because 'the poor Belgians expected to be pillaged', as was normally the case. Despite this, de Vatry recalled, 'We searched I don't know how many villages, finding more willingness than rations.'[23]

Some eight square miles were now filled with 150,000 troops, and more were arriving. Neither food nor shelter was available for latecomers. Former drummer-boy Corporal Louis Canler bivouacked with the 28th Line Regiment near La Belle Alliance and the high ground around Rossomme. 'Each started his preparations for dinner, and several left marauding,' he recalled. All they found was some wood and a small sheep. 'As, by all appearances, the next day was going to be rough' they kept the sheep for their next lunch and sat around the fire. On the other side of the Brussels road facing Hougoumont, 19-year-old Sergeant-Major Lerréguy de Civrieux, with the 93rd Line Regiment, remembered how the pouring rain made it 'impossible for us to light a fire, even to cook'. Soldiers had sabred slices of beef and mutton off what was available during the advance and the pieces lay raw, scattered around the bivouacs. 'The distribution of bread,' Canler recalled, 'was still awaited.'

Nervous anticipation and battle preparation did detract from some of the discomfort. 'Such was the interest of the moment, the grandeur of the stakes, the force of the excitement in the two armies,' remembered Sergeant de Mauduit, with the Imperial Guard, 'that the soldiers were almost insensible to physical suffering.' Nevertheless, de Mauduit was uneasy, as his experience at Ligny 36 hours before had been unsettling. He was reconciled to the prospect of injury from bayonet and musket balls, because these 'at least preserved a human form', but artillery strikes were another matter. 'Here, in contrast, it was limbs and scattered body parts, detached heads, torn out entrails and disembowelled horses.' Ligny had been a butcher's yard, and he would face artillery again in the morning.[24]

Arthur Wellesley, the 46-year-old Duke of Wellington, was at the peak of his career, whereas Napoleon at the same age was approaching the nadir of his. Wellington had successfully fought 24 battles and sieges, Napoleon had won all but 10 of his 72 battles. Physically Wellington was more vibrant than the increasingly flabby Napoleon, but on this morning the wily Napoleon had the edge on him. He had decisively outmanoeuvred the Anglo-Allied and Prussian armies at the very outset of the new campaign. Wellington had never confronted Napoleon before, and although he was outwardly confident, the auguries for the Anglo-Allied cause were not looking good. Wellington's soldiers could not predict what might happen after dawn, except that there would be a battle. 'Our conversation naturally turned on our present position,' the 32-year-old British horse battery commander Alexander Mercer recalled. He had never been in a major battle. 'After discussing all the pros and cons, we made up our minds to recommence the retreat with tomorrow's sun.' Nobody had told them what to do since arrival. 'When that retreat was to terminate' with Brussels at their backs and with the Forest of Soignes in between, it 'baffled all our powers of conjecture,' he admitted.[25]

Wellington sheltered at his headquarters in the inn, opposite the church in the village of Waterloo. He was not one to show concern and gave little away. Wellington's staff, as

Sergeant Cotton remarked, claimed 'it was impossible to learn from his countenance, voice or gesture, whether the affair in hand was trifling or important, quite safe, or extremely dangerous.' Behind that self-assured visage, Wellington had his concerns. He could not fight on this ground the next morning without Prussian support, and would that be forthcoming? Six weeks before, when Wellington first met with Blücher on 3 May to discuss future options, the Prussian commander's Saxon soldiers had mutinied outside the Prussian headquarters at Liège and 'obliged poor old Blücher to quit the town'. 'To hell with the Prussians!' the mob had chanted as they stoned the windows of the headquarters, and even more chillingly, *'Vive Napoléon!'* ('Long live Napoleon!') Blücher sent 20 Prussian battalions to disarm the Saxons. Seven of the ringleaders were shot and the colours of the mutinous regiments were publicly burned. Fourteen thousand Saxon troops were split into two contingents and relegated to garrison and guard duties along the Prussian lines of communication between Belgium and the Rhine. They would not see action.[26]

While Saxon morale plummeted, 10,000 Rhinelanders were also at odds with their new Prussian masters. They deserted in droves after Ligny and even now were sharing their doubts with their Saxon fellow malcontents on the line of retreat. Concerns over Prussian unreliability were mirroring those Wellington had over his own polyglot army of German, Dutch and Nassau contingents, many of whom had recently served with Napoleon. Indeed the Belgians were dressed the same as the French, having simply changed the badge on their shakos. There was bad feeling between the Belgians and Prussians. Culturally the Dutch and especially the Belgians were closer to the French than many of the Allied nations. On top of this Wellington was desperately short of trained men. Eleven thousand of his Peninsular War veterans had been sent to North America, and 47,000 soldiers had been struck from the active duty roster as part of the first peace dividend following Napoleon's abdication in 1814.

Wellington had been surprised and caught out by the Prussian retreat. He liked Blücher, but with an ingratiating air of British superiority he tended to show his suspicion that the Prussian army was inferior to his own. When he spoke with Blücher at Ligny he was tactless enough to comment that the Prussian reserve was over-exposed to French artillery and likely to be 'damnably mauled' if it did not move. Count von Gneisenau, Blücher's prickly chief of staff, was no lover of the British and had tersely responded, 'My men like to see the enemy.' Prussian inexperience resulted in huge casualties. They were an unknown commodity. Although expectations of performance were not high, Wellington intuitively grasped the grudge factor that applied. The Prussians hated the French, as did the Spanish, with whom Wellington had closely co-operated, because of the excesses of the French occupation. Hatred engendered a quality of resistance in itself. Wellington appreciated that whatever the Prussians might lack in tactical finesse, it would be more than compensated for by aggression. Baron Carl von Müffling, his Prussian liaison officer, had sought to allay some of these doubts, arguing Wellington's glass was more half full than half empty. The Prussians had retreated on Wavre, but 'von Bülow with his corps had taken no part in the battle, and Napoleon had not pursued'. With the Duke now realigned on a line with Wavre, 'things cannot be so bad', he argued.[27]

Some eight or ten miles further east, the flotsam of the retreating Prussian army was gathering in a box about seven miles across and four miles deep, with Wavre at its centre.

Sleeping rough and moving through or sheltering in outlying villages further east were 8,000 to 10,000 Prussian deserters, mainly disaffected Rhinelanders, who had recently come under Prussian control. Strung out from Sombreffe to Gembloux and converging on Wavre from the southeast was Marshal Grouchy's corps of 30,000 pursuing French troops, spread over columns eight miles long. Few of these elements were particularly aware of each other, struggling through roads knee-deep in mud in the pouring rain. One Prussian captain commanding a Westphalian Landwehr cavalry squadron with the Prussian I Corps was crossing the Dyle river near Wavre. Despite the awful weather 'the mood of the troops was certainly grave, but not in the least disheartened'. Although they were retreating, discipline was holding up, and 'the bearing of all but a few isolated units was still very good'. With every mile travelled north, unimpeded by pursuit, cohesion returned to the Prussian army. 'We have lost once, but the game is not up, and tomorrow is another day,' remarked one Pomeranian soldier to another who was grumbling within earshot of the squadron commander – 'and he was quite right'.

Blücher had ridden by, having bathed his bruised limbs in brandy after being pinned beneath his wounded horse at Ligny. 'Although riding must have been very painful,' the captain recalled, 'he rode alongside the troops, exchanging jokes and banter with many of them.' Progress was difficult, new saddles swelled with the persistent rain, 'and the troops, as young riders often do, sat unsteadily and lolled about during the march, with the unfortunate result that I soon had a number of horses with saddle sores.' These inexperienced troops were singled out and made to dismount 'and then go splashing through thick and thin on foot beside us', carrying their portmanteaus on their backs. Experience came at a price, and 'this was very unpleasant indeed for the rather easy going Westphalians'.[28]

Retreating infantry fared even worse. The Westphalian cavalry captain had watched them march by, 'terribly worn out after the fighting'. They had fought through sultry heat in the blazing villages of St Armund and Ligny for hours on end:

> *In the great heat, gunpowder smoke, sweat and mud had mixed into a thick crust of dirt, so that their faces looked almost like those of mulattos and one could hardly distinguish the green collars and facings on their tunics. Everybody had discarded his stock [collar]; grubby shirts or hairy brown chests stuck out from their open tunics; and many who had been unwilling to leave the ranks on account of a slight wound wore a bandage they had put on themselves. In a number of cases blood was soaking through.*

Temperatures had now fallen, and these lightly uniformed men had been lashed for hours during the summer storm by persistent freezing rain. Their clothes were in tatters from crawling through hedgerows during the village fighting, 'tunics and trousers had got torn, so that they hung in rags and their bare skin showed through'. Men accustomed to judge the efficiency of a unit from their appearance on a parade ground 'would have been appalled to watch the 4th Westphalian Infantry Regiment' pass by, the captain remarked. They disappeared into the curtain of cold rain that obscured the distinguishing features of many other units straggling painfully past, heading north. Major Carl Friccius, commanding the 3rd Westphalian Landwehr, remembered how difficult it was to assess in which direction to retreat, because there was no one left in the deserted villages they passed through to ask the way.

'Scattered troops passed through the village all night long,' recalled an officer on Gneisenau's staff during the retreat. 'No one knew whence they came or whither they were going.' Commanders attempted to set up assembly points where junior officers could halt stragglers, form them up into groups and march them off again. Prussian Colonel von Reiche wore himself out disentangling the mass to reform regiments drifting northward along the road between Tilly and Wavre. 'When one is so keyed up,' he recalled, 'one can stand unbelievable strains.' Carl Friccius realised 'we were on the right road' after directions from von Reiche. At first the withdrawal continued 'in wild disorder' until they were halted at the village of Tilly. 'The night was dark,' he recalled, 'and because of the great confusion and loud noise, the order could hardly be passed on, let alone carried out.' As the huge column came out of Tilly, Friccius and his ADC were waiting either side of the roadside shouting: 'East Frisians, out to the left!' The rally worked, 'a significant number of men started to gather', and within three hours three battalions of about 400 men each were formed up. 'Everyone was pleased to see us,' he remembered, and reformed, they continued the march. At the outset of the campaign the battalions numbered 750. 'Dispersion was as great as after the battle of Jena, and the night was just as dark,' remembered Gneisenau's staff officer, 'but morale had not sunk.' Prussian cohesion and leadership held them together. 'Each man was looking for his comrades so as to restore order.'[29]

When Wellington was seeking assurances, 12 hours before, that the Prussians would support him, Blücher's headquarters had only located half his army. The French completely missed the Prussian I and II Corps moving north, yet spotted elements of Thielman's III Corps moving east towards Gembloux, confirming the French expectation the Prussians would retreat east. III Corps then changed direction and also moved northwest to Wavre. Bülow's IV Corps had not yet arrived. During the evening of 17 June the missing ammunition wagons from the commissariat train appeared, which at least meant they could continue the battle. As Wellington considered his chances, I and II Corps were in the Wavre area with von Bülow's IV Corps, having missed Ligny, and filed into Dion le Mont, after a march of 90 miles to reach the area of operations.

Sixteen-year-old Franz Lieber, retreating with the remnants of the Colburg Regiment, had already been twice disturbed by the pursuing French, moving from bivouac to bivouac on the retreat from Ligny. Hunting for food through the surrounding villages, 'we made a meal of raw pork, having met with a hog,' he recalled, and later:

> We found a young woman with an infant, by the side of her father, who had been beaten and wounded by some marauding enemies. She asked us for a piece of bread; we had none. We gave her some potatoes which we had just found, but she said she had nothing to cook them with.

Rain fell in torrents until early on the morning of 18 June, when 'we found part of our regiment from which we had been separated'. It was an emotional reunion with 'soldiers rushing to each other, to find comrades whom we believed to be dead or missing'. Despite their exhaustion, there was to be no rest. They had already been warned they would be on the march again within a few hours.[30]

The last of the Prussian III Corps was closing on Wavre through the torrential rain. 'The paths had been washed away, so it took us considerable effort to find the right road,' remembered Major von Bornstedt, commanding the Fusilier

Battalion with the 1st Kurmark Landwehr Infantry Regiment. 'I tried extremely hard, despite my exhaustion, to find the right direction.' They were able to pick out the campfires of the newly arrived IV Corps. His men were at the end of their tether, 'not only because it was their third night in a row spent in bivouac, but also because the long march had exhausted them'. Von Bülow's last IV Corps brigade to arrive started to file into its bivouac sites during the early morning hours of 18 June. The 13th Brigade log reported that off the paved road 'the paths became very poor and, due to flooding, could in places only be crossed by planks in single file'. The Prussian army was mired by the same dreadful conditions as the French and Anglo-Allied armies, as the log described:

> As it was already so late at night, the men could be sent neither straw, nor wood, nor water and had to spend the whole night out in the rain on a field that turned to mud. Neither food nor brandy could be obtained, so the men were in a rather sorry situation.[31]

Von Bülow had already received his orders. The corps would march at daybreak. They had covered nearly 100 miles on foot since 15 June. Now they had to march another ten in the morning to reach Wellington at Waterloo, likely a six-hour forced march. They had missed the reverse at Ligny. Here was the opportunity, after days of marching and counter-marching, to prove their worth and close at last with the hated French.

CHAPTER 2

Twilight to Morning —•

2 am to 10 am

Dark and More Rain

Mrs Martha Deacon was in the last stages of pregnancy and struggling. She was marshalling three children as she made her ponderous way along the rutted and muddy Brussels road in the pouring rain. Thomas Morris knew her husband Ensign Thomas Deacon, with the 73rd, shot in the line next to him at Quatre-Bras. The man on his left had just gone down 'killed by a musket ball through the temple' when to his right another ball went through Deacon's arm, 'taking with it a portion of the shirt sleeve'. Deacon had stumbled back to the baggage train, where he searched for his wife. Eventually wearing himself out, he was picked up by a wagon and carried to Brussels. Martha Deacon had vainly looked for him amid the wounded the whole night long. By the time she realised he had been evacuated, the retreat was under way. As Morris remembers, 'conveyances, there was none to be got', so she had to make 'the best of her way on foot, with her children, exposed to the violence of the terrific storm of thunder, lightning and rain, which continued unabated'. By the time she neared the Forest of Soignes and Mont St Jean village, she was 'faint, exhausted, and wet to the skin, having no other clothes than a black silk dress, and light shawl'.

Being married to a soldier was a hard existence in normal circumstances and worse on campaign. Twenty-seven-year-old Rifleman Edward Costello, wounded with the 1/95th Rifles at Quatre-Bras, was on the same road in the teeming rain. 'The cries of the wounded, on their way, in cart-loads to Brussels were most distressing,' he recalled. Mrs Deacon would have been picking her way amid 'carts broke down through being overloaded', wrecked in their haste to escape the pursuing French. 'It is curious to observe the confusion and uproar that generally exists in the rear of an army in battle, while all in front is order and regularity,' Costello observed. Martha Deacon had to pass through 'wives and camp followers of all descriptions, who crowd in great numbers, making inquiries after their husbands and friends'. Processions of carts and horses thickly thronging the roadway 'were greeted on all sides by anxious faces and earnest enquiries'. This was a retreat and the French were closing.

Costello and his wounded companions had already picked up from the roadside a three-year-old boy, found 'by the side of its dead mother, who was still bleeding copiously from a wound in the head, occasioned most likely, by a random shot from the enemy'. The mother had to be left behind, dead or not. Martha Deacon struggled on, seeking her husband in Brussels, even though many of the wives and camp followers had turned off into the woods of Soignes or at villages and hamlets en route. As Daniel Gale bivouacked on the forward ridge line with the 3/95th Rifles, his wife Mary and five-year-old daughter Elizabeth began to cut and scrape lint, preparing dressings for the battle. Lint was spread over wounds and incisions, and scrapings were used to pack deep penetrations. Another wife in the 95th, whose young girl Barbara had been born on campaign in the Peninsula five years before, was helping her.[1]

The British army frowned on marriage. 'Marriage must be discouraged as much as possible,' the Rules and Regulations for the Cavalry emphasised. Soldiers required permission to marry and should be dissuaded. 'Officers must explain to the men the many miseries that women are exposed to and by every sort of persuasion they must prevent them from marrying if possible.' Some wives had little choice except to follow when their husbands enlisted. Life was hard, but even while caring for children, cooking, uniform repair and laundry work could be found, working for officers, which offered a precariously small extra income. Going on campaign was literally a lottery. Only a handful of women were allowed to go with their regiments, perhaps three or five per company, all decided on the roll of a dice, or drawing lots from the battalion's Marriage Roll. Being left behind was even worse, because they then became the responsibility of their native parishes for support, which meant the workhouse. Those that went were useful as cooks, laundrywomen and seamstresses and for their valuable, if unofficial role in nursing the wounded.

Whether they were on the Marriage Roll or not, women following the army would routinely clog roads, hindering discipline and slowing the movement of regiments. Edward Macready, an officer with the 30th Foot, recalled that their first forced march to Quatre-Bras was held up by a throng of baggage, animals, commissaries and the women. Many of the regimental wives had come up to bless and kiss their husbands, 'many for the last time'. Such occurrences were always unsettling, he observed, and 'agitate the hearts of soldiers' wives, the most callous and insensible creatures in existence'.[2]

The only concession the army made to their presence was a half-ration allowance, with a quarter for children. This created a multitude of expert foragers, who often beat the commissary to scarce supplies of food. Wellington once said, 'It is well known in all armies the women are at least as bad, if not worse, than the men as plunderers!' On one occasion he even threatened them with the lash. Dan Skiddy's wife Biddy, with the 34th Regiment, was uncompromising about her first loyalty. 'We must risk something to be in before the men,' she resolved, 'to have the fire and a dhrop of tay ready for the poor crathers after their load an' their labour.' Mathew Clay, with the 3rd Foot Guards, remembers the heroism of one of the company wives who 'fearlessly passed over the slain' at Quatre-Bras, 'bringing a supply of provisions for her husband and companions' inside the hotly contested Bossu Wood. Senior officers took a different view:

> *In time of war matrimony is a serious drawback to a soldier. Constant uneasiness about the family he has left at home, when he himself is called abroad, and their anxiety for him, are painful things to think of; his happiness and peace of mind are marred, and all his best exertions paralysed, by reflecting on his situation.*[3]

The decision rested with the soldiers and their lovers. Thomas Wheeler, with the 51st Foot, acknowledged, 'There are many sweets in having a pretty lovely young woman for a comrade, but then, I know from observation that there is an indefinite number of bitters attending it.' Wheeler was firmly of the view that 'when his cap is on, his family is covered, then he is free as air'. Private Thomas Plunkett, with the 1/95th Rifles, had his own philosophy. Plunkett was renowned for allegedly sniping a French general from his horse in the Peninsula, well beyond the normal range of the Baker rifle. Now his girlfriend had just been seriously disfigured by an exploding ammunition wagon the day before at Quatre-Bras. Nevertheless, he later married her.

Mathew Clay remarked on the poignant farewells prior to Quatre-Bras. Soldiers, he observed, 'desired that their expressions of affection might be communicated to their absent wives and families'. Those that were there managed parting embraces, even amid the sound of cannon fire. 'Although short [these were] sincere and affectionate and expressed with deep emotions of grief as though a state of widowhood had suddenly come upon them.' Thomas Morris's close friend Jack Parsons, with the 73rd Foot, an inveterate drinker but a lovable rogue, presented himself that morning to his captain. He wanted to make certain that if he did not survive the battle, any arrears of pay owed to him would be handed to the 'lovely Therese', his Flemish girlfriend, a popular beauty, who had been allowed to follow the regiment. She was to collect her money.[4]

As Mrs Martha Deacon continued her halting progress through the soaking Forest of Soignes, mustering her children by her side, they were passed by a huge column of 5,000 British and Hanoverian troops going in the opposite direction. The 6th British Infantry Division included three of Wellington's former Peninsula battalions with Lambert's 10th Brigade, nearly 2,300 men strong. Dorset soldier Sergeant William Lawrence could well have seen Mrs Deacon. 'All through the night,' he recalled, 'there was the clamour of thousands of camp followers, who fearful of sticking to the Allied army after Quatre-Bras, were retreating to Brussels with a stream of baggage wagons.' Conditions were miserable. 'It was quite a sight, the roads were almost impassable and some people got stuck in the mud.'

Wellington was tired. He had managed three hours' sleep following the Duchess of Richmond's ball on 15 June after discovering that Napoleon had entered Belgium. He directed operations from the saddle continuously until midnight the following day, covering between 30 and 40 miles from Brussels to Ligny, Frasnes, Genappe and then the battle of

Quatre-Bras. After snatching another three hours' sleep he covered the 12-mile retreat to Waterloo, again commanding from the saddle. He kept his plans and emotions to himself. If he was fatigued, his taut, athletic demeanour gave no sign of it. Little blame could be attached to Wellington for Napoleon's skilful emergence between the two armies, because the Duke had never publicly conjectured what might happen. Wellington was sensitive about his reputation. He might well have been depressed during the early hours of 18 June. He knew well he was operating at a disadvantage, but characteristically gave no sign of it.

Now, for the first time since this campaign had begun three days earlier, Wellington received some good news. A brigade of his former Peninsula veterans had arrived with the 6th Division, and at last contact had been re-established with Blücher's army, ten miles to the east at Wavre. A Prussian dispatch arrived at Wellington's headquarters at about 2 am, reassuring him that von Bülow's un-blooded IV Corps 'will leave Dion le Mont, and march through Wavre towards St Lambert to attack the enemy's right flank'. Not only had Blücher produced the corps' worth of support Wellington had requested; the dispatch went on to say that 'the II Corps will follow it immediately, and the I and III Corps will hold themselves ready to follow this movement'. Wellington had previously assured the Whig MP Thomas Creevey at Brussels that he and Blücher, even before the arrival of the Austrian and Russian armies, had sufficient manpower to 'do the business'. Reinforcements, he was now informed, would begin moving 'at daybreak', which in normal circumstances should be a six-hour forced march. 'As the troops are exhausted and some have yet to arrive, it is impossible to leave earlier.' That did not matter. Wellington could now afford to accept battle in his present position. There was always an issue of credibility and trust when dealing with allies. Would the Prussians arrive in sufficient time and strength to decide the issue? It was still raining and the roads were in an appalling state. Wellington could at least allow himself a few hours' sleep.[5]

Private Alexander Dunlop was striding through the soaking Forest of Soignes in the ranks of the 9th Company of the 1/27th Inniskillings commanded by Lieutenant Edward Drewe. Dunlop had served eight years with the Inniskillings, or 'Skins' as they were nicknamed. The former labourer according to his regimental records was 5 ft 7 ins tall, with brown hair and grey eyes. His round face and swarthy complexion had retained some of the tan from the regiment's recent stay in Bermuda. Dunlop and his comrades in the 27th had had a hectic year. In January they had been deployed outside the besieged town of Mobile, across the Atlantic in North America. When Wellington had needed his Peninsula veterans, 15,000 were in the wrong place. The regiment only just missed the bloodbath inflicted by the American revolutionaries on the British at New Orleans. Even though the war had officially been declared over, some 2,000 men had been lost, a third of the force, mown down in their rows by marksmen at a cost of seven American dead and six wounded. In April the regiment had shipped out of its exotic surroundings in Bermuda, but heavy storms in mid-Atlantic had scattered the troop ships, damaging some of them, so that the battalion staff and three of the battalion's ten companies had to put into the Bahamas for repair, and had still not arrived. The senior captain, John Hare, was now in charge of the Inniskillings, who were brigaded with the 4th 'Lions' and 40th 'Excellers', so named because of the XL on their regimental badge. Alongside them were four 'raw' Landwehr battalions with the 4th Hanoverian Brigade. Because of the absence of the pay staff in the Bahamas, pay was in disarray, as was also the repair of muskets, with the battalion armourer still absent somewhere at sea.

John Hare was motivated by the prospects of the coming battle in an era when rank was generally paid for in the British army. He had enlisted with the 1/27th as an ensign at the age of 16, had reached lieutenant without purchase by 1800 and captain by 1805, all likely as a consequence of casualties in the Peninsula. In 1813 he had been brevetted major for gallantry before Napoleon's abdication the next year meant, for him as for thousands of others, release on half pay and no prospect of promotion. The 'Great War', as the Revolutionary and Napoleonic wars were popularly called, was over. The battle this day could change all that.

Hare lacked the financial resources for quick promotion, as did one of his brother officers, Lieutenant William Faithful Fortescue, who had five children to support. He had been in the regiment since 1806 and had risen no further. He came from a military family, his father having stormed the Heights of Abraham at Quebec in 1759. Fortescue needed the money. Nobody was going to support his aspirations after he'd had the temerity to marry a Catholic, Honoria O'Brian, in 1798. Marrying for love had been a rash move and coincidental with the bloody rebellion that had shaken Ireland and further polarised the Catholic–Protestant divide. Fortescue, a disgraced Protestant gentleman in the regiment, probably appreciated that the coming battle might be his last chance to win preferment. He needed first to out-survive his brother officers.

Alexander Dunlop and his comrades in the 27th were dressed in scarlet short-tailed jackets with overall grey trousers and a high fronted shako headdress, which added to their height. The buff facing of their dripping wet uniforms was displayed on the collar, cuffs and shoulder straps, with square-ended shaped looped cuffs and shoulder straps. This was the last time gorgeously attired soldiers would fight such a decisive battle in Europe. Marching in the same column were Patrick Corbett, with the 1st Company, a former stone mason, and Thomas Hoyle, previously a weaver from County Armagh. Both were as wet as they were footsore. They had been on the road since daybreak on the 16 June, covering 30 miles that day and a further 21 the next, picking their way alongside the cobblestones, often reserved for artillery and wheeled transport. It had been a typically stop-start large formation move. Time spent standing in ranks alternated with spells of hurrying to close gaps in the march column, as they wound their way through the increased congestion they encountered on leaving Brussels and approaching Waterloo.

There was no rest on arrival in the darkness. Lieutenant Edward Drewe recalled that they were 'occupied some time clearing the road of provision carts containing bread, forage, and spirits that had been left on the road by the peasantry taking their animals from the carts, and concealing themselves in the woods'. A final splutter of artillery fire at dusk the previous day had initiated panic among the baggage wagons, upending and wrecking carts as they raced pell-mell to Brussels. Clearing a line of retreat became as important as ensuring a seamless re-supply from the city, so the road had to be disentangled. This normally obnoxious task was taken up with relish by men like Dunlop, Corbett and Hoyle. The men worked in scattered and generally unsupervised groups, and the combination of darkness, rain and separation from officers gave ample opportunity to pick up food and smash open the numerous abandoned gin and rum casks that they found. Very soon hundreds of canteens were filled with rum. So widespread was the resulting drunkenness that four sergeants and 12 corporals were demoted to private after the battle. Many of the NCOs took part in the drinking and certainly did not prevent their men from doing so. The regimental sergeant-major was still absent at sea alongside the regimental colonel. As daybreak began to lighten the sky, the Inniskillings took a brief salute from Wellington as they marched through Waterloo village, all tired but supremely content with a full canteen of rum slapping at their thighs. The men had their liquor, while officers such as Hare and Fortescue looked forward to the financial advancement that might come their way, along with honour and glory.[6]

On the Belle Alliance ridge, Napoleon Bonaparte was as tired as Wellington, but on the crest of a euphoric wave, convinced the enemy was in his grasp. The Anglo-Allies were backed up against the Forest of Soignes with no way out. Wellington was ignoring 'the most elementary rules of war' by remaining in his present position. 'If he were beaten,' Napoleon reflected, 'any retreat was impossible.' Napoleon was rumoured to be suffering from ill health: some claimed acromegaly, which generated a form of listless over-optimism. That night, it is said, his surgeon Baron Larrey treated him for collapsed haemorrhoids, bathing them with warm water and applying leeches. The Emperor was unquestionably overweight, but he had emerged from the inordinately harsh Russian winter campaign of 1812 with excellent health. Seventy-two hours before he had been in the saddle enduring sweltering heat while directing the initial invasion against the Prussians. He rode from 2 pm until nightfall the following day, another hot day, co-ordinating operations at Ligny. Any alleged torpor in following up the pursuit of Wellington and Blücher after Quatre-Bras resulted more from a conviction that he had shattered and divided his opponents, and that Brussels was his for the taking. If he was irritated by his ailments, which also allegedly included constipation, bladder and skin problems, they had little impact on his physical performance. All the old energy was clearly visible to his subordinates as he rode with the pursuing French vanguard, through the teeth of a summer storm, from Quatre-Bras to La Belle Alliance. Napoleon had lived a hard and fast life, energised by boundless ambition. He was on the cusp of success, as one of his officers observed following their entry into Belgium:

Wellington was so far out-generalled; he was disconcerted by an offensive movement which he had not foreseen, and he had thus lost the whole plan of the campaign.[7]

At 2 am Napoleon was woken at his headquarters at Le Caillou on the main Brussels road to read a dispatch from Marshal Grouchy, who was pursuing Blücher. Written four hours before, it suggested that 'one portion' of the Prussian army was going to join Wellington 'and that the centre, which is Blücher's army, is retiring on Liège', further east. Napoleon was not too concerned. Blücher's army was split and would be in no state after its mauling at Ligny to support Wellington. Napoleon was more fixated on destroying his remaining opponent, rather than any worries that the Prussians might move to prevent it. The immediate concern was that the weather might still intervene. But already the sky was clearing, Napoleon observed. Even so, with the French army spread across a large swathe of countryside, three to five miles apart, a delayed start to operations was inevitable. He ordered the army to be ready to attack at 9 am. Troops would have to close on their colours, and soaking wet conditions meant the rutted Brussels road offered the only main approach to the battlefield.

At about 4 am the sky began to lighten. 'At five o'clock I perceived a few rays of that sun which should, before going down, light up the defeat of the English army,' Napoleon recalled. 'The British oligarchy would be overthrown by it! France was going to rise, that day, more glorious, more powerful and greater than ever!'[8]

The Reluctant Reveille

As twilight gave way to an emerging drizzly dawn, the terrain in front of Mont St Jean came into focus. Sergeant Edward Cotton, with the 7th Hussars, saw that the ground:

> … *was covered with splendid crops of rye, wheat, barley, oats, beans, peas, potatoes, tares and clover; some of the grains were of great height. There were few patches of ploughed field.*

The veterans sensed there was nothing haphazard about this selection of ground. Today they would fight. 'The great advantage,' Cotton immediately saw:

> … *was that the troops could rest in rear of the crest of the ridge, screened in a great measure from the enemy's artillery and observation, whilst our guns were placed at points, from which they could sweep (they are wonderful brooms) the slope that descends to the valley in front.*

Thomas Morris, a Peninsula veteran with the nearby 73rd Foot, observed that 'our position was an extremely good defensive one' and 'as far as the selection of ground went, we were very favorably circumstanced'.[9]

Wellington had picked out this site as a potential battleground the year before. His appreciation of the suitability of the defensive value of its ridge line was confirmed during rides across the terrain during the weeks prior to the start of hostilities. The Mont St Jean ridge stood at the intersection of two of three ostensible routes Napoleon might use to march on Brussels, barring approaches from Charleroi and from Nivelles. The third conceivable route from Mons through Hal needed to be blocked by a separate force, which was duly inserted. So taken had Wellington been by this locality that he ordered the engineer staff to draw up a map of the area around Waterloo. It was not quite ready when called upon, so Major Oldfield with the engineer staff arranged to have the original sketches hastily pasted together. It was dispatched by courier, Lieutenant Marcus Waters, to Wellington's staff. Waters had an eventful ride. Apprehended by French cavalry, he escaped but was knocked senseless when he was thrown from his horse. On regaining consciousness he found his mount cropping at a carrot patch a half-mile away. The map and plans were still in the portmanteau.

The map has survived to this day and is on display at the Royal Engineers Museum at Chatham in England. Wellington was an astute observer of the tactical potential of landscape. Engineer maps of the period did not utilise the present system of contour lines to depict height; instead gradients were shaded with particular coloured densities and cross-hatching was used to systematically and scientifically represent slopes. Like many military maps, the vital ground was frustratingly at its edge. The farms of La Haye Sainte, the château of 'Goumont', or Hougoumont, and the Mont St Jean ridge are marked at the right-hand edge, including the main road leading from south to north through La Belle Alliance to Brussels. There are faded pencil lines to the north of La Haye Sainte, allegedly sketched in by Wellington himself before the battle, to depict the line he wished occupied and also where he anticipated the Prussians would appear. Ridge lines offered the opportunity to conceal infantry, not a generally accepted tactic at the time. Wellington's pencil traced the substantial outline of the Mont St Jean ridge, which was both long enough for his army to hold and difficult for the French to outflank. Sir William de Lancey, Wellington's quartermaster

-general, had the map in his possession when he was mortally wounded later that day. Major John Oldfield was to save the map and preserve it for posterity.

The Mont St Jean ridge ran southwest to northeast about 700 metres south of the farm and village of the same name. Although just 30 metres high, it offered an uninterrupted view across to the Belle Alliance ridge, variously between 350 and 1,400 metres away, obscured only by some undulations, tall standing crops and scattered trees. Most of the ground to the north of Wellington's ridge is reverse slope and in dead ground to the French, offering protection from view and to a lesser extent from artillery fire. All that Napoleon could observe from his front was what Wellington was prepared to let him see: only those troops on the forward slope or skyline. The French ridge line was lower than that of the Anglo-Allies.

To the right of Wellington's line was the walled château of Hougoumont, a natural strongpoint and anchor, 400 metres in front of the right flank. Wellington's pencil mark traversed the centre of the line, which was the crossroads, linking it to Brussels and Ohain. The east–west traverse and southern link was a sunken road, in some places 30 metres below ground, providing a steep sided cutting, which was both an infantry bastion and an obstacle to the movement of horses and guns. La Haye Sainte was another brick strongpoint, 250 metres in front of the centre. Both bastions, to the right and centre, were important outposts that would disrupt or delay any cohesive assault on the Mont St Jean ridge. Capturing La Haye Sainte was a prerequisite for any successful attack on Wellington's centre. On the far left of Wellington's line was an area of sturdily built farms around Papelotte, La Hai and Frichermont and the tiny village of Smohaine. This sector of deep sunken lanes, high banks and thick hedges created a natural bocage anchoring the left of the line, where it was anticipated the Prussians would appear. Wellington had chosen his ground well.

The morning was cold and showery. Captain William Verner's 7th Hussar picket behind Hougoumont to the right of the line was withdrawn. 'In all my experiences as a soldier,' he recalled, 'and I had some during the retreat to Corunna, I never saw the men so jaded as they were on the morning of the 18th.' When it became sufficiently light to distinguish the features of his men, Verner commented to the picket troop commander, 'Well, Shirley, if I look half as bad as you do, I must be a miserable looking object.' Wellington's pencil mark drawn through the Mont St Jean ridge line slowly but surely took on a tangible substance. Soldiers emerged stiffly from their wet bivouacs. 'One might imagine the whole plain itself to be undergoing a movement,' observed Sergeant Cotton nearby. Tens of thousands of specks began stirring like an animated ant colony along the whole length of the high ground. As they scurried to and fro, lighting fires and foraging for food, red British sections began to coalesce in between the darker colours of the foreign contingents. 'Imagine seventy thousand men huddled together,' recalled Cotton. 'The buzzing resembled the distant roar of the sea against a rocky coast.'[10]

It was a reluctant reveille for many. Corporal John Dickson, a Glaswegian with the Scots Greys, was woken by his friend MacGee. 'Damn your eyes, boys,' he exclaimed, 'there's the bugle!' Nobody wanted to hear it, especially Dickson, who claimed 'it's the horse's chains clanking'. 'Clankin'?' responded MacGee, 'what's that, then?' as according to Dickson 'a clear blast fell on our ears'. The dawn 'Stand To', ordered in case of surprise attack, created a brief coming together of unit lines. 'I never felt colder in my life,' remembered Sergeant Duncan Robertson, with the 92nd Gordon Highlanders, 'everyone of us was shaking like an aspen leaf … We seemed as if under a fit of ague,' he complained, until an issue of the gin allowance thawed them out, 'infusing warmth into our almost inanimate frames'. Many had been so tired that they had simply lain in the mud. Complaints about stiffness and cramp are universal to all the contemporary accounts of waking up on the dawn of Waterloo. One soldier named Thomas, with the 71st Regiment to the right of the line, claimed he was 'so stiff and sore from the rain I could not move with freedom for some time'. By six o'clock some brief snatches of golden sunlight began to pierce the clouds and a breeze developed. 'Under the cheering influence of which, we began to clean our muskets for the coming strife,' recalled Thomas Morris, with the 73rd. 'Having shaved myself and put on a clean shirt, I felt tolerable comfortable,' he reflected, 'although many around me were complaining much of cramps and agues.'[11]

With the French closing up on the opposite ridge at dawn, 150,000 men with 40,000 to 50,000 horses now filled eight square miles of countryside. There was a gap of between 1,300 to 400 yards between the opposing armies, adding to the crowding in the available space behind the ridge lines. The first requirement for a chilled soldier emerging from his wet shelter was to urinate. Regiments numbering between 600 and 750 men shared restricted space with thousands of horses, all needing to defecate. With no provision for latrine space, and orders to remain in situ as deployed, the whole area began to resemble a huge midden, as men engaged in traditional morning ablutions cheek by jowl. The distinctive odour of the nineteenth-century battlefield – pungent smells of excrement, manure and sweat-encrusted wet uniforms, mixed with those of wood smoke, cooking, trampled crops, dank straw and mud – permeated the entire area. All that was missing was the whiff of gunpowder and the distinctive odour of freshly spilled blood.

Soldiers gobble rather than eat food. Wellington had a known penchant for constantly adjusting deployments at the last minute, which meant the abandonment of any cooking under way. French soldiers generally prepared an all-in soup prior to battle. The British had 'stirabout', a porridge-like mess that broke down steely hard issue biscuits, mixed with raw and often hairy meat and anything else that was at hand. Should the drums suddenly beat 'To Arms!', pots were tipped onto fires while the men would quickly stuff anything edible into their haversacks, to chew on later. Private Mathew Clay, at the Hougoumont farm with the 3rd Guards Light Companies, was lucky enough that morning to get an ounce of bread from his sergeant and a share of a foraged pig, 'a portion of the head, in its rough state'. It was cooked over the same fire that was drying out their clothes. His 'separate portion of meat' was skewered over it. When it became 'warmed through and blackened with smoke I partook of a little, but finding it too raw and unsavoury (having neither bread or salt), I put the remainder in my haversack.' Hardly appetising by modern standards.

Muskets had to be serviced as the first priority on waking. Cartridges made wet by the rain had to be removed from loaded pieces and the wet powder residue cleared from the barrel. The simple solution, far easier than drawing the charge, was to fire the weapon off, which particularly irritated Wellington and alarmed nervous officers, but did not trouble the men. Clay discharged his into a bank. Sergeant Cotton was close by with the 7th Hussars and recalled 'a continual irregular popping along the line, not unlike a skirmish, occasioned by those who were cleaning their firearms'. Clay then ensured his musket was 'well flinted and oiled'. Damp conditions were affecting the lock springs, which had 'become wood-bound and would not act correctly', Clay explained, looking for 'clumsy flints' which 'became useless'. Clay thought he had better find a replacement for his defective one, 'from those that were laying about amongst the slain'. This would become an option within a few hours. At least he had a change of linen, taken from 'amongst the dead bodies of some of our German allies' at Quatre-Bras.[12]

Some of their German allies were finding conditions more difficult than their phlegmatic British veteran comrades. Sergeant Johann Doring, with the 28th Orange Nassau Regiment, recalled 'it was still raining cats and dogs' at dawn, but it did become clearer. A more resilient Captain von Scriba, with the Bremen Field Battalion in Kielmansegg's Hanoverian Brigade, remembered that by eight o'clock 'the sun's rays did their charitable work and enlivened the faces that had been marked by the chill, by hunger, wetness and exhaustion'. A moderate breeze began to dry out the ground. There was still no food for the Hanoverians and 'no thought of obtaining provisions, although one or the other were lucky to get something for their money'. Sergeant Doring's men benefited from constant readjustments of the line to the left of the ridge. 'There seemed no end to the corps' continuous marching back and forth,' which at least gave opportunities to forage. 'Our stomachs insisted on their right,' Doring stressed, 'and as our hunger was getting worse, the farms, mills etc. located between the lines were plundered, both by our troops and the French.' Livestock was stolen and vegetables were pilfered from the fields round about. Pieces of pig were 'half boiled or half grilled, [and] devoured with the greatest haste and appetite'. Plundering was a non-belligerent activity conducted alongside French soldiers, who were briefly 'the best of friends', Doring recalled. 'Nobody gave a thought to the prospect that in a few hours they would meet in a fight for life and death.' First, they had to eat.

Captain Carl Jacobi, with the Hanoverian Lüneburg Field Battalion, was at the fringes of exposure when he awoke. His feet were swollen and he only had the sodden blanket that his superior's orderly had given him to ward off the night's rain. His men 'rose, one by one, from their wet bedding, but there was no cheerful moving about of well-refreshed comrades in arms, instead only the sight of tired, pale faces and the sound of stifled groans'. 'If only we had some bread!' was the recurring undercurrent of opinion. Jacobi was irritated at the failure of the British commissariat chain to deliver. 'The prosperous city of Brussels was not too far away from the battlefield, where ample stores of navy biscuits and rum had been collected.' But this was unavailable 'because the Brussels highway was completely blocked by disabled carts and wagons'. The 27th Inniskillings were clearing the Waterloo side and pocketing and consuming all they could find. Jacobi moaned at the apparent inability to conclude local contacts, pointing out that they were in the middle of a densely populated 'and rich Brabant region'. His perception was petulantly coloured by discomfort and inexperience. 'The soldier's mettle was to decide the fate of Europe,' he grandiosely commented, 'but nothing was done to raise the morale of the fatigued men.' His men were actually more used to physical hardship than he was, and their attention was focused on the opposite and increasingly crowded ridge line. They like Jacobi began to appreciate 'that a bloody battle was about to be fought'. There was a sense of unreality about their predicament. It was after all a typical Sunday morning, Jacobi mused:

> *While many millions of Christians peacefully wended their way to the sacred houses of God for their Sunday worship, death and destruction were to be sown on these fields of trampled grains.*[13]

'The whole of the opposite heights were covered by the enemy,' observed Thomas, a soldier with the 71st Foot. Edmund Wheatley, a 22-year-old Ensign with the 5th King's German Legion Line Battalion, viewed the same scene from the centre of the Mont St Jean ridge line. 'On the opposite heights we could perceive large dark moving masses of something impossible to distinguish individually.' Wheatley, from Hammersmith in London, had served in the Peninsula and the final campaign in the south of France the year before. The opposite slope looked like a volcano where 'shoals of these gloomy bodies glided down'. There were a lot of French. An exuberant slap on the shoulder confirmed his suspicion. 'That's a battle, my boy!' exclaimed a comrade. 'That's something like a preparation!' Captain Alexander Mercer was also watching intently with his horse artillery battery, and observed that 'everything appeared perfectly quiet'. The French were doing much the same as them, preparing breakfast, 'people moving about individually, and no formation whatever'.[14]

The French like the Allies had slept fitfully, but not the latecomers. 'Ask a man who has been on campaign what the desire for sleep is when exhausted by forced marches and every sort of work involved with making war,' declared Second Lieutenant Jacques Martin, with the 45th Line, and 'he will tell you that in that case you would sleep on bayonets'. 'We awoke once dawn and the mist rising from the earth allowed us to see,' recalled Lieutenant J L Henckens, with the 6th Chasseurs à cheval somewhere between the villages of Plancenoit and Rossomme. It had been a dreadful night. 'There was no way either we or our horses could lie down on the soaked ground so I spent the night of the 17/18 June leaning against my horse which likewise preferred to sleep standing up,' he remembered. They scraped the mud from men and horses and waited for what would happen next.[15]

It was to be a long wait. There was no way the French army was going to be ready to resume operations at 9 am, as ordered by Napoleon. About 44,000 men and 168 cannon were still pressed together in a column two and a half miles long, stretching from Napoleon's headquarters at Le Caillou towards Genappe. They would need at least four and a half hours to negotiate deeply rutted, muddy roads to deploy, then another hour to clean weapons and eat. Colonel Toussaint-Jean Trefçon, a II Corps Division chief of staff, remembered that after setting off at 5 am, 'en route we received an order from the Major General to stop to wash ourselves and eat something'. This was welcome news 'because many of the soldiers were dying with hunger and, often, do not like to fight when they are dirty'. They got moving again at eight o'clock. The battle would have to start with part of the Armée du Nord still moving up. Provision caissons were still bogged down in the mud at Charleroi; it would take considerable time to reassemble units scattered about in miserable bivouacs across a wide swathe of countryside; and the Imperial Guard at the rear was unable to march up from Glabais before nine o'clock.

Foraging, moreover, took time and energy. As one French officer remembered:

> As soon as the troops had taken even a momentary position in the vicinity of a village, they rushed like water from a broken dam all over the country beneath; corn, cattle, bread, meat, even household furniture, linen and clothes disappeared in an instant.

If this was liberation, the local Belgian citizens wanted none of it. 'As our troops quitted these wretched villages, the inhabitants, a most miserable spectacle, reappeared' and surveyed the damage:

It was really miserable to see them collecting their broken furniture; and with their children in their hands look woefully at the cornfields trodden under feet, as if one short hour had destroyed the labours of their life; and reduced them from comfort to extreme poverty.

Both armies plundered, the only difference being that the Anglo-Allies had been directed not to; but hungry soldiers are rarely constrained if unsupervised.[16]

Jean-Baptiste Decoster, described as a 'sturdy, honest-looking countryman', was a Flemish peasant who worked a small farm south of La Belle Alliance that doubled as a tavern for carters on the Brussels road. Having hidden his wife and seven children for the night in Maransart wood nearby, he returned at five o'clock only to be apprehended by French foragers. A French patrol took him to Napoleon at Le Caillou nearby, to act as a guide. Decoster protested: 'Your soldiers are destroying all my property, and my family have nowhere to put their heads.' Napoleon was visibly unimpressed. 'I am Emperor, and can recompense you a hundred times as much,' he impatiently responded. Decoster was dubious about this, and about following Napoleon around during a day that was likely to become dangerous. This attitude was recognised; his hands were tied and he was hoisted onto a horse, whose saddle was attached by a halter to the saddle-bow to one of Napoleon's escorting cavalrymen. Napoleon intended to use his local knowledge. In the myths that have since emerged about Decoster's role, it is not entirely clear whether his information 'about every house, tree, wood and rising ground' was ever used. Many were to remark upon his forlorn presence later that day.[17]

Meanwhile, French soldiers breakfasted on the fruits of their plunder. 'We grilled several beef cutlets, which was truly delicious,' recalled Jacques Martin, with the 45th. Eighteen-year-old Louis Canler, with the 28th Line, remembered stripping muskets to grease them and change the priming. 'One of our corporals, being something of a butcher, killed, skinned and cut up our poor little sheep' captured the night before. As it was being cooked it soon attracted a ravenous audience, more interested in spitting meat than the build-up of battle. Fate dealt them a cruel blow. 'Instead of salt, which we totally lacked, our cook had decided to throw a handful of powder into the pot,' Canler recalled, which meant the outcome 'tasted foul'.[18]

Napoleon's breakfast, accompanied by his generals, was presented with infinitely more care. As they sat down shortly before eight o'clock the Prussian IV corps had already been marching toward them for four hours. The meal was important; Napoleon's Imperial Staff needed to hear how he proposed to fight the coming battle. They in turn had to report how long it was going to take to deploy. General Reille, his II Corps commander, was a Peninsula veteran, with a healthy respect for Wellington. He advised that the Englishman's army would be 'well posted'. 'I consider the English infantry to be impregnable,' he maintained, 'owing to its calm tenacity, and its superior aim in firing.' In order to get at them with the bayonet 'one may expect half the assailants to be brought to the ground'. Other generals argued that their opponent was less agile and less capable of manoeuvre than the French. 'If we cannot defeat them by a direct attack, we may do so by manoeuvring,' Reille urged. Such a frank appraisal was not what Napoleon wanted to hear:

> Because you have been beaten by Wellington, you consider him a great general. And I tell you that Wellington is a bad general, that the English are bad troops, and that this affair is nothing more serious than eating one's breakfast.

'I earnestly hope so,' said Marshal Soult, his chief of staff. Napoleon's peremptory dismissal of Wellington was designed to encourage his subordinates. Energy and personality had enabled him to quickly raise and arm an army within months of his return from Elba. He was well aware that it represented a shadow of the formations he had used to dominate the continent before, and that his present staff was not the best. Many of the great names were missing, leaving what was essentially a 'second eleven' command team. Soult, his chief of staff, was neither suited nor experienced in post. It was staff muddles 48 hours before that had prevented a successful annihilation of the Prussians at Ligny and enabled Wellington's escape. Marshal Grouchy, clumsily pursuing the Prussians, was actually a cavalry commander leading an infantry corps. Marshal Ney, 'the bravest of the brave', and popularly acclaimed as the 'red lion' or 'red-head' because of his distinctive hair, was not his best tactician, and had mismanaged the left wing at Quatre-Bras. Ney, the saviour of the French rearguard during the catastrophic winter retreat from Moscow in 1812, was displaying many of the characteristics of post-combat stress disorder. He was worn out and indifferent to death. Even Sergeant Hippolyte de Mauduit in the Imperial Guard had deduced 'it would have been preferable to force Wellington to manoeuvre rather than leave him to fight on ground of his own choosing'.[19]

In reality, Napoleon's past successes had been a product of his unpredictability. He was the consummate opportunist. Nobody ever knew what he would do next. Field Marshal Prince Karl Phillip Wrede, who served with him between 1805 and 1813, once asked him the secret of his brilliant tactical and strategic successes. His enigmatic response was typical. 'Je n'en ai pas. Je n'ai point de plan de campagne' ('I have no secret. I have no campaign plan'), he replied. Napoleon simply aimed his blows whenever and wherever they would achieve maximum effect. Buoyed by his initial success thus far, Napoleon had few doubts about what he would do next. Weather and the terrain before him precluded manoeuvre. The ground would take too long to dry out. He needed to bludgeon his way through whatever line Wellington had erected and seize Brussels, his political prize. Wellington 'has thrown the dice', Napoleon announced to his assembled staff, 'and our number has turned up!' There would be a feint attack to the right of Wellington's line, precisely where Wellington would anticipate manoeuvre. Meanwhile, he would aim a massive blow at the left centre of the Mont St Jean ridge line. Once he overran the farm at La Haye Sainte and the crossroads, the way to Brussels would be open.[20]

Wellington had been riding the ridge line with his staff since 6.30 that morning, cross-checking that the pencilled line on his map would commit his 73,000 men precisely where he had ordered. An astute defence tactician, he was the proven master of profiting from his opponent's mistakes. It remained to be seen if Napoleon would make any. Wellington was convinced Napoleon would attempt some form of creative manoeuvre. After being compromised at the very outset of the campaign, he had a healthy respect for what might happen next. Some 17,000 men, or 23 per cent of his army, had been posted around Hal and Tublize to the west, in the expectation the French might try to outflank his right wing via Mons and cut him off from the sea and the Royal Navy at Antwerp. This was a risk. A substantial element of his army was now further away than the Prussians.

Wellington rarely delegated, which was why he constantly rode to and fro co-ordinating and checking. The Prussians were anticipated to appear within a few hours, but this was not certain. Part of the staff ride was to tangibly demonstrate to his troops that he was in control. His dress was distinctive in its dullness, designed to project the image of a gentlemanly 'player'. He wore comfortable civilian clothes, white buckskin breeches and a blue coat over the knotted sash of a Spanish field marshal. The only concession to uniform was a low cocked hat adorned with the four cockades of Britain, Spain, Portugal and the Netherlands. Overall was a blue cloak, constantly removed and replaced, because, he said, 'I never get wet if I can help it.' This self-promotion was all part of his form, important in such a disparate army. British soldiers, who didn't care much for frippery, liked the irreverent approach, which hinted at a more practical professional. Lord Edward Somerset, at the head of the Household Cavalry, remembered Wellington's staff passing by as if 'riding for pleasure'. Ensign Rees Gronow, with the 1st Foot Guards, watched the staff sweep by near Hougoumont 'as gay and unconcerned as if they were riding to meet with the hounds in some quiet English county'. Wellington was, however, preoccupied. He might be considered the consummate defensive tactician, but now he was to meet the acknowledged master of manoeuvre and attack for the first time.[21]

Sunrise to 10 am

The Prize: Brussels

Brussels from first light exhibited all the unstable moods of a city about to be engulfed in conflict, alternating between shaky optimism and blind panic. Napoleon expected to sleep there that night. It was the capital of Europe's newest king, the fledgeling state of the Dutch Netherlands, barely months old, whose 80,000 inhabitants were ruled by the Prince of Orange. British society, excluded from Europe by the 'Great War', had flocked back to the continent, especially Brussels, after Napoleon's abdication in 1814. The cost of living was cheap. The past 48 hours had seen the city make the transition from the venue of the Duchess of Richmond's ball to a prospective battlefield, with the enemy barely 12 miles away. Charlotte Eaton (née Waldie), a British tourist, described the city's transformation:

> *The Parc! What a different scene did its green alleys present this evening from that which they exhibited at the same hour last night! Then it was crowded with the young and gay, and the gallant of the British army, with the very men who were now engaged in deadly strife, and perhaps bleeding on the ground. Then it was filled with female faces, sparkling with mirth and gaiety; now terror and anxiety, and grief, were marked upon every countenance we met.*

Whig MP Thomas Creevey heard the British army had retreated, and this appeared to be confirmed by 'the baggage of the army coming down the Rue de Namur, filling up my street, and horses were picketed all round the Parc'. Sunday, 18 June 'was of course a most anxious day for us' because 'it was clear there was going to be a desperate battle'.[22]

The night before, the wounded from Quatre-Bras and Ligny had started to arrive, recalled hospital assistant John Davy in Brussels; 'completely ignorant of what was passing, these unhappy ones bringing the worst accounts of defeat and disaster.' Injured troops were still coming in at dawn and were filling the city. 'An appalling spectacle,' an eyewitness recalled, soldiers 'I had so much admired at the review, now lying helpless and mutilated – their uniforms soiled with blood and dirt – their mouths blackened with biting their cartridges'. Many collapsed in the streets, drained by the physical effort of their journeys and loss of blood. The mayor of Brussels, Baron van der linden d'Hooghvorst, had already appealed to the citizens to bring mattresses, sheets, blankets and pillows to the town hall in the main square, the Grand Place. 'The pressing circumstances in which we find ourselves,' he announced, 'makes it imperative that people should come to the aid of the army.' Old linen and lint for bandages was passed on to priests. Many of the regiments based in Brussels had been Scottish, and the Highlanders with their distinctive kilts had been great favourites with the children. The youngsters used to take them home to their parents exclaiming 'Voici, notre brave Ecossois!' ('Here are our brave Scots!'). The population now responded generously, practically every house taking in wounded. Barracks and even churches were requisitioned as temporary hospitals. Doctors chalked the numbers and nationalities of the wounded outside on the doors.[23]

'Sunday morning was ushered in by one of the most dreadful tempests I ever remember,' recalled the eyewitness. 'The sky looked like that in Poussin's picture of the Deluge … a heavy black cloud spread, like the wings of a monstrous vulture over Brussels.' Rifleman Edward Costello, wounded with the 1/95th at Quatre-Bras, emerged from one of the side streets into the Grand Place 'gazing on some hundreds of wounded men who were stretched out on the straw'. A famous tourist spot today, the huge square was filled with the wounded, lying on straw across the cobblestones – with no shelter, they had been soaked by the summer storm. Wagons continually drew up to unload more mangled humanity. Friend and foe and different nationalities all lay indiscriminately side by side, with pathways left clear in between, for surgeons and attendants to treat them. Three miles away, at the Château de Walcheuse at Laeken, temporary visitor Caroline Capel would not forget 'the horrors of that night' as the 18 June dawned:

The rain and darkness and wind were frightful and our court-yard was filled during the night with poor wounded drenched soldiers and horses seeking for refuge and assistance.

'The 18th was a terrible day at Brussels,' recalled John Davy. 'The very elements seemed to be at war, we had thunder, lightning, rain and hail, in extent I hardly remember having witnessed.'[24]

Secretary of State Baron de Capellen had already issued three bulletins over the previous 24 hours. These were pasted up on the walls of Brussels and gave the latest information. When news emerged about Blücher's reverse at Ligny and Wellington's retreat to Waterloo, panic ensued. The first two bulletins had stated the Allies were going to attack the French; then the third, posted at seven o'clock the night before, announced Blücher was in Wavre and Wellington just 12 miles outside Brussels. There was now a general exodus, headed for the port of Antwerp. Charlotte Eaton, having already experienced a scare during the night, believing the French had entered Brussels, was off. 'It seemed to be the general opinion, that before morning the French would be here,' she remembered. There was unrest throughout the city. Staff officer Major Wylie was surrounded by a noisy crowd in the Place Royale, who demanded to know:

What is the reason that nothing is being done for our security? Are we to be left abandoned to the enemy? ...Why is not the City Guard ordered out to defend the town?

French prisoners were at first mistaken for conquerors –
because some, despite their injuries, conducted themselves
as such:

> *I noticed one, a fine fellow, who had had one arm shot off; and*
> *though the bloody and mangled tendons were still undressed,*
> *and had actually dried and blackened in the sun, he marched*
> *along with apparent indifference, carrying a loaf of bread under*
> *his remaining arm and shouting 'Vive l'Empereur!'.*

'Prepare the soup,' he recommended, because his friends
would be arriving that evening in Brussels and would join
them in the Grand Place. 'Don't believe him, sir,' a badly
wounded Scotsman whispered, in agony. 'It's all right – I –
assure you –' he haltingly gasped.

John Davy recalled that 'the most alarming reports were
spread and believed'. As a result, remembered Charlotte
Eaton, 'All Brussels seemed to be running away, and the only
competition appeared to be who should run the fastest.'
Fugitives soon clogged the Antwerp road. Riders slipping on
wet cobblestones were thrown into the path of hurrying
wagons in the panicky rush and crushed to death. Peasants
took advantage of the turmoil and began looting, alongside
deserters, who made off with valuables and abandoned
baggage. The more circumspect remained at home to await
developments, as short outbursts of panic became interspersed with longer periods of inactivity.[25]

Belgium had been one of the last places in Europe where
Napoleonic rule had prevailed, two months longer than
Paris, which had capitulated in March 1814. Now, according
to Major William Frye, caught up by the crisis in Brussels
while holidaying on leave, 'All the caricatures and satires
against Napoleon have disappeared from the windows and

stalls.' Shops were shut. Fanny Burney, a novelist and expat, married to a royalist general living north of the park, remembered that people virtually decamped to the streets so as not to miss what was going on. 'Doors seemed to be of no use, for they were never shut.' Business and normal social intercourse stopped. Even if an individual went indoors, it was in order to look back out through their windows. 'The whole population of the city seemed constantly in public view,' she recalled. Pessimism reigned, Frye commented:

> *The inhabitants in general wish well to the arms of Napoleon, but they know that the retreat of the English army must necessarily take place through their town.*

If that occurred, the British would fight, with consequences for the inhabitants, 'houses liable to be burned or pillaged by friend or foe'. The official bulletin, the latest issued at eight o'clock that morning, stated that the authorities were not abandoning the city. Wellington was defending along the Forest of Soignes, they were reassured, which according to Frye 'only serves to increase the confusion and consternation'. In the absence of news it was better to sit tight. 'All of which we seemed capable,' recalled Fanny Burney, 'was, to enquire or to relate, to speak or to hear.' The same information was re-processed and spun again as the latest news.[26]

Thomas Creevey's stepdaughter, living with him next to the park, had a clear view of the Namur Gate. At five o'clock that morning she saw 'a troop of horse gallop down into the Place with their swords drawn'. It was typical of the many crises that were to occur that day. 'Of course we imagined some detachment of French dragoons were in possession of Brussels', but nothing happened. 'Our fright you may have some idea of,' she recalled. The gate guard were called out and 'to our great surprise the guard came marching quietly back again and piled arms as if nothing had happened'. Sunday was developing into a miserable day. But it was not all bad. Martha Deacon completed her epic 16-mile struggle to reach Brussels despite being in the final stages of pregnancy, shepherding three bedraggled and very wet children. Her husband Ensign Thomas Deacon, wounded with the 73rd Foot, was found to be in comfortable accommodation and the whole family could join him. Within 24 hours Martha gave birth to a little girl, who would be christened 'Waterloo' Deacon.

At about 10 am church bells began ringing out all over Brussels, summoning the faithful to Sunday Mass. 'The churches in Flanders are usually little frequented,' observed John Davy, but on this day 'I had the curiosity to look into one in passing, it was full of people in fervid devotion.' Davy was a devout man and admitted, 'It is a humiliating and painful reflection, but is perfectly correct, that fear is the parent of natural religion.' The church of St Nicholas was no exception. First of all the preacher saw his restless flock was beginning to fidget. Very soon they started to hurry outside. In the distance the first sounds of cannon fire could be discerned, familiar to all those who had heard it further away 48 hours before. Now they had something tangible to pray about. The anticipated battle was starting.[27]

The Men —•

10 am to 11.30 am

11.30 AM The Opening Shots at Hougoumont

The battle opens with a French infantry assault on the British held farm at Hougoumont, to the right of Wellington's line.

Cpl Louis Canler
Lt Jacques Martin
Capt Pierre Duthilt

PAPELOTTE
FARM

Capt John Kinca
Lt George Simmo

Sgt Archibald Johnston
Cpl John Dickinson
Cornet Francis Kinchant
Sgt Charles Ewart

MONT S
FAR

PLANCENOIT
VILLAGE

Jean-Roch Coignet
Sgt Hippolyte de Mauduit

oleon Bonaparte
Baptiste Decoster

LA BELLE
ALLIANCE

Sgt Maj de Lerréguy Cívrieux
Lt Legros

Pte Mathew Clay
Capt Moritz Büsgen
Lt Col James Macdonell

LA HAYE SAINTE
FARM

CHÂTEAU HOUGOUMONT

Pte Friedrich Lindau
Maj George Baring

Sgt William Wheeler

Capt Carl Jacobi
Ensign Edward Wheatley

Pte Joseph Lord
Pte Thomas Playford

Mrs Martha Deacon
to Brussels

The Multi-Coloured Line: Wellington's Army

The entire Mont St Jean slope appeared to be in motion itself as the Anglo-Allied army made ready for battle. A moving mass of human beings went about their increasingly purposeful business, one officer recalling the sight of 'soldiers cleaning their arms and examining the locks, multitudes carrying wood, water and straw from the village and farm of Mont St Jean'. Breakfast was cooked for those fortunate enough to have any. More settled weather had raised spirits. The officer watching crowds of soldiers splashing through the ankle-deep mud also noted:

> *They were generally gay, and apparently thinking of everything but the approaching combat, which snapped the thread of existence of so many of them, deprived a few of legs and arms, and disabled many for life.*

After daybreak 'several hours passed quietly,' recalled Assistant Surgeon John Haddy James, with the 1st Life Guards:

> *The weather improved and later the sun came out. Nothing was heard except dropping shots now and then, principally from straggling parties of our own troops discharging their pieces, and at intervals the drums of different regiments beating along the line. A few alterations were made in the position of the troops, but mostly we were waiting and still.*[1]

'About ten o'clock,' Ensign Edmund Wheatley of the King's German Legion remembered, 'the order came to clean out the muskets and fresh load them.' With tension beginning to rise, 'half an allowance of rum was then issued, and we descended into the plain, and took our position in solid squares', to the right of the Brussels road facing the French. When they reached their position they were told they would fight from here, 'but if we like, to lay down'. The 1/27th Inniskillings, having reached Waterloo four hours before, were marched out into a field just west of the village of Mont St Jean. They were to await events, deployed as a centre reserve to the Anglo-Allied line. Exhausted and with canteens slopping with rum, they needed little bidding to finally stack arms, and soon most were asleep. Wheatley, forward of them, dwelled on the coming battle:

It is an awful situation to be in, to stand with a sharp edged instrument at one's side, waiting for the signal to drag it out of its peaceful innocent house to snap the thread of existence of those we never saw, never spoke to, never offended.

He glanced at the French opposite 'whose acquaintance would delight and conversation improve me, yet with all my soul I wished them dead as the earth they tramped on and anticipated their total annihilation'. Looking behind, he was reassured to see that 'shoals of cavalry and artillery suddenly in our rear' had been 'arranged in excellent order as if by magic wand'. Wheatley was from Hammersmith, and the impressive array of the 'whole of the Horse Guards' brought back memories of home. 'For my part I thought they were at Knightsbridge barracks or prancing on St James Street.'[2]

As Wellington's army drew up for battle it presented a motley multi-coloured line. There were scarlet and green British, blue Belgians and Dutch militia, Nassau soldiers with green jackets with yellow piping, Hanoverians in British red or green, and the 'Black Horde' Brunswickers with their distinctive silver death's head insignia mounted on black. Sir Henry Hardinge, a Peninsular War veteran, was moved to remark uncharitably that 'this army is not unlike a French pack of hounds: pointers, poodles, turnspits, all mixed up together and running in sad confusion'. Wellington had taken great care to mix contingents and add officers from veteran British and King's German Legion battalions. 'I had only about 35,000 men on whom I could thoroughly rely,' he was later to admit; 'the remainder were but too likely to run away.'[3]

When the news of Napoleon's return first broke and the crisis began, Wellington originally asked the government for 40,000 British infantry, 15,000 cavalry, 150 guns and a staff of his own choosing. He received only 30,000 in all and a four-page letter of apology from the Duke of York, the British Commander-in-Chief. 'To tell you the truth,' Wellington wrote back, 'I am not well pleased ... It will be admitted that the army is not a very good one.' Many of his Peninsula veterans were dispersed in Canada, Ireland and America, or were in transit back. 'I have got an infamous army, very weak and ill-equipped, and a very inexperienced staff,' declared a clearly irritated Wellington:

In my opinion they are doing nothing in England. They have not raised a man; they have not called out the militia either in England or Ireland.

In all Wellington had two infantry corps, a cavalry corps and a general reserve two divisions strong. It was an infantry-heavy formation, with 53,000 foot compared to 13,350 cavalry, or four to one. Wellington had 157 guns and howitzers deployed on the ridge, nearly 90 less than the French. Even so, 39 of his 84 infantry battalions were British or King's German Legion, a crack unit loyal to George III and the equal of any British formation. When Whig MP Thomas Creevey had asked Wellington at Brussels about his chances in the forthcoming battle, Wellington had pointed to a British soldier wandering through the Parc. 'There,' he said, 'it all depends on that article whether we do the business or not. Give me enough of it, and I am sure.'[4]

British soldiers shared Wellington's somewhat jaundiced opinion of 'foreigners'. Soldiers, as they do, swiftly reduced them to stereotypes: brave but nervous Frenchmen, brave but clumsy Prussians, cowardly Belgians, inexperienced Dutchmen and of course brave, stoic and courageous Englishmen. Valorous examples outside these rough parameters were regarded as exceptional. 'The foreign troops generally had disappointed expectation' was the caustic comment from one of Wellington's quartermaster staff at Quatre-Bras. The Netherlands contingent had actually borne the brunt of the fighting at the crossroads before the British appeared, suffering as many if not greater casualties. The British reinforced late, and then with just three eighths of their infantry, a third of the guns and a fraction of the cavalry. Lieutenant John Kincaid, with the 1/95th Rifles, thought the foreigners at Quatre-Bras were 'little better than raw militia'. 'Our foreign auxiliaries constituted more than half our numerical strength,' he explained, but despite exceptions they were like 'a body without a soul, or like an inflated pillow, that gives to the touch, and resumes its shape again when the pressure ceases'. In short, they were windy, 'not to mention the many who went clear out of the field'. The average British soldier accepted he was on his own and would need to be wary of what was going on within the integrated formations to his left and right. Lieutenant Donald Mackenzie, with the 42nd Foot, summed up the prevailing viewpoint on the Mont St Jean ridge:

> We knew the Prussians had been beaten; we felt no confidence in the Belgian troops with whom we were associated; we knew … that defeat meant complete rout. At the same time we had faith in our general and in ourselves, and were determined that the French would only take our next position with our lives.[5]

Following decisions taken at the Congress of Vienna in 1814, Wellington was commanding contingents from new states identifiable for the first time in a future, modern Europe. In effect they were the European genesis of the NATO armies that emerged after 1945 following a similarly destructive conflict in Europe. Forces from Britain, the Netherlands, Belgium, and principalities and states that would one day make up a united Germany, also formed part of the defence of Europe during the Cold War. Moreover Wellington's 'infamous army' was to share many of the characteristics and frictions that currently dog the international staffs of the present-day NATO organisation. Different cultures obliged to co-operate militarily often experience frustrations executing military decisions arrived at from differing national perspectives. Credibility and trust are essential prerequisites. How reliable was an ally in a tight spot?

The largest foreign contingent was the Hanoverians, which included Jacobi's battalion, at 17 per cent of the Allied army, or just under two of every ten men. Major William Frye, on leave in Belgium before the crisis, had seen them on manoeuvres at a 2nd British Division review. 'The British were perfect,' he predictably commented, 'the Hanoverians not so, they being for the most part new levies.' He watched as one of the battalions clumsily attempted to form echelon on the line of march. Its battalion commander was shouted at by the Brigade Major, demanding to know: 'Mein Gott, Herr Major, wo gehen Sie hin?' ('My God, Major – where are you going!'). Wellington was hardly reassured when, on the eve of hostilities, he was informed by the Commander of Ath in the Netherlands that the Hanoverian Brigade Reserve had 'many soldiers who have never fired a shot', and asked whether he could send powder and cartridges to 'exercise them'. Lieutenant-Colonel the Lord Saltoun, with the 1st Foot Guards, commented that the 'Hanoverian landwehr [militia], are tolerably good-looking men in general, but, of course being newly conscripted are a good deal in want of drill and other necessary training.' Their morale was good and they were pleased to be with the British. However, British soldiers preferred to keep their distance from the 'rid Jarmins', as they called them, because they too wore red uniforms.[6]

Captain Carl Jacobi, with the Hanoverian Lüneburg Field Battalion, may have given a false impression, slumbering in the front line with several of his exhausted comrades. Nothing appeared to be happening. With clearing skies and a little sunlight, 'a little dried spot soon enticed me to go to sleep'. There was even time to complete the sale of a horse to Captain von Schlutter, the aide-de-camp to his commanding officer General von Alten. Von Schlutter arrived with the selling price of 30 gold Napoleons. Such matters needed to be settled before the killing began; it was bad luck to leave money outstanding. The horse was for von Schlutter's brother, and he had only hours to live.

Jacobi was unhappy with the English. Many Hanoverian staff officers had lost appointments and seniority following Wellington's insistence of assigning Hanoverian brigades to British divisions. Jacobi very nearly missed the campaign, but was assigned a company at the last moment. 'At a stroke of a pen we no longer would appear on the battlefield as Hanoverians; we were now individual components of English divisions,' he complained. 'To us at least it was a severe blow to our morale', not helped by 'English generals totally unfamiliar with the traditions of the Hanoverians'. The English were unable to 'connect to the German soldier's nature'. Such frustrations are echoed within today's military alliances. Jacobi thought the British difficult and disdainful masters: 'In their eyes, everything was imperfect,' he insisted. Language differences and disparities in pay resulted in 'no camaraderie among the allied troops, not even among the officers', Jacobi recalled. The British were paid more, and the impact on local lifestyles stymied closer relationships. German became the first language spoken between the eight national contingents. Even the King's German Legion, making up 10 per cent of the whole, preferred to keep their distance. 'The fifteen-year-old ensign with the red sash,' Jacobi remembered, 'proudly looked down upon the older Hanoverian officers.' The lack of common understanding was to bedevil effective communications at times in the coming battle.[7]

The 'inexperienced Dutchmen', the next largest contingent at 13 per cent, were inextricably linked to the 6 per cent of 'cowardly Belgians'. In contemporary parlance they were called 'North Netherlands' and 'South Netherlands' respectively. There were some Dutch troops who were confused about their status; they had only recently been marching under Napoleon's banner. The Belgians, who had been promised independence in 1814, found they had exchanged the Napoleonic 'yoke' for that of annexation by Holland. The United Netherlands was barely 12 months old, and its new king the Prince of Orange had been installed as a client ruler by the British just three months earlier. It served as a buffer state between France and Germany and a corridor link to Britain's ally Prussia. 'Slender Billy', or the 'Young Frog' as the Prince was called, was totally out of his depth as a corps commander. It could have been worse; until replaced by Wellington he was the overall Allied commander. Even the lowliest private appreciated that this would have been a disaster. William Wheeler, with the 51st Foot, had already commented, 'He is not the man for us,' adding, 'Surely we shall not be led to battle by that boy.' Wellington's laconic appraisal was simply 'The Prince is a brave young man, but that's all.' Now he was a corps commander.[8]

Major Friedrich von Gagern, serving with the staff of the 2nd Netherlands Division, acknowledged that 'our troops were generally very willing', but had 'insufficient time to know their commanders on the field of battle'. As a consequence 'there was not the mutual trust and self assurance that one can see in experienced armies'. This was echoed by Prince Bernard of Saxe-Weimar, commanding the division's 2nd Brigade. Like many of the Hanoverians, he bristled at the off-hand treatment they received from British staffs. 'Of course, my dear Captain,' he later wrote to Ernst van Löben Sels, when requesting historical information, 'you may have noticed that the officers in our army who served in the campaign of 1815 do not like to discuss it.' He had 'bitter' memories 'of the wrong and half measures that preceded the outbreak of hostilities, the confusion which characterised the operations'. In particular he felt that Wellington was cold and disdainful when dealing with Dutch commanders, and that they received scant recognition in his famous subsequent report. Some of the Dutch felt they were relegated to the role of cannon fodder that the English needed to hold the line, while they won the battle.

'After ten o'clock word arrived that the French were coming,' recalled von Gagern. He had spent much of the morning checking and ensuring that his young soldiers had cleaned their muskets. 'They would not have been able to fire a single shot,' he observed 'because they were all wet and rusty inside and out.' He saw Wellington riding the line and giving orders for the positioning of each regiment. 'What I could see of our army had all been formed in squares,' he remembered; the tension was palpably increasing. Like the British, von Gagern hoped his new conscripts would prove steady.

In contrast to the Hanoverians and Dutch, the King's German Legion was regarded by the British as being effective enough. They were established in 1803 from refugees that had fled the Electorate of Hanover after the French had overrun their country. Now they were an integral part of the British army, with their own depot and base at Bexhill-on-Sea, and were inter-marrying with the local women.

The 27-year-old Friedrich Lindau, who according to the recruiting record was blond, blue-eyed and quite tall at 5 ft 9 ins, epitomised the typical Legion infantryman. At about 10.30 am he was pushing a cart onto the Brussels road at La Haye Sainte to help build an *abatis* of sloped wooden stakes to block the road to cavalry. He and his men were thickening it up with farm implements they had gathered. A shoe-maker by trade, he had run away from Hamelin and joined the 2nd Light Battalion in 1809. He was a hard-bitten Peninsula veteran and had allegedly killed a man in a bar brawl the year before. Lindau had fond memories of the English coastline, where 'we caught crabs on the shore when it was ebb tide, cooked them in the barracks and ate them with much pleasure'. Like many exiles, Lindau was an adventurer and made a tough, uncompromising soldier. They had their personal reasons for fighting the French.

Simon Lehman, in Lindau's battalion, was another Peninsula veteran, having fought six battles, and was renowned as the hero of the Adour river crossing near Bayonne in February 1814, when he swam to capture the flag of a de-masted French corvette. Having been discharged and returned to Hanover after Napoleon's exile, he had re-enlisted six weeks before Waterloo, after 'Boney' came back. It was the response of a typical veteran, more likely stemming from the need to stand with his comrades rather than the lure of battle, whose bloody risks he knew only too well. Why else did he return? Many had fallen on hard economic times, which the prospect of loot could assuage. Recruiting records offer tantalising facts but no motives. Was it unfinished business with the French?[9]

As acceptable as the Legion was, recently it had lost much of its Hanoverian flavour and discipline. There were now many other central European nationalities serving alongside Germans. However, as Ensign Edmund Wheatley was to discover, it was still an unsuitable corps for an English gentleman to join, which had complicated his relationship with the love of his life, Miss Eliza Brookes. Wheatley used to meet her at the Hyde Park turnpike in London. Her family was unimpressed by Wheatley's choice of regiment. 'Not an individual related to you approves of me,' he sadly lamented. Wheatley's diary is full of affirmations of love for Eliza, but he already had a reputation for being headstrong. He had fought a duel with a young man who had gone to his school. When

Wheatley shifted his attention to the French on the opposite ridge, he considered they were 'by far, more commendable characters than these heavy selfish Germans'. British officers regarded themselves in a class of their own, and Wheatley spent his leisure time with the other English officers in the brigade. He had no close German friends and was going to feel isolated in the coming battle.[10]

For every one of 'that article' – the British soldier identified by Wellington – there were two Germans, Dutch or Belgians, seven nationalities in all, and eight counting the Prussians. The heterogeneous contingents had little in common, neither language, nor customs nor ideals. But as they stood on the Mont St Jean ridge they knew they needed each other. The genial British soldier was able to mix with anyone. There was more dissension between the varying national contingents than unhappiness with the fact of overall British command. Wellington and his staff and soldiers were well used to working with allies in Spain and Flanders. When confronted with an unknown potential, the British soldier characteristically resorted to scepticism. The British actually formed only about 36 per cent of the whole, so were reliant on 64 per cent of the line being held by foreigners. Ironically, facing a desperate battle, they were going to be relying on the 'brave but clumsy Prussians' arriving in time.

Such detail was lost on the average British soldier, who tended to have an air of arrogant superiority when dealing with over-dressed foreigners. 'Ah yes, and to look at them marching forward as proud as a Spaniard on sentry,' recalled Private James Gunn as a contingent of Hanoverians and Brunswick troops passed their front, looking like 'a turkey cock in a farmyard, dressed in dark uniform, something like a horse's tail in their helmets with the shape of a scalped face and a man's shin bone'. Gunn sardonically commented, 'If they did not frighten the French, most assuredly the French frightened them.' He had been unimpressed by their performance at Quatre-Bras:

On the French coming forward to attack without minding what became of their commander the duke of Brunswick who was killed and that some of them did not stop until they reached Antwerp about 40 miles from the battlefield.

They looked good, some cynical British soldiers observed, but could they fight?[11]

British soldiers were not totally homogenous themselves: some were Scottish, others were Irish and a few were black. The latter included 24-year-old George Rose, who according to his discharge papers was originally recruited as a labourer. He was 5 ft 6 ins tall, with black hair and black eyes, a 'man of colour' with a 'copper complexion'. He stood alongside Thomas Morris in the ranks of the 73rd Foot, between Hougoumont and La Haye Sainte. Rose was attested in London in August 1809, but Morris, who joined three years later, makes no mention of him in his detailed and very observant diary. This suggests his presence was either unremarkable or, more likely, by the time Thomas Morris's diary was published in 1847, the so-called 'golden age' for black soldiers serving in the British army was over. He was either ignored or air-brushed from the text. After the mid 1840s black men were no longer recruited.

Rose was born into slavery at Spanish Town, Jamaica, in 1787. By 1809 he had escaped, narrowly avoiding capture on the way. Enlisting in the 73rd Foot was the safest and best way of avoiding a return to shackles. Thousands of enslaved and free blacks had arrived in London after the Somerset case of 1772 had ruled that slavery was unsupported by the existing law in England. Some black sailors had fought at Trafalgar in 1805. When Rose enlisted he was asserting control over his destiny, because all recruits had to be volunteers and were paid the same as their white counterparts. The alternatives were bleak: either employment as a servant or a life of begging.

George Rose had suffered considerably the night before. The climate in northern Europe was hardly suited to men used to hot Caribbean temperatures, and for this reason many black soldiers tended to serve in the Far East. Trumpeter William Affleck, with the 10th Hussars, was born at St Kitts in the West Indies and likewise had a very uncomfortable night. Taller than Rose at 5 ft 9 ins, he had a 'black complexion' and had also been a labourer. Not only was he to lose his teeth that day, fatal for a bugler, he was already in the advanced stages of pneumonia. One of the reasons given for his subsequent discharge four years later was 'pain of the chest, since exposed to wet and cold service in France 1815'. At 36, Affleck was an old war horse, and may well have been the most decorated black soldier at Waterloo. He had four clasps on his General Service Medal for battles fought on the Spanish Peninsula and in southern France between 1808 and 1814.

George Rose could well have walked across to the 13th Light Dragoon lines to their right and rear to speak with Private William Wilson, another black soldier. He was the same height as Rose and also quite old at 36. Wilson was probably tired of campaigning, and the coming day would make up his mind to leave the army. He would survive and be discharged on a pension of 9d a day 'as worn out'. Wilson was a musician by trade and likely a trumpeter. If Rose had sought advice, Wilson's extensive experience would have enabled him to provide it. He had first enlisted with the 55th Foot during the Revolutionary War in 1795 and served with the 28th Light Dragoons three years later. Since 1803 he had been with the 13th, black military musicians supposedly being much sought after in the high status Household and cavalry regiments, because of their 'natural propensity for music'. In reality they were often employed to promote the regimental image, rather than for their musical capabilities, being shown off as exotic mounted bandsmen.

Rose would have learned from men like Wilson and Affleck that the only way to get on as a black man in the ranks was to demonstrate competency through extensive campaign experience. Rose served in the ranks with 1st company and had 'something about him'. He was resourceful enough to escape as a slave and get to London. He had seen action with the regiment already in Germany in 1813 and had been wounded at Merxem in the Netherlands in 1814. While recruiting in Ireland four years before, he had converted to Methodism, likely because of its pro-abolition slavery stance; he was abstemious and avoided the slippery road of an excess of liquor. The Methodists would have taught him to write, an essential skill if he was ever to be promoted. Rose had been in the thick of the action at Quatre-Bras, where the 73rd lost 52 dead, wounded and missing. He probably viewed the approaching battle as an opportunity, for he was competent and likely to do well, and with his campaign experience was probably measuring the odds against his survival. While soldiers were sensitive to 'racial hierarchy', it was an issue that Rose had already overcome. All that his mates in the line required of him was to be steady in a fight. If Rose was ever to progress, he had first to survive.[12]

The Irish differed from the Scots in terms of their acceptability in the ranks. They were looked down upon. Religion, namely the Anglican Church as distinct from Roman Catholicism, was at the heart of the issue, along with loyalty to the British crown. Catholics remained disenfranchised, and the bungled rebellion of 1798, which spawned atrocities and counter atrocities, together with a tiny French invasion force that landed in Mayo, served to remind everyone it mattered. The murder rate in County Armagh was four times that seen in the English county of Kent. The 1/27th Inniskilling Regiment was recruited from a violent region, the product of centuries of conflict, where 95 per cent of the land was controlled by a 5 per cent (Protestant) minority of the population. Artillery Captain Alexander Mercer was disdainful of the 'childish mummery' of Catholicism and had labelled the Inniskilling Dragoons he encountered on the line of march as 'rollicking Paddies'.

Nevertheless, men like Alexander Dunlop, waiting in reserve to the west of the Mont St Jean farm before 10 am, had been raised on the oral tradition of great warriors and epic battles, a culture honouring brave men who fought and died in battle. Surviving recruitment records show that 90 per cent of the soldiers of the 1/27th Inniskillings were Irish, with just 4 per cent from England and 2 per cent from Scotland. The majority of recruits came from a background of wretched deprivation. Small wonder that Dunlop preferred to give up life as an agricultural labourer to become a British soldier. They fed and clothed him. Despite the mix of religions – there were two Catholics for every Protestant – and differences in language, literacy and social opportunity, these men bonded. The fact that 200 men in the regiment were illiterate, and over 30 could only speak Irish, made them even more likely to mix with each other than the British were. Comrades could share a newspaper or pass on the local news by reading it out of letters from home. The officer corps, dominated by Wellington's strident views on Catholic Emancipation, which no 'gentleman' could support, did not produce division. The men were pragmatic soldiers, hardened by service on the Spanish Peninsula and newly arrived from North America. It was to the same God that they would all pray for mercy in the coming battle.[13]

With just a third of his infantry British, and half the cavalry and guns, Wellington was convinced that his motley line would hold until the Prussians arrived. His core British element had been hastily assembled over four months. Captain Verner, with the 7th Hussars, had been policing the 'No Corn Bill' riots in London when they heard that Napoleon had escaped from Elba. His regiment marched to Brighton and embarked to Flanders within 12 hours. Sergeant Thomas Morris, standing in line to his left, had been comfortably billeted locally, near Waterloo, with a miller and two pretty daughters, but had been 'tired of the monotony'. All the units already in Flanders had shared the 'restlessness' of the 73rd Foot, along with 'an anxiety to know what the French were about, and how soon our services would be required'. That moment had arrived.[14]

Morris and his comrades in the line regiments risked their lives for a shilling (5p) a day. The cavalry, gun crews and Guards infantry regiments got two shillings (10p). Stoppages for 'necessaries' like uniform, equipment and subsistence reduced this to virtually nothing, something like 1s 6d (7½p) per week. This should be compared to the 12s (60p) that a civilian agricultural worker received. Skilled weavers got £2 4s 6d (£2.27½ p) for a week's labour. An ensign might receive 5s 3d (over 25p) per day compared to 27s (£1.35p) for his regimental commander. Fiscal motivation came from pay and, more important, from pensions, but above all from prize money and plunder. It was anticipated in the British ranks that potential pickings this day would be considerable.

Economics inevitably played a part in the decision to join the army, as did also a sense of tradition and the expectation of adventure. 'TOO MUCH WIFE?' asked one 14th Light Dragoon recruiting poster in capital letters, alongside an appeal reading 'DEATH OR GLORY BOYS WANTED'. Alcohol blurred the distinction between these attractions but assisted in the decision-making process, normally to the benefit of the crown. Recruiting sergeants earned 16 shillings (80p) for every recruit added to the regiment's strength, while the 'bringer of the recruit', often the local innkeeper, received £2 12s 6d (£2.63p). There were also 'crimps' or middlemen involved, who offered up potential recruits for cash in hand, a system vulnerable to abuse. One crimp, Richard Kedgson, was hanged at Ipswich in 1787 after admitting he enlisted himself 49 times into different regiments in England, Scotland and Ireland.[15]

Recruiting was assisted by the advent of enclosures, which was dispossessing agricultural families. Likewise the mechanisation and centralising of weaving, a feature of the Industrial Revolution, was depressing wages in the textile industry, as weaving became a declining occupation. Sergeant William Lawrence, resting next to the Inniskillings with the 40th Regiment, admitted that his entry to the army was due to a mixture of tantalising bounty payments and the decision-making qualities of alcohol. 'Straight away [a soldier] said that he could enlist me in the 40th Foot which gave 16 guineas bounty ... it sounded like a great deal of money,' Lawrence, who was barely 16 years old, remembered. 'I thought that if I got hold of it I would not want money for a long time.' The rendezvous point was not surprisingly the local inn, and 'I paraded around town with the other recruits, entering almost every public-house, treating someone or other.' Sergeant Thomas Morris, forward on the ridge line with the 73rd Regiment, recalled that his attraction was a fondness for 'reading heart-stirring accounts of sieges and battles; and the glorious achievements of the British troops in Spain'. He volunteered firstly for the militia, '... and oh! How proud did I feel when having gone through my course of drill, I was permitted to join the ranks.' The process was not, however, as haphazard as it appeared. Sergeant Harry Hopkins recalled recruiting for the 28th Foot:

> There are no men so good soldiers as the man who comes from the plough. We would never take a weaver while they were there. Townsmen require all the means in the power of their officers ... to teach them that subordination is the first duty of the profession into which they have entered.

Wellington, observing the field mid-morning, was about to field the finest physical body of men that England would recruit for some time. They were generally hardy, big-boned men, adept at wielding the bayonet and rifle butt in close combat, as well as marksmen. 'The standard for men raised for the heavy cavalry, is to be five feet seven inches, and for the light cavalry and infantry five feet five inches' was the official ruling:

> But no recruits are to be taken even of those sizes , who exceed 35 years of age, or who are not stout and well made. Lads between 16 and 18 years of age, who are well-limbed and likely to grow, may be taken as low as five feet six inches for the

heavy cavalry, and five feet four inches for the light cavalry and infantry.[16]

Wellington's conviction that he could rely on his 35,000, whatever Napoleon threw at him that morning, was based on his belief that honour, grit and the threat of corporal punishment would hold his battalions in line. Punishment for officers was about honour; for the enlisted men it was the lash. Officers could be suspended, reprimanded, replaced, cashiered or in extremis hanged. Sergeants and corporals could be reduced to the ranks or flogged. The only punishment that could be imposed on a private soldier was flogging or death. The number of lashes was determined by regimental custom or the whim of the commanding officer. The average sentence inflicted on 136 men of the 10th Hussars during the Peninsular War in Spain between 1812 and 1814 was over 250 lashes, rising from 50 for stealing to 600 for plundering. One soldier who underwent flogging recalled that the first stroke felt 'as if a knife had gone through my body', and in describing the second he called 'the former stroke sweet and agreeable compared to that one'. Drummers wielded the cat-o'-nine-tails, whose metal ends could trash a wooden plank.

Lieutenant-Colonel John Colborne, commanding the 52nd Regiment, in reserve just north of the Nivelles road to the right of the line, believed:

The system of recruiting is so defective and so radically bad in every regiment one must say there are 50 to 100 bad characters that neither punishment nor any kind of discipline can restrain.[17]

These were the men who invariably slipped away in pursuit of drink and plunder. Taken literally, this might represent between 6 and 13 per cent of the army, so it took more than the lash to control what were nicknamed the 'King's hard bargains'.

Wellington's troops were required to defend the ridge line, which was less demanding than to attack, bearing in mind the polyglot nature of the Anglo-Allied army. Two fundamental skills were needed to do this well during the Napoleonic era: proficient musketry and impeccable foot drill. Sergeant William Lawrence remembered that as soon as he was attested and in the 40th Regiment, 'I had begun to drill twice a day.' This was all they did for the first month. 'I soon learnt the foot drill and was then put on musketry drill.' The British army was adept at both.

Co-ordinated drill movements were required to tactically deploy British defence lines across the Mont St Jean ridge when and where they were needed. The process had already begun an hour before and was complete but for minor adjustments by 10 am. The colours were in the centre of the line, and officers stood behind the second rank. Movement was at about 75 paces per minute, enabling a British battalion to cover 100 metres ready to level 550 muskets. Engagement outcomes were normally decided at this sort of distance; artillery killed more men up to 100 metres. After concentrated volley fire the line might surge forward to close with the bayonet. This had a triangular sectioned, 15 to 17-inch long blade that fitted into a cylindrical socket at the end of the musket barrel. Its effectiveness was more psychological than physical.

These were systematic drills carried out by lines of individual soldiers at the roll of a drum or shouted command. Each man was part of a machine, the cogs of which were set in motion by officers. Soldiers often did not know what was going on, and in the absence of effective commands, they simply had to stick to the last instruction ordered. 'Hanged if I know anything at all about the matter,' Captain John Kincaid with the 1/95th Rifles was later to admit, 'for I was all day trodden in the mud and galloped over by every scoundrel who had a horse.' Wellington was convinced that the fear of corporal punishment played a role. This was not so remarkable, bearing in mind that harsh physical punishment formed an integral part of the eighteenth-century justice system. Interestingly, the crack King's German Legion did not flog, nor did the French.

'Honour' and 'grit' were two other primary characteristics that Wellington would have to draw upon to hold the ridge. An officer was judged more on his ability to endure wounds rather than inflict them. Refusing to leave his post when struck, returning once his wounds were dressed and punctiliously obeying orders, which meant certain injury or death, was how an officer consummated his honour. He was not yet the paternal officer, constantly caring for his men, that characterises the modern British army. His abstract sense of 'honour' was as tough a bond as 'mate-ship' was to the simple private soldier. Peer pressure motivated soldiers. 'Let him seek death, and we welcome it from the hand of a foe, rather than give room for any surmise respecting his courage,' recalled Corporal James Anton, with the 42nd Highlanders, soon to be in the heart of the action at the centre of the ridge line. Whatever the carnage, he must stand firm. An officer's reputation upheld his position in society, while an enlisted man's society was the small but harsher world of his battalion.

The key to success on the ridge lay in the expectation each group had of the other. Officers would expect obedience from their men, and the soldiers anticipated bravery and skill from their officers. Wellington instinctively appreciated that honour and grit would differentiate his troops from the other foreign contingents and that he could rely on them implicitly. The irony was that success depended on mutual trust and performance from 64 per cent of 'foreigners', 'rid Jarmins' and the like. The British could not do it alone.[18]

The French in Review

As the British cavalry began to form behind the Mont St Jean ridge, they were still trying to clarify the losses accrued during the confusing retreat and rearguard actions amid pouring rain the night before. Captain Elphinstone, with the 7th Hussars, had been stabbed in the breast by a French lancer during the cavalry mêlée on the muddy Genappe high street and taken captive. It was the same skirmish that saw the disappearance of Major Edward Hodge. Elphinstone was interrogated by Napoleon himself, volunteering information that the British cavalry numbered seven to eight thousand, an under-statement. He was obliged to hand across his copy of the *Morning Post* to Count Flahault, one of Napoleon's aides, who commented with a hint of self-satisfaction that he had been in London himself, just four days before 'and everything was going on very well there'. By one of those coincidences of fate, the Count, clearly a spy, was destined to marry a relative, Miss Mereer Elphinstone, recalled by brother officer William Verner to be 'a very beautiful person with a large fortune'. Elphinstone was attended by Napoleon's personal physician and confined to a nearby loft.

Elphinstone could see what his comrades in the 7th Hussars would be up against long before the French plan of attack would begin to unfold. Peering through a gap in the rafters, he watched endless columns of 'the whole of the French cavalry' clatter by in the morning light. He later told Verner that something like 22,000 horsemen filed past and that 'he could not help comparing their force with our 7,000 or 8,000, thinking how little chance we had against such a force'. In reality Wellington had some 13,350 cavalry. When the last regiment clattered by, Elphinstone realised he had been forgotten and painfully made good his escape.[19]

The soldiers of Wellington's Anglo-Allied army watched closely as the amorphous mass of French soldiers on the opposite slope began to form up into recognisably military shapes and patterns. Shortly after 10 am four massive French columns, preceded by officer outriders, began to approach their deployment areas to left and right. Behind them in the middle distance came seven additional columns debouching from the low ridge. Sergeant Edward Cotton, with the 7th Hussars on the right of Wellington's line, observed 'the flashing of bayonets over dark masses at different points, accompanied by the rattling of drums and the clang of trumpets'. The Armée du Nord began to manoeuvre its three infantry corps, the I and II Corps and the Imperial Guard of around 20,000, each with its integral cavalry and artillery. There was a smaller 10,600 strong VI Corps and a reserve of two corps of heavy cavalry numbering over 3,000 troopers each. In all, the onlookers witnessed the approach of 53,400 infantry and 15,600 cavalry, while 246 guns were being hauled into position by horses and manhandled by 6,500 crews with 2,000 staff through thick, viscous mud. An army of 77,500 men was on the move, seemingly in review order.

'The music resounded with airs which brought back memories of a hundred victories' to Napoleon. 'This was a magnificent spectacle,' he recalled, precisely what it was meant to be. 'The army must have seemed to them twice as big as it really was.' Napoleon's normal modus operandi was to suddenly appear, where least expected, delivering a brutal blow to the flanks or rear. With so few options for manoeuvre and stymied by the soggy ground but confident of victory in any case, Napoleon was exerting psychological pressure. 'Could anyone behold so imposing a spectacle without awe, or without extreme excitement?' asked an admiring Sergeant Cotton. It was not the convention to mass one's troops directly in sight of the opposing army. Just the day before, Napoleon had used posters and proclamations to appeal to the Belgians, who represented 6 per cent of Wellington's army. 'The phenomenal success of my enemies has separated you for a moment from my Empire,' he announced. After mauling the Prussians and pushing Wellington back to Brussels, Napoleon suggested he was on the cusp of victory. 'Rally to my invincible ranks and destroy the barbarians,' he appealed. 'They are your enemies as well as mine.'

Napoleon was filling the anxious time that precedes any battle and raising the morale of his men, as he had done with his officers over breakfast. The ground needed some time to dry out before positioning the heavy artillery, and the bonus was the chance for a degree of mental intimidation. Napoleon remembered how:

These eleven columns deployed with such precision that there was no confusion; and each man took up exactly the place which had been planned for him in the very mind of his leader. Never had such huge masses moved about with such ease.

By about 11 am the French army had drawn up in six lines, forming six figure 'V's. In front were two lines of infantry with light cavalry on their wings. The third and fourth lines were cuirassiers, and the fifth and sixth were the Guard cavalry. The waiting Imperial Guard was still forming behind, at right angles to the forward lines assembling either side of the Brussels road, behind the inn of La Belle Alliance. Observing opposite was Sergeant Duncan Robertson, with the 92nd Highlanders, and he could hardly believe his eyes. 'Nor do I believe any man in the British army had ever seen such a host,' he later said. The clinical precision of the French army's form-up suggested to the Allied onlookers that this force knew what it was about. 'When I saw them taking up their ground in such a regular manner, and everything appearing so correct about all their movements,' Robertson admitted, 'I could not help wishing that we had had more troops with which to oppose the thousands that were collecting in our front.'[20]

Men like Robertson in the Anglo-Allied army had a spectacular view of the French review. In contrast, try as they might, the French could see very little. One French officer recalled that apart from on the plateau, around the Mont St Jean farm, 'we saw but a few troops; but naturally supposed', as was to be the case, 'that they were stationed, and thereby hidden, in the gorges which separated the plats from the forest, and in the forest itself'. Major Fée, a medical aide with the I Corps, had climbed on top of the small thatched roof leaning against the Belle Alliance inn 'to better see the situation of the troops'. With too many others likewise straining for a view, the roof collapsed under their weight. Captain Jean-Roch Coignet of the Imperial Guard was sent forward by Napoleon to get a better view. He soon appreciated how much of Wellington's force was waiting in dead ground, while much of the army still assumed they faced only a rearguard. As he approached a ravine edge, Coignet recalled, 'I saw columns of infantry closely massed in the lower part of it.' There were artillery batteries standing amid fields of rye, 'but no one was moving'. When he edged closer to the rye he picked out a body of cavalry hiding behind. 'I had seen enough,' he decided – much of Wellington's force was out of sight. 'On the right,' he reported to Napoleon, 'their cavalry was concealed behind the rye-fields, their infantry masked by a ravine.' All this was unconventional; it was considered unmanly to skulk out of sight.[21]

'The Emperor passed us in review,' recalled Colonel Trefçon, the veteran chief of staff of the 5th Infantry Division. Not one to display his feelings, he later admitted, 'I cannot recall without great emotion this last review.' Not since crossing the Nieman river prior to the fateful invasion of Russia in 1812 had Trefçon been so affected. 'The enthusiasm of the soldiers was great, the music played, the drums beat and a shiver excited all the men for many of whom this was to be their last day.' The moment seemed to encapsulate past glories, suggesting even more were to come. 'They cheered the Emperor with all their might,' Trefçon observed. Corporal Canler, with the 28th Line, was similarly caught up in the enthusiasm. When Napoleon rode by there was 'a spontaneous movement that resembled an electric shock, helmets, shakos, fur caps, were put onto sabres or bayonets to frenetic shouts of "*Vive l'Empereur!*"' Napoleon had deliberately set up this rallying pageant.[22]

During the brief period of Napoleon's abdication and return, the royalist French army had remained Bonapartist, virtually to a man. The Bourbons were unpopular. Royalists filled high positions in church and state and reprisals and petty injustices were practised in an army that resented its toppling from favour. 'Greedy old' Louis XVIII was called Le Cochon (the Pig), and that was even how the King in a pack of cards was referred to as bored soldiers amused themselves with games in the cafés and inns outside the barracks. Amid tobacco smoke, stories abounded about the 'Little Corporal' who, like his iconic violet, would return in the spring. 'The government sent us off to plant cabbages in our départements on half-pay,' complained Captain Jean-Roch Coignet, 'seventy-three francs a month.' Finding just 200,000 men under arms when he returned, Napoleon raised 300,000 in eight weeks. Coignet recalled that the advance guard that set off from Auxerre to arrest the returning Napoleon left with 'white (royalist) cockades in the morning' and were back with 'tricoloured ones in the evening'. One French officer described the hectic activity that followed the decision of the Allies to declare war on Napoleon – the man – rather than the French state:

> From all parts, troops were levied, counted and dispatched towards the frontiers; the battalions were filled with restored prisoners; with pensionaries, with new levies. The National Guard were organised. Arms of all kinds, artillery of all calibre, and equipages innumerable, seemed to issue as if by magic from arsenals and foundries; and within days France was transformed into a vast camp. The first and that a numerous army filed towards Belgium.[23]

This was the formation that was marshalling with such precision before a visibly impressed Anglo-Allied army at 10.30 am. The enthusiasm and ardour permeating the blue-uniformed ranks stood in stark contrast to the watchful and silent multi-coloured ranks facing them. These Frenchmen were the enthusiastic successors of the Revolutionary armies that had preceded them. They had a different status to the monarchical *ancien régime* opponents they faced. Drawn by mass conscription from the population at large, they were the protégé of a social and partisan revolution, with a level of political awareness unparalleled by former generations. The French Revolution had taught them to think of themselves as citizens, men with rights and opinions. Unlike their opponents, they were soldiers with a different relationship to society and the state. The mass levy made no concessions to wealth or regional identity. Conscription, which followed it, created huge field armies that had transformed the nature of warfare in Europe. At the same time the Revolution transformed the popular image of the army, abolishing many of the ordinances and regulations that had tied the officer class so tightly to the landed aristocracy. However, while conscription was by ballot, it was still vulnerable to corruption. Waivers could be bought, resulting in commonplace fraud and 'no shows'. With public opinion increasingly hostile, the system of conscription was teetering.

There were four distinct types of soldier in Napoleon's army, which derived its power from the cumulative impact of shared experience. At its heart there were still a number of older soldiers, bas officiers NCOs and officers who like Napoleon himself had served the pre-Revolutionary *ancien régime*. It was they who brought discipline and a certain technical precision in training. They served alongside the second element volunteers from 1792 and 1793, men like Captain Pierre Charles Duthilt with the 45th Line, who had fought with the Revolutionary armies of the North, Sambre and Meuse, before joining Napoleon's Army of Italy. These men, aged between 30 and 36, were seasoned by years of service, solid, alert and still retaining elements of their republican enthusiasm. The grognards or 'grousers', as they were called, had covered huge distances in campaigns stretching from snow-covered Alpine passes to the hot plains of Castile, from vineyards in Italy and the Rhineland through to the deserts of North Africa and Egypt. 'Of what importance to us was the number of our enemies?' asked Lieutenant Jacques Martin, also in the 45th Line. 'We counted in our ranks soldiers grown old in victory, who had spent some years as prisoners, which made them even more formidable.' These men thirsted for revenge.

Then there were the conscripts of Year VII of the call-up, the third element, who had opted to remain in uniform years after the climactic battles of Hohenlinden or Marengo. Napoleon's failing imperial fortunes produced ever larger waves of mass conscription, the fourth element numbering 63,000 in 1803 and rising to 80,000 two years later. It ended disastrously in 1812, smothered by Russian snow. Conscripts fighting the final campaigns in 1813 and 1814 seemed like children to the old campaigners. The 'grousers' thought the youngsters tended to play about and lie too much about drink and women, but saw them as good soldiers. One of these was the young Corporal Canler, with the 28th Line, who had barely transitioned from drummer boy. Lieutenant Jacques Martin had never intended to remain long in the army, because 'to be a soldier of the Bourbons did not appear to me the same as being a soldier of Napoleon', and in 1814 he left after a year's service. Abdication, he felt, had been 'a death blow to a military career'. Back with the colours, he could look forward to 'prospects of glory and rapid promotion'. Many of the teen-agers conscripted the year before were the orphans of dead soldiers, the minimum age being 14 years for drummer boys and 17 for the ranks. Nicknamed the 'Marie Louises', after the Empress, or simply the 'Emperor's infants', they had been impelled to join by industrial recession and poor harvests. Large-scale food riots had been bloodily suppressed at Caen in March 1812.[24]

The Armée du Nord was homogenous, unlike Wellington's army. The various elements were well integrated within their units and shared both a common esprit de corps and a dislike of the foreign invader. Soldiers popularly believed that the invasions of 1814 were the consequence of treason. Fear of foreign intervention in 1815 at least dissipated some of the venom surrounding the political debate over the Bourbons, the French royal family, imposed by force of arms after Napoleon's abdication. Napoleon's invasion of Belgium met with the army's approval; it was better to take the fight to the invader. All four categories in Napoleon's army also served for material gain, loot, and embraced the pride that came from generously awarded medals. Above all else the men placed Napoleon on a pedestal by virtue of his tactical prowess; he was regarded as a brilliant commander. After all, the campaign was virtually over, they believed. That night they would be carousing and womanising in Brussels.

Wellington, looking on at 11 am, may have envied the homogeneity of the French army in contrast to his own multi-national contingents drawn up around him, but the strength it derived from the cohesion of its diverse nature also made it more volatile. There was friction, for example, between the privileged Imperial Guard and the rest of the army. They were Napoleon's personal elite creation and had never lost a battle. The Guard's pay was double that of line regiments, and each Guard rank was one higher. They had the best barracks and better food, with civilian cooks in camp and their own unique supply chain in the field. Other regiments had to give way to Guard units on the line of march. The standing joke among line regiments was that even the Guard 'asses have the rank of mules'. Napoleon's previous battlefield success was built around his proven ability to fight the various component elements of his corps d'armée – infantry, cavalry and artillery – in tandem. Practice, however, was falling short of theory in the Armée du Nord. One officer even referred to 'an implacable hatred' that 'animated one corps against another'. Disputes were often about food or loot:

> *The different arms of cavalry were equally jealous and contentious of each other and of the infantry; whilst the latter, confident of its strength and numbers, threatened the cavalry with their bayonet; and insisted upon their own equality of rights and respect.*[25]

At the core of this implicit fragmentation lay suspicions of political treachery. The breathless cycle of events since April 1814, with first the abdication and then the restoration of the Emperor, had placed enormous tensions on individual and collective loyalties. Isolation at Elba had de-sensitised Napoleon to the impact that the former betrayal neurosis was having on his own soldiers. Apparently hysterical switches of allegiance from imperialist to royalist before this battle and then back again had undermined the confidence and trust of soldiers in their leaders and among commanders themselves. Intent forms the vital component of any military message, yet the Armée du Nord had repeatedly wrong-footed itself on this campaign by misinterpreting key commands, compromising decisive success at both Ligny and Quatre-Bras.

The young soldiers remained intensely enthusiastic and patriotic. They were raring for action. Newly joined, they were certain the war would be quickly won by this battle and were impatient to get the job done. Army life was not so dazzling for the 'grousers', no longer impressed by rousing speeches. By 1813 they had been worn down and embittered by the constant presence of death in their lives, dismayed by the sheer scale of human destruction that had accompanied debacles such as the winter retreat from Moscow. They instinctively appreciated that carnage on an awful scale was the inevitable outcome of decisive victories, having been lucky enough to survive so far. They had paraded this morning to face the spectre of yet another costly battle. 'Swear to defend your Eagles! Do you swear it?' had been Napoleon's challenge on presenting new eagles to the army and National Guard. 'But the vows were made without warmth,' recalled 'grouser' Jean-Roch Coignet of the Imperial Guard, 'there was but little enthusiasm,' he observed. 'The shouts were not like those of Austerlitz and Wagram,' he presciently remarked, 'and, the Emperor perceived it.'

Such reservations were not noticeable to the Allies. They were visibly impressed by the precise roll-out of the massive French army before them, and the French themselves were as caught up in the emotion of the spectacle as their opponents. 'Since morning the weather has been fine,' recalled Lieutenant Jacques Martin, with the 45th Line, 'and now a splendid sun shone on the lines of combatants and reflected off their arms. It was a magnificent spectacle.' On the opposite ridge line was Corporal John Dickson of the Scots Greys, who recalled:

> *The grandest sight was a regiment of cuirassiers dashing at full gallop over the brow of the hill opposite me, with the sun shining on their steel breastplates. It was a splendid show. Every now and then the sun lit up the whole country. No one who saw it could ever forget it.*

His attention was aroused by 'a sudden roll of drums along the whole of the enemy's line'. Listening intently he thought he could detect the strains of the 'Marseillaise', but it was obscured by a sudden uproar that rose up from the French side. It appeared the French were moving into position for battle. 'On our side perfect silence reigned,' he observed as the troops waited.

At about 11 am Colonel Auguste-Louis Pétiet found he was more interested in watching Napoleon than the deployment. He had noticed how much 'during his stay on Elba, Napoleon's stoutness had increased; his pot belly was unusually pronounced for a man of forty-five'. This was not what Pétiet, a veteran Hussar officer, serving with Soult's staff, had anticipated. He had seen Napoleon during the iconic battles of Austerlitz and Eylau, totally unlike this preoccupied man now spreading a map over his traditional little table:

> *From the foot of the mound where I stood, I found it hard to keep my eyes off the extraordinary man upon whom victory had for so long showered her gifts. His stoutness, his dull white complexion, his heavy walk made him appear very different from the General Bonaparte I had seen at the start of my career during the campaign of 1800 in Italy.*

Napoleon then had been so alarmingly thin that the soldiers questioned how such a frail body could withstand such fatigue. The Napoleon he observed now seemed very ordinary indeed.[26]

At about 11.20 am there was a sudden flurry of cannon fire off to the left of the French line. All heads turned and officers glanced at their timepieces. One by one, three French infantry battalions peeled away and started to move forward towards the château of Hougoumont to the right of Wellington's line. There was a pause, and then another four battalions detached themselves from the same area of the French line and followed on. Over 4,000 French infantry were on the move, seemingly in slow motion when viewed at distance. After all the posturing the battle was actually going to start. All the French soldiers could see of their objective was a wood to their front. Allied artillery began to engage the approaching mass, and gaps began to appear in the serried columns. Still a localised affair, it looked too detached to be a battle; more people were watching than participating.

11.30 am

The Prussians: Wavre to St Lambert

Count Friedrich von Bülow's IV Corps had been on the move since 4 am. They had already marched three days nonstop. Today, they had the furthest to go of all the Prussian corps. Concentrated around Liège when the crisis began, some units had slogged 50 miles from Maastricht. Arriving at Wavre in the rain the night before, at 2 am they were warned off to march again at twilight, and it was still raining. The vanguard 18th Regiment heading the corps was led by a shepherd through the unfamiliar narrow winding streets of Wavre, crossing the Dyle river at the single small bridge. The 15th Brigade found their exit from the town blocked by a broken-down 12-pound cannon, but they squeezed through. Having cleared the town and started to ascend the undulating and hilly terrain to the northwest, they looked back and were surprised to see a column of smoke rising up from Wavre below. Now they struggled up meandering paths leading to Chapelle St Lambert.

They had about ten miles to go to reach Wellington's army at Waterloo, which would be six hours' forced marching under normal conditions. But the narrow country paths had been washed away by the heavy rain and a glutinous lime soil stuck to everything. Artillery wheels and axles became clogged with mud sticky enough to suck the boots off their feet. Men were hungry and wet through. At any moment they expected to be attacked by the French, while the sight of the smoke lazily climbing into the sky behind them was hardly reassuring – they weren't to know that it was just a fire in a bakery. A supply train provost named Diedrichs looked back from the high ground. 'We suddenly noticed that the town had caught light,' he recalled, 'and were most concerned that the march could be delayed by this event.'[27]

Steep ridges had to be traversed, and Prussian artillerymen whipped their horses and put their shoulders to the wheel at every ascent. It was hard going, and even more difficult on the downward slope as gun-carriage limbers skidded and slipped down, running over the unwary. Tracks were so deeply rutted that the infantry had to straggle along the borders. Eventually the vanguard had to abandon its heavy 12-pounders, which were left behind to rejoin the reserve artillery. Cavalry picked their way forward to take their place. The column barely managed one mile per hour.

'Sunken lanes cut through deep ravines had to be negotiated,' recalled Lieutenant-Colonel Ludwig von Reiche, the I Corps chief of staff, who was following a northern route, separate from Bülow's IV Corps. 'Almost impenetrable forest grew on each side, so that there was no question of avoiding the road, and progress was very slow, all the more so because in many places men and horses could get through only one at a time.' Hans von Ziethen's I Corps did not get going before 12 am. His men were still recovering from the traumatic fighting around St Amand village at Ligny 48 hours before. A quarter of his men were missing. Those remaining were worn out, with no food and little ammunition.

Many Prussian soldiers were inexperienced Landwehr militia, like Franz Lieber, who had been with the Colberg Regiment for only about six weeks. He was barely 16 years old, having lied about his age on joining up. Two thirds of von Bülow's leading corps, 23 of 34 battalions, were composed of such men. There was a fair proportion of veterans from the 1813/14 advance on Paris, but it was primarily the quality of its leadership that sustained the green Prussian army. Lieber's regiment 'was composed of brave and sturdy Pomeranians, a short, broad-shouldered healthy race', he remembered. 'Go!' was all his distraught mother could manage when Lieber and his brother had marched off through the Brandenburg Gate. There was only time for the most basic of training, which was conducted by their colonel, nick-named 'Old Iron'. His demeanour exuded 'a calmness which bordered on coldness', Lieber recalled, and his 'face betrayed no emotion'. Each volunteer was required to provide his own musket, which meant every man cast his own lead balls prior to battle. The absence of a standard calibre proved a logistic nightmare at Ligny. Individually casting musket balls was 'one of the most peculiar situations a man of reflecting mind can be in' before going into battle, Lieber observed.

Ligny, fought 48 hours before, had been an 'indelible horror'. Lieber had trampled across 'three or four layers of dead and living' as the village changed hands three times. 'Wounded enemies, imploring them to give some assistance', had to be ignored with 'a deaf ear'. This was his first battle, indelibly printing haunting images on his receptive mind: 'called upon to assist in getting a cannon over the mangled bodies of comrades and enemies, leaping in agony when the heavy wheel crossed over them'. When his supply of musket balls ran out, 'I was obliged for more than an hour to be present at the fire as a mere spectator.' At the end of the day his company, originally 150 men strong, was reduced to about 20 or 30, and no longer would the likes of Lieber be regarded by their seniors as 'beardless boys'. 'The old soldiers of our regiment treated us ever after this battle with signal regard,' Lieber remembered.

There was plenty of time to dwell on bad memories, because Pirch's II Corps, to which Lieber belonged, was still waiting for the congestion around Wavre to ease, so they could get moving.[28] The uniforms of the marching troops were filthy and torn, bearing bloody marks from light wounds. Some men nursed bruises and cracked ribs from spent musket balls and grapeshot. Owing to the undulating ground, columns became increasingly split and dispersed. Ludwig von Reiche remembered 'the heads of the columns had to halt so as to give time for the detachments to collect themselves again'.[29]

'The firm bearing of the army owed not a little to the cheerful spirit and freshness of our 74-year-old Field Marshal [Blücher],' recalled a Westphalian Landwehr captain, referring to their intact morale, despite privations. Blücher was not known for his intelligence – for that he relied upon his chief of staff, von Gneisenau – but he was 'a soldier's man', immensely popular with the men. 'His humour spread like wildfire down the columns,' the officer observed. 'Forward, boys!' shouted Blücher. 'I hear some say it can't be done! I have promised my brother Wellington. Would you make me a liar?' The men of the lead 18th Regiment had determined not to, jettisoning their stiff collars in the heat of the march. They would later proudly wear ceremonial pink ones to commemorate the event. Blücher's aide, Count von Nositz, watched private soldiers slap the old field marshal's knee as he rode past. 'Bring us lots of luck today, Papa Blücher!' they shouted. 'Only exert yourselves a little longer, children,' exhorted the old commander 'and certain victory is ours.' But stragglers were falling out by the wayside.[30]

Two and a half hours earlier the lead elements of von Bülow's corps had reached Chapelle St Lambert. As each brigade reached the high point it was allowed to flop gratefully to the ground. The pause was to enable trailing units to catch up. Von Bülow's corps of 30,000 men and 86 cannon was strung out from St Lambert to the outskirts of Wavre. Meanwhile a troop of Prussian Hussars had penetrated forward as far as Frischermont wood, to the left of Wellington's line. An hour later they met a patrol of the 10th British Hussars under Captain Taylor, who immediately dispatched a subaltern to Wellington's headquarters with the welcome news that von Bülow was at St Lambert, just four miles away. There was much relief that contact had at least been made with the Prussians, but when would they be ready to play a part? Nobody appreciated the extent of their dispersion, but at least contact with the Prussians was now assured.

Back at Wavre the fire had caused real problems. 'The scene was simply dreadful,' recalled Lieutenant Elsner. 'On the left of the road, clouds of smoke and flames were shooting out of a roof, and a strong wind was blowing down the street, into the town.' There was mayhem. 'Whole battalions were running at full pelt' to clear the fire, which was in danger of exploding ammunition-carrying wagons as they passed through. 'The cannon and powder wagons were galloping away … everybody was screaming and pushing.' The solitary bridge across the Dyle became a choke-point:

When the infantry and artillery reached this bridge, they got mixed together and there was a great danger of men being run over. A powder wagon, driven badly, blocked the bridge for a time, cutting off part of my company from the battalion, which then had to wade across the river.[31]

A pioneer company managed to extinguish the flames, which had engulfed two whole houses. The rest of the army started to cross the Dyle downriver. The combination of the fire, baggage trains snarled up in Wavre and primitive paths eroded by rain meant that at eleven o'clock von Bülow's corps was spread across eight miles.

At the moment the Prussians discovered that their left flank and approach route was clear of the French, they seemed unable to get moving. Even the Lasne brook defile, ahead of St Lambert, a Rubicon in miniature, where just a few Frenchmen could hold up the entire Prussian advance, seemed empty. The prospect of success was tantalising, but it hung by a mere thread. With the entire IV Corps, extended and struggling laboriously through the mud, it would only take a handful of Frenchmen allied with geography to stop them.

Up ahead they heard the sounds of heavy cannon fire. This attracted everyone's attention. Two days before, Franz Lieber with the Colberg Regiment had stood in line 15 paces from the French, experiencing his first fight. 'Aim well, my boy,' his sergeant-major had advised as a musket ball grazed his scalp. He felled his assailant with a return shot through the smoke. Examining the awful mess his musket ball had done to the Frenchman's face had done little to diminish his ardour, but it did give pause for thought about what might happen to him, throughout the punishing march towards Waterloo. Playing cards stowed in knapsacks were being thrown away, the soldiers thinking they were bad luck. 'This poor instance of timid superstition disgusted me,' Lieber recalled, 'so I purposely picked up a pack and put it in my knapsack.' There were scores to settle with the French. They had devastated Prussia and now it was their turn. They marched on to the sound of a 'dull half-suffocated drum, from within the deep column', its muted beat as interminable as the march. Despite all the frictions and hindrances, the Prussians were coming.[32]

CHAPTER 4

First Shots —

11.30 am to 1.50 pm

The Wooded Château: Hougoumont

Two centuries since the battle, the château farm of Hougoumont still nestles in the fields at the base of the ridge to the right of Wellington's line. It is a haunting sight, its crumbling whitewashed walls and red-tiled roofs still sufficiently preserved to give some idea of its former grandeur. Marked 'Château Goumont' on Wellington's original surviving map, it was owned by Chevalier Gouret de Louville, an officer retired from Austrian service and an occasional visitor. The farmer, Antoine Demonceau, abandoned the site when soldiers appeared and entrusted its safekeeping to his servant, Guillaume van Cutsem, who reluctantly remained behind. Wellington had twice visited the buildings, at dawn and again at 10.30 am, to oversee the four light companies of the Guards under Lieutenant-Colonel James Macdonell, charged with preparing its defence. He considered the château vital ground. Its construction and layout made it a veritable fortress, which would serve to break up French formations attacking the Mont St Jean ridge.

There were 12 buildings and outhouses arranged around a courtyard in typical Brabant style. The dwellings inside were enclosed by walls, ditches and thick hedges, with a château at the centre, and the farmer's house to the south. A substantial wood of mature trees over 270 yards wide and 380 yards deep obscured the buildings on the south side. To the east

was a large orchard and a beautifully laid-out formal orna-
mental garden. The south side of the château facing the
French was enclosed by a wall 7 to 8 ft high. These walls gave
the quadrangle-shaped site its fort-like appearance, with con-
centrically arranged buildings forming a bastion on its west
side. There were two main entrances, a carriage gate, overlooked by buildings and the garden wall facing the French,
and another gateway at the back, leading onto a tree-lined
avenue to the Nivelles road. The château securely anchored
Wellington's line on the right, covering the valley that ran
deep into his flank. It was a precarious breakwater for the
defenders, situated midway between the French and British
lines. Despite being easily observed and covered by cannon
from the Allied-occupied ridge behind, the soldiers defending it felt isolated.

Captain Moritz Büsgen's 800-man battalion from the 2nd
Nassau Regiment was ordered to replace the Guards detachments in the château and orchard early on the morning of the
18 June. This was probably on orders from the inexperienced
'Young Frog', the Prince of Orange, and without Wellington's
knowledge or consent. The unexpected directive encapsulated
the difficulties of commanding Allied units with varying levels
of professional and language competence. Büsgen knew that a
battalion's worth of 'English Guards of the Coldstream
Regiment under command of Colonel Macdonell was partly
deployed behind the farm', but little else. 'From the existing
defence preparations' – gates had been barricaded and walls
loopholed – 'it was obvious that this post had already been
occupied by other troops.' In the woods to his front Büsgen
could see that German light infantry jaegers had already
deployed. 'Neither upon my being detached, nor during this
entire period,' he recalled, 'was a commander named to me
under whose orders I was to operate.'

It was not surprising that the Nassau commander felt isolated. 'No allied troops were drawn up near Hougoumont to either its right or left,' he explained. Napoleon's whole army appeared to be lined up in review order and he and his Nassauers were protruding out towards this approaching mass. Having been hastily deployed, they would immediately have to fight. 'I had seen no other troops sent in support of the battalion under my command,' he later complained, and 'I do not know if and what other troops were later detached to reinforce this position.' Both the Nassau soldiers and German jaegers were to fight this battle in blissful ignorance about what was going on around them. 'I was unable to observe what was happening at a distance,' Büsgen recalled. All that lay ahead was walls, hedges and trees.

In all there were 200 British Guardsmen under Macdonell positioned to the west of the château buildings. Büsgen's 800 defended the complex, garden and great orchard, and 200 Hanoverian Germans were forward in the woods. Seven battalions of French infantry numbering 4,000 men converged on the woods to the south. Both sides were screened from each other at ground level by the trees. Wellington, meanwhile, came across the two light companies of Guards, who under Lieutenant-Colonel Lord Saltoun had just been relieved by the Nassau contingent. They were somewhat aggrieved, having spent the night barricading and loopholing apparently for nothing. Wellington told them to wait where they were, and not rejoin the brigade. The first French attacks were already coming in.

'The farm was now occupied at the greatest speed by us Nassauers,' recalled Private Johann Peter Leonhard, who was in Büsgen's 3rd Company. After a miserably inactive night, events moved swiftly. 'This big farm was surrounded by a wall,' they noticed as they hurried inside, and 'the doors were open.' A quick glance revealed freshly broken loopholes, gouged out with bayonets. It was an exposed position. '*Ha*, I thought to myself, here you'll settle in but leave nevermore, good night world!'

We had hardly taken up position at the loopholes when masses of French came out of the wood, apparently all set to capture the farm, but they were too late![1]

'A ball whizzed up in the air,' recalled Ensign Edmund Wheatley, standing in the centre of the Mont St Jean ridge, and 'up we started simultaneously'. Glancing at his watch he saw 'it was just eleven o'clock, Sunday morning'. His sweetheart Eliza Brookes, never far from his mind, would be 'just in church at Wallingford or at Abingdon'.

Early nineteenth-century timepieces were notoriously inaccurate. 'We heard the first cannon shot of the battle fired in the direction of Hougoumont,' remembered Lieutenant G Gawler, with the 52nd Regiment on the other side of the Nivelles road, behind the château. 'An officer near me pulled out his watch, and said it was "twenty minutes past eleven o'clock".' Reports of the opening shots at Waterloo vary in their time estimates. Lieutenant H Lane, nearby with the 15th Hussars, claimed, 'I saw the first shot fired from our lines about eleven o'clock.' He watched its howling trajectory, striking the French column advancing upon Hougoumont and 'causing confusion and delay'. Lieutenant-Colonel Francis Home, observing from the ridge with the 3rd Guards, was convinced 'the first shot that was fired on the 18th was by the English' and 'it was exactly half past eleven'. Fifteen nine-pound cannon-balls shrieked past from the British ridge line and were immediately on target, bouncing through the French files, each ball scouring a succession of mud splats as they passed through up to 1,200 yards away. Home saw that 'large openings were instantly formed in the column into which almost every shot fell'. The grisly impacts were muted when viewed at such distance. A French officer later told Sergeant Edward Cotton with the 7th Hussars that 17 men were carried away by the first shot. The carnage had begun.

'Very pretty practice indeed,' commented Wellington watching nearby. These opening shots were the precursor to nine uninterrupted hours of an unearthly din that was distinctly audible in Brussels, 11 miles away. Edmund Wheatley recalled that 'in five minutes a stunning noise took place and a shocking havoc commenced'. Johann Leonhard and his Nassau comrades opened fire through the loopholes of the walled Hougoumont as the first French columns approached. 'A shower of balls that we loosed off on the French was so terrible,' he recalled, 'that the grass in front was soon covered with French corpses.'[2]

Prince Jérôme Bonaparte had been instructed by Napoleon to distract Wellington's attention to the right while he later drove up the centre with his main effort. The attack, pressed home with élan and an aggressive determination to close after such heavy casualties, developed an irresistible emotional momentum of its own. General Bauduin's 1st and 2nd Légère or Line regiments with 4,000 men took an hour to clear through 400 or so Nassau and Hanoverian jaegers, fighting stubbornly from tree to tree. Marshal Ney's ADC, Chef de Bataillon Levavasseur, sent ahead to energise the faltering advance, 'found all the infantrymen posted behind trees, begging for support'. The two regiments were running out of momentum and 'were not able to go further because the enemy were shooting them down'. Some of the Hanoverian jaegers had their own private hunting rifles and these inflicted serious casualties with their accurately aimed fire. They did not have bayonets fitted, however, and the need to use heavy rammers and tap with mallets while loading, slowed their rate of fire – but it was still effective. 'The fire of the enemy was so sharp and heavy,' commented General Foy, that 'for us the wood was a death trap.'

Büsgen recalled 'swarms of tirailleurs [skirmishers] then pressed forward, supported by formed troop bodies'. The three Allied companies began to give way. 'Closely pursued by the enemy, the retiring troops fell back,' Büsgen remembered, 'partly to the right around the buildings, partly to the left between the garden wall and the hedge of the orchard into the orchard.' Wellington, clearly irritated to have lost the wood so quickly, remarked to the Russian attaché on his staff that 'it is with these scoundrels that a battle must be won'. This characteristically disdainful comment was to smear the reputation of the Nassau defenders of Hougoumont that day, when in reality they had stood their ground for an hour against odds approaching ten to one. Lord Saltoun's two Guards companies were ordered to counter-attack back into the orchard, where they established themselves on the southern hedge line, and British Guardsmen reoccupied the château buildings.[3]

British artillery fire meanwhile created a bloody gauntlet through which any advancing French had to pass, to reach the dubious cover provided by the large wood. Jolyet, commanding one of the attacking battalions, recalled that the English batteries 'opened a lively fire which knocked over 20 men of the second battalion, and more balls followed so rapidly that it was obliged to drop back into the shelter of the lane'. As 19-year-old Sergeant-Major Lerréguy de Civrieux, with the 93rd Line Regiment, waiting to be ordered forward, recalled, 'Balls reached us after an occasional ricochet from a fold in the ground that allowed us to distinguish

the arc the projectiles took before decimating our ranks.'
Low velocity round shot followed a wispy curved trail occasionally visible to the eye. As such it might conceivably be
dodged, but this was considered unmanly in closed ranks.
De Civrieux observed:

> *Our true courage was put to the test; and it is very trying to wait
> for death in such circumstances, the most complete inaction, sur-
> rounded by death and horribly mutilated bodies.*

Off shoots bounced into a brigade of mounted carabineers
standing behind Foy's division. Moving left to avoid destruction, General Foy caustically remarked, '*Ah ha!* The big boots
do not like le brutal, the "*rough stuff*".' Lemonnier-Delafosse,
his chief of staff, remembered they stood their ground and
'received this fire stoically; they covered us with mud'. It was
not long before the ground around them resembled 'a field
that had been ploughed up by vehicle wheels' as ricocheting
round shot gouged tracks through the mud around them.[4]

French infantrymen approaching the château through the
wood were disorientated by smoke and trees, buffeted by
noise and explosions and distracted by screaming soldiers
dropping about them. By the time they cleared the wood,
line cohesion was lost, fragmented into loose crowds. Before
they knew it they were in a killing ground, an open space
stretching 30 yards ahead and more than 200 yards wide.
This had to be traversed in a rush to gain the perpendicular
buildings or the 7 to 8 ft-high wall on the other side. Volleys
of murderous musket fire spat out from loopholes or from
English and Nassau soldiers firing out of windows or over the
top of the wall. The French were so densely packed they
could not miss. The attackers were taken aback by the situation in which they found themselves. There had been no

orders to scale buildings and no ladders provided; few indeed even knew there was a farmhouse complex at the back of the wood. They hurled themselves at the wall in blind faith, counting on comrades to keep their nerve as they clambered over their backs and shoulders to clear the obstacle. 'Some of the more daring, and there were many in their ranks,' recalled Sergeant Edward Cotton with the 7th Hussars, 'rushed over the hedge up to the wall and seized the muskets which protruded through the loop holes.'

British Guardsmen poured in musket fire from loopholes and the upper windows of the gardener's house next to the south gate. Others stood on fire steps made from piled furniture and planks supported on bricks, stacked against the reverse wall. The wall was 'so peppered' with French fire, recalled Cotton, that it 'led one to suppose they had the idea of battering it down with musketry, or mistook the red bricks for our red coats'. Crouched on their fire steps above, the British waited as struggling Frenchmen gradually exposed themselves, climbing up on a comrade's shoulders, just to discharge a musket over the wall. This was as physically daunting as it was time-consuming. As heads followed by neck and torso became visible, they were shot off by muskets, pierced with bayonets or clubbed from the wall. Bodies piled up in the killing zone, adding to the anguish of those following, who had to trample over the inert forms of their comrades to reach the British. Of 1,852 officers and men of the 1st Line Regiment that mounted the first attacks on Hougoumont, only 607 were able to muster six days later.

Within an hour of the beginning of the attack, Bauduin's 1st Brigade from Jérôme's 6th Division was attacking the walls of the formal garden. Bauduin was killed in the first assaults. The inability to climb the vertical walls channelled the French onrush to the left, where it began to lap against the west side of the complex. Private Mathew Clay, with the Coldstream 3rd Foot Guards light company, was kneeling and firing from cover at their approach, 'but annoyed by a most galling fire' pouring in from the left as more and more French soldiers enveloped the west corner of the buildings. Incoming fire was heavy, and 'the spreading of their small shots rarely escaped contact with our knapsacks and accoutrements,' Clay recalled. 'Even the heels of our shoes whilst kneeling, were struck by them.' Ensign David Baird in his company was struck on the jaw bone by a musket ball, which knocked out some teeth on the opposite side of his mouth. The bone was left protruding with some teeth still embedded in it. Staunching the blood flow in the first instance would have required an experienced surgeon, and with only two surgical assistants in an average infantry battalion, this was unlikely. Nevertheless someone succeded, and Baird must have led a charmed life, for he did not finally die until 1851, while out hunting.[5]

By midday, Lieutenant-Colonel Charles Dashwood's light company of the 3rd Guards, which included Mathew Clay, numbered less than 100 men. It now took the full force of the second major French attack, which enveloped the west side of the building complex. They steadily withdrew under pressure along the lane and in through the back gate into the northern courtyard of the château. Clay, distracted by his malfunctioning musket, was 'earnestly engaged' with a companion. Before they realised it, they were cut off, 'the intervening objects being the cause of our not perceiving the movement and retreat of our comrades'. Clay had been uneasy about his musket since breakfast, the spring was 'wood bound' and 'would not act correctly', a consequence of the prolonged soaking it had received the night before. He could not get another until men started to drop. He picked up one from a dead 1st Foot Guardsman, 'in exchange for my old one', and found that it 'was warm from recent use and proved an excellent one'. But Clay and his companion were isolated. 'We were for a moment or two quite at a loss to act,' he wrote, 'but on turning my eyes towards the lower gates I saw that they were open.' They ran for the back gate, deliberately left open to allow free and speedy access for friendly troops coming into the back of the complex. The French saw it too as it was swinging shut. Clay and his companion were probably the last British soldiers to squeeze through in time.[6]

French axes hacked away at the gate during a violent French assault, which smashed through its beams before they could be properly secured. Guards Captain Evelyn's arm was shattered by musket balls puncturing the woodwork as he and others desperately tried to force it shut. Lieutenant Legros, with the 1st Line Regiment, nicknamed L'enforceur or the 'Smasher', suddenly burst through the woodwork wielding an axe. He was an engineer who had risen through the ranks and a powerful, inspirational leader. Legros and his men levered the gates apart and some 30 or 40 Frenchmen broke into the courtyard, where desperate hand-to-hand fighting ensued. Some defenders fled into the surrounding buildings, barns and low pigsties to turn about and fire point-blank into the mêlée developing across the courtyard. Lieutenant Diedrich von Wilder, a Nassau officer attached to the guards, was chased by an axe-wielding French sapper as far as the farmer's house on the other side of the courtyard. The Frenchman, quite possibly Legros, chopped his hand off at the wrist when he attempted to secure the house door. At last the French were inside.

Lieutenant-Colonel James Macdonell, the 34-year-old Peninsula veteran in charge of the defence, kept his head.

Appreciating the north gate had to be closed at any cost, he yelled at three officers nearby who joined him with six Guardsmen to form a ragged group that rushed the gate. Some heaved and pushed at the doors, while others savagely tackled Frenchmen seeking to get through with sword and bayonet. More and more Guardsmen were firing inwardly into the courtyard from the upper windows and side buildings. It was a vulnerable moment. French infantrymen rampaging about inside were temporarily ignored as, slowly and inexorably, the gates were pushed together. Macdonell, described as 'a gigantic broad-shouldered Highlander from Invergarry', heaved alongside the equally powerfully built 24-year-old Corporal James Graham, assisted by his brother Joseph. Graham finally dropped the cross-bar into position. Attention then focused on the Frenchmen trapped inside, who were shot and bayoneted to the ground. Mathew Clay described the scene at the gate:

> *On entering the courtyard I saw the doors or rather gates were riddled with shot-holes, and it was also very wet and dirty; in its entrance lay many dead bodies of the enemy; one I particularly noticed which appeared to have been a French officer, but they were scarcely distinguishable, being to all appearance as though they had been very much trodden upon, and covered with mud.*

Clay saw Macdonell carrying a large tree trunk in his arms, 'one of his cheeks marked with blood'. All the French were slaughtered, with the poignant exception of a lone drummer boy, without his drum, who was shown mercy and led away. Men piled flagstones, carts and debris up against the gate to make it doubly secure. Frustrated at its closure, at least one Frenchman had clambered onto his comrade's shoulders outside and was in the process of levelling his musket over the wall at Lieutenant-Colonel Wyndham, who had just helped close the gate and was holding Corporal Graham's musket. This was calmly passed back to Graham, who fired in the same instant, and the Frenchman's brain splashed open as he toppled backwards from the wall. After the battle Wyndham could never bear to shut a door and was prepared to subject himself to howling draughts for hours on end. Like so many others he stoically endured post-combat stress disorder for the rest of his life, living on to reach 70 years of age.[7]

Among the casualties at Hougoumont was French infantryman Domenic de Lorraine, with the 1st Line Regiment. The musket ball that struck him on the left side of his forehead was partially spent, but it dropped him with a bone-smashing blow. The ball barely missed his frontal sinus before traversing part of his skull and lodging inside his brain. The force of the impact fractured the bone, which protruded vertically. For the next three days he was to lie unattended on the battlefield, before reaching hospital 12 days later. British surgeon Charles Bell subsequently treated him and recorded his sulky-looking countenance on a medical water-colour, which survives. His half-shaven head can be seen resting on his hands in a resigned posture, and the picture shows the small entry wound. Bell records that the ball was extracted 17 days later and de Lorraine was apparently to make a remarkable recovery within two months.[8]

Shortly before 1 pm six further French battalions from Jérôme's 6th Division were fed into the battle for Hougoumont from General Soye's 2nd Brigade. At the same time, Major General Byng, in command of the 2nd Guards Brigade, anxiously watching the mêlée around the north gate, ordered an additional seven Guards companies to move forward and counter-attack the French who had got around the back of the complex. This additional 600 or so men meant that about 7,500 Frenchmen were now up against 1,850 Allied soldiers, odds of almost four to one. Hougoumont was becoming less of a French deception, more a battle within a battle.

1 pm to 1.30 pm

The Objective: The Mont St Jean Ridge

At about 13.00 General Desalles, controlling Napoleon's Grande Batterie, ordered that all the guns were to open fire in unison 'to surprise and shake the morale of the enemy'. 'The earth shook,' he later claimed, as the centre of Wellington's line was enveloped in concentrated artillery fire. This was to be Napoleon's main effort of the day. From this moment onwards the battle steadily enveloped the Mont St Jean ridge in its entirety. Hougoumont had become a side show – now, for most men, the battle of Waterloo began.

Wellington's mix of British, Hanoverian, German and Dutch-Belgian battalions manning the east side of the ridge had seen it coming. Captain Carl Jacobi, standing in line with the Lüneburg Battalion of the 1st Hanoverian Brigade just to the west of the Brussels–Genappe road, had uneasily observed the steady enemy build-up. 'The conviction took hold more and more,' he recalled, 'that a bloody battle was about to be fought.' Standing to the left of the brigade he had 'an excellent view of the area in front of us from the plateau on which we were posted'. Clearly visible below was the main road leading south to Quatre-Bras. Just beyond was the farm at La Haye Sainte. French artillery caissons had been seen struggling through the mud up onto the intermediate ridge ever since eleven o'clock. 'A marvellous sublime feeling gripped all of us,' Jacobi recalled:

We had courageously fought many a battle, but never before had
we been part of as great a body of troops as this one; never before
had we taken part in a battle which was to decide the fate of
countries near and far.

Captain John Kincaid, with the 1/95th Rifles, spread along
the hedge line that stretched east from the sand pit to the left
of the farm at La Haye Sainte, was easily visible to Jacobi.
Both had been watching the heavy build-up of smoke and
firing around the wooded château of Hougoumont to their
right. Kincaid was momentarily distracted by a cannon-ball
'from Lord knows where' that decapitated the man on his
extreme right, nearest La Haye Sainte. He too was observing
the ridge, where the French Grande Batterie was being
assembled. He later wrote:

It had hitherto been looking suspiciously innocent with scarcely
a human being on it; but innumerable black specks were now
seen taking post at regular distances in its front.

They were identified as artillery pieces. Kincaid knew from
experience that 'although nothing else was yet visible, that
they were unerring symptoms of our not being destined to
be idle spectators'. Some form of bombardment was clearly
imminent.[9]

Across the road in the farm of La Haye Sainte, Friedrich
Lindau was still at work, with the 2nd Light Battalion of the
King's German Legion commanded by Major George Baring,
constructing an *abatis* to block the Brussels road to French
access. The men hurried, aware the storm rumbling around
Hougoumont, to their right, was about to burst over them.
'We pushed half a cart onto the road,' he recalled, while
'others brought ladders and farm implements, and three

spiked French cannon were pushed there.' Lindau was trying to cheer up his friend Harz, who was convinced he would be killed that day. 'Today is going to be a tough day,' he confided to Lindau, 'and I am going to die because I dreamed quite definitely that I would get a bullet through my body.' Lindau was less convinced – as a veteran he had heard countless such gloomy predictions before. 'Dreams don't matter,' he insisted and got Harz to help him to take his mind off his premonitions.

Lieutenant Emanuel Biedermann, with the same battalion, was also gravely reflecting on his survival chances. 'I was confronted with the question: will you see your homeland and loved ones again, or will your restless life be cut short by an enemy's sword?' Soldiers often dwelled on the trauma of an anonymous death, craving reassurance that their loved ones would at least remember them. Biedermann philosophically reflected that 'man is always at the threshold of eternity; it is only that the world around does not always remind him of it in all its earnestness'. He was reacquainted with the fickle nature of his own mortality when the Grande Batterie suddenly opened fire. 'Soon the balls from the artillery on both sides were flying over and beyond us.' There was activity both to their right at Hougoumont and to their left. For the moment their sector of the line remained quiet except for 'the incessant buzz of the cannon-balls which only caused broken tree branches to shower on our heads'. Major Baring pointed out the sector of ridge line behind them that they had occupied the night before. It was to there, in extremis, that they were they were to pull back.[10]

'One could almost feel the undulation of the air from the multitude of cannon shot,' remembered Ensign Edmund Wheatley, at the centre of the Mont St Jean ridge with the King's German Legion.

*The first man who fell was five files on my left. With the utmost
distortion of feature he lay on his side shrivelling up every muscle
of his body, he twirled his elbow round and round in acute
agony, then dropped lifeless.*

Wheatley reflected on the ugliness of his passing, 'dying as it's
called a death of glory'. Yet the horrors were only beginning.[11]

The battle was starting to engulf the Mont St Jean ridge in
its entirety. Men squatted, knelt, crouched and lay in lines
amid a sonic symphony of howling, booming and crashing
impacts as solid shot rained down. Overhead shells burst
open with sharp cracks, leaving dirty smudges hanging over
the ridge line. This was hardly the grandeur of Napoleonic
warfare; they had to wallow in the mud to seek cover. Unable
to leave the line, soldiers relieved themselves where they
stood or lay, the stench of human waste mingling with the
earthy tang of wet mud. It was the great clods of mud flying
in all directions as each solid shot bounced down that kept
casualties down. Even so, the dreadful impact of strikes, and
the screams that emanated from the massively injured few,
did little to lessen the acute anxiety among the many.

Albrecht Heifer, in the King's German Legion, was
bowled over by an enormous punch to his chest, which
snatched his breath away and left him breathing with pain
and difficulty. The flesh of his right breast had been torn
away by a glancing blow from round shot, eviscerating fat
skin and muscle from the chest wall. Iron powder stained
the skin area around the bright red gouge mark visible
through his torn uniform breast coat. It was rare for soldiers
to survive a direct hit on the torso, but Albrecht, remarkably, would do so.[12]

'It is with artillery that one makes war,' declared Napoleon.
Eighty of Napoleon's jeune filles – his 'daughters', i.e. guns,

from the Grande Batterie – were lined up along a small spur on the eastern side of the battlefield. The employment of 'Grandes Batteries', such as at Lutzen in 1813, was a favoured tactic. The 6-, 8- and 12-pounders were now being fired at the Mont St Jean ridge only 700 yards away. Feverishly working gunners wreathed in smoke could hardly discern the fall of shot, but about five out of every eight rounds were hitting the forward slope of the ridge, while the remainder bounced, showering mud over the crest line. Most of the Allied troops hugged the ground in the lee of the crest. As one French observer recalled, despite the spectacular effect, enemy 'masses could only be aimed at by approximation because they were almost entirely hidden by the lie of the land'. For 30 minutes about 2,700 round shot howled over, displacing the air with a noise like ripping canvas, while another 900 shells burst open with reverberating cracks overhead. The distinctive rotten-egg smell of gunpowder pervaded the air.

It was the shells, with their wispy signatures of white smoke trailing across the crest line, that were the main killers. Sergeant William Lawrence, crouching with the 40th Regiment of Foot, to the west of Mont St Jean farm, recalled:

A shell from the enemy cut our deputy Sergeant-Major in two, and having passed on to take the head off one of my company of grenadiers named William Hooper, exploded in the rear not more than one yard from me, hurling me at least two yards into the air.

Lawrence was shaken; the blast scorched the skin from the side of his face and burned off the tail of his sash, scorching his sword handle 'perfectly black'. He picked himself up and remarked to a sergeant close by, 'This is sharp work to begin with – I hope it will end better.' A new recruit, Bartram, had been badly shaken. It was his very first action. He cried out to Lawrence that 'he must fall out of rank, as he was taken very ill'. Lawrence shoved him back into line and told him to forget this whiff of gunpowder; but Bartram was having none of it. 'He fell down and would not proceed another inch.' Exasperated, Lawrence left him, thinking, 'He ought to have been shot.'[13]

Shells were roaming killers, but at least they were invisible. Round shot was a different matter. The muzzle velocity of a 12-pounder was about 1,700 yards per second. Air resistance then slowed its progress, so that they could often be seen. On contact they might bounce three or more times. The arrival of these howling projectiles was so frequent and their effect on human flesh so destructive that apprehension bordering on terror affected everyone, convinced survival could only be for a matter of time. Sergeant Anthony Tuittmeyer, standing in the 2nd Line Battalion of the King's German Legion in du Plat's brigade behind the Nivelles road, had his left arm torn off at the shoulder by round shot. Hardly a stump remained, with just a small piece of the humerus adhering to the shoulder socket. It was a massive injury. Tuittmeyer was put on a horse, which he proceeded to ride upright all the way to the St Elizabeth Hospital at Brussels. This incredible feat of stoic endurance got him to the hospital alive and he was still living one month later, but whether he eventually succumbed is not known. Captain Robert Adair, with the 1st Guards near Sergeant Lawrence's position, was fatally struck in the hip by a cannon-ball, tearing away the flesh on his thigh and exposing his splintered hip bone. Surgeons described such wounds as 'macerating', pulping flesh tissue and tearing off limbs. As many as nine or more men could be knocked down by a ball passaging the lines, smashing skulls and disembowelling torsos with direct hits. Raw recruits were instructed not to casually block spent rolling balls, because they still retained sufficient energy to take off a foot.[14]

With no recoil action, the huge French 12-pounder guns had to be manhandled back to their original firing position after each shot. The gun might be jerked back by as much as 12 feet, where its 3,400-pound weight often stuck in the mud. As time went on, the rate of fire began to perceptibly slacken, since hot barrels had to be allowed to cool down to avoid premature powder explosions during loading. Crews became increasingly tired from the constant shoving and pulling needed to realign violently recoiled guns back on target. Eight specialist and seven non-specialist crew were needed to serve these guns, creating a tangle of men and equipment on the firing line, through which d'Erlon's attacking troops would have to pass.

'Columns do not break through lines, unless they are supported by artillery fire,' declared Napoleon, unleashing the major effort of the day. The French columns of Count d'Erlon's I Corps had been steadily moving into the hollow between Napoleon's La Belle Alliance ridge and the intermediate ridge upon which stood the Grande Batterie. Among them was Lieutenant Jacques Martin with the 45th Line Regiment, part of Baron Marcognet's 3rd Infantry Division. His men had marched and counter-marched for three days previously, between Ligny and Quatre-Bras, without once meeting the enemy. Of Ligny he recalled: 'We waited a long time for the order to attack, which was finally given to us by Napoleon himself,' but 'it was still not our turn to prove what we could do because on arrival we found the position vacated.' They had been deeply disappointed. Now on this Sunday morning they had been waiting for the

order to go yet again. After an exceedingly wet and uncomfortable night they had managed to dry their muskets,
which were clean and ready for action. They assembled in
front of the Mont St Jean ridge. 'We waited with impatience for the signal to depart, that we imagined should be
very soon; but to our great surprise, the hours passed
without anyone making us change position,' Martin complained. Now with the time approaching one o'clock they
could see the château of Hougoumont to their left, where 'a
furious combat raged'. After missing the Prussian reverses
at Ligny and then chasing the British back to within ten
miles of Brussels, d'Erlon's corps was itching to administer
the *coup de grâce*. 'We deployed in massed brigades,' Martin
recalled, 'and halted at the foot of a small rise which hid the
enemy from us.'[15]

Napoleon, with his Hougoumont deception well under
way, was about to grapple with Wellington's centre. By
pushing up the line of the two farms on the Brussels road at
La Haye Sainte and Mont St Jean, he would sever Wellington's
line of communication with Brussels and the Prussians to the
east. Wellington was vulnerable here, because for every gun,
infantry or cavalryman he had deployed east of the Brussels
road, there were two to the west, in the wrong place. Napoleon
was confident he had wrong-footed Wellington again.

Seventeen-year-old former drummer boy Corporal Louis
Canler, with the 28th Line Regiment, remembered that 'three
beats of the drumstick' amid the unearthly din of artillery fire
'sufficed to get the corps ready to march'. As the columns
formed he noticed that Adjutant-Major Hubant, 'an old
soldier who had taken part in all the campaigns of the Empire,
was pre-occupied and very pale'. He knew well what to
expect. Nevertheless, a wave of fervour swept the line. 'Today
it is necessary to vanquish or die!' grandly announced General

FIRST SHOTS

Drouet d'Erlon. 'The cry of "*Vive l'Empereur!*" left our mouths in reply,' Canler remembered, followed by the shout '*L'arme au bras!*' ('Shoulder arms!'). As the massed drums beat out the charge, they set off.[16]

D'Erlon's corps of 17,000 infantry advanced on a massive front of 1,000 yards, with 800 heavy cavalry supporting its left flank, just west of the Brussels road. They had to first move out of the hollow beneath the Belle Alliance ridge and make their way through hundreds of artillery caissons and horses drawn up behind the gun line of the Grande Batterie. This meant crossing five lines of re-supply wagons, caissons and gun limbers, with nearly 1,500 horses waiting in their traces in between. With senses dulled by the noise from the terrific cannonade crashing out ahead, which 'was terrible from the beginning,' Lieutenant Martin recalled, columns and files groped their way through clouds of stinking cordite smoke as they negotiated the wagon parks. Shouted commands became indistinct as they neared the gun line, energetically crewed by up to 1,000 gunners. Direction and pace was controlled by drum roll, rattled out by the drummer boys, who stuck closely to their company commanders. Guns belching fire flashed through the gloom, and the soldiers opened their mouths to equalise the pressure in their ears at each crashing report as they passed by.

To Captain Carl Jacobi, with the Hanoverian Lüneburg Battalion, 'the cannonade became ever more violent, as we beheld the enemy's attack columns descending into the plain'. Masses of French infantry were now moving beyond the guns as far left as the eye could see. Jacobi's men, soaked through the night before, had been verging on hypothermia that bitterly cold morning. At last shafts of watery sunlight were beginning to illuminate the impressive scene. 'As the foremost French battalions began to deploy,' he recalled, 'all of this caused the mind to triumph over the frailty of the body; all the misery of the night and morning were forgotten.' They were now scared instead – battle was about to engulf them.

At ground level east of La Haye Sainte, Captain John Kincaid's green-uniformed 1/95th riflemen witnessed the mass emergence of the French line infantry from beneath the fiery curtain of the spitting gun line. 'Countless columns began to advance under the cover of it,' he recalled. 'The scene at that moment was grand and imposing, and we had a few minutes to spare for observation.' It looked as though the whole ridge line had taken on a motion of its own, moving on them. 'A smaller body of infantry and one of cavalry moved on their right,' he could see, 'and, on their left, another column of infantry and a formidable body of cuirassiers.' Napoleon stood on the side of the road to their front, and as each regiment passed they roared '*Vive l'Empereur!*'. Kincaid and his men could barely take in the scene, but there was more. 'Beyond them,' he chillingly observed, 'it seemed one moving mass.'

'At last we left,' recalled Lieutenant Jacques Martin, 'the weather had cleared up; the sun shining brightly illuminated an imposing spectacle.' Masses of blue-coated infantry, imposingly tall with brightly badged shakos, gave a momentary glimpse of the grandeur of Napoleonic war. White cross-belts stained by the night's rain brightened in the sun, which enriched the blue hue of their jackets. 'The army was deployed magnificently before the enemy's positions,' Martin saw, 16 eagles were held aloft, and 33 battalions were on the march. As swarms of *voltigeur* skirmishers moved forward, d'Erlon's men began to form in column of battalions. They had little doubt they would smash through Wellington's centre as they finally stepped off. The spectacle and pageantry had yet to meet reality.

1.35 pm

The Prussians: Chapelle St Lambert

At about the same time Napoleon Bonaparte traversed his telescope along the Mont St Jean ridge line, for one last look before the artillery obscured everything with smoke. D'Erlon's corps had been released for the decisive attack of the day, and he needed to confirm that nothing was going to compromise the outcome. Looking toward St Lambert, the Emperor picked out something which could have been a cloud but 'which looked to me like troops'. He turned to Soult, his chief of staff, and asked his opinion.

> All the glasses of the general staff were fixed on this point. The weather was rather misty. Some maintained, as often happens on such occasions, that they were not troops, but trees; others that they were columns in position; some others that they were troops on the march.

Whatever they were, they were about five miles away. Napoleon could only see the open ground in front of Chapelle St Robert behind St Lambert at this point. The tell-tale spindly black trails might well be troops, and this disconcerted Napoleon. Three thousand cavalry were dispatched to investigate. These would be able to effect a junction with Marshal Grouchy if they were his troops or screen against the Prussians if not. Fifteen minutes later a Prussian Black Hussar prisoner brought the discouraging news that it was indeed General von Bülow's IV Corps approaching, with some 30,000 fresh men, who had not fought at Ligny. With his staff at breakfast that morning Napoleon had assessed the odds of success as being 'nine to one in our favour'. Now 'Bülow's arrival deprives us of three,' he calculated, 'but that still leaves us with six to four in our favour.' If Grouchy, who was supposed to be pursuing the Prussians, did put in an appearance at this moment the victory would be even more decisive, Napoleon assessed, 'because Bülow's Corps will be entirely destroyed'.[17]

It was not just the blazing building blocking the main street at Wavre that was enforcing rest on the Prussians at Chapelle St Lambert. The Grande Batterie opening fire was clearly audible, but galvanised nobody. Columns did need to close up but there was another more subtle psychological obstacle. The deep and muddy Lasne defile had yet to be traversed, the most difficult terrain en route. Gneisenau, Blücher's chief of staff, considered this a Rubicon moment. Once over, they were irrevocably committed, whatever happened to Wellington, and Gneisenau for unknown reasons mistrusted the Allied commander. His cumbersome route selection and illogical order of march seemed to suggest a desire not to arrive too soon. The addled Blücher depended heavily on Gneisenau's consummate planning proficiency, a man he affectionately nicknamed 'The Brain'. 'I will do what none of you can,' the old field marshal would announce as his dinner party trick: 'I will kiss my own head!' Then, without further ado, he would lean forward and kiss his chief of staff on the head, triumphantly announcing 'This is the way!' Gneisenau practically ran the Prussian army and was senior to three of its four corps commanders. He was the master of strategy but not a battlefield tactician, while it was no secret that Blücher understood nothing about the conduct of war. Blücher rarely formed a judgement about a plan, but instinctively understood the battlefield; he admired Wellington as a fighter, and his sense of honour and instinct led him to support him.

Co-ordination would be needed with Wellington before pressing on. How would they know the outcome of the heavy French attack audibly going ahead? Where would the French right be when they reached Wellington? Blücher finally convinced Gneisenau that further delays were not in their interest. They must press on at best speed. Napoleon by contrast had no such doubts. He had calculated the odds and instinctively appreciated he must quickly finish off Wellington's army.

Nevertheless, the troops resting at Chapelle St Lambert brought immediate relief to Wellington, though they were barely visible. Napoleon ordered two divisions of cavalry to move 3,500 yards eastward towards the Prussians. Behind came Count Lobau's two infantry divisions with 8,000 men and 32 guns. D'Erlon's corps needed to shatter Wellington's centre before the Prussians arrived. They had been launched and Napoleon was confident, but if the attack did not succeed there was no further infantry reserve. All that would be left was the Imperial Guard, and they were only ever deployed at the point of victory.

Just before two o'clock in the afternoon Prussian troops began their precarious crossing of the Lasne valley. The stream had been swollen by torrential rain the day before. Steep valley sides proved a slippery nightmare for Prussian gunners manhandling cannon. Even in dry weather local carts found this a difficult descent. Tree trunks were laid at successive points to enable horses to pause and rest. Wellington had been informed at 11 am that the Prussians were in St Lambert; now three hours later the vanguard was traversing the Lasne valley. He was already three hours out in his calculation of the anticipated Prussian arrival, and the first major French assault was bearing down on his centre.

Within an hour French cavalry was beginning to appear

ahead of the Prussians, making their way through the Wood of Paris, which covered the plateau opposite the Lasne defile. One of the first Prussians to crest the other side was Count Wilhelm von Schwerin, one of Blücher's cavalry commanders with the 6th Hussars. He was ripped apart by the opening salvo of a French horse artillery battery. Skirmishing broke out on the near side of the Lasne valley. The French appeared at last to be reacting. To Wellington this was an ominous and unwelcome development, even if not unanticipated. Von Bülow's IV Corps column was several hours long and hardly in a position to deploy for a formal attack. Units were configured to push rapidly along narrow muddy tracks, impeded on both sides by trees. Artillery could not be brought up easily. Von Ziethen's I Corps was marching through similarly difficult terrain on a parallel northern route, but had only been on the march for an hour and had a long way to go. They were in no position to assist. Decisions needed to be made, but whatever the outcome, Wellington would not get his reinforcements for some time yet.

CHAPTER 5

The Muddy Slope —●

1.50 pm to 2.15 pm

Advance: The Intermediate Valley before Mont St Jean

Captain Pierre-Charles Duthilt was with the 45th Line, the lead regiment in Marcognet's division column of eight battalions, advancing against the Mont St Jean ridge. The speedy assembly took about five to ten minutes before the divisions stepped off at five-minute intervals. 'Our turn came eventually,' recalled Duthilt. With a frenzied shout of '*Vive l'Empereur!*' they set off, eagles on high and 'with ported arms and serried ranks'.

When the 44-year-old Pierre Guillot had uncased the eagle of the 45th, he knew what to expect. He had suffered considerably in Spain, shot in the right foot in 1809, lanced in the left flank in 1811, and two years later he was wounded in the right thigh and captured by the British. His time had come again. As he hoisted the eagle, he may have briefly reflected that it was precisely one year since he had been released by the British. Ahead of the columns trotted *voltigeur* skirmishers, preceding a phalanx of bayonets, all moving in time with the menacing drumbeat that tapped out the pace. These were the veterans of battles from Austerlitz in Bohemia to Borodino in Russia, from Wagram in Germany to the final battles for France the year before. It was their first opportunity to prove themselves in this campaign, and now the sun emerged, bathing the ranks in glorious colour. 'All combined to make more majestic the terrible scene which was unfolding,' recalled Jacques Martin.

Each battalion had about 514 men, and these quickly formed frontages of 130 to 140 men wide, three ranks deep, as soon as they cleared the wagon trains of the Grande Batterie. An imposing column then came together, 130 yards wide and stretching back 24 ranks or 80 metres long. It was one of four such solid wedges, each about 270 yards apart, that set off to bludgeon their way through Wellington's centre line. They were in effect human battering rams advancing across 1,300 yards of front. Duthilt was four paces behind the battalion up ahead. 'A strange formation,' he commented, 'and one which was to cost us dear.' His soldiers felt vulnerable, unable to form square against cavalry, 'while the enemy's artillery could plough our formations to a depth of 20 ranks'. His opinion was echoed by Brigadier Noguès, who felt so vulnerable at the lack of a reserve square following on behind, that he suggested to d'Erlon that he keep one back. It could wait behind in the valley of corn they were traversing. 'Keep going,' d'Erlon insisted. 'Do not fear.'[1]

There were about 27 guns, howitzers and rockets within range on the Allied ridge to contest the advance; the majority were 6-pounders, along with 9-pounders and 5.5-inch howitzers. It took about 30 minutes for d'Erlon's divisions to clear the gun line and form up. Before them was a short walk of about six minutes to climb the ridge, but the tall crops and mud was to make it last twice as long. 'The distance was not great,' Duthilt estimated:

> But the soft and rain sodden earth and tall rye slowed up our progress appreciably. As a result the English gunners had plenty of time in which to work destruction upon us.

The British, Dutch-Belgian and Hanoverian guns could fire two to three rounds per minute. Ground and smoke obscuration of targets reduced the rate, but there was time for 1,000 round shot, 500 shells and finally 500 canister to play along the ranks of the four approaching columns. They would have to endure a storm of artillery fire for about 25 minutes. Doubling ahead were 3,000 *voltigeur* skirmishers, producing a density of about three men per metre of front.

Suddenly the Grande Batterie ceased firing and a cheer went up from the Allied ridge as their guns set to work with a will. Until now they had been forbidden to duel with the heavier French guns, waiting for their preferred prey, advancing infantry.

Ensign Rees Howe Gronow, an 18-year-old 1st Guards officer with Picton's 5th Division, heard the discordant sounds of band music from the French regiments amid the din of artillery fire. 'The rapid beating of the *pas de charge,* which I had often heard in Spain – and which few men, however brave they may be, can listen to without a somewhat unpleasant sensation – announced that the enemy's columns were fast approaching.' The beat was known to Peninsula veterans as 'Old Trousers'. Captain John Kincaid, manning the hedge line facing the advance, became more aware of 'the rubidub of drums, and the tantarara of trumpets' in between more resonant shouts of '*Vive l'Empereur!*' 'It looked at first, as if they have some hopes of scaring us off the ground,' he recalled, 'for it was a singular contrast to the stern silence reigning on our side.' This was indeed the intent. Napoleon's Grande Armée had already used these tactics, as much psychological as physical, to batter their way through defending lines of infantry all over Europe. They seemed to physically exude tangible might. Kincaid commented: 'The voices of our great guns told that we had mouths to open when we chose to use them.'[2]

'Then the cannonade started and was terrible from the beginning,' declared Lieutenant Jacques Martin, with the

45th Line, 'because once we had appeared from behind the rise, the distance between the two armies became very small.' For the first half of their soggy 1,200-yard walk, columns were hit by bouncing 6- and 9-pound solid shot as air-burst shells cracked overhead. Nine-pound balls tended to plough into the ground at about 400 yards on firing, bounce out to 760 yards, and then to 100 yards, as momentum petered out. First strikes howled in at head height, splattering mud and body parts in all directions before bouncing back up at knee or chest level to wreak further destruction. Projectiles whooshed in at subsonic speed; a whistling rush cut short by a sickening crump, followed by the sound of equipment splintering and screams and muffled cries. 'Death flew all around,' remembered Martin, 'entire ranks disappeared under the hail, but nothing could stop our march.' When they reached the bottom of the valley in front, the Grande Batterie's 80 guns crashed out again, shooting directly over their heads at the ridge line beyond.

The impact of bouncing shot was intimidating. Men on horses were snatched away, saddlebags bursting open with the shock of impact, spewing contents in all directions. Fragments from smashed muskets, equipment and flying body parts brought men down in the immediate vicinity. Up to a dozen men might be felled by one shot ploughing through packed human ranks. Parade lines of soldiers were bowled over like so many rag dolls. 'The dead were immediately replaced by those who followed,' Martin recalled; 'the ranks, although becoming fewer, remained in good order.'[3]

Allied artillery crews feverishly worked their guns on the ridge. Sponge men extinguished burning powder and canvas in the barrels before the next shot. Powder bags and shot were fed into the barrel and rammed home. '*Ready!*' shouted the crew to the vent man, who then touched the quill with his port fire and ignited the powder charge. The blast recoiled the gun trail violently backwards and to the side, as the commander, peering through smoke, tried to discern the fall of shot. Two men pushed and levered at the trail to roughly realign the gun. Up to eight men were at work, five crewing and three bringing up the ammunition. A further two might be reassuring the horses in their traces attached to the limber. Crews had to keep their heads as the columns approached. French skirmishers would seek them out. Guns tended to fire at the mass to their front, rather than attempting convergence with other guns. This took time and a cool head. With the attackers closing, aiming became less important than the number of projectiles they could bang off . It was the weight of fire that mattered – they could hardly miss as the massive columns bore down on them.

The second bounce of the ball generally cleared the target column and smashed into whatever was following on behind. Lower grazes took men down at leg height; even a seemingly slow-rolling ball might cause massive leg injuries. Shells arcing overhead exploded and lashed the surface of the columns like hail over water. Shakos disintegrated or were snatched away in a splash effect, rippling as men went down, before the files ebbed back into place as the men closed up again.

The columns laboured more and more as the slope of the Mont St Jean ridge perceptibly increased. Artillery range closed to 500 yards and then 400 yards – canister range. Many soldiers lost their shoes in the mud of the ridge basin. Recovery was impossible. There could be no pauses or going back, the inexorable mass pushing from behind and seeking to passage this torment as soon as possible. Captain Duthilt recalled that a soldier was 'soon tired out by the difficulty of crossing the greasy and waterlogged ground, in which he broke the straps of his gaiters and even lost shoes, weighed down by the amount of dirt that attached itself to them'. Men could hardly discern words of command above the constant drumming, shouting and gun fire. 'The corn was breast high,' observed Ensign Charles Dallas on the ridge line ahead with the 1/32nd Foot, 'so that they got pretty close before they came in sight.' The French slipped and struggled in the long rye stalks, which ensnared legs and feet already balled in mud. Few could see what was up ahead from the depths of the column, and the leading ranks anxiously sought to keep their powder pans dry as they struggled through the long wet corn.

Canister was, as the name implied, a thin-walled bucket-shaped container made of tin, leather or heavy canvas. Each one was filled with 85 solid 1½-ounce iron balls. When fired, the canister ruptured, spraying out balls like a gigantic shot-gun. Grapeshot was similar but fired at slightly longer range, stabilised by a spindle, to which the shot was attached like a paper towel holder, wrapped in cloth and laced together. When it fired, a bundle of balls burst from the cannon mouth, resembling a bunch of grapes – hence the name – which slashed through the ranks. Its distinctive signature was a rattling sound like hail, which occurred when the balls struck muskets and equipment, as well as eviscerating flesh from bones, as it blasted through.

'A great number of the wounds are from cannon-balls,' observed Assistant Surgeon Donald Finlayson, serving with the 33rd Foot on the ridge. 'Most wounds of the limbs are in the lower extremities. There are perhaps 15 or 16 legs taken off for one arm, there are not many bayonet wounds.' In his experience 'one in seven or eight may be killed; the rest are wounded'.[4]

Within a hundred paces under canister or case shot, first Corporal Canler's battalion commander, Marins, fell mortally wounded; next, his company commander M Duzer went down, struck by two balls, followed by the colour-bearer

Crosse, who was also killed; and Adjutant Hubant, the pale veteran of countless campaigns, disappeared beneath their feet. 'In the middle of this,' Canler remembered, 'the calm and serious voices of our chiefs called out the single command *"Serrez les rangs!"* ("Close Up!").'

The second discharge of case shot took off their drummer's right arm, 'but he continued to march at our head beating the charge with his left', with the taps becoming progressively weaker until he fell over. A third discharge of the murderous canister 'reduced the frontage of the battalion to that of a company; the terrible cry *"Serrez les rangs!"* was heard again.' The company grimly laboured onward through this storm of shot and steel, a silent rage galvanising their determination 'to avenge our unhappy brothers in arms who died before our eyes'. When Canler bent down to adjust a broken gaiter, a massive blow yanked back his shako, still attached by his chin-strap. A musket ball had punctured his regimental nameplate, adding a zero to the 28th Line title and shaving the top of his head.

'As we mounted on the other side,' a French conscript with the 25th Line Regiment recalled, 'we were met by a hail of balls from above the road at the left.' Canister raked the ranks at decreasingly shorter ranges. 'If we had not been so crowded together,' he recalled, 'this terrible volley would have checked us.' They pressed on, with more commands to close up, encouraging each other by shouts of '*Vive l'Empereur!*' 'Two batteries now swept our ranks,' the conscript continued, 'and the shot from the hedges a hundred feet distant pierced us through and through.' Double shot was loaded next, solid shot on top of canister, and fired into them at point-blank range.[5]

Only the first three ranks of the column could level their muskets, and they were the only ones able to see. Climbing the slope, Lieutenant Jacques Martin saw 'the mountain was peppered with their cannons and covered with their troops; it looked impregnable'. The 45th Line could only see Bijlandt's Dutch-Belgian brigade to their left. The ridge directly ahead seemed empty, although obscured by smoke. The files in depth saw nothing; they could only feel, as another howling rush of shot carried off more of their number, buffeted by the pressure waves as it flashed past. Martin started to chuckle hysterically. Ahead of him was a very tall thin officer who had acquired the dubious reputation in Spain of being less than steadfast. He was bent double, sheltering behind the short burly soldier to his front. Sensing that the ranks had detected the ridiculous spectacle, the officer turned about to march backwards, raising his sword above his head with two hands as if to correct the line. But he was still bent forwards. This pathetic cover-up raised a few droll grins.[6]

2 pm →

The Breakwater: La Haye Sainte

As d'Erlon's columns ascended the Mont St Jean ridge, a cluster of buildings next to the Brussels road hemmed in Quiot's 1st Infantry Division on the left. The obstacle, hidden in a hollow, was not immediately obvious to the advancing French. They were surprised to be confronted by several companies of the King's German Legion in the orchard and more in the buildings behind, well in front of the Allied line. The farm of La Haye Sainte ('the sacred hedge') was a rectangular configuration of barn, stables, cow-shed and farmhouse, grouped around a courtyard. It was enclosed by a substantial wall, eight to ten feet high, and a hedge. The farm belonged to Count Charles-Henri Boot de Vellhem, who had purchased it 40 years before. He rented to his tenant farmer Pierre Moreau, who had already been ruined by the total destruction of the crops around the farm.

La Haye Sainte was defended by the 2nd Light Battalion of the King's German Legion, with 400 men under the command of Major George Baring. An experienced veteran, Baring had put three of his companies in the orchard facing the French, two in the complex itself and another in the back kitchen garden on the Allied side. La Haye Sainte was the second breakwater, like Hougoumont to its right, protruding 270 yards out beyond the Allied ridge line. It was an impediment to any attacker seeking to force Wellington's centre, being able to delay or inflict damaging flanking fire on any advance. The farm bastion was mutually supported by two companies of the 1/95th Rifles located in the sand pit just beyond the kitchen garden, on the other side of the Brussels road. Both Baring's men and the 1/95th were equipped with the more accurate Baker rifle. The farm's Achilles heel was the completely open large barn door on the French approach side. Baring and his officers for some inexplicable reason had allowed its destruction for firewood, during the rainy night the evening before. They had perhaps assumed that their occupancy would not be long – before being tasked with its defence.

Quiot's 1st Brigade, with 2,000 men under Charlet, was attempting to wash around both sides of the building as Bourgeois's 2nd Brigade swept on, ejecting Captain John Kincaid's 1/95th riflemen from the sandpit position. The impetus on d'Erlon's left flank was slowed and somewhat deflected. Illogically, the only way for the French to survive was to keep moving forward in order to get beyond the beaten fire zone of Allied artillery. Kincaid saw they had checked the French skirmishers ahead of the main column, 'but their columns advanced steadily through them'. Accurate Baker rifle fire levelled an 'incessant tirilade', which 'was telling in the centre with fearful exactness'. With his line turned at both ends, Kincaid's men fell back. They were impressed at the dogged persistence with which the French attacked, 'encouraged by the gallantry of their officers, who were dancing and flourishing their swords in front'. Bourgeois's men carried on, leaving the untidy business of reducing the farm to Charlet's 1st Brigade to his left. La Haye Sainte became an isolated and besieged outpost.[7]

At first Major Baring was taken aback at the sheer ferocity of the French onslaught. He had 'forbad all firing until the enemy were quite near', but the first shot shattered the bridle on his horse, close to his hand, and the second felled his second in command Major Bösewiel. Within view of Lieutenant Emanuel Biedermann, he was 'struck by several bullets and sank off his horse, the first of us to be killed'. Two dense French columns from the 54th and 55th Line rapidly closed in, 'one of which attacked the buildings,' Baring recalled, 'and the other threw itself in mass into the orchard', to their front, 'showing the greatest contempt for our fire'.

Private Friedrich Lindau, who was by the vulnerable open barn door, remembered a jubilant cry of *En avant!* as the French rushed forward. 'The French are in such a hurry, it's as if they wanted to eat in Brussels today,' he sarcastically confided to his close companions. 'We opened such a murderous fire on the dense crowd' of packed Frenchmen, he recalled, 'that the ground was immediately covered with a mass of wounded and dead.' It was not without cost. Emanuel Biedermann described how 'we vigorously returned the fire for some time, but our men fell by the dozens'. The French impetus seemed irresistible. Baring, appreciating they were becoming increasingly exposed, realised 'it was not possible for our small disjointed numbers fully to withstand this furious attack of such a superior force'. A bugle call summoned all to fall back on the barn, 'in a more united position, in order to continue the defence'.

Men were falling left and right around Lindau. 'For a moment the French halted,' he recalled, 'then they fired causing major destruction on us.' Harz, whose premonition of death had been scoffed at by Lindau, 'collapsed at my side with a bullet through his body'. The wounded Major Bösewiel, the second in command, had struggled unsteadily to his feet and 'then fell on his face and died'. A line was hastily assembled inside the farm courtyard, which 'gave such unbroken fire in the barn behind, towards the open entrance', according to Lindau, that the 'thickly massed' French 'did not attempt to enter'. Both sides blazed away at point-blank range, Baker rifle versus French musket. 'The French stood so closely packed here,' Lindau observed, 'that several times I saw three or four enemy fall by one bullet.' The superior muzzle velocity of the Baker rifle was beginning to tell. When the French failed to disperse, the King's German Legion went in with the bayonet. 'I stabbed and cut blindly into the crowd,' Lindau remembered, and 'they did not hold their position as we pressed forward with overpowering boldness.'[8]

Captain Carl Jacobi, with the Lüneburg Field Battalion of the 1st Hanoverian Brigade, virtually overlooked the farm at La Haye Sainte from the Mont St Jean ridge. 'We were idle spectators for hours of the fighting that surged before us,' he recalled, but when the French began to flow around the buildings below, 'our lieutenant colonel [von Klencke] led us down from our position to confront the enemy.' The division commander Lieutenant General Alten had decided to intervene before the situation, with the French climbing the slope to his left, got worse. Carl Jacobi, who had endured wet and miserable conditions all night long, remembered that the sight of the approaching French 'caused the mind to triumph over the frailty of the body'. Animated by the sight, he felt impelled to do his duty. 'Full of determination and in good order we advanced,' Jacobi recalled, and the Lüneburg Battalion enjoyed a brief moment of glory as they 'threw ourselves upon the enemy who fell back'.

Major George Baring, observing the arrival of fresh reinforcements, ordered his King's German Legion to counter-attack again, and 'made the enemy give way'. At the same time he uneasily 'perceived a strong line of cuirassiers forming in front of the orchard on the French side', a potentially catastrophic development. The Hanoverians greatly outnumbered his own men, and as the two forces joined there was considerable confusion, marked by clumsy attempts to rally. With an uncertain number of as yet unseen enemy cavalry lurking on the periphery, the situation started to slip beyond Major Baring's control. The Hanoverians were caught off balance by the arrival of even more columns of French infantry. They had to pause, fall back and rally. Dimly perceived French cavalry suddenly surged through the smoke and rode at them. Carl Jacobi suddenly realised they were 'in the midst of the French cavalry', who had appeared as if from nowhere. Baring saw that the Lüneburgers, 'seeing the cuirassiers in the cornfield, imagined that their only chance of safety lay in gaining the main position of the army' back on the ridge. So they ran.

Colonel Ordner's 1st French Cuirassiers had been moving with the 4th Cuirassiers as part of a cavalry screen protecting the left flank of d'Erlon's corps attack. 'I set my regiment off at a trot, in column, by squadron at deploying distance,' he recalled. His armoured cuirassiers were skirting the left side of

Charlet's brigade attack on the farm buildings. They moved off at walking pace and descended into the dead ground of the small re-entrant just south of La Haye Sainte, wading through the wet standing crops. Strung out in two ranks with sabres drawn, they could neither see nor be seen by the enemy. When they crested the slope, Ordner could dimly see infantry in the smoke ahead, and then, as he put it, 'the Hanoverian battalion Lüneburg and the 2nd German [King's German Legion] were encountered en route'. They were a cavalryman's dream target: infantry dispersed in the open. The Lüneburgers were trying to gain entry into La Haye Sainte, but broke and ran when they spotted the advancing cavalry. The charge was sounded and Ordner's cuirassiers pushed on at a brisk trot, approaching like a bow wave through the high crops. 'We passed over them,' Ordner recalled with characteristic brevity. 'I overthrew three officers with my own hand, their colour remained in our possession.'[9]

Baring did his best to avert catastrophe. 'My voice, unknown to them [the Hanoverians], and also not sufficiently penetrating, was, not withstanding all my exertions, unequal to halt and collect my men together.' Fleeing to the main Allied ridge line was not an option, for it was too late, they were 'already overtaken by the cavalry'.

'Nobody among us really knew how he had escaped the horses' hooves or the horsemen's swords,' Carl Jacobi recalled. In the ensuing debacle, the officers lost control. Before they realised what was happening the heavily armoured cuirassiers were slashing down and bowling over the Hanoverians with their heavy horses. Jacobi watched helplessly as 'French Cuirassiers trotted past myself, ten to twelve paces away'. They were on them before they could form square. 'There are moments when the senses of hearing and sight had in fact shut down,' he later admitted. 'Only faintly do I remember that I had told some men fleeing next to me to fire on individual horsemen among the pursuers.' He later guilty reflected:

Would it not have been possible to observe in good time the approach of the enemy cavalry? Or to form with calmness and circumspection, if not a regular square, at least a compact mass?

Lieutenant Emanuel Biedermann remembered suddenly hearing the call: *'Cuirassiers! Cuirassiers!'* The young King's German Legion officer was caught outside the farm complex with his scattered command: 'Now we had to take to our heels. Many of us were shot or sabered. Whoever was unable to reach the squares behind in time was to suffer that fate.'

As Biedermann ran towards the square, he saw a phalanx of friendly rifles levelled at them. 'There was nothing left for me [to do] but quickly drop to the ground,' he recalled, 'and to crawl for a few more paces to get there.' Behind him his captain had been cut and ridden down alongside three of his company sergeants.

Jacobi and a few scattered survivors managed to flee back to one of their brigade's squares, but the battalion was decimated. 'The Lüneburger Battalion had ceased to exist,' he dolefully recalled, 'not even the smallest gathering of its troops could be found anywhere.'

Ordner's 1st Cuirassiers chased the remnants back to the main Allied line. 'There I found myself ten paces from a square,' he recalled. Part of it 'opened a murderous fire on us; my horse was killed, I was struck by a ball in the neck.' It was deflected by his armoured cuirass, which enabled him to get away. Biedermann and a few others got inside the square 'and soon were glad to see how the cuirassiers, clanking up in their sabre flourishing charge, were forced by a well directed fire to flee in their turn with heavy losses'. Rarely could cavalry collapse a disciplined square.

Ordner felt they were on the cusp of a victory. 'This was, I have to say,' he recalled, 'a great fault not to support my successful charge with all the cavalry.' In his opinion:

> The plateau of Mont St Jean [would have been taken], without great loss, the English army cut in two, and completely compromised as it would not have been able to conduct its retreat by the Brussels road.[10]

The Crest of the Mont St Jean Ridge

General d'Erlon's men were at the point of sealing that victory further to the right, enduring punishing cannon fire as they approached the crest of the ridge. What kept the French going amid such carnage? Many British observers attest to the gallantry displayed by French officers, leading by example and pushing and shoving shell-shocked survivors back into the grisly gaps created by the storm of shot. The size and extent of this attack suggested they were at the vanguard of the main French effort of the day. Having fruitlessly marched back and forth 48 hours before and missed both the battles of Ligny and Quatre-Bras, here was their chance to resurrect their honour. Driven by élan and the power of their bloody-minded urge to avenge their dead comrades, the soldiers sensed that one more supreme effort could well decide this battle.

These men were veterans and had witnessed similar carnage in battles before. Familiarity with death had to some extent defrayed the impact of risk and pain. Early nineteenth-century life was generally harsh and precarious, with injury and loss of livelihood leading to starvation and death. Women often died in childbirth, and children were highly vulnerable if they fell ill. Hard labour with the expectation of little reward was the norm. Soldiers had been on half or no pay since Napoleon's abdication the year before and were constantly irritated by the petty injustices meted out by the restored Bourbon regime. Life in the military was not half so bad. They could forage and freely loot, as they had done for the previous two decades. The price was exacted in battle, and d'Erlon's men were willing to pay. Nevertheless, as they crested the ridge of Mont St Jean, there was every expectation from the opposite ridge line of La Belle Alliance that they had done enough. Napoleon's staff sensed victory as d'Erlon's battering rams struck home.

Major-General Willem van Bijlandt's Dutch-Belgian brigade was the only Allied formation visible to the French on the ridge, and Baron Donzelot's division was heading straight for it. Directly behind Bijlandt's brigade, which had been pulled back slightly before the Grande Batterie could do its worse, was the 1/42nd Foot. Lieutenant Donald Mackenzie, standing with them, remembered 'the gloom and doubt apparent in the faces of officers and men' following the retreat from Quatre-Bras. 'We knew the Prussians had been beaten' and 'we felt no confidence in the Belgian troops with whom we were associated'. Ensign George Gerard in the same regiment concurred, claiming that 'people pretend to be attached to the House of Orange' but actually 'the great majority of them really were not so'. They kept their opinion to themselves because of the presence of Allied soldiers. Gerard had been told by an English resident in Brussels that the Belgian soldiers were 'not to be trusted as the greater part of them had served under Bonaparte, to whom they were much attached, and that he had little doubt the most of them would go over to him as good opportunities occurred'. As a consequence he was 'astonished under these circumstances that they should be kept in front as they are at present' – precisely where the French storm was to break.[11]

Bijlandt's brigade had already been severely bloodied at Quatre-Bras, 48 hours before, where it and the 2nd Netherlands brigade had lost 1,100 men. They were the first to arrive and bore the brunt of the French attacks until British reinforcements arrived. Bijlandt was realistic about the mood among his troops and later wrote that their performance should be viewed in the light of 'the short amount of time they had been formed and the inexperience of the officers of a young army'. They were doing their best under trying circumstances, but officers unfamiliar with their superiors and doubting the qualities of their own troops 'were at a great disadvantage when facing an intrepid enemy [like the French] accustomed to victory,' he explained.[12]

Victory certainly appeared to be in the French grasp. The tightly packed French columns pushed the English Rifles out of the sandpit and hedge line and poured into the orchard at La Haye Sainte. Papelotte farm was captured by the furthest French division to the right, as Donzelot's division, the furthest forward, closed with Bijlandt's Dutch-Belgian Brigade in the centre. Twenty-four French battalions were about to converge on 13 Allied ones, but apart from skirmishers only four or five of these were actually in view. Corporal Dickinson, with the Scots Greys, observed Bijlandt's brigade standing near the crest. 'They numbered at least 3,000 men,' he recalled, 'and looked well in their blue coats with orange and red facings', but he shared the slightly jaundiced British view of what happened next.

'The Belgian troops assailed with terrible fury, returned the fire of the enemy for some time with great spirit,' recalled

Lieutenant James Hope, with the 92nd Gordon Highlanders. But as the column pushed remorselessly on, 'they shifted their ground and retired behind the hedge, which, although it afforded them no shelter from the enemy's fire, yet concealed them from their view'. Looking to their rear they were reassured to see the British battalions and 'seeing themselves well supported, they showed a little more courage' and 'maintained their ground with considerable fierceness'.[13] Earlier that morning the brigade had withdrawn across the sunken road, which was lined by two hedges, to reduce their exposure to the 80 guns of the Grande Batterie. The road, in effect a hedge-lined shallow ditch, could only be penetrated here and there by groups, not in formation. This caused the head of the French column to start to widen into line, an awkward and prolonged manoeuvre that required the rear battalions to march out from behind the leaders.

For a while the Dutch-Belgians stood their ground, pouring fire into the halted and reorganising columns. 'We were so close,' recounted Lieutenant Chrétien Scheltens, a young Dutch-Belgian grenadier with the 7th Line Battalion, 'that Captain Henry l'Olivier, commanding our grenadier company, was struck on the arm by a ball, of which the wad or cartridge paper remained smoking in the cloth of his tunic'. Bijlandt the brigade commander remembered 'the confusion was so great, the mêlée horrific, and it was in this confusion that I received a bayonet thrust in my thigh'. He was out of the battle and so was his chief of staff, Colonel Zuylen van Nyevelt, who was also wounded. The Belgians were being rendered virtually leaderless. Lieutenant van Haren, with the brigade staff, was killed, and the division commander General Baron Henri de Perponcher had two horses shot dead under him. Scheltens saw a French battalion commander pathetically trying to rearrange his nose, which slashed by a sabre cut was 'hanging down over his mouth'. '"Look," he said to me in shock, "how they do for us!"' Scheltens's immediate reaction was to think 'the good fellow might have fared much worse'.

Lieutenant Hope saw the Dutch-Belgians starting to fall back from the hedge. 'At the entreaty of their officers, the greater part of them again returned to their posts, but it was merely to satisfy their curiosity,' he ironically explained, 'for they almost immediately again retired without firing a shot.' This is precisely what the British onlookers expected. 'The officers exerted themselves to the utmost,' Hope remembered, 'but their efforts were fruitless and at length the whole corps took fairly to their heels.' A collective groan with hisses and cat-calls rose up from the British lines to their rear. Four of Bijlandt's five battalions fell back, exposing a 250-yard gap on the crest of Mont St Jean.[14]

It all depended now on Lieutenant-General Sir Thomas Picton's 5th British Division battalions to plug the gap. Picton was described by one of his ensigns as being 'a strong-built man with a red face, small black eyes, and a large nose', and was incongruously dressed in civilian clothes. Picton was immensely popular with his troops, who recognised him for the character he was. He was reputed to be as brave as a lion and even now was nursing internal bleeding and two undeclared broken ribs he had suffered at Quatre-Bras two days before. Combat strain during his final year of the Peninsula campaign had exacted a toll; he was suffering from post-combat traumatic stress disorder. In Spain he had begged Wellington, 'My lord, I must give up.' He was at the end of his tether, admitting, 'I am grown so nervous, that when there is any service to be done it works upon my mind.' The spectres had doubtless reappeared at Quatre-Bras. 'It is impossible for me to sleep at nights,' he had told Wellington.

'I cannot possibly stand it, and I shall be forced to retire.' He was recalled for the Hundred Days Campaign, Now, dressed in a shabby greatcoat and dusty top hat, Picton waved his umbrella to signal the advance. His troops loved him, but the general had long resigned himself to the certainty he would not survive this battle.[15]

Viewed from the Belle Alliance ridge, the skyline and forward slope of the Mont St Jean ridge was dark with swarms of d'Erlon's infantry. Four great rectangular shadows were beginning to converge on the distant crest line. Another masterstroke, it seemed, initiated and executed by the Emperor. Concentration had been achieved: 17,000 French infantry moving irresistibly up the slope, fired in by 80 guns and supported to their left by nearly 800 elite French heavy cavalry. 'We were on the plateau, victory was ours!' declared Lieutenant Jacques Martin with the 45th Line. Ahead was a sunken road. 'Our soldiers did not await the order to cross it; they rushed over it, jumped over the hedges and broke ranks to run against the enemy.' Their impetus appeared unstoppable.

As Donzelot's lead division crossed the ridge line, they began to ponderously extend their 500-musket column front into line, moving across the sunken road and into the deserted hedge line in front. To their right Marcognet's division, having crested the slope, increased the drumbeat tempo to a charge. 'Our pace quickened,' recalled Captain Duthilt with the 45th Line, 'and to repeated shouts of "*Vive l'Empereur!*" we rushed at the batteries.' As they did, seven red-coated battalions suddenly came into view just 100 yards behind the crest line. The rippling crackle and crash of 3,000 muskets sounded along the line as Kempt and Pack's brigades belonging to Picton's 5th Infantry Division opened fire. The French columns froze and staggered as virtually the entire front ranks crumpled and fell to the ground. 'Suddenly our path was blocked,' recalled Duthilt. 'English battalions, concealed in a hollow road, stood up and fired at us at close range.' Massively checked, the 45th Line Regiment still managed to press on. 'A Colonel stopped his regiment to get it back into order,' remembered Captain Pierre Duthilt. 'In the circumstances his command was too forcefully given and was clumsily repeated.' It was too late, they were too close to the enemy and 'the disaster was irreparable'. The men were in a tangled mass.

'At this critical moment I did not see a single cowardly thought show on the faces of our soldiers,' insisted Lieutenant Jacques Martin. 'Bullets had already killed many and it was when we arrived at their guns that the carnage became terrible.' Low velocity musket balls frequently fragmented or deformed on striking solid objects such as equipment or splintering bone. Strikes on the torso compacted fragments of filthy uniform into substantial sucking wounds destined to turn gangrenous. Most hits on the body's core proved fatal, which was why the vast majority of battlefield surgery involved the treatment and amputation of limbs. The advance 'carried on with the same order, the same precision', recalled Martin. 'Dead men were replaced on the field by those who survived; the ranks were thinner, but were no less formed.'

Even as the rolling fire of 3,000 muskets scythed into the leading ranks, the Highlanders in front of the 45th Line shouted 'Hurrah!' and came at them with the bayonet, running through the hedge gaps lining the sunken road. They charged in a ragged line only two deep, the only infantry between the French and Brussels. Picton, their commanding general, was shouting 'Charge! Charge! Charge! Hurrah!' until the crown of his black top hat disintegrated as a musket ball struck him on the right temple. He fell forward onto the neck of his horse and slid to the ground. The misshapen musket ball that killed him is on display today at London's National Army Museum.

Pierre Duthilt was shoving and pushing soldiers into line, 'since a disordered group can achieve nothing'. Jacques Martin had 'at last arrived at the summit', anticipating 'the prize for such bravery'. He was convinced they had the English on the run, and like Duthilt was trying to re-establish order in the confusing crossing of the sunken road. 'Fatal mistake! We had to enforce good order,' he later wrote, which meant a momentary pause to rally. Men were roughly pushed and shoved into formation amid the noisy mêlée of fighting and men falling. 'Just as I was pushing one of our men back into the ranks I saw him fall at my feet from a sabre slash,' Duthilt remembered. 'I turned round instantly – to see English cavalry forcing their way into our midst and hacking us to pieces.'[16]

Where on earth had they come from?

CHAPTER 6

A Cascade of Cavalry →

2 pm to 3 pm

2 PM The Mass French Infantry Assault

D'Érlon attacks the Allied centre to the right of the crossroads and is repelled by the British cavalry brigades.

PAPELOTTE
FARM

Cpl Louis Canler
Lt Jacques Martin
Capt Pierre Duthilt
Pierre Guillot

Lt Chrétien Scheltens
Sgt Robertson

Sgt Archibald Johnston
Cpl John Dickinson
Cornet Francis Kinchant
Sgt Charles Ewart

MONT ST
FAR

PLANCENOIT
VILLAGE

Napoleon Bonaparte

LA BELLE
ALLIANCE

LA HAYE SAINTE
FARM

CHÂTEAU HOUGOUMONT

Pte Friedrich Lindau
Maj George Baring

Capt John Kincaid
Lt George Simmons

Capt Carl Jacobi
Ensign Edward Wheatley

John Shaw

S
E ⊕ W
N

Behind the Mont St Jean Ridge

Hidden beneath the ridge lay two brigades of English heavy cavalry, with Lord Somerset's Household Brigade to the right of the Brussels road and Sir William Ponsonby's Union Brigade to the left. Bunched together, in close column of squadrons, the force numbered some 2,600 sabres. Thus far, their day had been uneventful.

Sergeant Archibald Johnston of the Scots Greys remembered trading foraged food for liquor from the Highland regiments also hiding behind the ridge line. Cannonades from the Grande Batterie necessitated frequent changes of location to avoid shellfire and round shot bouncing over the ridge. 'We were ordered to retire a short distance under cover of a hill,' Johnston recalled, 'where we had continued but a short time, when the shot and shell began to wreak dreadful havoc amongst us.' The frustrated Sir William Ponsonby yelled, 'Greys, they have found us out again!' and the cavalry dispersed into open columns of half squadrons to reduce vulnerability. 'But all was in vain,' noted Johnston, as the cannon continued to seek them out and 'we were then halted and ordered to wheel into line'. Action of some kind was clearly becoming imminent. Across the road, Private Joseph Lord of the 2nd Life Guards recalled the round shot passing over and through the ranks, while 'others struck the ground a few yards in front of us. At last one struck a man and horse and killed them both.' The kinetic energy from such a strike could lift both man and horse clear from the ground.

'There is no part of an action more disagreeable than looking on,' wrote Captain William Verner, further west with the 7th Hussars:

> When engaged the mind is employed and the attention is taken up with what is going forward; to be exposed to fire without being able to return it, is like receiving a personal insult, and not having the power to resent it.

Verner and his men felt vulnerable to the 'galling' fire. They were moved by the Squadron Captain Thomas Wildman, but:

> Hardly had we taken up the new ground when a shot came, went thro' the breast of the man beside me, passed thro' the knee of the Sergeant close behind, and broke the leg of a horse in his rear.

It was over in a terrifying instant. There was no medical assistance and the sergeant quickly bled to death. The soldier had been killed instantly and the wounded horse was shot through the head. 'I could not help wishing that Wildman had left us where we were,' Verner commented.[1]

Both brigades either side of the Brussels road had dispatched riders to the ridgeline to observe what was happening over the crest. Corporal John Dickinson of the Scots Greys rode forward to confer with the 92nd Highlanders and noticed that 'all were intently watching the movements going on about them'. More than half of the 92nd had fallen at Quatre-Bras two days before and 'they began to tell me about the battle'. The men had every reason to be apprehensive at what was about to happen, but remained stoical. Dickinson had learned that 'every regiment in brave old [General] Picton's division had lost more than one-third of its men'. The men were lying in the same sodden ploughed field they had occupied since the previous afternoon. Lieutenant James Kerr Ross remembered it was 'one of trodden down crops' but 'at all events some way down the slope from the crest of the position, with a view, to our avoiding the cannonade as much as practicable'.

'The French cannoniers could not hit us with their shot, but they made some shells to bear upon us,' recalled Sergeant Robertson of the 92nd, 'which made great havoc in our ranks.' Canny veterans knew best where to stand and when to move. 'It is remarkable that recruits in action are generally more unfortunate than the old soldiers,' observed one veteran. Recruits newly joined, just before leaving England, seemed uncannily vulnerable. 'The reason for this is that an old rifleman will seek shelter if there be any near his post,' remarked the veteran, 'while the inexperienced recruit appears as if petrified to the spot by the whizzing balls, and unnecessarily exposes himself to the enemy's fire.' The slow and the unwary died first.[2]

The 92nd were watching the French; Robertson could see them 'forming columns to their right, which was directly in our front, and we were expecting every moment to be attacked'. At Quatre-Bras they had seen other regiments overwhelmed by cuirassiers and lancers before they could form square and assumed 'in all likelihood, we would be first attacked by cavalry, who would try to break our line'. It was therefore comforting to observe that their own heavy cavalry had formed up behind them. When Napoleon's forces suddenly appeared at Quatre-Bras the British cavalry had to cover immense distances from their cantonments and were conspicuously absent from the battle. The infantry had been dreadfully exposed.[3]

Private Joseph Lord of the 2nd Life Guards, stationed to the right of the Brussels road, was looking for his brother, John, also with the same unit. He was reassured to spot him nearby. They had always been close. John Lord later recalled how they had been 'brought up from infancy together, the companion of my riper years, my comrade as a soldier, my friend in misfortune [and] my consoler in distress'. Joseph likewise regarded John as 'a very affectionate brother' who 'was respected by all who knew him in the regiment'.

Earlier that morning Sergeant William Clarke with the Scots Greys had fleetingly managed to meet his brother Mark, also to exchange farewells. 'He was permitted by the Colonel to come down the hill to our lines,' he remembered. Their exchange was all too brief. 'We had just time to take a dram of each other's flask, as other warriors do, when the word was given to arms.' There was a brief handshake and they 'took more than a common farewell with each other', promising that 'if we are both spared we must be sure to send word to each other as soon as possible after the battle, which we knew well was to be a serious one'.

'This was Sunday morning and church time,' recalled Private Thomas Hasker, a stocking weaver by trade serving with the 1st Dragoon Guards. But instead of church bells 'the balls came whistling over the hills, occasionally striking one or other of our men and horses'. Hasker's thoughts strayed to 'how many thousands of my countrymen are at this moment assembling to worship God!' back home while here he was, sword in hand, awaiting battle.

Cornet (cavalry Ensign) Francis Kinchant was a carefree, bawdy young officer whose animated letters to his friend John in England suggest he would likely have been chattering away in the ranks. His troop sergeant Charles Ewart kept a benign and paternal eye on him. He was attached to this bubbly young officer, who worked hard and enjoyed life to the full. 'Three drills a day on horseback and on foot I assure you,' Francis wrote to John, 'did not a little fatigue my bones, however I trust I am now a tolerable good match for a Frenchman.' The coming battle was viewed with youthful optimism, for there might well be a lieutenancy to be derived from this opportunity.

Kinchant liked the girls, but Belgium had been a disappointment. 'The women are very plain,' he complained, 'with mouths that reach from ear to ear and are extremely ignorant, it is with great difficulty I can make them understand my wants.' Despite his non-existent Flemish he tried his luck. 'The only answer I can ever obtain is *"Yaw"*, an English "Yes",' he explained to his friend. 'I asked a girl one day if she would let me *manoeuvre* her, she answered *"Yaw, Yaw"*.' Plunging in, 'I proceeded to action; when lo! To my astonishment she kicked [up] such a row in Dutch that I never before had' and beat a hasty and tumultuous retreat. Kinchant likely shared these bawdy tales with fellow subalterns, with the ranks listening appreciatively. 'Some of our lads have pieces [prostitutes] and I wish I was of their number,' Kinchant confided to John, 'so much for that.' He could well identify with his men:

> *There are, however, the most excellent pieces to be had at Brussels, Ghent and other large towns at regular licensed bawdy houses, indeed some of the French girls are beautiful and their action surpasses anything I have before met with at Drury Lane or Covent Garden.*

Kinchant had lived his short life to the full. Sergeant Ewart, smilingly looking on, decided he would keep an eye on his young sir.

Trepidation nagged at the men. One Scots Grey sergeant had written to his wife about the carnage he had witnessed 48 hours earlier when camping among the wounded in a wheat field at Quatre-Bras. Arriving too late to participate in the action, they had seen enough to unsettle them.

Believe me, Dear Mary, the cries of those poor creatures to God almighty to take them out of this world frightened the horses. I will leave you to judge whether we could sleep or rest, every man praying to God for morning light to get at those French murderers.

Horses were not impervious to the sights, smells and sounds of the battlefield. Captain William Verner remembered how musket balls 'produced a whistling noise not very agreeable to the ear'. His horse was affected the same way. 'It is a remarkable fact,' he later explained, 'that horses soon become reconciled to the noise of cannon, but never to the whistling of bullets.' His horse served him well and saved his life and lived on for a further 20 years; 'she was a fine animal, and a faithful soldier to me'. Despite not being wounded, she became 'ever afterwards fidgety and uncomfortable when she heard a shot or smelt powder' even long after in rural England.[4]

Men were nervous, but suffering was not unfamiliar. They lived harsh lives in a society where death was commonplace. The heavy cavalry in Somerset's Household Brigade across the Brussels road were phlegmatic about their chances. 'We are only 15 miles from Mr Boney,' Private Charles Stanley with the King's Dragoon Guards had written to his cousin the previous month, 'and we expect to have a rap at him every day.' Like many of his working-class contemporaries Stanley had resigned himself to accept whatever life dealt in the battle ahead. 'At present there is no doubt of us beating the confounded rascal,' he added blithely, 'we have the most cavalry of the English that ever was known at one time and in good condition and good spirits. It may cost me my life and many more. That will only be the fortune of war ... my life I set no store by at all.' Charles Stanley would be dead within the hour.[5]

Mounted in squadron file to his left was the imposing figure of Life Guardsman Corporal John Shaw: fair-haired, large-limbed, the very epitome of a Guards cavalryman. A former prize-fighter, Shaw was completely at home in an endemically violent English society where bear baiting, ratting and duels were regarded as sport. A scrapper and street-fighting cockney hero of the London mob, his ability to handle himself in a fracas had commended him to the colonel of the Life Guards, who had adopted him as a sort of regimental mascot. Just two months before he had floored the last prize-fighting contender for the English Championship at Hounslow Heath. The 30-minute contest was so one-sided that one witness claimed that he 'seemed to be able to do what he liked with him'.

Corporal Shaw enjoyed a drink, and was even now helping himself to grog in the commissariat wagons to the rear. Picking up the regimental allowance attracted volunteers but was not without its dangers. Retrieving his company allowance of 'Hollands', Thomas Morris of the 1/73rd Foot recalled that 'we had scarcely received it, when a cannon-shot went through the cask and man too'. This was excruciating news for thirsty soldiers, who often cheered when the barrels rolled up. Friends now pointed out 'Shaw the fighting man' nearby and Morris saw that he had drunk 'a considerable portion of the raw spirit'. Nobody was going to question a man like Shaw for helping himself, and Morris watched the corporal climb unsteadily back onto his horse.

The troopers were buoyed by their sheer splendour and huge horses. Double-breasted red coats contrasted with blue trousers and scarlet waist sashes, while a man's height was further accentuated by brass helmets with nodding blue and red crested, scarlet and white plumes. Swords were drawn – 35 inches of heavy steel looped around wrist gauntlets by leather straps – the blades honed by armourers the night before. 'Shaw's regiment was composed of tall, muscular men about six feet in height,' wrote a contemporary commentator, 'and the powerful black horses which they rode exceeded sixteen hands high.' The artist Benjamin Robert Haydon had used Shaw and other Life Guardsmen as models, and Shaw's companion, Corporal William Hodgeson, had been declared 'the finest man of all, a perfect Achilles'. But a subdued Hodgeson was now feeling hardly epic. He had never fought anyone with a sword before and was about to face some of 'Boney's' consummate experts. The men's attention focused on a flurry of activity to their right as a succession of senior officers and aides-de-camp galloped up and took post to their front.[6]

Corporal Dickinson with the Scots Greys had barely returned to the squadron lines when 'a great fusillade commenced just in front of us'. He watched the 79th Cameron Highlanders moving up in a red and tartan column to the sunken road on the right. Things were clearly happening. 'Then, suddenly, a great noise of firing and hisses and shouting commenced, and the whole Belgian brigade, of those whom I had seen in the morning, came rushing along and across the road in full flight.' There was a great commotion in the ranks of the heavy brigades drawn up behind them. 'Our men began to shout and groan at them too. They had bolted almost without firing a shot, and left the brigade of Highlanders to meet the whole French attack on the British left centre,' Dickinson complained. The Belgian departure had opened up a 250-yard gap on the Mont St Jean crest.

Sergeant Robertson was with the Gordons further up the slope towards the crest. 'Everyone was eager to be led on ... they could see what was going to happen next, because the gap would have to be closed.' Donzelot's French column was cresting the ridge at the gap and another under Marcognet was about to appear on the Gordons' right. Watching with the cavalry, Dickinson saw 'three regiments of Highlanders, only a thousand in all, bravely firing down on the advancing masses of Frenchmen'. At this point the Gordons' brigadier 'shouted out with great energy "Ninety-second, you must advance! All in front of you have given way!"'. Robertson's Gordons 'cheered loudly, and called over to the Scots Greys "Scotland forever!"'.

A bugle call rang out to the right of the heavy cavalry – Somerset's Household Brigade had sounded the 'Walk March'. Cavalry attacks aimed to strike the enemy in unison across his front. Squadrons riding two deep closed in a series of pummelling blows designed to break through. It was a disciplined approach, controlled to maximise the power and weight of man and horse. Each rippling line of sabres buffeted the enemy like waves on a sea-shore. The Earl of Uxbridge, commanding the British cavalry, had been monitoring the battle and chose his moment with consummate timing. He had exhaustively drilled the cavalry in Belgium, often before a dubious Wellington, jaundiced by his Peninsula experience that suggested cavalry exercised little control. Uxbridge was mostly left to it, and Wellington never interfered; he concentrated on his infantry and artillery.

Trooper Thomas Playford with the 2nd Life Guards remembered 'a slight murmur of gladness passed along the ranks' when they were given the command to 'Mount' and 'Form Line'. They could not see what was happening beyond the crest line to their front. Battle noises could at first be heard towards Hougoumont on their right and then again to their left. 'At length,' he remembered, 'there was a tremendous thunder of cannon which drowned every other sound, immediately in front of us.' But they still could not see. 'The roar of artillery with the report of small arms was incessant,' he recalled. After 'Advance' the trumpet sounded 'Walk', but no enemy were in sight. 'Yet there was a strange medley of shouts, musket shots, and the roar of cannon beyond the rising ground in front of us,' recalled Playford.

The mass of British cavalry now began to advance up the reverse slope of the ridge, flowing around the infantry squares, which had formed to let them pass. As they fanned out for the attack, buglers sounded the 'Advance', but when the distinctive blasts of the 'Charge' followed, the slope of the ground meant they could do little more than raise a ponderous canter, throwing great clods of mud into the air. Even so, these were big men on big horses, able to produce a weight of charge of half a ton each.

They passed a number of English foot-soldiers that Playford assumed were 'running for their lives'. It was confused artillerymen and riflemen, who hastened to get out of the way and reformed behind them. Then ahead 'I noticed the soldiers of a battalion of Belgian infantry, formed under the brow of the hill, run away'. Playford 'supposed they were very young soldiers, for no veterans would have done so'. All in all, 'It was a magnificent sight,' he reminisced, 'the charge of the Life Guards was tremendous!'[7]

'Now then, Scots Greys, charge!' shouted Colonel Inglis Hamilton, smoothly jumping the hedges bordering the sunken road. 'At once a great cheer rose from our ranks, and we too waved our swords and followed him', recalled Dickinson, who almost immediately saw one of his officers, Major Hankin, snatched from his saddle by shot. 'I felt a strange thrill run through me, and I am sure my noble beast felt the same, for after rearing for a moment, she sprang forward, uttering loud neighings and snortings, and leapt over the holly hedge at a terrific speed.' The Greys managed to negotiate the sunken road, after which the long lines of giant horses were 'dashing along with flowing manes and heads down, tearing up the turf about them as they went'. Dickinson was cantering as fast as he could in the second rank. Having cleared the crest they had to tighten their grip on the horses' thighs as they descended the hillside, swishing through corn. Stray Highlanders were knocked out of the way and Dickinson recalled one crying out, 'Eh! But I didna think ye wad ha'e hurt me sae!' Some Scottish soldiers grabbed hold of stirrups in the fierce exuberance of the Greys' charge, to be whisked in among the startled French.

Dickinson heard 'loud discordant yells' coming up ahead and 'just then I saw the first Frenchman'. A young Fusilier officer slashed at him with his sword, but Dickinson parried and broke the man's arm. 'The next second we were in the thick of them' but 'we could not see five yards ahead for the smoke'. Galloping alongside, Archibald Johnston remembered the Highlanders 'mingled amongst us' and 'running like bucks down the hill after us'. Half a ton of man and beast had made short work of the French front ranks, who bounced off in all directions. The Highlanders 'were very busily employed with those whom we had rode down,' Johnston remembered, 'crying out to us "ne'er mind that chiel, Grey, I'll do him" as they went in with the bayonet.'[8]

As they broke into the ranks of the 21st Line Regiment, a British officer punched his short sword into the base of conscript 'Trois Louis' Célestine's throat. The blade was likely arrested by his cervical vertebrae, just missing the windpipe, and Célestine escaped death by a fraction of an inch. Seven of the eight French battalion commanders and at least one regimental commander in this column went down as the British cavalry swept across the slope.

Somerset's Household Brigade struck the French columns and cuirassiers around La Haye Sainte. 'The head of the column appeared to be seized with a panic,' Captain Clark Kennedy of the 7th Dragoon Guards recalled, because they 'gave us a fire which brought down about twenty men' then fled through the hedges on the sunken road, 'but we were upon and amongst them before this could be effected'. James Alexander, with the 1st Dragoons, was blasted from his saddle by grapeshot, which tore a fist-size hole on the lower part of his neck. The shock of the impact reduced his arterial blood pressure to such an extent that blood congealed rather than spurting out. His surgeon was amazed at the size of the wound, which he said 'will admit a hand', exposing the quivering nerves in his neck. Alexander would linger on for two months.[9]

Clark Kennedy saw that the French infantry in the column were compressed so tightly by the impetus of the charge that they couldn't react, 'one dense mass, the men between the advancing and retiring parts getting so jammed together that the men could not bring down their arms, or use them effectively'. The sheer weight of men and horses from the heavy brigade began to push them down the slope.

On his left, Joseph Lord was trying to keep his brother in sight. 'I was very close to him all day,' he later wrote to his wife, 'two or three men distant only and we every now and then looked to see whether each other was present as they were falling continuously.' He had been lucky to find him. 'We might be spared,' Joseph had shouted. 'Don't fret yourself,' his brother responded, 'but should I fall, write home, give my kind love to them all [and] desire them not to fret.' It was agreed that if one of them died the other would take their possessions and sell them to their fellows at the unit auction, conducted by the survivors after any battle. '"God bless you," says he, "God bless you," says I, and we shook hands and mounted again.' John Lord would live for about another two and a half hours. Joseph saw a cannon-ball shatter the right side of his brother's forehead during a subsequent charge. 'He fell from his horse uttering "O Lord, have mercy on me", his body immediately disappearing from sight.' The charge continued over him.[10]

2.30 pm

The Other Side of the Hill: Grande Batterie Ridge

'The warning call *Attention, cavalerie!*' rang out,' recalled a French conscript with the 25th Line Regiment, but it was too late. 'Almost at the same instant a crowd of red dragoons on grey horses swept down on us', piling into the lead regiment of Marcognet's division column. 'Once the ranks have been broken and penetrated, then resistance is useless,' explained Captain Pierre Duthilt of the 45th Line; 'nothing remains for the cavalry to do but to slaughter at almost no risk to themselves. This is what happened.'

The Scots Greys were quickly inside the column 'slashing right and left with their sabres,' recalled the French conscript, 'and spurring their horses into the flanks of the columns in order to break them. They were too deep and massive for that [but] they killed great numbers and threw us into confusion.' The 25th Line benefited from their depth in the column, many ranks were ahead, or 'we should have been dispersed over the hillside like a swarm of ants. Only the first two ranks made a stand ... it was shameful to form our men in that manner.' Stragglers were mercilessly cut down or finished off by the Gordon Highlanders charging in among them. Sergeant Robertson saw dragoons:

> ... *lopping off heads at every stroke, while the French were calling for quarter. We were also among them busy with the bayonet and what the cavalry did not execute we completed.*

Sergeant Charles Ewart crashed into the French column just ahead of his protégé, Cornet Francis Kinchant. Ewart was an accomplished swordsman and quickly disarmed a French officer who shrieked, 'Ah mercy, mercy Angleterre' as he was about to cut him down from his horse. 'Sergeant Ewart, spare his life,' Kinchant instructed, 'and let us take him prisoner.' The battle-wise Ewart was reluctant, 'considering that moment as a period for slaughter and destruction,' he remembered, 'and not the proper time for taking prisoners.' Kinchant, his superior officer, was adamant and Ewart relented. 'As it is your wish, sir,' he responded, 'it shall be done.' The Frenchman was ordered to the rear.

As Ewart spurred his mount to rejoin the charge he heard a sharp pistol report behind and turned in time to see Kinchant topple over the back of his horse. The French officer was 'attempting to hide his pistol under his coat'. The enraged Ewart turned on him as 'the villain' begged for mercy 'in the same supplicating terms as before,' the sergeant recalled. 'Ask mercy of God for the devil a bit will ye get at my hands,' he bellowed, and 'with one stroke of his sabre severed his head from his body'. The lifeless trunk briefly rode on. Kinchant's death was to haunt Ewart for the rest of his life. Two years later an acquaintance remarked he was still 'very much affected at this distant period of time'. Ewart was known to be 'strongly attached' to Kinchant and 'to have more respect [for him] than any other officer under whom he might have served during the 24 years that he had been in the regiment'. Now he sought revenge.[11]

'The enemy's column, near which I was, on arriving at the crest of the position seemed very helpless,' recalled Major de Lacy Evans, Ponsonby's ADC. It had 'very little fire to give from its front or flanks, was incapable of deploying, must have already lost many of its officers coming up [and] was fired into, close, with impunity by stragglers of our infantry who remained behind'. The column recoiled, pathetically trying to make itself smaller. 'The front and flanks began to turn their backs inwards' while 'the rear of the columns had already begun to run away'. At the back of Marcognet's column to the right, Brigadier Noguès recalled the closely packed soldiers were unable to fire a single shot. They 'raised their bayonets above their heads to parry the sabre blows' and then a musket ball shattered his left hand.[12]

The French gunners on their small ridge opposite Mont St Jean were at first bewildered, then aghast. The slopes ahead of them had been teeming with French infantry, clearly silhouetted crossing the skyline. There had even been cries of 'Victoire!' ahead. Now a cascade of some 2,600 red-coated British heavy cavalry was plunging down the slope towards them, just minutes away if they overflowed the blue columns of French infantry lying between.

Lieutenant Jacques Martin with the 45th Line threw himself to the ground amid the flood of riders and let the cavalry ride over, counting on the traditional reluctance of horses to trample human bodies. The gunners of the Grande Batterie faced the dilemma of whether or not to open up friendly fire on their comrades, but the issue was swiftly resolved in favour of survival. Cannon blasted away at anything to their front. Martin saw that they 'poured fire into the mêlée and killed many of us – we too, in the mayhem of a confused and agitated crowd, shot many of our own people with shots aimed at the enemy'. Pierre Duthilt described the sheer desperation of being unable to 'reach far enough to bayonet those cavalrymen mounted on powerful horses'. In the free-for-all, Martin saw that 'hands and muskets fell together' as the British lopped off limbs attached to any weapon and 'sabred without pity even the children who served as drummers and fifers in the regiment, who asked in vain for mercy'.

Corporal Louis Canler saw the 1st Dragoons carve their way through the ranks of the 105th Line directly ahead; they were on the 28th before they realised what was happening, 'and fell on us with wild cheering'. The division was broken and:

> A real carnage then ensued. Everyone saw he was separated from his comrades and fought for his own life. Sabres and bayonets slashed at the quivering flesh for we were too close to each other to use firearms.

They were soon cut off. Canler was taken prisoner and disarmed.

'The French were fighting like tigers,' recalled Corporal Dickinson, as he barged through tumbling soldiers on Rattler, his grey mare. 'Some of the wounded were firing at us as we passed.' Lieutenant Wyndham saw 'several killed and wounded' pitching from saddles as they went in and the 'extraordinary' high-pitched metallic pings coming from small shot and bullets that 'struck our swords as we ascended'. Captain William Tomkinson remembered Frenchmen crying for mercy as they started to jettison muskets and claw off cross belts, throwing them down as the cavalry swept towards them, the accoutrements falling neatly 'in two lines, nearly as regularly as if laid on parade'.

The swirl of movement now approached the French rear, interspersed with eddies of frenzied fighting around retreating colours. Sergeant Charles Ewart, with the Scots Greys, smarting at the death of Cornet Francis Kinchant, took the eagle of the 45th Line. It displayed past honours at Austerlitz, Jena, Friedland, Essling and Wagram. 'I had a hard contest for it,' wrote Ewart, 'the bearer thrust for my groin – I parried it off, and I cut him through the head.' Standard-bearer Pierre Guillot went down and was unable to get up again in the press. A French lancer threw his lance at Ewart like a spear, which he knocked aside with his sword and then swung and 'cut him from the chin upwards, which cut went through his teeth'. A foot-soldier fired at point-blank range, then came at him with the bayonet, which he parried and then slashed down through his head and, suddenly, the eagle was his and immediately borne off the field. Today the eagle resides in Edinburgh Castle. In later years, when Ewart was asked how he felt about achieving the honour, he 'always seemed to speak of it with much indifference'. His focus had been to avenge Kinchant. Asked whose regiment the colour had belonged to, he would respond vaguely, 'The Invincible or the like.'

Away to his right Captain Kennedy-Clark and Corporal Francis Stiles took the eagle of the 105th Line Regiment. 'I ran my sword into the officer's right side, who carried the eagle,' Kennedy-Clark recalled. A tussle over the colours occurred when the Frenchman fell forward, held off the ground by the press of bodies about him. Corporal Stiles managed to scoop it up before it fell through. Only two eagles had been captured during the entire Peninsula campaign in Spain, whereas two were secured here within as many minutes during the headlong rush down the slope of Mont St Jean.[13]

'We continued to charge until we broke through the second line,' recalled Sergeant Archibald Johnston, 'which we dispersed in the same manner.' Corporal Dickinson remembered the 'sharp fire of musketry' that preceded the clash with the second column. By now they were galloping into the depth of the French lines with the Enniskillings and Royals and 'began a furious onslaught on this obstacle, and soon made an impression; the battalions seemed to open out for us to pass through, and so it happened that in five minutes we had cut our way through as many thousands of Frenchmen'.

'In fact,' admitted Major de Lacy Evans, 'our men were out of hand. The enemy fled as a flock of sheep across the valley – quite at the mercy of the dragoons.' But their momentum began to peter out as they crossed the bottom of the valley basin, 'slippery with deep mud', and began to charge up the other side towards the Grande Batterie. French gunners were now firing directly into their faces, heedless of the consequences for their own fleeing comrades. 'We suffered greatly in men and horses,' Johnston remembered, while Dickinson noted how 'the ground was very difficult, and especially where we crossed the edge of a ploughed field, so that our horses sank to the knees as we struggled on'. Rattler was now panting and wheezing. '*Charge! Charge the guns!*' shouted Colonel Hamilton, who was last seen galloping through the Grande Batterie 'going at full speed, with the bridle-reins between his teeth,' according to one witness, 'after he had lost his hands'.

Officers had lost control. 'The General of the [Union] Brigade, his staff, and every officer within hearing, exerted themselves to the utmost to reform the men,' remembered de Lacy Evans, but it was hopeless. 'The helplessness of the enemy offered too great a temptation to the dragoons, and our efforts were abortive.' The impetuosity of the charge was propelled by pure blood lust. Artillery fire ceased once the troopers were in among the Grande Batterie. 'There was nothing to be heard but the clashing of swords and bayonets, and the cries of the dying and wounded,' recalled Sergeant Archibald Johnston. 'We sabred the gunners, lamed the horses, and cut their traces and harness.' The French gunners watched the progress of the British cavalry and despaired once they cleared their infantry, knowing there would be no escape. 'The artillery drivers sat on their horses weeping aloud as we went among them,' recalled Dickinson. 'They were mere boys, we thought' – but, nevertheless, they were hacked down from their horses. Even Dickinson's horse succumbed to the madness: 'Rattler lost her temper and bit and tore at everything that came in her way.' From his vantage-point Napoleon watched the Greys plunging into the Grande Batterie gun line. 'These terrible Greys,' he conceded with some awe, 'how they *fight*!'[14]

Thomas Playford, with the 2nd Life Guards, saw men who 'had become decidedly insane during the hot work of war'. Out of control, 'they shouted, raved, and rushed recklessly into battle where several of them perished'. Trooper Samuel Godly had his horse shot under him and lost his helmet. 'He raved about the field of battle on foot until he met a cuirassier, whom he slew and rode off with his horse to new scenes of conflict.' Playford saw another Guardsman, 'of nervous infirmity', who dropped his own sword in panic and seized that of his opponent. Others were brutalised to the extent they were 'ready for any act of barbarity':

I saw one soldier, who had always before appeared to be of a humane disposition, slay a grey-haired French officer, who had surrendered, in a most savage manner. Some men appeared anxious to shed blood whether there was any occasion for it or not.

'Many of our brigade after dispersing the second line advanced as far as the third,' remembered Sergeant Johnston, and this was the point at which the Union Brigade ran out of momentum. A high price would be exacted for their recklessness. Johnston observed that the new third line of French cavalry 'was chiefly composed of lancers and cuirassiers, whose horses were quite fresh'. The British horses were blown, the squadrons fragmented and weakened by huge losses. The veteran French lancers made an oblique movement 'and got round between us and the British lines'. This would be no blind charge; they sought to first ensnare their quarry. To get back, the exhausted men on their winded horses now realised, they would have to fight their way out. Ensign Mounsteven, with the 28th Regiment, saw the approaching catastrophe from the ridge of Mont St Jean. 'I well remember the intense anxiety we felt when we saw some of our gallant, but over-rash fellows, without stopping to form again, ride on headlong at what appeared to me an immense corps of support in perfect order.'[15]

'Everyone saw what must happen,' Major de Lacy Evans later wrote. 'Those whose horses were best or least blown got away. Some attempted to escape back to our position by going round the left of the French lancers.' Men with short sabres on tired-out horses were helpless against lancers. Nearly 2,400 horsemen rode into the disorganised and exhausted British cavalry. A remorseless door swung shut from their front and east.

The Scots Greys were quickly in trouble. Corporal Dickinson glanced back over the valley through which they had charged and saw 'a couple of regiments of cuirassiers on the right, and away to the left a regiment of lancers. I shall never forget the sight,' he recalled. They were galloping to close the gap, throwing up great clods of earth, 'trumpets blowing wild notes in the midst of the discharges of grape and canister' emanating from the Grande Batterie ridge line. 'We had no chance,' he remembered. 'I saw the lances rise and fall for a moment, and Sam Tar, the leading man of ours, go down amid the flash of steel.' The lance's blade was a smooth spike of polished steel, nine inches long, sharpened to a point like a needle. It was jabbed with a gloved hand tight on the cord grip wound around the long ash staff. Still in a fighting frenzy, but on flagging horses, the British tried to sabre their way through. Men were soon down. 'I saw them trying to ward off the lances with their hands,' Dickinson recalled, until his horse also fell, pierced by a lance, 'and I thought I was done for.'

Colonel Bro de Commères, leading the 4th French Lancers, swept down on the spent British cavalry with 700 lancers from the fields south of Frischermont, and charged westward. 'Come, children, we must overrun this rabble,' he called out to rouse his troops. '*En avant!*' shouted back the lancers. '*Vive l'Empereur!*'

Two minutes later the shock occurred. Three enemy ranks were bowled over. We struck into the others terribly! The mêlée became dreadful. Our horses crushed corpses and screams rose from the wounded on all sides.

He was briefly disorientated by powder smoke:

When I came out of it, I noticed some English officers surrounding second Lieutenant Verrand, eagle bearer. Rallying some horsemen, I rushed to help him. Sergeant Urban killed General Ponsonby with a lance thrust. My sabre cut down three of his captains. Two others were able to flee.

Lances, held rigid against the body by the pressure of the right elbow, were rammed home. Caught in the cloying mud at the base of the valley on blown horses, the British stood little chance. 'On no occasion, was it so clearly seen as in this encounter, the superiority of the lance over the sabre,' commented General Duratte, commanding the 4th Division. The British cavalry were to re-role a number of light dragoon regiments to lancers after this searing experience at Waterloo.[16]

Trooper Peltier, with the French 3rd Lancers, was sabered across the upper abdomen by a British dragoon. He gasped and tensed his abdominal muscles by grunting and straining. As his horse moved away, part of his viscera fell out, an ugly partial disembowelling. Fortitude was much admired, but surgery for Peltier was going to be nigh impossible with the post-operative shortcomings of the day.

Once down, a cavalryman's chances of survival, often surrounded by vengeful infantry, were slim. Private Thomas Hasker, with the 1st Dragoon Guards, who had earlier reflected on the irony of missing Sunday church, was instead caught up amid a group of pursuing French cuirassiers. 'Many of them on our right flank got behind us, and thus we were at once pursuing and pursued,' he recalled. His horse went down and he was immediately cut about on foot by one of the cuirassiers, who 'rode up and begun cutting and slashing at my head with his sword'. His helmet was bashed off and he received wounds about the head and face. When he raised his right hand to protect himself his little finger was slashed off and the blade cut 'halfway through the rest' of his hand. He flung himself to the ground to escape further punishment.

One of the lancers rode by, and stabbed me in the back with his lance. I then turned, and lay with my face upward, and a foot soldier stabbed me with his sword as he walked by. Immediately after, another, with his firelock and bayonet gave me a terrible plunge, and while doing it with all his might, exclaimed 'Sacré nom de Dieu!'

The bayonet snagged in one of the brass eyes of his coat, which deflected the blade. French soldiers swarmed over his inert body, manhandling and tugging to plunder his watch, money, canteen, haversack, even his trousers. British round shot still exploded to the left and right and soon covered his body with great splashes of mud. Hasker was to lie amid the dead and dying 'bleeding from at least a dozen places' for three days.[17]

Whether it was best to cut or thrust on horseback was the interminable professional cavalry debate during the Napoleonic wars. A stab to the torso was invariably mortal but required cool presence of mind to execute during the hack and thrust of fighting on horseback, when it was an achievement to simply remain in control of the horse. One could survive as many as twenty sabre cuts, the immediate and instinctive action during clashing, brawling exchanges. Surgeon Charles Bell recalled treating the typical outcome, in this case a soldier with the 1st Dragoons, repeatedly sabered from above, with cuts to the chin, ear and scalp. His worst injury was a deep slash across the centre of the skull, which after a dicing blow to the rear, had created a grisly flap. The trooper had been chopped about the head, first one way, then the other. 'On being urged to speak,' Bell noted, 'he makes painful effort to speak but cannot.' He could sit unsupported, 'but stoops languidly and with a vacant and indifferent expression of countenance'. Bell removed a piece of bone from the skull, which 'considerably relieved in his symptoms the day after the operation, but [the man] could still give no account of himself'.[18]

The noted French cavalryman Colonel Antoine de Brack routinely advised subordinates that 'it is the point alone that kills; the others serve only to wound, so *thrust! thrust!* as often as you can, you will overthrow all whom you touch, and demoralise those who escape your attack'. The British 1796 pattern heavy cavalry sabre was a compromise, with a sharp edge and point, neither of which satisfactorily fitted the bill. Unit armourers had honed some down to a narrower and sharper point.

Life Guardsman Corporal William Hodgeson was fighting with a sword for the first time in his life. Luckily he was an adept horseman. He nearly broke his arm with the shock rebound from a cuirassier's breastplate he mistakenly thought was 'silver lace'. The cuirassier appeared to know what he was doing, but Hodgeson found that he could manoeuvre his horse faster if he dropped the reins and guided his mount by knee alone. When his opponent thrust he lopped off the Frenchman's sword arm, then plunged the point of his own blade into his throat and 'turned it round and round'. 'Damn me, sir,' he said, exhilarated by his new-found skill, 'now I had found the way, I soon gave it them.'

Thomas Playford's experience by contrast was bizarre. He could not find any Frenchmen to fight:

I have a painful recollection of the pursuit, of shots, of clashing swords and mangled bodies and groaning men; yet strange to say, no enemy confronted me.

Whichever direction he turned, the enemy got out of the way. 'Those who first looked me in the face rode off before we crossed swords.' He was like a spectator, side-lined from this dreamlike procession of nightmarish events. There was 'fearful carnage taking place on the main road to Brussels', but when he spurred his horse 'under a hot impulse' to get there, the fighting was over before he arrived. 'All I could do was to ride after some cuirassiers who, however, contrived to escape.' He fought in a bubble: 'I rode among conflict and slaughter,' he recalled, 'and every enemy avoided me.'

One Scots Grey sergeant found himself 'within 20 yards of them, then with sword in hand everyone killing another, so awful was the sight that it could be compared to nothing but the day of judgement'. To keep one's head in the middle of a mêlée and then act with the precision prescribed by de Brack required considerable presence of mind. The sergeant described the ensuing fight in a letter to his wife:

> God forgive me for such an expression dear Mary, I was the orderly sergeant so I was covering my captain and while he was engaged with a lancer a spearman came up to run him through, I struck the man and wounded him and saved my captain's life, he immediately made a push at me but I struck him again and just as the spear was entering my breast I cut his arm off. When I was galloping off a rifleman shot my poor horse in the head which killed him on the spot, he fell and me under him.

Hodgeson had to fight his way out, at one point behaving in a way that he later regretted, unusual amid the normal plethora of bellicose or phlegmatic contemporary accounts of the battle. The corporal, a clumsy swordsman, was confronted by an elderly French officer, whom he unhorsed by slashing at his mount's neck. Losing his helmet during the fall, the bald officer begged for mercy. But with a troop of lancers bearing down 'at full gallop', Hodgeson 'clove his head in two and escaped'. This was not something he was proud of, admitting in later years that 'the recollection of the old man ... pained him often'. Post-combat trauma was unrecognised in this age, but is not totally unfamiliar according to many eyewitness accounts. Even by the ghastly standards of the day Waterloo was universally regarded as being extremely violent.[19]

Life Guardsman Shaw, the prize-fighting toast of his regiment, was now fighting for his life. Shaw's exploits were later whitewashed for the benefit of Victorian audiences – he would be depicted as the staunchly brave working-class hero, precisely the ideal, steadfast warrior underpinning the leadership of the Duke of Wellington. Shaw was undoubtedly a vicious scrapper, whose edge that day had been dulled by the vast quantity of grog he had indulged before the charge. Corporal Webster, who fought alongside, saw him parry one cuirassier's thrust and cut him through his brass helmet to the chin, so that 'his face fell off him like an apple'. Lieutenant Waymouth recalled that 'Our famed Shaw was very conspicuous ... dealing deadly blows all around him'. But Sergeant Thomas Morris with the 1/73rd was unimpressed, believing that Shaw had had far too much to drink 'and running a-muck at the enemy, was cut down by them as a madman. I admire, as much as any man can do, individual acts of bravery,' Morris insisted, 'but Shaw certainly falls very far short of my definition of the term *hero*.' If he had been sober Shaw might have had the presence of mind to stick with his regiment, thereby adding to their effectiveness, rather than rushing, 'in such a way, on to certain death', which 'in my opinion was as much an act of suicide, as if he had plunged with his horse from the cliffs of Dover'. One witness claimed Shaw was taken down by a lone cuirassier who, standing clear of the mêlée, 'occupied himself by shooting our people with his carbine, taking very deliberate aim'. But Shaw was overpowered and 'almost cut to pieces, scarcely able to move' near the farm buildings at La Haye Sainte. Victor Hugo claims that a French drummer boy gave him the *coup de grâce*. In reality the champion of Hounslow Heath bled to death that night and was found the following morning on a dung heap. John Shaw, pugnacious victor of many a gang brawl, died as violently as he had lived.[20]

Corporal Louis Canler knew he was saved when he heard a shouted French command and crowds of French lancers and cuirassiers galloped by. He hid inside a tall wheat field nearby as the British were chased off by the French cavalry 'furiously sabering and lancing them in such a wild manner' that the English retreated, 'leaving a good number of their men on the battlefield'. He detoured out of their way to regain d'Erlon's corps, which was beginning to reorganise in the rear. Surrounded by the grisly detritus of battle, he noticed a dead English dragoon officer. 'A sabre cut had split his head open and the brains had burst out of the skull.' Macabre though this was, Canler had eyes only for the 'superb golden chain' attached to a splendid watch that hung from the fob around his neck. 'I applied the law of an eye for an eye,' he recalled. The British had taken his knapsack and weapons, so he helped himself to the watch.

Lieutenant Jacques Martin, with the 45th Line, managed to straggle back to the French lines in an apathetic haze. He had 'fought like a machine', all the time 'awaiting the fatal blow'. Being bowled over by a fast-moving dragoon was probably his saving. 'It was there that I saw death closest,' he recalled, while 'my best friends fell at my side'. He made his way back in a semi-concussed state.

I staggered between the cavalry who were remounting around our guns. I looked around me and saw nothing but enemies and without hope, kept walking. It was this unbelievable apathy which saved me, although I should have been lost a thousand times. Actually I survived the fire of our artillery, which was firing at me as well as them, because we were getting up together, how could I escape from them? Three or four times I saw those who were closest turn as if to chase me. I do not know what restrained them, if they thought me too weak, or probably the bullets and balls that flew around drew their attention.

Martin moved beyond the desperate sword fights raging around the Grande Batterie, grateful not to have jettisoned the haversack and greatcoat strapped to his back, which had absorbed many sabre cuts. He turned towards the formed French units to his left that were still fighting. 'Our lancers gave them such good work,' he observed with renewed relish, pursuing the British cavalry across the battlefield, 'where they rode over a great number of our wounded, and they retook many prisoners'.[21]

By 3 pm there was not a live French infantryman on the slopes of Mont St Jean. D'Erlon's corps attack was Napoleon's main point of effort and it had been repulsed with severe losses – anything up to 4,000 men. But, as Jacques Martin recalled, when he returned to the French line, 'the rest of the army corps were regrouped'. Canler was carrying a man across his back whose fibia had been shattered by a musket ball. He was confronted by his colonel, riding frantically back and forth 'like a madman' shouting out '*To me, 28th! To me!*' The anguish in his voice reflected 'the greatest despair', for the destruction of his regiment had been 'a blow to his own honour'. 'It took more than an hour to recover from the first check and to reform the attack columns,' recalled Captain Pierre Duthilt. He saw that the 28th and 105th Line Regiments from Bourgeois's 2nd Brigade, that had by-passed La Haye Sainte, 'were entirely torn to pieces'. Remnants could only be rallied with difficulty. Major Dupuy, with the

7th Hussars, had persuaded at least one forlorn retreating standard-bearer to stop. 'I do not wish to dishonour you, monsieur,' he said, thinking he ought to rescue the colours, but 'display your flag and move ahead calling "*Vive l'Empereur*" with me'. 'He did it immediately', he recalled, 'the brave man'. They turned around some 3,000 men.

The Grande Batterie was considerably shaken. Perhaps seven or eight 12-pounders had been taken out of the fight. Although the charge that briefly overran it had been repulsed, some crews had fled to the rear and were not about to come back. General Desalles, the I Corps artillery commander, acknowledged that 'this check was grave'.[22]

In reality only two and a half of the four attacking divisions had actually been thrown back from the ridge line and the corps would recover. The soldiers were veterans; there had been setbacks before, and they would participate in further attacks. But, by mid-afternoon, Napoleon was short of infantry. Comte Reille's II Corps was still hammering away in profligate piecemeal attacks on Hougoumont. Wellington lost two brigades of heavy cavalry, reduced to fewer than 50 per cent of their effective strengths, but they had swept the ridge clear of 11,000 French infantry. It would take another two hours before the depleted French corps could even begin to threaten the ridge line again.

Trooper Thomas Playford had the painful events of that day etched on his mind in perpetuity. He rejoined the remnants of the 2nd Life Guards and other survivors of Somerset's brigade to the rear. 'When our regiment was again formed,' he recalled, 'I looked round to see who was there, and I found that about three out of four were not present.' It had been a shocking day – 'our loss altogether was dreadful,' he reflected. Like many other Waterloo veterans he would stoically endure post-combat stress disorder, without anyone understanding the symptoms, for the rest of his life. 'I have a confused, disjointed recollection of many things,' he was later to write, 'yet no clear, comprehensive idea of them as a whole.'[23]

Napoleon was back to where he had started at 11.30 that morning. Both sides had fewer men, but the French, with the Prussians in sight, were now short of time.

CHAPTER 7

'En Avant!'
The Cavalry Charges

3 pm to 6 pm

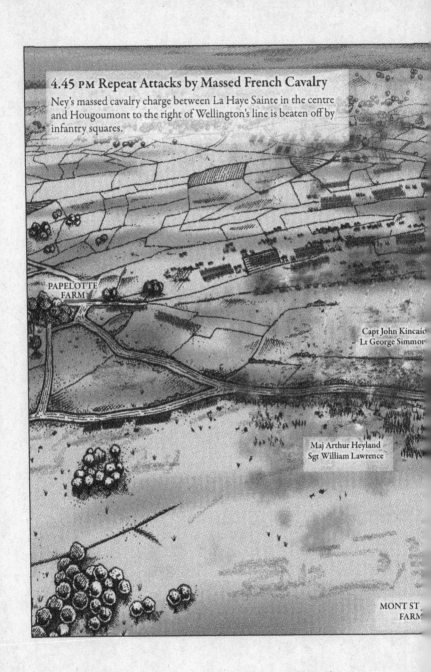

4.45 PM Repeat Attacks by Massed French Cavalry

Ney's massed cavalry charge between La Haye Sainte in the centre and Hougoumont to the right of Wellington's line is beaten off by infantry squares.

PAPELOTTE
FARM

Capt John Kincaid
Lt George Simmon

Maj Arthur Heyland
Sgt William Lawrence

MONT ST
FARM

PLANCENOIT
VILLAGE

S
E ⊕ W
N

Napoleon Bonaparte

LA BELLE
ALLIANCE

Capt Fortuné de Brack
Pte Melet

Sgt Maj de Lerréguy Civrieux
Pte Mathew Clay
Maj Moritz Büsgen

CHÂTEAU HOUGOUMONT

Lt Col James Macdonell
Guillaume van Cutsem

LA HAYE SAINTE
FARM

Pte Friedrich Lindau
Maj George Baring
Cpl Henry Müller

Sgt William Wheeler

Ensign Edward Wheatley

Sgt Thomas Morris
Pte George Rose

Capt John Hare
t William Fortescue
Lt Edward Drewe

Ensign Rees Gronow

Lt Heinrich von Gagern
Capt Friedrich Weiz
Capt von Scriba

Capt William Verner

Twin Breakwaters: Hougoumont and La Haye Sainte

The battle within a battle around Hougoumont continued unabated at the southwest corner of the Mont St Jean ridge line. Nobody had seen the decisive repulse of d'Erlon's corps to the right, which was out of sight. Half an hour earlier Foy's 9th Division was brought forward to back up Jérôme's already committed 6th Division. As there was little point reinforcing the chaotic fight for the building complex, Foy's division came up on the right through the fields until they reached the hedges and ditches of the great orchard. The French raised the stakes to nearly 13,000 men; the British responded by sending the 2nd Battalion of the 3rd Guards to bolster the garrison. Now 13,000 Frenchmen were pitted against less than 3,000 British. To Sergeant William Wheeler, with the 51st Regiment overlooking Hougoumont, 'so fierce was the combat that a spectator would imagine a mouse could not live near the spot'. The Guards were hanging on, but 'the slaughter was dreadful', he recalled.[1]

'The division of the King of Westphalia [Jérôme] had disappeared under the enemy's fire,' recalled Sergeant-Major Lerréguy de Civrieux, advancing on the right with the 93rd Line. 'Around this farm were heaps of thousands of dead, wounded and dying, which we soon doubled in number.' Captain Moritz Büsgen's 2nd Nassau Regiment saw this 'great rush against the buildings and gardens' as de Civrieux's men 'attempted to escalade the garden wall' and 'gain a footing behind the orchard hedge'. They were 'mown down,' de Civrieux recalled, 'by the English and Scottish fusillade from their formidable positions'. Büsgen's Nassauers claimed they were 'repulsed at all points'. The number of men falling shook de Civrieux. 'Soon we had our feet bathed in blood,' he remembered; 'in less than half an hour our ranks were reduced by more than half'. They were getting nowhere.

'I never saw such a "bull fincher" of a hedge,' recalled Ensign Standen, with the 3rd Guards. It was particularly thick and high, with a ditch on the other side. The assault was to be 'à la baïonette', remembered Lieutenant Puvis, with the 93rd; 'we tried to get through this hedge in vain' and 'suffered enormous casualties'. The carnage was such that the 93rd men resigned themselves to the increasing likelihood of death. 'Each stoically awaited death or horrible wounds,' de Civrieux recalled, being continually splattered with blood as musket balls thudded home with distinctive and unsettling thuds. 'My Captain, shot through by two balls and losing blood', urged them on with 'his failing voice, until he fell in the middle of this butchery'. Puvis was abruptly flung onto his backside from the impact of a ball striking the visor of his shako. 'I thought I had been wounded; but there was no blood,' he recalled, shaking his head before pressing on. They needed reinforcements. Marshal Ney rode up and ordered Puvis to bring up the 100th Regiment, waiting just behind, but the older officers urged him to reconsider. 'We could not take the position,' they insisted, 'it needs cannon.'[2]

French Sergeant Hippolyte de Mauduit would later question how it could be 'that it had not occurred to any of the senior officers to send for even two twelve-pounders, to break down the walls to open a passage for our soldiers'. Napoleon allegedly ordered them up, but staff confusion stymied the deployment. Lieutenant-Colonel Saltoun of the 1st Foot

Guards, however, recalled that when his men were pushed back into the hollow way at the back of the orchard, the French 'brought up a gun'. 'This gun I endeavoured to take, but failed.' Moritz Büsgen, fighting in the same orchard with the Nassauers, concurred:

> Between two and three o'clock, the enemy then moved up a battery to the right of the farm and started a heavy cannonade with his guns and howitzers on the buildings.

'Carcass' incendiary shells splashed fire amid the buildings, and soon 'they were all in flames'.[3]

The blazing buildings became apparent all over the battlefield. Sergeant Cotton with the 7th Hussars, saw 'from the right of the Allied line the appearance was awfully grand'. It quickly attracted Wellington's attention and he dispatched a message, hastily scrawled on a slip of ass's skin, which has survived to this day. Hougoumont, he repeated, was to be held at all costs. 'Still keep your men in those parts to which the fire does not reach,' Macdonell was urged, and 'take care that no men are lost by the falling-in of the roof or floors'. After the collapse the ruins had to be defended. He did not want the French to 'pass through the embers'; the Guards were to get in and fortify the hot rubble.[4]

The defence of the burning buildings took on a Dantesque quality. Private Johann Leonhard, with Büsgen's 2nd Nassauers, remembers that 'the fifth attack that the French launched against the Hougoumont farm was beyond description'. Trees around them 'were razed by the immense cannonade, as if mown down'. Private Mathew Clay of the 3rd Guards, firing out of one of the upper rooms of the blazing château, found their escape barred by Lieutenant Gough of the Coldstream Guards, who:

Would not permit anyone to quit his post, until our position became hopeless and too perilous to remain, fully expecting the floor to sink with us every moment, and in our escape several of us were more or less injured.

With the whole of the barn and cart house containing the wounded in flames, Ensign George Standen saw 'three or four officers' horses rushed out into the yard from the barn', panicked by the glare from the surrounding buildings, but within minutes they 'rushed back into the flames and were burned'. Johann Leonhard recalled that 'the skies seemed to have been changed into an ocean of fire; all of the farm's buildings were aflame'. Hideous screams were heard above the crackle of the flames, as the English and German wounded burned to death in the barn, rescue attempts beaten back by the heat.[5]

Corporal James Graham approached Colonel Macdonell and asked for permission to leave his firing post in the garden. Graham had impressed him when he helped close the gate, but the colonel could not understand why he insisted on leaving at such a critical moment. 'I would not,' the corporal argued, 'only my brother lies wounded in that building which has just caught fire.' Macdonell let him go because his brother Joseph was another that had closed the gate. They got him out and Graham returned to his post. Joseph was exceedingly lucky, because as Sergeant Wheeler later observed:

Many who had been wounded inside or near the building were roasted, some who endeavoured to crawl out from the fire lay dead with their legs burnt to a cinder.

Under the cover of artillery and raging fires, the French broke in again. Clay recalled that, 'the enemy's artillery having forced the upper gates, a party of them rushed in who were as quickly driven back'. Shortly after, round shot bounced the gates open, and 'the gates were again secured', Clay recalled, 'although much shattered'. 'Aided by the smoke and flames' French grenadiers 'forced their way into the upper courtyard through a small side door,' Major Büsgen remembered. Musket fire poured down from the windows of the building, and the attack was broken up and driven out by a detachment of British. 'Some intruders were taken prisoner, but seven of our grenadiers were also captured by the enemy during this skirmish,' Büsgen admitted.

The defenders were desperately short of ammunition. Captain Horace Seymour, ADC to Lord Uxbridge, ordered Private Joseph Brewer of the Royal Wagon Train to drive his tumbril load of ammunition to the farm to replenish them. This was a virtual suicide mission because the buildings were clearly under intense fire. 'I merely pointed out to him where he was wanted,' Seymour recalled, and 'he gallantly started his horses and drove straight down the hill to the farm gate'. The mission was touch and go, and coolly executed. 'He must have lost his horses,' Seymour remembered, 'as there was a severe fire kept on him', but the Guards got their ammunition.[6]

The flames gutted many of the buildings to the north, east and west of the chapel. Roofs collapsed, but the walls remained standing and kept the French infantry out. The blazing château was linked to the chapel by a door. Inside, wounded soldiers watched anxiously as the flames licked beneath it and burned the feet of a wooden crucifix hanging above the door. One leg was burned off and the other ankle was charred before the flames ceased to spread. They were convinced that divine intervention had spared them, because the chapel did not burn down. It survives to this day, still joined to the ruined château staircase.

The attacking French infantry were becoming exhausted and disorganised. Many of their officers had fallen. Wounded Frenchmen, sprawled around the killing area before the garden wall, piteously beseeched Lieutenant-Colonel Francis Home of the 3rd Foot Guards 'to order his men to fire upon them and put them out of their misery'. Attacks continued but tactics changed, by necessity, to maintain an annoying skirmishing fire on the defenders. It appeared impossible amid all the confusion and disorganisation to attempt a general escalade.

During the afternoon, Hougoumont's resident servant and gardener, Guillaume van Cutsem, who had been asked to remain behind by the farmer, decided to leave during a lull in the battle. He took his daughter with him and they made their way, virtually unnoticed, through suffocating smoke and flying embers. Van Cutsem led his little five-year-old girl by the hand, preceded through the back gate by a Guards sergeant into the hollow way. The young girl was to grow up with fond memories of kind British soldiers 'who treated her as a pet, and kept throwing her bits of biscuit out of their haversacks wherewith to amuse her'. The forlorn couple picked their way across the ridge line to find shelter in the Forest of Soignes. British and Nassau soldiers watched them go with mixed feelings. The small child was the last vestige of domestic normality many would ever see.[7]

Corporal Henry Müller, with the 1st Battalion of the King's German Legion, had the prism down on the pan of his loaded Baker rifle, with the cocking piece pulled back for safety. He was lying at the extreme end of the garden of La Haye Sainte, with skirmishers Sasse and Schüllermann next to him, spotting for targets. Müller did the shooting, the other two loaded. His bullets were carefully 'patched', with powder poured down the barrel and a ball wrapped in a circular piece of greased cloth forcefully rammed down the barrel. A mallet tap at the end of the ramrod was sometimes needed when powder residue built up. The Baker rifle with its threequarter-turned rifled barrel imparted greater velocity and thereby accuracy than the Brown Bess musket, but took three times longer to load. Tightly loaded, the weapon with its leaf sight could be deadly in the hands of a well-trained, competent marksman.

Müller had lined up on a French officer on foot, who was waving his sword for the column to advance. He pulled the cocking lever fully back. Earlier that day he had picked off a column commander from his horse and then inflicted considerable damage, dropping individual soldiers at ranges out to 300 yards. This new target held higher rank. The average combat range was 150 yards but Müller was firing well beyond that. Only the briefest flash fired the main charge as the rifle cracked. The officer dropped and pandemonium erupted within the French column.[8]

The Baker rifle could be loaded and fired as quickly as the Brown Bess when a smaller paper cartridge was used. Friedrich Lindau, firing through a loophole near the gateway under Captain Graeme, 'shot at the enemy where they were densest, then quickly stepped back to load and make room for the others'. Fighting here was so intense that attacking Frenchmen were sticking their own muskets through defending loopholes and firing. 'More of my comrades fell near me,' Lindau recalled, as well as men who 'came falling down from the stand above, from which our people were shooting over the wall'. The King's German Legion men kept the French at bay with fire. 'I could hardly wait until I fired another round,' Lindau recalled; loading as fast as he could, 'I shot over a hundred rounds that day.'

Special targets were engaged by the slower loading compacted patched bullet. Lindau had been watching an enemy officer 'constantly riding the battlefield in front of us and showing the way to the advancing columns'. He was a difficult target to register. 'I had him in my sights,' he recalled, with his rifle at full cock, but the target constantly moved out of the way. 'At last, just as he was leading up new troops, he came into my fire' and Lindau squeezed off a ball. Through the smoke he could see that 'his horse made a bound, reared up and fell with the rider beneath it'. He had his man, an officer, who would be worth money, so 'soon afterwards we made a sally'. Lindau grabbed at his gold watch chain, but the Frenchman was not quite dead and raised his sabre to ward him off, so Lindau reversed his rifle and cracked his skull with the brass butt plate. Off came a gold ring, and the officer's purse containing gold coins was cut away. After Lindau ran back to the farm, his comrades warned him 30 French cavalry were approaching. Lindau was well satisfied. Life on the battlefield could be nasty, brutish and short, as all veterans knew. Loot was the only compensation, for which they were prepared to risk all.

Across the road, Captain John Kincaid and his 1/95th riflemen returned and re-occupied their sandpit after d'Erlon's men had been ridden down by the British Heavy Brigades' counter-attack. Of the regiment's six companies, two were in the sandpit, one was 50 yards back in depth, and the remaining three were holding along the Ohain sunken road, the main Allied position. 'Some one asked me what had become of my horse's ear,' Kincaid remembered, which 'was the first intimation I had of his being wounded'. One ear was missing, 'I suppose by cannon shot', while a musket ball had furrowed his forehead, and another had passed between his legs, 'but he did not seem much the worse for either of them'.

There had been some bizarre moments during the ebb and flow of the action around the sandpit. 'I had not hitherto drawn my sword,' Kincaid recalled, until French cavalry appeared. Now he urgently needed it, but 'having been exposed to the last nights' rain, it had now got rusted in the scabbard, and refused to come forth'. It was not his finest moment. 'I was in a precious scrape,' he recalled. But now he and his men were back, firing at the road leading to La Haye Sainte, in support of the besieged King's German Legion garrison. Inside the farm, peering through his loophole, Friedrich Lindau appreciated the support. 'I was glad to see heaps of dead enemy lying more than a foot high near the *abatis* on the Brussels road,' he remembered.[9]

Napoleon faced a dilemma. Hougoumont showed no signs of being close to capture, d'Erlon had been decisively repulsed and the Prussians were coming. These twin break-waters were impeding and breaking up the cohesion of his advance. D'Erlon had very nearly forced the ridge line and La Haye Sainte was the key to his regaining the initiative. He instinctively appreciated what Wellington – fixated on Hougoumont, to his right – had missed. La Haye Sainte in the centre was the more important objective. Ney was ordered to take it.

Quiot's 1st Division troops, already repulsed once, were opposite the farm and familiar with the ground. During the pause in the battle, two companies of the 1st Battalion the King's German Legion were fed into the farm. Major Baring was down to about 550 men, even with these reinforcements; he had lost a quarter of his men. Colonel Charlet's 54th Line Regiment attacked with two close columns from both sides. Over the next few hours Ney committed a total of 7,000 men from 13 battalions, even though there was only room for about 2,000 to attack at any one time. Ney's ADC Levavasseur recalls the general being unimpressed at the lack of élan shown by the men repeatedly thrown back. 'Tell him to storm the position with a charge,' Ney ordered. An engineer captain 'had the charge beaten' by drum and ran forward with cries of 'En avant!' as the ADC tried to organise more men. Looking back he saw 'the engineers had already seized the gardens and hedges, and driven the enemy back' as more columns came up to apply more pressure. A barrier of bodies rapidly piled up outside the west barn door.

'We soon ran short of cartridges,' Friedrich Lindau recalled, 'so that as soon as one of our men fell we immediately went through his pockets.' Baring reassured his men that ammunition was on the way. Five appeals for re-supply had been dispatched, without response.

Lindau was struck on the back of the head by a musket ball. Rugged and resourceful as ever, 'I undid my scarf, wet it with rum and asked one of my comrades to pour rum into the wound' and tie it up. He pulled his shako over the head-scarf and refused to leave his position.[10]

Across the road the green 'grasshoppers', as the 1/95th riflemen were nicknamed, were being flailed by incoming fire. 'I have been shot through the cap, my jacket torn across the breast by a ball and a spent ball which hit my thigh and partially lamed me,' complained Lieutenant Orlando Felix to fellow subaltern George Simmons, concluding, 'I shall be killed today.' Simmons, who just two days before had breakfasted in the sun with the Duke of Wellington on the same stretch of road, replied 'Nonsense!' Ever the optimist, he declared, 'I have a charmed life and feeling myself in the full vigour of manhood, the devil a feather will they touch of me.' It was not to be the case. When a musket ball did strike Simmons, Felix recalled, he 'jumped as high as myself and fell near the hedge of La Haye Sainte'. The projectile entered his side, snapping two ribs and penetrated his liver before lodging in his chest. 'The shock I received brought my watch to a full stop at four o'clock,' Simmons remembered, 'the works were broken.' He was in serious trouble. 'I had great difficulty in breathing,' he admitted, 'the warm blood was still oozing from my side into my trousers, [and] the ends of the broken ribs gave me excruciating pain.'[11]

'Soon after I heard a cry at the door of the barn,' recalled Friedrich Lindau, who was inside La Haye Sainte; 'the enemy mean to get through here'. The French had set fire to the barn, producing 'thick smoke under the beam'. Loopholes were left thinly manned as large cooking kettles the red-coated Nassau reinforcements had brought in with them were used to pour water on the flames. As Lindau fired out 'a Frenchman seized my rifle to snatch it away'. 'Look, the dog has seized my rifle,' he yelled to his neighbour, who promptly shot the French soldier. When another man grabbed at his rifle again his right-hand neighbour 'stabbed him in the face'. Fighting was as pitiless as it was intense. 'A mass of bullets flew by me,' Lindau recalled, 'rattling on the stone of the wall.' One ball snatched away the worsted tuft on his uniform shoulder, while another 'shattered the cock on my rifle'. Ammunition was running out. Lindau picked up another rifle, but 'before I could shoot again I had to search the pockets of my fallen comrades for ammunition, but they were mostly empty by now'. The fire that had spat out from the farm buildings and kept the French at bay became progressively weaker.

George Baring well remembered the indomitable Lindau, 'bleeding from two wounds in the head and carrying in his pocket a considerable bag of gold which he had taken from an enemy officer'. The resistance his men were putting up inspired Major Baring. 'He would be a scoundrel that deserted you, so long as his head is on his shoulders,' Lindau reassured him, but Baring was increasingly anxious. 'What must have been my feelings,' he recalled, 'when, on counting the cartridges, I found that, on average, there were not more than from three to four each!' Glancing outside, he could see two French columns moving up. Then off to the right, a huge dark mass of cavalry passed by, seemingly covering the entire valley bottom.

'All this I could see,' Baring remembered, 'and confess freely that now and then I felt some apprehension'. It was more cavalry than his men had ever seen. 'I brought all the fire possible to bear upon them; many men and horses were over-thrown,' he recalled, 'but they were not discouraged.' The cavalry did not even turn about to acknowledge their pres-ence, but stolidly carried on 'with the greatest intrepidity'. Squadron after squadron cantered by, heading towards the Mont St Jean ridge. It was a particularly bleak moment.[12]

3 pm to 4.15 pm

Charge à la Sauvage

At about 3 pm the 1/27th Inniskillings and the rest of Lambert's 10th Brigade, Peninsula veterans, newly arrived from North America, were ordered forward. They had had plenty of time to reflect on their mortality. As Lieutenant Edward Drewe with the 1/27th remembered, the battle had begun to their right at Hougoumont, 'gradually extended to the left, apparently extremely hot in the centre on each side of the road leading towards La Haye Sainte'. The men, he observed, had been 'quite unconscious and apparently care-less of the part they were shortly to take'. Many were sleeping off the effects of the march and the rum they had plundered while clearing the Brussels road through the Forest of Soignes the night before. 'Some of them were wounded by a few straggling shot that passed from the enemy over or through our advanced lines,' he recalled, 'and a few killed.' Thus far, they were relatively unscathed by this battle.

Major Arthur Rowley Heyland, commanding the 40th Regiment in the brigade, was a sober and consummate professional. 'It appears to me of no consequence whether a man dies young or old,' he had just written to his wife, 'provided he be employed in fulfilling the duties of the situation he is placed in this world.' Heyland had written this to his wife, Mary, the day before. She was the same age as he, 34 years, and pregnant again. Arthur Heyland had six other children and loved them all. 'What dear children, my Mary, I leave you,' he wrote, because despite having 'no desponding ideas on entering the field', he was convinced and 'cannot help thinking it almost impossible I should escape either wounds or death'. He had witnessed battles as intense as this before in Portugal and the Spanish Peninsula. After being wounded at Talavera in 1809 he was back for the epic and costly sieges of Ciudad Rodrigo and Badajoz three years later, when his company had suffered over 400 casualties and he was wounded a second time. In 1813 he survived the bloody battle of Vittoria, but was seriously wounded again a month later in July. Heyland knew he was lucky to be alive, so much so, that on his return to Cork in 1814 he sought permission to retire. When Napoleon escaped Elba, he was however, recalled to command the 40th.

After so many close shaves, Heyland did not rate his survival chances highly. His letter to Mary was therefore composed with infinite care. He wanted two of his sons, John and Alfred, to join the infantry, while Kyffin 'might try the artillery service'. His wife was advised to invest 60 per cent of his income and not scruple to accept 'the usual government allowance for officer's children and widows' and take up residence in Wales. 'Let my children console you, my love, my Mary,' he wrote, assuring her 'that the happiest days of my life have been from your love and affection, and that I die loving only you'. Heyland had regularly confronted his mortality and was to do so again. Sentimental thoughts were banished from his mind as he focused in on the 40th Regiment following behind the 1/27th Inniskillings as they marched to the east side of the Brussels road, near La Haye Sainte.[13]

'At about quarter past three o'clock the welcome and anxiously sought for tidings to advance reached us,' recalled Private Alexander Dunlop's company commander, Captain Edward Drewe. 'Every man grasped his firelock and moved forward with a decided, firm and confident step.' They passed close to the Mont St Jean farm and began to 'ascend the gradual rising ground on the left of the Brussels road', where the three regiments formed column of companies. The Inniskillings immediately realised how much more vulnerable they were than their two sister regiments. Drewe observed that the others 'were in great measure covered by the rising ground in front [from the French], whilst the 27th was exposed from being on the highest ground to all that came'.

Captain John Hare, the senior captain, was commanding the 27th, because their commander was absent, his ship refitting after storm damage at sea. Hare anticipated promotion might well come from this battle, as did also Lieutenant William Fortescue, with one of the companies, who had five children and a Catholic wife to support. Lieutenant Charles Crowe, with the 3rd Battalion of the regiment, had commented that 'it was really disgusting to hear the levity of remarks' about the possible loss of the battalion headquarters at sea; 'and the great promotion resulting, made with unblushing front by some individuals'. Everyone needed, in any case, to outlive their brother officers in order to benefit. They had not the slightest comprehension of what was to follow.[14]

On the other side of the ridge, Marshal Ney had come forward at about the same time to observe the Allied line. He saw movement, which he interpreted as rearward. Wellington was adjusting his central deployment, in the vicinity of La Haye Sainte. The battle had reached a tipping point; no outcome was visible either at Hougoumont or La Haye Sainte. D'Erlon's infantry attack had been decisively repelled, but a punishing reverse inflicted on the British heavy cavalry brigades that had done so. It was not clear what should happen next. Ney thought the Allies were likely retreating in the centre and took Napoleon's decision for him. Whatever else Napoleon might have decided on, it would have been an attack. There could be no going back because they were fully committed; either the Prussians attacked or they finished Wellington first.

Ney was convinced that Napoleon's assembled cavalry, massed just to his rear, could be decisive. If a brigade of cuirassiers could anchor itself on the plateau just over the ridge line, panic might transform a retreat into a rout. Like Lambert's brigade moving towards them, the French cavalry were champing at the bit, considering their role and inevitably their survival chances. Many of them were seasoned veterans of Marengo, Austerlitz, Eylau and Friedland. They had been at their zenith between 1805 and 1807: the shock troops of Napoleon's Empire. In their heyday, when the enemy was closely engaged by French infantry and unable to form squares, they were irresistible. Having broken a British square at Quatre-Bras 48 hours before, they could do it again. Their cool courage was legendary. Colonel Leipic had shouted to the mounted grenadiers of the Guard at Eylau: 'Heads up, by God! Those are bullets – not turds!' French casualties had been high, but the cavalry had turned the battle.

The cavalry exuded an arrogant confidence. Unique to the Guard cavalry were the *grosse bottes* or 'big boots' of the *grenadiers à cheval*. On the one hand admiringly referred to as 'the gods' or 'Invincibles', on the other, when Napoleon was reluctant to expose his favourites to combat, they might be called the 'brats' or 'pets'. Napoleon's unwillingness to commit them had sometimes cost the opportunity for a decisive victory, for example at Borodino in Russia in 1812.

The quality of the mounts on this day was nothing like the massive chargers employed during their heyday. Losing 200,000 trained horses three years before in Russia had virtually annihilated Napoleon's cavalry and taken away much of its veteran core. The Emperor's interregnum at Elba resulted in 110 line cavalry regiments being reduced to 56, while the dragoons lost 9 regiments, the chasseurs 16 and the cuirassiers two. A cursory glance through the ranks at Waterloo would reveal cloth caps instead of bearskin shakos, and there were severe shortages of weapons, armour and trained horses.

Swaggering cuirassier officers could, nevertheless, be relied upon to carry the day. One regiment boasted its own unique initiation system. Potential new officers were given three bottles of champagne, three willing wenches and three horses. They were given three hours to drink, whore and ride the horses 20 miles. Endurance was tested alongside judgement, as it was up to them to decide in which order.

The Grande Batterie had already redoubled fire against the left centre of Wellington's line. Some English battalions in the first Allied line retired a hundred paces to shelter behind the plateau crest, further raising Ney's hopes and the urgency to commit the cavalry. At 3 pm Ney urgently galloped up to summon his cavalry. There was still everything to play for in this battle. Napoleon could still reasonably expect to win.

Sitting erect on his horse 'Bijou' in the ranks was an old sergeant in the cavalry. He had originally captured Bijou from the Mamelukes at the Battle of the Pyramids in 1798 and since then the pair had been inseparable. The horse had saved the sergeant's life on 20 occasions and brought him out of Russia. 'Bijou only lacked speech,' the sergeant explained, and 'had all the intelligence and loyalty of a poodle dog'. They stood alongside other veteran campaigners, such as Private Melet with the Dragoons of the Imperial Guard and his horse 'Cadet'. Such combinations encapsulated Ney's hopes. Melet and Cadet had fought together since 1806, from Prussia to Poland, to Spain and Austria, back again to Spain then across the frozen wastes of Russia to Saxony until the dreadful days of the final campaign in France the year before. In 1812 Melet had raided Russian lines at night, to provide Cadet with forage, at a time when the death of one's horse was widely regarded as a blessing. It would have ended his obligation as a cavalry soldier and the horse could have been eaten into the bargain. Melet and Cadet had seen 12 major battles and 30 lesser ones. Small wonder Ney was hopeful. They formed part of a tightly knit group dedicated to the service of the Emperor, and the Emperor needed them once again.[15]

On the Mont St Jean ridge the precocious Second Lieutenant Heinrich Gagern, with the 1st Nassau Light Infantry Regiment, was experiencing a series of 'firsts' in his limited military career: he'd had his first night in the open in the unforgiving weather the night before and his first ever day's foot march. He had missed Quatre-Bras, so today was to be his first grim indoctrination into battle. 'Most of the balls flew over our heads,' he remembered of earlier that day; now 'things were heating up'. Round shot killed the man standing directly in front. 'I received such a blow on my arm that I was tossed aside for several files.' The French had realigned their artillery and had become wilier in their selection of targets. They homed in on the left of Wellington's line, where more troops were visible. 'Never,' claimed General Alten, commanding the 3rd British Division, 'had the oldest soldiers heard such a cannonade.' The bombardment presaged the most intense period of artillery fire throughout the battle.

'The screaming and the groans of the wounded were so pitiful on this day that I can not even put it on paper!' wrote Private Ernst Christian Schacht, in Vincke's 5th Hanoverian Brigade. The young Landwehr soldier estimated 'more than 80 large balls flew quite low over our heads', until eventually the lower trajectories ploughed in amongst them. Deeply shocked, he admitted nearly two months later, 'I am still shaking, my pen is too weak to describe this pitiable misery.' More groups of wounded, convoys of prisoners, empty caissons and crowds of fugitives streamed towards the Forest of Soignes. It looked almost like a retreat.

Von Gagern experienced one close shave after another. With his arm numbed by the near miss from round shot, 'a stupid ball from a canister shot hit the upper yellow fitting of my sword scabbard and ripped the sword belt apart'. He threw it away, 'but that was not all of it yet':

Before long, there comes a shell which has the impertinence to explode at the very corner where I am standing; it kills three soldiers and slashes at my foot, which still gives me trouble, tears apart my trousers and moreover shatters my sword that I stick in the ground next to me.

He was angry and frightened, the shell 'had hellishly burned me, and at first I could not step down on this foot'. In shock, he examined himself with some trepidation and 'saw that everything was still in its right place, the skin as well as the flesh'. With his trousers in tatters he picked up a musket from a dead soldier and returned to the ranks, which had moved forward 40 paces to get out of the fire.[16]

Ney, the Prince of the Moskva, was convinced immense results would come from this cavalry charge, if delivered now, but he was hindered by frustrations at every turn. Lieutenant-General Baron Jacques Delort, one of Milhaud's experienced division commanders, refused to attack without orders from his corps commander. Delort recalled that Ney 'was bubbling over with impatience', insisting that not only his division attack, but both divisions in Milhaud's corps. 'I pointed out that heavy cavalry should not attack infantry which was posted on heights, had not been shaken and was well placed to defend itself.' Ney was unhappy at this, having been forward personally and *seen* the enemy retire. '*En avant!*' he roared. 'The salvation of France is at stake!' 'I obeyed, reluctantly,' Delort remembered.

The reasoning behind the charge and its initiation is steeped in controversy. The cavalry were keyed up to go, in fact all the psychological hallmarks of cavalry regiments about to charge were there: excitement, expectation, pumping adrenalin and an inflated arrogance that they should not be seen as hanging back. 'A man did not think himself … a Hussar if he did not model himself on Lasalle,' the famous cavalry general Marbot claimed, 'and become like him, a reckless, drinking, swearing rowdy.' These men were the progeny of the French cavalry legend. 'Any Hussar not dead at thirty' was 'a scoundrel or malingerer', Lasalle had proclaimed, and by 34 he had perished at the head of his cavalry at Wagram.

Elan and esprit de corps prized action over contemplation. Little encouragement was needed to charge. As Milhaud's corps set off, the light cavalry division of the Imperial Guard almost immediately followed. 'No one knows by what rush of blood to the head it was followed by all the reserves,' remembered Ney's ADC, Colonel Heymès. 'Not even forgetting those of the Guard', who, as Heymès commented, 'everybody knows only followed the orders of its own officers, or the orders of the Emperor'. Milhaud allegedly asked its commander Lefebvre-Desnoëttes: 'I am going to charge, support me.' Assuming Milhaud was giving him the Emperor's order, the Guard duly complied.[17]

The reverse he had seen inflicted on the British heavy cavalry had excited Captain Fortuné de Brack, with the 2nd Chevau-Légers lancers, who shouted 'The English are lost!' from the ranks. 'There – look,' he said, indicating British cannon on the ridge, 'they have uncoupled their guns.' The guns were actually coming into action. 'I was ignorant of the fact that the English batteries usually fought uncoupled' from their horses,' he later admitted. His shouts drew the attention of a number of officers, 'who pushed forward to join our group'. De Brack later asserted that a subsequent general move forward to restore the alignment in the line made everyone think that the order to charge had been given. Although unproven, this is as credible an explanation as others for the ensuing sequence of events:

The right hand file of our regimental line followed them; the movement was copied in the squadrons to the left to restore the alignment, and then by the chasseurs à cheval of the Guard. This movement, of only a few paces at the right, became more pronounced [as it was copied] to the left.

De Brack offered his explanation in 1835, twenty years after the event. It would be odd to attract the opprobrium of its seemingly illogical launch by admitting he was partly responsible. What is credible is the depiction of adrenalin-fuelled pent-up expectation, the precursor to any cavalry attack. Whatever the reason, an attack of some description would no doubt have been forthcoming. In the event no fewer than 43 squadrons of heavy cavalry, comprising some 5,000 men and horses, began to canter across to the west side of the Charleroi–Brussels road. All that Napoleon could say, helplessly watching at this moment, was 'This is a premature movement which may well lead to fatal results.'[18]

Every Allied veteran at Waterloo took the awesome sight of the massed French cavalry attacks with him to the grave. 'Not a man present who survived could have forgotten in after life the awful grandeur of that charge,' recalled Ensign Rees Gronow of the 1st Foot Guards:

> You perceived at a distance what appeared to be an overwhelming, long moving line, which ever advancing, glittered like a storming wave of the sea when it catches the sunlight.

Alexander Mercer, with the Royal Horse Artillery, described the same inexorable wave, 'reminding me of an enormous surf bursting over the prostrate hull of a stranded vessel, and then running, hissing and foaming up the beach'. The hollow between the armies 'became in a twinkling covered with horsemen'. There were sudden upturned faces all along the Allied line. This made no sense and was unexpected. 'The spectacle was imposing, and if ever the word sublime was appropriately applied, it might surely be to it,' thought Mercer. 'On came the mounted host until they got near enough,' recalled Gronow, 'whilst the very earth seemed to vibrate beneath their thundering tramp.' Soldiers quickly formed square. Ensign Edmund Wheatley, to the right of the charge, heard shouts of 'Stand firm! Stand fast!' all around:

> *No words can convey the sensation we felt on seeing these heavy-*
> *armed bodies advancing at full gallop against us, flourishing*
> *their sabres in the air, striking their armour with the handles,*
> *the sun gleaming on the steel.*[19]

French squadron officers rode forward, generally five per squadron. Unlike British cavalry officers, they exercised control from the front. Each squadron was about 120 men strong, advancing at the 'Walk-Trot' and two ranks deep, with sabres drawn. They had to cover 1,000 yards. Speed was kept well under the gallop for maximum effect. This preserved a solid and aligned formation, kept the horses relatively fresh until impact and allowed men to use their arms more precisely. The canter or fast trot was the optimum. Here, however, there were problems with space. The Allied breakwaters at La Haye Sainte and Hougoumont constricted the 5,000 horse to a 700-yard front, punishing the advance on the flanks as they flowed past. The norm for the line was two files deep with an interval of at least 100 yards before the next. If the first two lines did not achieve the penetration, adding more men in echelon was not going to help. Each horseman occupied a space just under a yard wide, and the largest squadrons were over 100 yards across. So tight was the line, with the pressure of fire from the flanks, that horses and riders in the centre might be bodily borne aloft by their neighbours.

From the front the attack looked more like a column of horses than a charging line. Second Lieutenant Richard Eyre, with the 2/95th Rifles, thought he was being assaulted by 'about thirty thousand' not 5,000 cavalry. Napoleon had often used mass in the past, far beyond the requirements of military efficiency, to achieve a psychological impact. Over 60 per cent of the attacking force was armoured cavalry. To Cockney Sergeant Thomas Morris, with the 73rd Regiment, 'Their appearance was of such a formidable nature, that I thought we could not have the slightest chance with them.'[20]

Wellington had unlimbered 65 guns forward on the ridge to oppose them, compared to the 75 French cannon that were 'shooting in' the attack. He accepted risks in order to inflict maximum damage on any French advance traversing the valley bottom. If cavalry reached them, the gunners would have to run back to the safety of the squares, carrying port fires, rams and spikes. Spread over 1,500 yards of ridge line, there was one artillery piece for every 20 yards. 'Fire!' yelled Mercer at his horse artillery battery, double loaded with shot and canister:

> *The effect was terrible. Nearly the whole leading rank fell at once; and the round shot penetrating the column carried confusion throughout its extent ... The discharge of every gun was followed by a fall of men and horses like that of grass before the mower's scythe.*

En Fourrageurs, or extended open order, the conventional tactic used to reduce target frontages to grapeshot, was not possible with the constricted space. 'I have seen four or five men and horses piled upon each other like cards,' remembered Royal Artillery Captain Samuel Rudyard, blazing away with 9-pounders, 'the men not having even been displaced from the saddle, the effect of canister.'

'They moved in profound silence,' recalled an awed Alexander Mercer, 'their pace was a slow but steady trot.' Silence was imposed in the ranks to better hear the shouted words of command above battle noises. Equally impressive were the answering shouts, bellowed in unison, to confirm the receipt of an order. Such control could be intimidating. 'None of your furious galloping charges was this,' Mercer remembered, 'but a deliberate advance, at a deliberate pace, as of men resolved to carry their point.' The mass approach came in slightly obliquely, the first echelons on the right manoeuvring to approach the level section of the Ohain road, while the left had to skirt Hougoumont. Soon they were splashing through the swampy, rain-drenched valley bottom. Horses occasionally sank knee-deep, impeded by the tall rye that swept their chests. The rye was flattened by an unstoppable bow wave, with no flexibility to change direction in the centre. The pace perceptibly slowed as the tidal wave surmounted the steep slopes of the Mont St Jean ridge, still reasonably passable at this stage. Obstacles, inclines and boggy ground soaked up much of the momentum.

At about 150 yards the buglers sounded the gallop, but the pace could barely pick up much beyond a canter. Artillery fire was causing havoc, especially flanking fire coming from northeast of Hougoumont, which bowled over squadron lines in enfilade. Even as they approached the gun line the French were astonished to be blasted yet again with double-shot from the totally exposed British and King's German Legion guns. 'Now I thought those gunners would be cut to pieces,' recalled one French cavalryman; 'but no, the devils kept firing with grape, which mowed them down like grass.' Still the cavalry came on, and exhilaration surged through the ranks as they burst through the gun line. It was a heady moment. The Peninsula cavalry veterans had never captured and retained a single gun of Wellington's cannon in Spain. Now they swept past some 65, with 6,000 pounds of armoured cavalryman and horse.[21]

Still 'boot to boot', the *charge à la sauvage* or the 'wild charge' was sounded by bugle. Troopers stood up in their stirrups en masse to give their horses free rein. Those in front held sabres outstretched, pointing at the enemy.

'*Avancez!*' ('Forward!') they shouted in acknowledgement of the command, amid cries of '*Vive l'Empereur!*' Officers fell back in line as the NCOs spurred forward from the rear ranks, to position themselves for the impact. Up ahead they anticipated a target-rich cavalry environment, in which Wellington's retreating army would be dealt the *coup de grâce*; but as they breasted the ridge and entered the reverse slope plateau, they were confronted by something totally unexpected: a chequer-board configuration of infantry squares.

On the rise to the right of the Belle Alliance inn, the Emperor and his staff had been transfixed by the magnificent charge. They saw the cannon abandoned and masses of horsemen galloping out of sight over the plateau. It seemed as though the enemy's line had been breached. Napoleon had been vexed and surprised that his cavalry had been pitted probably against unbroken infantry. 'It is too soon by an hour,' he suspected – 'but it is necessary to follow up what has already been done,' he said to Soult. Once launched, a cavalry charge can never be recalled.[22]

4 pm to 4.30 pm

Chequer-Board Battle

Ensign Rees Gronow heard the clear command above the thunder of hooves: '*Prepare to receive cavalry.*' Every man in the front rank knelt and dug the butt of his musket into the ground to present a phalanx of bayonets. 'One might suppose that nothing could have resisted the shock of this terrible moving mass,' he recalled. 'They were the famous cuirassiers, almost all old soldiers, who had distinguished themselves on most battlefields of Europe.' They were virtually upon them.

'In an almost incredibly short period they were within twenty yards of us, shouting "*Vive l'Empereur!*"'

Soldiers who the night before had nervously discussed the prospect of facing cavalry again, after witnessing squares shattered at Quatre-Bras, were confronted with their worse fears. Sergeant Thomas Morris and his friends had little faith in the leadership of 60-year-old Captain Robertson, whose dithering 48 hours before had very nearly got them all killed. Neither were they reassured now. 'Our poor old captain was horribly frightened,' Morris recalled, 'and several times came to me for a drop of something to keep his spirits up.' The other primary topic of conversation had been 'rid Jarmins' and the like. How would the casually disdained, under-trained foreign contingents perform now? They manned about two thirds of the squares facing the French.[23]

Apart from the near success of d'Erlon's infantry attack repelled two hours ago, this was only the second point at which the French might have carried the battle. After sweeping through Wellington's guns, the French cavalry were taken aback at the chequer-board of some 22 to 25 infantry squares that lay before them. Wellington was clearly not in retreat. There was a sinking feeling that this was not going to go well. With no way of changing direction and no space on the level plateau beyond the crest, they were up against a phalanx of menacing infantry squares bristling bayonets. The first line of squares was directly ahead. If the seemingly irresistible line cantering boot to boot had kamikazed a few squares head-on, they might have won. Cuirassiers were large men, averaging 309 pounds, mounted on powerful Flemish and Norman horses. Crashing 2,000-pound projectiles into squares would have broken any battalion. Napoleon would certainly have favoured this; he was no cavalryman and regarded horses as expendable. 'Take no heed of the complaints of the cavalry,' he once argued, 'for if such great objects may be obtained as the destruction of a whole hostile army, the state can afford to lose a few hundred horses from exhaustion.'

It was a well-known and scientifically proven fact that it is not in the nature of horses to ride roughshod over human beings, particularly if they are shouting and stabbing from behind a phalanx of bayonets. The only recourse was to get so close that if the horse went down, the momentum of the fall might collapse a small part of the square. Dying horses, thrashing around, made it impossible for infantry to remain in line, which was why horses were immediately and ruthlessly dispatched with shot and bayonet when it occurred. Both man and horse baulked short of these squares. One British witness described the impossibility of directing a horse 'against the terrible face of the infantry square, more resembling a living volcano than any phalanx of human intervention'. The impetus of the charge could not be maintained. 'The animal becomes bewildered with terror, and wheeling round, in spite of rein and spur, rushes from the unequal conflict.' Both man and horse instinctively recoil from death.

Major Létang, with the 7th French Dragoons, later admitted they were defeated by seemingly invincible and coolly delivered volley fire. 'The steadfastness of the English infantry was made more remarkable still by the absence of the volley that we awaited and that to our great surprise we did not receive.' This insidious flinching effect slowed the momentum of the advance as the troopers realised the British were simply waiting for them to get nearer. 'This disconcerted our troops' as the range closed, Létang confessed, as they realised 'they would be exposed to a fire that would be much more murderous from being at point-blank range'. Self-preservation took over. These were veterans, aware their heavy cavalry successes at Wagram, Eylau and Austerlitz had been achieved against enemies too hotly pressed by French infantry to form square. 'Fright seized them,' Létang recalled, 'and probably to escape such a fire, the first squadron wheeled to the right and caused a similar movement by all the following squadrons.' With the break-up of squadron lines evading squares, echelons following on simply rode around the chequer-board alignment of infantry squares in depth. There were many ghosts riding with the veterans, but few Lasalles, willing to dash themselves against an intact square.[24]

The value of the deployment was akin to a game of draughts. French cavalry could be taken by fire from any of two directions, as they rode deeper into the Allied line. Two sides of every square they avoided could bring fire to bear, mutually supported beyond by yet more squares. Ensign Edward Macready, with the 30th Foot, recalled:

> Not a shot was fired until they were within 30 yards, when the word was given and our boys peppered away at them. The effect was magical. Through the smoke we could see helmets falling – cavaliers starting from their seats with convulsive springs as they received our balls, horses plunging and rearing in agonies of fright and pain.

The French had arrived in line, thinking they were in pursuit. What should they do now? They were also not prepared to deal with captured artillery. Overrunning all the English batteries proved an illusory success. 'We rode through the batteries,' recalled Captain Fortuné de Brack, 'which we were unable to drag back with us.' Neither were mallets and spikes available to put them out of action. When time was of the essence the gunners were sabred and support troops spared to haul the guns out. Otherwise the guns were overturned and rams broken. No ropes had been prepared to drag them away; the objective had been to pursue and harry. 'For several minutes some few cuirassiers were in possession of several of our guns,' observed Uxbridge, the British cavalry commander. Foiled by fire from the squares, 'desperate men' trying to haul them off 'remained there to be picked off'. Uxbridge felt the French cavalry lacked 'that vigour and speed which would have given them some chance of penetrating' the squares. 'No heavy mass having a well formed front actually came collectively against our bayonets.'[25]

Wellington had astutely set out his draughts pieces on the board with five squares of British infantry, two King's German Legion and four Brunswick and two Hanoverian squares soaking up the shock of the first contact with French cavalry. The second line in depth were nine German-speaking Hanoverian, Brunswick and Nassau squares and one King's German Legion square. His non-British contingents took on the flotsam of the initial failed charge. Ninety per cent of the squares occupied the compacted triangular area of the three roads leading to Ohain, Brussels and Nivelle. This meant there was one square for every 100 yards of front. Mixing the nationalities was to prove crucial in maintaining overall resolve. The fragmentation of the first charge, in hindsight, may have been decisive. How long would the foreign units have been able to soak up a degree of punishment never previously endured?

Company commander Captain Friedrich Weiz, in square with the 1st Nassau Regiment, was anxious about his survival prospects. He thought his commanding officer Major von Weyhers was 'energetic and brave' but lacking the barest competency.

To this day, this officer must be blamed for never for a single moment having commanded and exercised the battalion entrusted to him, from the day it was mobilised until this day of battle.

Their sister battalions around them, 'moving all the time by their commanders through ployments and deployments', avoided the worst of the artillery fire. Not only did they demonstrate proficiency, the 'procedure had the advantage that the men paid less attention to any danger' because they were kept busy. The 1st Nassau by contrast was left 'to face the death dealing gunfire for hours on end'. The battalion had barely escaped a spectacular explosion from a blazing artillery caisson that had passed near their front. Fortunately 'some dragoons rode up in a hurry and, while racing along, stabbed and brought down the horses'. When it exploded, the Verden Battalion to their left lost a number of men. Weiz's CO had done nothing.

It was therefore with considerable trepidation that they viewed the onset of masses of French cavalry. 'At first, only their helmets could be seen,' recalled Weiz, 'an instant later their cuirasses, and, finally, did the men and their horses come into full view.' A storm was about to be unleashed against their front. Orders were given not to fire too soon; 'our young soldiers,' Weiz recalled, 'were still unfamiliar with using their weapons effectively'. Officers moved in front of their companies to prevent any premature firing. Weiz realised with some relief that the three echelons of cuirassiers bearing down on them were going to first attack the English 73rd Regiment to their right.

Thomas Morris of the 73rd observed the approach. 'Their appearance, as an enemy, was certainly enough to inspire a feeling of dread – none of them under six feet; defended by steel helmets and breastplates, made pigeon breasted to throw off the balls.' They were allowed to approach within ten or twelve paces. The unreliable Captain Robertson did not have to direct the first volley; that was the prerogative of the commanding officer of the 73rd, the square commander:

> *Our rear ranks poured into them a well directed fire, which put them into confusion, and they retired; the two front ranks kneeling then discharged their pieces at them. Some of the cuirassiers fell wounded and several were killed.*

Those unhorsed immediately shed their armour and ponderously made off through the mud.

Weiz and his men witnessed the 'exemplary behaviour' of the 73rd's first volley, 'fired at a distance of 60 to 80 paces'. 'The effect was spectacular, many riders and horses fell, and the remainder of the squadrons scattered like chaff.' They were reloaded in time for the incoming second echelon, which was also successfully seen off. Weiz could see that his young and inexperienced soldiers had been impressed. 'These examples happening in our immediate vicinity were of the highest significance for our young soldiers.' When the third French echelon reached their battalion and that of the Hanoverian Bremen Field Battalion to their left, they were 'most forcefully repulsed'. The cockney Morris did not see it that way, predictably claiming 'they were unfortunately broken into and retired in confusion'. The British soldier could be unkind in any assessment of a foreigner. Weiz on the contrary, felt his men were gaining confidence, inspired by the resilience of the British example. There were, however, 'precarious' situations when aggressive cuirassier squadrons surging between squares struck out at the soldiers on the periphery. Morris might have witnessed such a pass. Weiz claimed that occasionally 'they could not fire their muskets because of our own troops before them', and when that happened, 'they had to face the attack with only their raised bayonets'.[26]

Captain von Scriba was with the Bremen Battalion to the left of Weiz. His commander waved a pistol and threatened to shoot anyone who opened fire without his order. Together with the Verden Battalion in square, they waited until the cuirassiers were 40 to 50 paces away before blasting off a volley. 'They were sent off with a loud Hurrah!' von Scriba recalled, everyone 'gladdened by the calm, laudable conduct of our men'. They were benefiting from the deployment in depth of their squares, which broke up the impetus of the first charges and funnelled the fragmented French squadron lines into a gauntlet of murderous close-range musket fire, as they rode ever deeper into the Allied line. Von Scriba saw winded French horses 'halted at 70 to 80 paces away as if to catch their breath'. The French cavalrymen 'were brave but too slow'. 'The temptation to shoot was great,' he remembered, 'but the entire square stood motionless with cocked weapons' – waiting, as did the other squares nearby, in order to conserve ammunition. No French cavalry would close, knowing the square was loaded with weapons cocked. They were too wily. Von Scriba had already seen a French brigadier who 'lay flat on his horse when the right flank was ordered to take aim' and got away. He remained uneasy; they seemed to be hitting too few men at close range. 'Our men were aiming too high,' he suspected, and he gave the order to aim at the horses.[27]

French cavalry had to cover 1,000 yards under artillery fire to reach the batteries, then endure a gauntlet of volley fire from several directions amid a patchwork quilt of infantry squares up to 600 yards in depth. It was beyond human endeavour. Those surviving this ordeal were then faced by the 8,000 Allied cavalry Uxbridge had deployed in reserve to counter-attack. Within an hour Napoleon decided to commit another 5,000 men, so that shortly after 5 pm 9,000 French cavalry had been committed. The French were attacking 22,000 men with 9,000, with no hint of surprise to equalise the force ratio. There was insufficient room for more than 18 cuirassiers to attempt to force one side of an infantry square, which was 34 bayonets wide and four deep. Each square outnumbered its attackers on average by four to one, and as General Guyot, commanding the 2nd Cavalry Division, pointed out, 'We only had sabres to oppose the fire of the squares and to the volleys of case shot that we received as we approached.' Allied cavalry snapped at the heels of squadrons disordered by fire. Guyot was unhorsed and caught on foot. 'I had not gone ten paces backwards when I was knocked down and ridden over by cavalry that sabered me as it passed by'. He got away only when his own cavalry counter-attacked. When he climbed back into the saddle of a procured horse, 'I received a ball in the chest and a shell splinter in the left elbow.' He was out of the battle.[28]

William Verner, attacking with a 7th Hussars foray from behind Wellington's line, waved his sword enthusiastically toward a party of cuirassiers. 'Come along,' he shouted to his men, 'now is the time to cut them off.' The Allied cavalry had been positioned to pick off over-extended French cavalry attacks. Chasing them down a road to their rear, he jabbed at one of them in the neck, eliciting a loud *'Sacre!'*, but his sword ricocheted off the man's armoured collar and his arm was left completely numbed. Momentarily stunned, Verner suddenly realised that in the confusion of battle only one officer, Captain O'Grady, had followed him. 'Whether the men had not heard me or whether they did not understand what I said, I cannot say.' He was out on a limb and completely outnumbered until suddenly he found that he had chased the cuirassiers directly into a British infantry ambush:

> I heard a fire on both sides and in one moment the whole party were sprawling on the road and amongst the trees placed to intercept any troops that may have come down the road.

Soldiers of the 1/51st had ensnared them, and among them was Sergeant William Wheeler. 'There were nearly one hundred of them, all cuirassiers,' he recalled with some relish; 'down they rode at full gallop.' The opening volley cut down the fleeing French cavalry careering down the road, creating total carnage – 'the work was done in an instant'.

> Those who were shot dead were fortunate, for the wounded horses in their struggles by plunging and kicking soon finished what we had began.

So desperate were the cuirassiers to escape, Verner recalled, that two troopers whose horses were shot, fell or jumped down from the high road and 'kept running on'. To stop them, 'the soldiers placed their muskets close to their bodies and fired'. Even this only momentarily checked their flight and 'they received several shots before they fell'.

The 51st men were soon amongst them searching for loot. 'We could not find one that would be like to recover,' remembered Wheeler, and doubtless some were helped on their way. Verner found one unwounded officer, whom he promised to protect. 'I had scarcely done so when a private of the Brunswick Oels in green uniform and buff belts came up and began to rifle his pockets.' When Verner remonstrated, raising his sword, the Brunswick soldier levelled his musket at him. Loot was loot, but he hesitated to fire when he spotted O'Grady.[29]

This ambush was part of the gauntlet the survivors of the first charge had to run, having penetrated the depth of the Allied line, in order to get back. 'The charges of our fine cavalry were certainly the most admirable thing I have ever seen', recalled Colonel Trefçon, chief of staff of the 5th Division. It was emotionally as much an iconic event for the French as for the Allies. 'I had tears in my eyes,' Trefçon admitted, 'and I cried out my admiration to them!'

Courage was not enough. Captain Lemonnier-Delafosse in Foy's division remembered how one particular squadron from the 1st Cuirassiers, caught up in the chequer-board of volleying squares, 'was obliged to move through the centre of the British army as far as its right!' Ensign Rees Gronow recalled the impact of their volleys as the cuirassiers galloped by. 'I can only compare it to the noise of a violent hail storm beating upon panes of glass.' It was an epic death-ride. Delafosse tracked their dramatic progress from afar: 'One suddenly saw smoke rise like that from a haystack or pile of straw,' he observed, as volley fire marked their latest position. The result of one such broadside volley from a square was 15 to 18 cuirassiers, men and horses slashed down, 'covered in blood, black with mud, just a shapeless mass'. The death-ride continued, shedding cuirassiers knocked from their horses as the squadron mass was steadily whittled down by further volleys jetting out from infantry squares within the chequer-board framework in depth. The survivors had to charge, led back by a sous-lieutenant 'through most of the [Allied] army'.

When they got back they reported, standing next to their horses 'covered in sweat', Delafosse recalled. 'The smoke we had noticed was nothing other than the water vapour rising from their bodies.' The chef d'escadron had not survived. He must have felt they had gone in far too deep to consider going back now. They had to attack to retreat, which they did, shouting '*Conquer or die!*' Eighty cuirassiers with three officers and their fanatical commander were left lying behind on the battlefield, and only 30 to 40 men got back. 'But what a charge!' said Delafosse.[30]

CHAPTER 8

Death of a Regiment

4.30 pm to 7.30 pm

6.30 PM The Fall of La Haye Sainte and a Teetering Allied Centre

Ney attacks and captures La Haye Sainte, threatening to pierce the Allied line.

Baron Jean Pel
Gen Duhesm

Maj Gen Carl von Müffling
Franz Lieber

PAPELOTTE
FARM

Capt John Hare
Lt William Fortescu
Lt Edward Drewe

Maj Arthur Heyland
Sgt William Lawrence

Capt William Vern
Lt George Simmo
Edward Heeley
Capt Carl Jacobi

MONT ST
FARM

PLANCENOIT VILLAGE

Cpl Louis Canler

Sgt Hippolyte de Mauduit

LA BELLE ALLIANCE

Napoleon Bonaparte
Jean-Baptiste Decoster

CHÂTEAU HOUGOUMONT

LA HAYE SAINTE FARM

Tpr François Faveau

Pte Friedrich Lindau
Maj George Baring
Lt George Graeme

Sgt William Wheeler

Ensign Edward Wheatley
Baron Christian Von Ompteda

Ensign William Leeke
Capt Alexander Mercer

Sgt Thomas Morris
Pte George Rose

Capt Friedrich Weiz
Maj Von Weyhers
Capt Von Scriba

'A Mere Pounder After All.' The Ridge

The 1/27th Inniskilling Regiment formed a square 50 feet wide and 200 feet deep with 700 men. Major-General Sir John Lambert, the 10th Brigade commander, had placed them on a pronounced mound, with the 1/4th and 1/40th Regiments behind and to their left. The Inniskillings held a vital part of the centre of Wellington's line, covering the northeast corner of the crossroads on the Brussels road, the axis of the French attack. Captain Edward Drewe, commanding the 9th Company, had already noticed the other two regiments were in dead ground to the ridge crest, whereas the 27th were out on a limb. They formed up just prior to the massed French cavalry attacks.

Captain Sempronious Stretton, with the 40th Regiment about 250 yards away, was occasionally able to see the 1/27th square through the smoke. 'The field immediately around the 40th was thickly scattered with horses and men of the French cavalry who repeatedly charged our squares,' he remembered. They galloped between the three squares 'without making any impression' and 'suffered severely from the fire of each'. 'We were told not to fire at the men, who wore armour, but at their horses,' recalled Sergeant William Lawrence in the 40th square. 'We opened a deadly fire on them,' he claimed, 'and very few escaped.' Frenchmen trying to haul away abandoned artillery pieces were shot down. 'It was almost funny to see these Guards in their chimney armour trying to run away after their horses had been shot from under them,' Lawrence remembered.

Junior officers and men standing in these squares had no idea 'of knowing anything beyond their own division or brigade,' remembered Lieutenant Browne, with 4th Regiment. 'The smoke, the bustle, which I fear is almost inseparable to regiments when close to the enemy' meant they had no idea of the big picture. 'Particularly,' Browne emphasised, 'the intention which is required from the company officers to their men, intercepts all possibility of their giving any correct account of the battles in which they may be engaged.' The fight to their front, only fleetingly visible, had their entire focus. Battle was fought simply left and right of what could be seen.[1]

The Inniskilling fight in square was becoming a very personal one. Private Alexander Dunlop in Drewe's company would have seen men falling rapidly. Examination of the regimental rosters reveals two men named John Collins were wounded with the 1st Company. One survived, the other lingered on until 2nd August before dying of his wounds. Two brothers, Privates Neil and Thomas McHugh, were wounded, whereas two other likely siblings, Arthur and George McCormick, were to emerge unscathed. Lieutenant William Grattan, who served with the Connaught Rangers, vividly recalled the advice his commanding officer gave a square threatened by charging cavalry:

Mind the square; you know how I often told you that if ever you had to form it from line, in face of an enemy, you'd be in a damned ugly way, and have plenty of noise about you; mind the tellings off; and don't give the false touch to your right or left hand man; for by God, if you are once broken, you'll be running here and there like a parcel of frightened pullets!

Captain John Hare, standing in the centre by the colours, decided when the square should open fire. Soon men like Lieutenant William Fortescue began directing company volleys. Edward Drewe was soon wounded, whereas Alexander Dunlop in the same company remained on his feet, cringing at every shocking artillery impact on the square.

Proficiency at loading and firing the India pattern Brown Bess musket was vital; anything less than two to three shots per minute was considered poor. Precision from men firing from lines four deep is questionable. One man is priming, another comes up to the present, a third is trying to aim, while a fourth is ramming down his cartridge. The weapon was only effective at short range. The year before, Colonel George Hunger had assessed that a musket ball 'will strike a figure of a man at 80 yards', anyone hit at 150 yards 'must be very unfortunate indeed', and a man attempting to aim at 200 yards 'may as well fire at the moon'. Hitting a galloping cavalryman, unless he was approaching head on, would be an equally difficult enterprise. Volley fire provided a solution of sorts through its scatter-gun effect. All this, however, had to be conducted amid smoke, appalling noise and in a virtual storm of incoming musket, grape or cannon shot. Small wonder that immature young recruits might sometimes fumble the complex reloading cycle. Terribly mutilated men began to fall and be assisted by comrades into the centre of the square, near the colours. Noise, smoke and fleeting targets crossing undulating ground encouraged men to simply shoot outwards, quantity compensating for accuracy or direction. The very act of standing in line, packed together, sharing the rhythmic group activity of loading and firing, while enduring suffering, bonded the Inniskillings together. Each man occupied roughly two feet of space, with elbows touching either side.[2]

The 27th were in line of sight to four French batteries, totalling a mix of 32 guns and howitzers, varying from 12-pound heavy cannon to 6-inch howitzers. From half past three until six thirty they were intermittently attacked by cavalry, and when not so, raked by artillery. Their isolated mound position required them to stand vulnerably in square against cavalry for virtually the entire time.

Ensign William Leeke, with the 52nd Regiment, described what it was like to see slow moving cannon-balls pitch into their squares.

It is much more easy to see a round-shot passing away from you over your head, than to catch sight of one coming through the air towards you, though this also occurs occasionally.

Drawn up tightly in four ranks in square like the Inniskillings, Leeke 'caught sight of the ball, which appeared to be in direct line for me'. This posed a dilemma in the crowded ranks. 'Shall I move? No! I gathered myself up, and stood firm.' The catastrophic consequences seemed to play out before him in slow motion:

I do not exactly know the rapidity with which cannon balls fly, but I think that two seconds elapsed from the time that I saw this shot leave the gun until it struck the front face of the square. It did not strike the four men in rear of whom I was standing, but the poor fellows on their right. It was fired at some eleva- tion, and struck the front man about the knees, and coming to the ground under the feet of the rear man of the four, whom it most severely wounded, it rose and, passing within an inch or two of the colour pole [where he was standing], went over the rear face of the square without doing further injury.

Two men in the first and second rank fell outward, horribly mangled, and two others fell inside the square. One of the rear men screamed out in agony, but one of the officers reproached him in a kindly fashion: '*Oh man, don't make a noise*' – and 'he instantly recollected himself,' Leeke recalled, 'and was quiet'.[3]

Lieutenant James Mill, with the 40th just behind the Inniskillings, could only occasionally make them out through the storm of shot and shell. 'A very tremendous cannonade was commenced by the French on our lines, and uninterruptedly continued,' he remembered. The 40th lay down in square to offset the worse destructive effects. 'Half the Inniskillings were mowed down in a similar position, without having the power to return a shot.' Sergeant Lawrence remembered 'the men were very tired and did begin to despair, but the officers cheered them on'. The British squares remained unbending. 'Keep your ground!' the officers shouted. 'It's a mystery to me how it was accomplished,' Lawrence recalled, 'for there were scarcely enough of us left to form a square.'

The French were becoming equally disconsolate. Colonel Ordner, commanding the 1st Cuirassiers, remembered with some frustration, 'We were almost masters of the plateau, but the English, although three quarters destroyed, were rooted to the spot; it was necessary to kill every last one of them.'

Wellington, anticipating manoeuvre, had expected Napoleon to be far more creative than this. Turning to Colonel Andrew Barnard, one of his Peninsula officers, he drawled, 'Damn the fellow, he is a mere pounder after all.'[4]

So far as the French cavalry were concerned, with 9,000 men flung at over 22 infantry squares for two hours between four and six o'clock, it had indeed deteriorated into a pounding match. Napoleon prided himself on his superior willpower, and he was convinced that, as with the successful storming of the Russian redoubt at Borodino in 1812, his will would prevail. But he was fast running out of time. His later memoir gives the impression that he was focused more on the Prussian approach to his right flank than the conduct of the mass cavalry attacks. 'Various infantry and cavalry charges took place,' he wrote, glossing over this two-hour period; 'the detailed narration belongs rather to the history of each regiment than to the general history of the battle.' Little explanation is offered. 'These accounts if multiplied would only bring confusion,' he insisted. Napoleon still thought the battle was going his way. 'Confusion reigned in the English Army,' he claimed and after committing Kellerman's Cavalry Corps after five o'clock, 'the enemy for the second time that day, thought the battle lost', and was contemplating retreat. Napoleon was optimistic he could block the arrival of von Bülow's Prussian Corps. Grouchy behind him in pursuit would likely persevere because '40,000 or 45,000 Prussians beaten and disheartened, could not impose their will on 28,000 [Grouchy's] Frenchmen, well placed and victorious'.[5]

Jean-Baptiste Decoster, the Flemish peasant pressed into service as Napoleon's guide early that morning, observed Napoleon's behaviour during the battle, remarking:

He issued his orders with great vehemence, and even impatience: he took snuff incessantly, but in a hurried manner, and apparently from habit and without being conscious he was doing so: he talked a great deal and very rapidly – his manner of speaking was abrupt, quick and hurried; he was extremely nervous and agitated at times, though his anticipations of victory were most confident.

Decoster sat on a large charger attached to the saddlebow of an escorting cuirassier by a long strap. He was closely watched, as he appeared anxious to escape. He was also ducking and wriggling in the saddle at the fall of each shot, as Napoleon himself noticed. 'My friend, do not be so restless,' advised the Emperor. 'A musket shot may kill you just as well from behind as from the front, and will make a worse wound.'

Decoster was unimpressed, and apparently useless as a source of information. Another guide, Joseph Bourgeois, was picked up, but stuttering with fear kept his eyes obstinately fixed to the ground. Napoleon sent him away. 'If his face had been the face of a clock,' Bourgeois later claimed, 'nobody would have dared to look at it to tell the time.' Napoleon was extremely frustrated, Decoster recalled, by the obstinacy and gallantry of stubborn British resistance. 'These English certainly fight well,' he commented to Soult, his chief of staff, 'but they must soon give way.' Decoster overheard Soult respond that they probably would not, whereupon Napoleon peremptorily demanded, 'And why?' 'Because,' Soult drily replied, 'I believe they will be first cut to pieces.' All Decoster wanted to do was live and go home, but for the moment his life hung on the strap that was attached to his unsympathetic cuirassier captor.[6]

Napoleon's pounding of the ridge line was an exercise of willpower. 'In war there are sometimes mistakes that can only be repaired by persevering in the same line,' he confided to General Flahault, one of his senior ADCs. Napoleon was an unpredictable and unconventional commander. Conventional military wisdom acknowledged it was pointless to try and reduce determined infantry squares with cavalry alone. Napoleon was short of the infantry that would otherwise have obliged the Allies to deploy vulnerably in line. D'Erlon's infantry corps was mauled, Reille's II Corps dissipated by the battle of attrition around Hougoumont, and Lobau's smaller VI Corps committed to block the Prussian approach on the right flank. Incessant cavalry attacks kept the Allied squares formed and vulnerable to artillery, such as in the case of the 1/27th Inniskillings. Napoleon was an artilleryman, and more Allied soldiers would die this day from the effects of artillery than from any other arm. Napoleon aimed to crack Allied resistance with artillery and then his reserves. When this happened, if successful, the Prussians would hesitate to grapple with his right flank. He was a gambler. Forty-eight hours earlier he had been at the pinnacle of success, having worsted the same opponents at Ligny and Quatre-Bras. Prussian performance had been unpredictable, while many of Wellington's foreign contingents were unlikely to share British resolve. The British would fight to the death, but her allies might be another matter. There was much, therefore, to be gained from a brutal pounding.

Soldiers were completely unsighted regarding grand decisions. With confusion all around, the Allied soldiers simply continued with the last given task, which was to defend. They were as aware of this as the French, who appreciated they had to attack, a more complex mission requiring more instructions. Command and control was exceedingly difficult, and there was scant opportunity to manoeuvre, so at regimental and battalion level on both sides, the incessant pounding went on.

Confusion was the primary characteristic that governed this nightmarish conflict, fought in atmospheric conditions worthy of Dante's *Inferno*. The hot afternoon, following on from the wet and cold conditions of the night before, raised the moisture content in the air. This combined with enormous quantities of gunpowder smoke and fires produced a 'greenhouse' smog effect that hung in the air over eight square miles of battlefield. 'We breathed a new atmosphere,' recalled Captain Alexander Mercer, when his battery ascended the reverse slope of the main position. The temperature palpably rose. 'The air was suffocatingly hot, resembling that issuing from an oven.' The nightmare of the battlefield was assuming a tangible reality, fought in an environment that pre-dated twentieth-century industrial smog. Mercer and his gun teams were enveloped by thick smoke, and all around they 'could distinctly hear a mysterious humming noise, like that which one hears of a summer's evening proceeding from myriads of black beetles'. 'My God, Mercer,' called out Surgeon Hitchins, who had briefly joined them, 'what *is* this noise?' 'How curious!' he exclaimed, when 'a cannon shot rushed hissing past'. He had never been in battle before. 'There! – *there!* What is it all?' After over six hours of pounding, it was beyond most soldiers' comprehension.[7]

Mercer's gun teams lashing their horses rode up into this garish scene. 'From time to time' Mercer saw 'still more dense columns of smoke rising straight into the air like a great pillar, then spreading out into a mushroom cloud'. The bizarre here was a nightmarish norm. One of his gun crew, Butterworth, lost his footing in the mud after sponging the gun, pitched forward and caught the blast when it went off. Throwing out his arms to steady himself, he lost them – blown off at the elbows. 'He raised himself a little on his two stumps and looked up most piteously in my face,' Mercer remembered. Butterworth was sent staggering to the rear to seek medical assistance. The next the crews saw of him was 'his body lying by the roadside near the farm of Mont St Jean – bled to death!'

Mercer was puzzled to observe a horse, unharnessed from one of the guns and chased away by the crew. This was the normal procedure if they were wounded, but this one 'stood and moved with firmness, going from one carriage to the other, where I noticed he was always eagerly driven away'.

His first indication of something wrong was a gasp of horror to his rear, which indicated the horse, so often chased away, was back at the gun line again. 'A sickening sensation came over me,' he admitted, 'mixed with a deep feeling of pity.' The poor horse was pressing his panting body against the leaders of the ammunition wagon horse team just behind, 'as though eager to identify himself as their society'. The driver, 'a kind hearted lad', was trying to drive the horse away, horror written 'on every feature', but could not bring himself to strike the animal. Mercer saw why: 'a cannon ball had completely carried away the lower part of the animal's head, immediately below the eyes,' and his clear eye seemed to be imploring them not to chase him away. Price, the farrier, was ordered to put the beast out of his misery and he ran a sabre through its heart. 'Even he,' Mercer recalled, 'evinced feeling on this occasion.'[8]

Between four and six o'clock Ney led six to eight general French cavalry attacks. This meant individual infantry squares received 23 or more squadron level charges. Napoleon's III Cavalry Corps Commander Kellerman described their predicament between Hougoumont and La Haye Sainte as 'awful'. They were 'unable to retire in order not to drag along the army with it, nor able to charge, because it had no quarry', and the squares remained intact. They were therefore condemned to 'receiving death without being able to fight back' as well as being exposed to their own cannon fire. Counter cavalry sweeps constantly fell upon them, when their own horses were blown by the incessant attacks. 'We were driven back brutally by the Hanoverians,' recalled Major Baron de Laussat in the 2nd Dragoons. 'I had the honour to be hit there by a musket ball, which pierced the leather part of my helmet, and received a sabre slash that would have sliced deeply into me if it had not struck the visor of my helmet.' He had to hand his horse over to his colonel and move back on foot.

One private soldier, in square with the 71st Regiment, recalls how the whole square applauded just such a fight, conducted by the 13th Dragoons. The description was like a prize-fight, 'we cheering the 13th and feeling every blow they received'. 'When a Frenchman fell, we shouted; and when one of the 13th, we groaned.' Sergeant Thomas Morris of the 73rd watched a similar contest, with a Guards cavalryman fighting off two cuirassiers. One was dropped 'by a deadly thrust to the throat', while the other took part in a thrilling five-minute bout that ended with the cuirassier's helmet flying off for some distance 'with the head inside it'. As a finale, 'the horse galloped away with the headless rider still sitting erect in the saddle, the blood sprouting out of his arteries like so many fountains'.

After the first hour the French cavalry realised their super-human efforts were destined to result in a bloody stalemate. Kellerman raged at having to simply maintain a cavalry presence on the ridge, 'condemned to watch defenceless men and horses fall around them'. Captain Fortuné de Brack, with the 2nd Chevau-Légers lancers, saw involuntary truces induced by 'the complete exhaustion of the troops'. 'Half of our squadrons dismounted in half-musket range,' he recalled. Ensign Rees Gronow, with the 1st Foot Guards, observed the horses of the first rank of cuirassiers opposite his square 'come to a stand-still, shaking and covered with foam, about 20 yards distance'. Despite the considerable efforts of their riders, they would not charge. The French could see the Allies were equally exhausted. Major Rigau, with the 2nd Dragoons, could see the soldiers in square were 'so tired from holding the position of *appretez armes* that all the time you could hear officers warning men who had sunk to the ground, to get up'.[9]

Ney found the 1,000 man strong Brigade of Carabiniers still uncommitted, and according to Kellerman 'rushed over to it, indignant at its inaction'. Kellerman felt they should be retained as a reserve, but Ney flung them against eight British squares placed in echelon on the Hougoumont side of the ridge. 'The carabiniers had to obey,' he recalled, and 'either through impotence, or clumsiness their charge had no success'. When it advanced it was engulfed by fire from numerous batteries ensconced on the slope near to Hougoumont. A 23-year old trooper named François Antoine Faveau was struck by a cannon-ball on the right side of his breast. In civilian life he had been a butter dealer. Any aspirations for glory were punctured along with his armoured breastplate, torn like paper as the solid shot passed straight through him, punching a similar size hole in the rear plate as it exited. Snatched from his horse, Faveau has long disappeared into the anonymity of a mass grave, but for the regimental number printed on the padding inside his armour, opened up like a food can. It can still be seen today at the Museé de l'Armée in Paris. Kellerman recalled 'three butcher's cheers' from the squares amid 'the thunder of their fire', and 'within seconds the Carabiniers had vanished, in death or flight'. Most of the brigade were strewn about the field.

'Five times we repeated the charge,' recalled lancer Captain de Brack, 'but since the conditions remained unchanged, we returned to our position at the rear five times.' The going was becoming progressively worse. The ground was a quagmire. They had to ride over palisades of dead men and horses to get at the squares. 'Our men began to lose heart,' he admitted. 'It has been said that the Dragoons and Mounted Grenadiers to our left broke several squares; personally I did not see it.' Occasionally lances clattered against bayonets, but 'in vain', said de Brack. 'At 150 paces from the enemy infantry, we were exposed to the most murderous fire' as well as howling solid shot and shrapnel shells cracking open as murderous smoke puffs overhead. Each time they moved back to the rear 'at ordinary pace and formed up again', they began to dolefully appreciate they would never break the impasse.

Bijoux the horse carried his old cavalry sergeant back to the French lines. His master's left thigh was torn apart by a shell fragment. The sergeant's 'best friend' carried him with difficulty back to the Imperial Guard. Sergeant de Mauduit watched them approach. The horse had been riddled with case shot, 'parts of his entrails hanging out announced the gravity of his wound'. Bijoux had saved his master for the last time. The long partnership of Private Melet and his horse Cadet, with the Imperial Guard Dragoons, was also at an end. They had campaigned together since 1806 and now formed an anonymous part of the grisly debris covering the slopes of Mont St Jean. Melet, severely wounded, was barely clinging on to life.[10]

'At four o'clock,' remembered Ensign Gronow of the 1st Foot Guards, 'our square was a perfect hospital, being full of dead, dying and mutilated soldiers':

> Inside we were nearly suffocated by the smoke and smell from burnt cartridges. It was impossible to move a yard without treading upon a wounded comrade, or upon the bodies of the dead; and the loud groans of the wounded and dying was most appalling.

Most of the carnage was from artillery shot. Private John Lewis of the 2/95th recalled that 'my first rank man was wounded by part of a shell through his foot, and he dropt'. The next man he was due to cover was taken down by a musket shot that 'came sideways and took his nose clean off'.

As the third man filled the file, 'the man that stood next to me on my left had his left arm shot off by a nine-pounder shot, just above his elbow, and he turned round and caught hold of me with his right hand'. His dance with death carried on as another cuirassier attack came in and this time 'the man on my right hand was shot through the body, and the blood run out of his belly and back like a pig stuck in the throat'. As he dropped 'I spoke to him; he just said, "Lewis, I'm done!" and died.' Lewis confronted a new terror with each passing minute. A bullet struck his rifle as he rammed down the next ball, 'not two inches above my left hand'. This left him unarmed, at which point his company sergeant was spliced cleanly in two by round shot, just three files away. Lewis jettisoned his shattered rifle for his sergeant's, which was still intact.[11]

Sergeant Morris, with the 73rd Regiment, recalled the irony of his friend Sergeant Burton, who 'had a trifling defect in his speech', calling out each time the cuirassiers charged, 'Tom, Tom, here comes the calvary.' Calvary was an apt description for what followed. The square was subjected to the devilish attention of French horse artillery, brought up to fire at them from virtually point-blank range. 'Complete lanes' were pulverised through their square as the cavalry stood cold-bloodedly by, to await their advantage. 'We saw the match applied, and again and again it came thick as hail upon us.' The black Private George Rose, with the 1st Company nearby, who had been born into slavery at Spanish Town, Jamaica, had his promotion prospects lessened when a musket ball struck his right arm. Captain Alexander Robertson, Morris's 'poor old Captain', frightened and inept to the last, 'was cut in two by a cannon shot'. Morris was as much enveloped by a storm of steel as Lewis in his square nearby. 'On looking round, I saw my left hand man falling backwards, the blood gushing from his left eye', while the man on his right 'by the same discharge, got a ball through his right thigh'. He was to linger on for a few days. 'Men were falling by dozens every fire,' he remembered, when to their horror a large shell fell fizzing just in front of the square. 'We were wondering how many of us it would destroy,' he recalled, 'when it burst.' Seventeen men were swept away by the blast, and a small piece of rough cast iron 'about the size of a horse-bean' stuck in his left cheek, which immediately began gushing blood.

It was not all bad. During one of those odd incidents that characterise intense battle, a commissary wagon trundled down the slope to the 3rd Division squares. On board was Assistant Commissary Alexander Dallas, fulfilling a promise he had made to a wounded General Alten in the rear. 'Mr Dallas, my brave fellows are famished for thirst and support, where are the spirits you promised to send them?' the general had asked. In the back of the wagon was a barrel of rum, and Dallas and his storekeeper had run a gauntlet of fire to get it forward. 'At the time I came to Mont St Jean cannon shot were constantly passing over the road,' he remembered, 'and some falling short, tore up the road itself.' His storekeeper was hit by a stray shot but they gained access to the back of one of the squares. Dallas informed an officer he was delivering spirits 'by special order from the General'. He need do no more, 'the barrel was rolled into the centre amidst a shout from the men, who opened ranks to admit it', and soon began passing liquor around. Morale perceptibly increased, even as a sergeant laid the wounded storekeeper on the cart and led him off to the rear.

Sergeant William Wheeler of the 51st remembered the 'grape and shells were dupping about like hail'. Graphic images of spectacular violence were to be imprinted on these men's minds in perpetuity. Wheeler saw a shell burst amidst the assembled 15th Hussars nearby and was mesmerised when he saw 'a sword and scabbard fly out from the column'. Another shell struck the breast of a man a few files to his right and 'he was knocked to atoms'. Each man going down was a further psychological blow to survivors, who cringed at the prospect of their own imminent demise, and every loss was known to dozens of comrades. 'Tom', an unknown veteran private standing in square with the 71st Regiment, had often listened to premonitions of impending death during the Peninsula campaign. He felt he ought to reassure 'a young lad who had joined but a short time before' that everything would not be all bad. 'I grew dull myself, but gave him all the heart I could.' The young lad had his legs swept away by shot; 'they were cut very close,' he remembered. The injured man entreated Tom:

Remember your charge: my mother wept sore when my brother died in her arms. Do not tell her all how I died. If she saw me thus, it would break her heart.

His lips quivered as he breathed 'God bless my parents!' and there in front of Tom 'he ceased to breathe'.[12]

One of the youngest regiments standing in square was the un-blooded 14th Regiment, formed just two years before. No fewer than 14 of its officers and 300 of its rank and file were under 18 years old. So young were these lads, straight from the plough, that they were nicknamed 'the Peasants'. It had taken an impassioned plea from Major Frank Tidy, their commander, to get them on the battlefield at all, away from line of communication duties. Lord Hill, their corps commander, viewed their deployment as virtual infanticide, but Wellington, who reviewed the regiment, considered them 'a very pretty little battalion' and released them for active service.

Among them was Ensign George Keppel, barely 16 years old, 'a boy in every sense of the word', his commanding officer recalled. Four months earlier he had been thrashed by a master at Westminster School. When the square was ordered to lie flat to avoid shot, Keppel, unable to find a vacant spot amid the battalion 'packed together like herrings in a barrel', seated himself on a drum in the centre. The colonel's charger started to reassuringly nuzzle his epaulette, while he patted its cheek.

Suddenly my drum capsized and I was thrown prostrate, with the feeling of a blow on the right cheek. I put my hand to my head thinking half my face was shot away, but the skin was not even abraded. A piece of shell had struck the horse on the nose exactly between my hand and my head and killed him instantly.

He was not the only one covered in gore. The regimental colour was borne in the centre by a young dandy named Charles Fraser, who was often accused of being effeminate because of his stylish dress and appearance. A young bugler from the 51st nearby had scurried into the square for safety and was congratulating himself, saying, 'I am all right now', when his head burst apart on contact with a cannon ball. Fraser was liberally splattered across his face with blood and brains. He raised a dark laugh from the ranks and impressed many by drawling, 'How extremely disgusting!' before quietly remarking, 'I should like to wash my face and hands after this!'[13]

The squares soon became confident that it would not be cavalry that would break them. The 71st had scarcely formed, before cuirassiers were upon them. Changing formation from column to square took a battalion about 30 seconds on average to achieve. 'Many of our men were out of place,' recalled Tom, the veteran private, 'there was a good deal of jostling for a minute or two, and a good deal of laughing.' Their quartermaster lost his bonnet riding into square, and after it was hastily retrieved, wore it back to front for the rest of the day. Familiarity with the failure of the cavalry to penetrate engendered some contempt. An old soldier with the 1/30th nearby, on seeing another attack on its way, growled, 'Here come those damned fools again.'

The impact of artillery, however, was an entirely different proposition. Many veterans were even to comment later that cavalry attacks were welcome, because they provided some relief from the pulverising impacts of artillery. At about six o'clock, recalled Ensign Edward Macready, two French guns unlimbered only 70 paces from their square and 'by their first discharge of grape, blew seven men into the centre'. Such cold-blooded execution could be traumatic. 'It was noble to see our fellows fill up the gaps after every discharge,' Macready claimed, but distressing. Three of his own men were ordered up and had hardly taken station 'when two of them fell horribly lacerated'. One of them to his horror 'uttered a sort of reproachful groan' after Macready had guiltily looked at his face, 'and I involuntarily exclaimed, "By God, I couldn't help it!"'

'Not a single square could they break,' claimed Sergeant William Wheeler with the 1/51st, but nearby some of the foreign squares were teetering.[14]

4.30 pm to 7.30 pm

'Night or the Prussians Must Come.' Plancenoit

Wellington was glancing habitually at his timepiece. The hands were crawling round its face inordinately slowly, and by four o'clock he was willing it on. He had been anticipating the arrival of the Prussians at every hour, since the battle had been under way. Von Bülow's corps, at 31,000 men, was the largest in the Prussian army, and thus far uncommitted. It had marched for three days in suffocating heat and drenched in cold rain, with units covering an average of 50 to 60 miles over the past two days, so it was hardly fresh. Nine hours had been needed to get to Chapelle St Lambert, three to four miles away. Wellington was out by about six hours in his calculation of Blücher's arrival. Napoleon had first spotted the Prussians at Chapelle St Robert, not Chapelle St Lambert, which was what he thought he was looking at, and this meant he was three hours out with his calculation. The Prussians were much closer than he envisaged; they were already across the Lasne defile. Wellington had been heard to mutter in exasperation, 'Night or the Prussians must come.'

Von Bülow, leading the vanguard of the Prussian army, encountered immense difficulties. Water-logged and rutted sunken lanes and treacherous slopes seriously impeded progress. His corps needed to arrive in the formation he intended to fight. Somehow infantry, cavalry and artillery had to be sorted out in the front, with sufficient resupply wagons behind. The resolve to overcome these physical problems was fuelled by their intense desire to close with the hated French and avenge the depredations inflicted by years of occupation. Nobody sought vengeance more avidly than Blücher and his chief of staff, Gneisenau, who would glorify in a ruthless and cruel retribution. Franz Lieber, marching with the Colburg Regiment, hurrahed the 'old one' as he cantered past. 'Be quiet, my lads,' Blücher answered, 'hold your tongues; time enough after victory is gained.' It was a remarkable comeback for an army which Napoleon was certain he had shattered. Hate and blood lust had kept them together. 'We shall conquer because we must conquer,' Blücher shouted to the Colburg Regiment.[15]

Back at Le Caillou, Napoleon's base headquarters, about 1.8 miles from the battlefield, his valet Louis Marchand was uneasy at the reported presence of the approaching Prussians. One of the servants had told him, 'Things are going badly, masses can be seen in the distance.' At first their arrival had been accompanied by exclamations of joy, until the dark tentacles crawling across the distant slopes were identified as Prussian and not Grouchy's. Mameluke Ali, Napoleon's personal servant, had been back on an errand. On the way he noticed that cannon-balls were skipping across the road for the first time; on the way back 'they were falling faster'.

Corporal Louis Canler, with the 28th Line, had returned to the rear, after the failure of d'Erlon's attack, to find that his regiment had been broken up. He was put on the Brussels–Charleroi road to the south with three lancers to check that nobody capable of bearing arms was slipping away amid the flow of wounded. 'In less than an hour we had stopped more than 400 fugitives,' he recalled. Major Jean Duuring, commanding the 1st Chasseurs further along the same road, was securing Napoleon's baggage at Le Caillou. He saw that soldiers coming in from the east 'were scattering, without their arms', and he set up another checkpoint to halt the rearward flow. Artillery gun caissons came rattling back, drivers claiming they had run out of ammunition, but not all were empty when checked. Duuring felt it might be prudent to harness the Emperor's gold to the horses in case it was necessary to move quickly. Louis Marchand inside the headquarters remained anxious, as 'the sound of artillery and musketry seemed to get distinctly closer'. The numbers of able-bodied men flowing past assisting the wounded 'took on an alarming character'. He knew the Emperor's carriage was still forward on the battlefield, which 'made me very worried as it contained a large amount of gold'. He too decided to pack up everything else, just in case.[16]

Sergeant Hippolyte de Mauduit, with the 2nd Grenadier Imperial Guard Battalion, had been sitting on his knapsack with the rest of his men all day, in reserve. Trees around were bending with the weight of officers and men trying to get a better view of the battle. 'A ball coming at full force, firmly struck an apple tree twenty paces from us,' shaking out at least five or six grenadiers like falling apples. 'We all laughed at their misadventure.' Nobody really knew what was happening. 'Numerous *bravos* were shouted by us', watching charges in the distance, but the main view was of a distant ridge line, malevolently spitting flashes through massive clouds of rolling smoke like some spluttering distant storm. The sight of the Emperor, observing 400 yards away from a small rise, offered reassurance that nothing untoward was happening.

Suddenly about twenty white clouds banged out in the distance, to the east. At first they were thought to be French cannon. Seconds later – 'above our heads, the whistling of balls!' Nearly all the balls of the second discharge 'landed either in our square, or in that of the *Sapeurs* and Marines of the Guard' next to them. Trees to the right hid them from Prussian view and the observers swiftly climbed down. One of de Mauduit's comrades was dismayed to find 'seven of the grenadiers of his company spread lifeless and horribly mutilated' in their square. 'It was the ravages of a single, cruel ball that had fallen among the company!'[17]

At half past four von Bülow's corps dramatically erupted from the Forest of Paris into open ground on the French right flank. Ahead of the Prussians stretched the track from Lasne to Plancenoit, their axis of advance. 'After a dreadful hard march the whole day, in spite of the great battle of the

16 June, and only one day rest, and privation for men and horses,' remembered volunteer Henry Nieman, with the 6th Uhlan Regiment, 'we arrived at last in full trot at the field of battle at Mont St Jean.' Close behind the cavalry screen came Bülow's 16th and 15th Brigades, 9,000 men and 1,000 cavalry supported by 24 guns. Facing them was Lobau's weak corps of 7,000 infantry and 2,000 cavalry with 28 guns. The dramatic surge of Prussians into view on open ground more than compensated for their low numbers at this point. Even more were pouring out of the woods behind them. Apart from dismaying the French it provided an enormous psychological boost for Wellington's men to the left of the line. Captain Thomas Dyneley, with E Troop Royal Horse Artillery, saw that the Prussians 'advanced with a very heavy body of cavalry in front, with which they charged the moment they came on the ground'. The British were elated. 'This was a remarkably fine sight and our army gave them three cheers.' But the day was not over yet.[18]

With the 16th Brigade to the left and the 15th to the right of the Lasne road, von Bülow's corps began to bear down on the Brussels road in the far distance. Four battalions were wheeled right towards Papelotte and Frichermont to begin the link-up with the left of Wellington's line. Von Losthin's 15th Brigade was ordered to fix Lobau's corps in place with 6,500 men and provide flank protection for the 16th Brigade's assault on Plancenoit, led by Colonel Hiller von Gartringen with nearly 6,300 men. By five o'clock von Bülow's corps of 30,000 was complete on the battlefield, and one hour later they had advanced about a mile, just short of Plancenoit, a low-lying village at the head of the Lasne road. The Prussians did not know Napoleon's headquarters was at the Belle Alliance inn, but its distinctive white walls and red roof at the high point on the western horizon was used as the marker to direct the advance. 'Our artillery fire and that of our skir-mishers,' recalled von Bülow, 'chased the enemy from one undulation to another.' They made good progress despite stiff opposition from Lobau's 6,000 infantry, whose Frenchmen belonged to tough old regiments.

The church spire at Plancenoit provided clear orienta-tion for Hiller's 16th Brigade. Once Lobau's men were ejected from the slight rise in front of it, a clear panorama of the rest of the battlefield opened up before the Prussians. To the right was the Mont St Jean ridge with the 'Elm Tree' crossroads and the farm at La Haye Sainte, blazing just below. Beneath the tall column of smoke the whole of the Mont St Jean ridge was seething with swarms of French cavalry. Clouds of rising light grey gunpowder smoke denoted where infantry squares fought for their existence. The Prussians had arrived at the height of the French cavalry attacks. The French line was far to the Prussian right, and the advancing Prussians could clearly see the deep penetra-tion they were about to make in their flank. Hiller's 16th Brigade formed six battalions into three heavy assault columns, which attacked Plancenoit together with four battalions from the 15th. Six battalions of artillery were brought up and began to pound the village and its sur-rounds, while 4,000 Frenchmen with another 3,000 covering the open ground to the north defended it.

The Prussians entered the village, which had contained 520 inhabitants, and began to bash in the doors to evict the French. Each house was fought through with musket, bayonet and swinging rifle butt. The Prussians battered their way through the outlying farm buildings and into the maze of village streets, until the Silesian Landwehr came up against the high walls of the church. 'The open square around the churchyard was surrounded by houses,' Hiller recalled, 'from which the enemy could not be dislodged in spite of our brave attempt.' Colonel Roussille's 5th Line Regiment savagely checked them. 'A fire-fight continued at 15 to 30 paces range,' in the narrow streets, Hiller remembered, 'which ultimately decimated the Prussian battalions.' Roussille fell dead at the head of his men. The irony of it was that far from being a supporter of Napoleon on his return from exile, Roussille had refused him access to Grenoble. His soldiers, however, had forced him to give way. He begged Napoleon to let him keep his command, stating, 'My regiment abandoned me, but I will not abandon it.' Three months later at Plancenoit, Roussille demonstrated this allegiance until death. He died for them, not Napoleon. Plancenoit had fallen.

Just to the north of Plancenoit, French Fusilier Verdurel, from the 47th Line Regiment, lay sprawled in the mud. According to records, the 47th was not even present at Waterloo. Verdurel died an anonymous death, felled as Lobau's corps was pushed back towards the Brussels road. He had been conscripted in Picardy, and was barely 24 years old. During the German campaign in 1813 he had been taken prisoner yet was back in the ranks again by February 1815, before Napoleon's return. Now his body was turned over and looted by the Prussians. The pages of his small service book fluttering in the breeze caught somebody's attention and this preserved his memory. Across the bottom of the cover an inked comment is scrawled in English: 'I found this book on the battlefield of Waterloo' and then 'June 1815', underlined. The yellowed pages and faded ink made Verdurel's passing less anonymous, despite the fact that he was likely tumbled into an unmarked mass grave.[19]

With the Prussians within 1,000 yards of the Brussels road, and his primary line of communications, Napoleon appreciated that if he did not get them out of Plancenoit, it could cost him the battle. At around 6 pm Napoleon directed the eight battalions of the Young Guard, waiting patiently on the Brussels road, to the rear of La Belle Alliance, to take the village back. Their commander, the incorrigible looter Duhesme, a brutal general who had been removed from Spain because of involvement in torture, was just the remorseless man for the job. He double marched the 4,750 Young Guardsmen, mostly volunteers from Paris and Lyons, down into the village valley. These were some of Napoleon's best troops, eager for action and glory, because with it came promotion to the Old Guard. They hit the exhausted Prussians just at the moment of maximum confusion, when they were fragmented and disorganised, having barely captured the village. Inside 30 minutes Plancenoit was back in French hands, cleared at the point of the bayonet.

The Prussians were soon back. Two battalions from the 14th Brigade were beaten off alongside the battle-weary 16th Brigade. By now the entire Prussian IV Corps had arrived on the battlefield and another 12,000 infantry were brought up. Two columns of primarily the 14th Brigade hurled themselves at the furiously blazing village. Most of the houses including the churchyard were wrested back by a quarter past seven o'clock. Only the church was held by the French.

Blücher was becoming obsessed with Plancenoit, which he too viewed as the key to the battle. Wellington, meanwhile, was desperately trying to shore up his centre. Von Ziethen's I Corps was only 30 minutes away and could provide immediate relief, but Blücher felt he needed to concentrate and redirected him towards Plancenoit, where a decision had to be forced. Events were heading for a repeat of the debacle 48 hours earlier when d'Erlon's misdirected meanderings cost a decisive outcome at Quatre-Bras. Von Ziethen might well miss the main battle. Napoleon had no doubts that Plancenoit could not be allowed to fall. Brigadier-General Baron Jean Pelet, commanding the 2nd Chasseurs of the Old Guard, was personally summoned. 'Go with your 1st Battalion to Plancenoit, where the Young Guard is entirely overthrown ... Support it,' Napoleon commanded, and 'keep your troops closed up under control'.

Following on behind was a second Guard battalion, with specific instructions. There were no tactical handbooks for fighting in built-up areas in the nineteenth century; but Napoleon instinctively realised that momentum amid streets and houses could only be maintained if troops did not halt to form line, so as to reduce the opposition by volley fire. 'If you clash with the enemy,' he insisted, 'let it be with the bayonet.' Mobility was essential to turn flanks and panic the enemy. 'Do not fire a shot,' they were instructed. As Lieutenant-Colonel Golzio's 2nd Battalion quick-marched by, Napoleon reiterated: 'Fall on the enemy with the bayonet.'[20]

During the Napoleonic era it was thought that fighting among buildings was to be avoided if possible, because it fragmented the cohesion of columns and lines. Better to dominate such hamlets with skirmishers. Occupying houses conferred an intrinsic advantage to the defender. Once entered, the fight was man against man. Inexperienced Landwehr could therefore match experienced Imperial Guard professionals in the confused turmoil of breaking down doors and fighting through blazing buildings. Once inside a village it was difficult to direct an attack, consolidate or reorganise; men were frequently disorientated.

The Prussians had fought through the buildings without ladders or ropes. Men had to balance on shoulders to gain access to burning buildings through constricted windows, with head and shoulders vulnerable to bayonet and rifle butt. Buildings swallowed whole units, who had to break ranks and line to enter. Also, out of sight and vision, it was all too easy for the 'skulkers' to hide away until the worst was over. The streets, churchyard and cemetery were covered by thousands of bodies. Five Prussian brigades were to lose between 15 and 30 per cent of their strength – over 6,000 casualties – fighting for this village. The French would lose 4,500. When the two Imperial Guard battalions arrived, the streets of Plancenoit were liberally coated with between 5,000 and 6,000 dead and whimpering wounded.

As Pelet doubled into the village at the head of his troops, they passed the mortally wounded General Duhesme, being held up on his horse by his men. The Prussian vanguard was descending the street opposite, and his lead Guard company attacked them with the bayonet. When the Prussians dispersed, the Guards paused to shoot and lost momentum. Each Guard company coming up did the same. 'Hardly had the enemy turned his back than the men began to skirmish,' Pelet recalled. They could not be induced to fight in the open streets with the bayonet. 'I could not rally a single platoon,' he complained. Hardly surprising, as they were firing back at point-blank range. The Prussians were swept to the edges of the village, where, Pelet recalled, 'in each interval between the gardens, I saw muskets aiming at me from forty paces'. He was lucky to be still on his feet. 'I do not know why I was not struck down twenty times.'

With directionless, hand-to-hand combat going on amid the din and blazing embers floating down from burning buildings, the hostility felt by both sides manifested itself in bitter fighting. Quarter was neither asked nor given. Prussians hanged or slit the throats of their prisoners and the French reciprocated. Pelet lost control of his own men. 'I rushed to them to prevent it,' he recalled, but 'saw them perish under my own eyes'. The violence was brutal and dispassionate. 'I was revolted,' Pelet admitted, as Prussians 'faced having their throats cut with *sang froid*', after which the dying prisoners 'hung on to my men'. He rescued those he could, including one French officer 'who prostrated himself, telling me of his French friends and those of his family'.

Pelet became increasingly anxious. Although the initial Prussian resistance had been cracked, his men had skirmished out of sight into the buildings.

> *Certainly, I still held the village; I came, I went, I had the charge beaten, the rally, then the drum roll; nothing brought together even a platoon.*

It was vital they hold this village. He cantered up and down the street on his horse, but 'men did not seem to recognise me as a general officer'. Despite not being able to form up, 'we held like demons'. Hidden away, his men maintained a sufficiently murderous fire to keep the Prussians at bay. 'They were stopped,' he explained, 'despite the numbers that should have overwhelmed us.' Just at the point when he felt the balance was shifting against them, the lead elements of the second Old Guard battalion arrived.

Pelet halted them and used the pause to rally some of his own chasseurs. 'Then I had [them] charge with the bayonet, without firing a shot.' Their momentum proved irresistible. 'They went forward like a wall and overthrew everything they encountered.' Even so, over-exuberance took some of the grenadiers clear beyond the village confines, where a waiting squadron of the 6th Prussian Hussars cut them down.[21]

Plancenoit was French again and Napoleon had achieved a breathing space.

4.30 pm to 7 pm

'Rid Jarmins and the Like'

The cart containing the reserve rifle ammunition for Major Baring's King's German Legion battalion at La Haye Sainte was overturned in a ditch in the confusion behind Wellington's lines. Baring watched the approach of another two French columns bearing down on the farm with acute unease. 'I was not capable of sustaining another attack in the present condition,' he appreciated. He exhorted his men to economise on ammunition but not courage. 'No man will desert you,' they insisted, 'we will fight and die with you.' Baring found it difficult to contain his emotions; 'never had I felt myself so elevated,' he confessed. Racked by guilt at his inability to procure ammunition, he reflected that 'at this moment I would have blessed the ball that came to deprive me of life'.

Beyond the heroics, it had been a gross error on the part of Wellington, his staff and Baring to run out of ammunition. Across the road the 1/95th Rifles had plenty of Baker rifle ammunition, but no request came. Wellington, having just reinforced the garrison with an extra two companies of Nassau troops with muskets, should have appreciated that ammunition was running low. It was to prove a costly error of judgement.

Napoleon wanted La Haye Sainte quickly reduced. Ney deployed Pégot's fairly fresh brigade from Durotte's 4th Infantry Division. Spearheaded by three battalions from the famous 13th Line Regiment, the attackers broke down the outer door of the passage through the stables. Engineer troops axed their way through the wooden door and wild fighting with butt and bayonet ensued inside.

'*Defend yourselves! Defend yourselves!* They are coming over everywhere, come together,' Friedrich Lindau heard. He bent the blade of his sword bayonet ramming it into the chest of a Frenchman and had to discard it. 'Now I used the butt of my rifle and hit out in all directions around me.' Soon all he had left was a splintered gun barrel in his hands. The doorway into the farmhouse on the other side of the courtyard was held for several minutes with just bayonets. 'Our fire gradually diminished,' Major Baring recalled, 'and in the same proportion did our perplexity increase.' He called out encouragement to stand. 'But we must have the means of defending ourselves!' was the agitated response. Baring realised that ominously 'the enemy, who too soon observed our wants' pressed on. They could take virtually any liberties with the unarmed riflemen now and climbed on top of a cart to better shoot into the passageway at a range of under ten yards. 'They now mounted the roofs and walls, from which my unfortunate men were certain marks.' King's German Legion men were shot down like sitting ducks. Unable to clear the roofs of Frenchmen with the bayonet, having climbed up, Baring's men were reduced to hurling roof tiles at them and the enemy below.

The defenceless Lindau grappled a Frenchman with his bare hands, and managed to heave his assailant into the path of another bayonet thrust. 'He let go of me and with the cry "*Mon Dieu, Mon Dieu!*" fell down.' Lieutenant George Graeme 'wanted to halt the men and make one last charge' down the narrow passage. 'Take care,' he was warned by another officer who had seen a French soldier level his musket five yards away. 'Never mind, let the blackguard fire,' responded Graeme, preoccupied with stopping his men. The King's German Legion officer 'stabbed him in the mouth and out through his neck' killing him instantly. Chaos ensued, as Lindau fled chased by a Frenchman shrieking '*Couyons!*' ('Scoundrels!'). Ensign George Frank, nursing an arm broken by a musket shot, ran into a room in the farmer's house and hid under the bed. Two other soldiers came in seeking to hide, but the French were on their heels and shot them, shouting, 'No mercy for you bastard greens!' Frank remained undiscovered until after the battle.[22]

Baring saw the situation was hopeless. 'I made the men retire singly to the main position' on the slope behind the farm. The French, realising they had won and intimidated to some extent by the ferocity of the hand-to-hand resistance, let them go unmolested. Sometimes the attackers could be more fearful than the defenders. Lieutenant Graeme was hiding under a bed while the French shot and bayoneted the wounded above. He was eventually discovered by a French officer and four others who exclaimed, '*C'est ce coquin!*' ('Here's the rascal') and came at him with the bayonet. Graeme parried with his sword and shook off the officer, who had grabbed him by the collar. 'They all looked so frightened and pale as ashes, I thought, "You shan't keep me"' – and he bolted off through the lobby. Shouts and a couple of shots followed him, but little else. Only 42 of Baring's 400 men were able to rally on the main position; the rest were dispersed, dead, wounded or prisoners. Many would rejoin later. Not among them, however, was Simon Lehman from Lindau's battalion, the hero of the Adour river crossing. He had returned from Hanover just six weeks before, after discharge, choosing to go back and join his friends about to go into action. He was dead, sprawled somewhere in the farmyard below.[23]

Lindau and his surviving companions were captured and taken out onto the Brussels road outside the farm, 'where many of the French crowded round us, seized hold of us and plundered us'. His bag of gold and the gold and silver watches they themselves had stolen were soon found. 'A violent quarrel instantly developed' and his knapsack was snatched from his shoulders in a feeding frenzy. Thoroughly irritated by his change of fortune, Lindau punched one over-enterprising Frenchman in the face, as he grappled for more. The brief stand-off was settled when two round shot fired from the Allied side came crashing in, 'striking down a crowd of Frenchmen and taking away some of ours'. Then, with their hands bound, they were led off by a wounded cuirassier, who brooked no opposition. 'They forced us to run as fast as their horses and stabbed a man from the 1st Battalion dead through the loins because he could not run fast enough.' La Haye Sainte, perhaps the most important bastion on the battlefield and the only one in the centre, had now fallen to Napoleon.[24]

Few men, whatever their nationality, could endure point-blank exposure to deliberate artillery fire. When several horse artillery guns protected by cavalry rolled up towards the square of the 1st Nassau Regiment, Captain Friedrich Weiz realised his battle was about to enter a new and particularly painful stage. Two guns unlimbered in front of his battalion at a distance of 200 to 300 paces. They were so close the troops could clearly see the movement of the port fires to ignite the cannon fire holes, at which point 'a certain uneasiness or painful sensation could be noticed in our soldiers' eyes'. Case shot was fired point-blank into their ranks. Cuirassiers patiently waited 100 paces off to the right, for 'that disarray [which] threatened to happen any minute now under the increased cannonade of case shot'. The butchery was relentless:

The first rounds from the two guns went too high and caused no losses to the battalion; all the more terrible were the following ones. From now on, so many men were levelled by each shot that it took superhuman efforts by the officers to have the dead removed and to close the ranks and to keep them closed.

Three officers in 1st Company were killed 'and all it had left were some young inexperienced NCOs'. Weiz, commanding the 5th Company, was ordered to step forward and take over. His company had also lost two officers, leaving one surviving inexperienced officer to be helped by the old NCOs. Goaded beyond endurance, Major von Weyhers, who had never practically commanded his battalion before, ordered an advance against the two murderous cannon. His senior captain, the battle-wise Schuler, argued strenuously against compromising the symmetry of the square: the French cavalry were too close. Weyhers haughtily ignored him and gave the order.

As Weyhers led the battalion forward to attack, two more rounds of case shot shredded the line after 50 paces, and 'levelled the major and his horse and many soldiers'. Not only were they leaderless, the two forward companies had just changed commanders. 'The resulting disarray and gaps caused an unforeseen halt,' Weiz recalled, 'before order could be restored.' Wellington noticed the apparent collapse of their square and sent an ADC across to get the battalion back to its former position at once, but no Allied cavalry was sent to support. Weiz remarked that Weyhers had led them to disaster with the best intentions, but 'the absence of any effort to rescue [the isolated detachment] was a much graver mistake'.

Colonel von Hagen, dispatched from the regimental staff, rode up to replace the unfortunate Weyhers, and immediately ordered the battalion to retreat to the main line. As the rearmost companies marched off, Weiz and Captain Schuler, ironically, who had advised against the rash advance in the first place, were left behind with two companies, which kept firing. Weiz may have missed the message, but in all the turmoil they were completely preoccupied with beating back the enemy. The isolated cluster of 130 to 140 men left behind was quickly surrounded by swarms of cuirassiers, waiting for just such an opportunity. 'Now started a most severe and bloody battle,' Weiz remembered. More and more cuirassiers galloped up to take advantage of this choice morsel and Weiz's men were soon fighting for their very lives. His group included the grenadier company, who with '30 to 40 older intrepid soldiers', gave as good as they got in the savage mêlée.

Private Peter Henninger saw Schuler go down, cut about by a French major, with three sabre slashes to the head and stabbed in the hand while defending himself. Henninger and two other grenadiers pulled the Frenchman over, still on his horse, and he 'was killed by a shot in the head from one of my comrades'. Sergeant Jorg, Weiz remembered, bayoneted two cuirassiers from their horses, one after the other, although he was 'wounded by several saber cuts and had his right eye stabbed from its socket, which then hung down his face'. Nobody was going to come to their rescue, and the line would not be compromised to rectify the mistake. The other squares bleakly observed that 'with every passing moment the situation of the detachment became more desperate and hopeless'. Even more cuirassiers joined the frenzy to annihilate the remnants, which were finally ridden down and dispersed. A few individuals made it back to other squares, while Weiz and the severely cut-about Schuler were taken prisoner. The surviving four companies were so severely depleted by the debacle, they 'could no longer serve as an independent unit'.[25]

What happened confirmed Wellington's impression that some of the foreign squares in the depth of his position were teetering. He was not the only one. Captain von Scriba, in square with the Bremen and Verden Battalions left of Weiz, had also recognised, after the first few heady moments of repelling cavalry, that French artillery was far more lethal. 'We saw to our great consternation our neighbours on our right, the Nassauers, begin to yield in disorder,' he recalled. They watched uneasily as the cuirassiers finished off the isolated detachment. 'This misfortune recurred, later, one or two times under similar circumstances,' von Scriba remembered. Forty-eight hours earlier he had been the fifth senior officer in the battalion; now he was in command. Artillery fire was steadily whittling away their numbers and, more ominously, 'I must remark' that alongside each wounded man, 'one, sometimes two left the ranks', ostensibly to help, which 'reduced our strength considerably'. 'Our square, under artillery fire again, was losing its original shape,' he observed; 'at first it became an irregular triangle, then only a mass closed on all sides without a distinct shape.'

Other foreign battalions were similarly being shredded by artillery. Lieutenant Henry Dehnel, with the 3rd King's German Legion line battalion to von Scriba's right, likewise accelerated in seniority due to horrific casualties. Four captains including the battalion commander had already been killed or mortally wounded. 'At the same time,' he recalled, 'grapeshot blew down a corner of the now small square so that from that moment on the battalion changed to more of a round formation than a square one, as the men were drawing together.'[26]

'The Brunswickers were falling fast,' Captain Alexander Mercer saw, 'the shot every moment making great gaps in their squares.' Collapse seemed imminent. Sergeants were pushing men together, 'thumping them ere they could make them move!' Mercer shared the same prevailing jaundiced British view of foreign contingents. 'They were in such a state that I momentarily expected to see them disband,' he recalled. After Quatre-Bras he had seen one such unit run, spooked only by the sound of his horse battery's hooves. The Brunswick Battalion looked very green. 'I should add that they were all perfect children. None of the privates, perhaps, were above 18 years of age.' They had been reduced to a state of shock; 'there they stood,' he observed, 'with recovered arms, like so many logs'. Mercer was so convinced that they were about to break, that he chose to disregard Wellington's order to fall back on the squares at the approach of cavalry. 'Our coming up seemed to re-animate them,' so he ordered his crews to remain at their guns. The cuirassier charge bearing down on them was reduced to 'a complete mob, into which we kept a steady fire of case-shot from our six pieces', he recalled. 'Every discharge was followed by the fall of numbers' as the French cavalry momentum stalled:

> *The survivors struggled with each other, and I actually saw them using the pommels of their swords to fight their way out of the mêlée … intent only on saving themselves.*

Allied squares fought as bitterly to live as the British. Ensign Rees Gronow saw two Brunswick riflemen leave their square to plunder a French Hussar colonel pinned beneath his dead horse in front of their square. After rifling his pockets and purse 'they deliberately put the colonel's pistols to the poor fellow's head and blew out his brains' to cries of 'Shame! Shame!' from Gronow's indignant square. 'But,' as he remarked, 'the deed was done.' Brunswick Company Surgeon Wilhelm Schutte recalled that despite losing nearly half their men, they 'fought most valiantly because our men were full of hellish wrath'. Their commander the Duke of Brunswick had been killed at Quatre-Bras. 'Wherever they could do in a Frenchman, they would do it,' Schutte claimed, including prisoners. He remembered one French prisoner who broke away from a group of about one hundred:

> *A Hussar chased him and with his pistol shot him through his head, others ran towards him and everybody stabbed at him, and even the wounded took a piece of wood or whatever they could find and clubbed him, until no single piece of him hung to another.*

This was bordering on collective mass hysteria. The nightmarish battle was perverting men and producing an intensity of violence exceptional even by the harsh standards of the century. 'The battlefield was entirely covered with corpses,' Surgeon Schutte continued; 'one could hardly move through all the dead bodies', and these were piled about the squares.[27]

The 1/27th Inniskillings was suffering appalling casualties in square, on the isolated mound next to the Brussels road. Few would survive to give their account of the death of their regiment. Officers were dropping at an alarming rate. Lieutenant Tom Craddock was thrown off his feet when a musket round splatted through both cheeks, carrying away the roof of his mouth. Brother officer Lieutenant Charles Manley was struck in the thigh, and Thomas Charlton Smith, who had been wounded three times during his brief service with the Royal Navy, was hit again and severely injured. At one stage, Captain John Hare, the acting commanding officer, rode across to the 40th Regiment's square to liaise and informed them he had barely any officers of any rank left to command each company. Lieutenant James Mill overheard his commander Major Browne offer to lend him some, but Hare politely declined. 'The sergeants of the regiment like to command the companies,' he explained, 'and he would be loath to deprive them of the honour'.[28]

Sergeant William Lawrence was ordered to take up the colours of the 40th Regiment at about four o'clock. He was not enthusiastic; 14 sergeants and officers had been cut down standing with the colours in the centre of the square, 'and the staff and colours were almost cut to pieces,' he recalled. Lawrence stood next to a captain, almost touching, and within 15 minutes 'a cannon shot came and took his head off, splattering me all over with his blood'. The traumatic event 'will never be blotted from my memory. I am an old man now but I remember it as if it were yesterday,' he would later write. 'There goes my best friend,' muttered Private Martin from the ranks. 'Never mind,' insisted the idealistic young officer who took his place, 'I will be as good a friend to you as the captain.' This produced a few wry gins because Martin, as Sergeant Lawrence well recalled, was one of the 'notorious characters', whom the dead captain had, despite his best efforts, never been able to reform.

Any pause in artillery fire resulted in finding 'ourselves surrounded and beset by hordes of horsemen', James Mill recalled, 'who were slashing and cutting at our kneeling ranks'. They held their ground and allowed the standing ranks to fire over their heads, 'and both horse and rider were to be constantly discerned rolling over on the plain'. While the Inniskillings could beat off the French cavalry with relative ease, they were obliged to remain in square even as they were punished by artillery. 'A round shot from the enemy took off the head of Captain Fraser near me,' recalled Captain Sempronius Stretton, with the 1/40th alongside, 'and striking his company on the left flank, put *hors de combat* more than 25 men.' Stretton, a soldier since 1806, claimed 'this was the most destructive shot I ever witnessed'.[29]

At about 6.30 pm the King's German Legion battalion defending La Haye Sainte, in the foreground, had run out of ammunition. Landau and his comrades had been overrun. The few survivors not caught by the massacre inside hurried out. Intermittent glimpses of this fight through the smoke surrounding the 1/27th square, and the sudden intensification – then dropping off – of firing, signalled its collapse. The loss of the strongpoint placed the regiment in an untenable position. They were the only square directly blocking access to the Brussels road and had to remain in formation as such, because of the cavalry threat. They now became the target of opportunity for the French regiment ensconced in La Haye Sainte.

It was not long before a storm of musket and close-range artillery fire, directed from less than 300 yards away, began to flay the 27th Regiment. The 4th and 40th Regiments nearby, indirectly protected by the ridge line, could barely see it through the surrounding thick smoke. Only periodic glimpses were seen of inert scarlet forms forming the ghostly outline of a grisly palisade of corpses.

The 1/27th was dying in square, and with them, Wellington's centre.

CHAPTER 9

The Crisis —•

7.30 pm to 8.30 pm

7.30 PM The Final Assault and Repulse of Napoleon's Elite Imperial Guard

Napoleon's Imperial Guard attacks the right of Wellington's line and is repelled. The French retreat, assailed to their right by Prussians entering the field in ever greater numbers from the east.

Franz Lieber
Henri Nieman

PAPELOTTE
FARM

Pte Thomas Hask

Lt Col Frederick Ponsonby

Maj Arthur Heyland
Sgt William Lawrenc

MONT ST
FARM

PLANCENOIT
VILLAGE

Ensign Eward Wheatley
Pte Friedrich Lindau

S
E ⊕ W
N

LA BELLE
ALLIANCE

Sgt Maj de Civrieux

CHÂTEAU HOUGOUMONT

Sgt Hippolyte de Mauduit

Pte Mathew Clay

LA HAYE SAINTE
FARM

Ensign William Leeke

Commander Guillemin

Capt John Kincaid

Capt Alexander Mercer
Capt Harry Powell
Wellington

Capt John Hare
William Fortescue
t Edward Drewe

Sgt Thomas Morris
Pte George Rose

ary Gale

The 'Via Dolorosa' to Brussels

Captain Horace Seymour, ADC to Uxbridge, commanding the Allied cavalry, held the unfortunate Hanoverian Colonel Hake by the collar. Hake, commanding 500 or so troopers with the Duke of Cumberland's Hussars, had refused to halt the rearward drift of the Hanoverian cavalry around them. Sergeant Cotton of the 7th Hussars claimed Seymour 'nearly shook him out of his saddle', demanding to know who was the second in command. Seymour was an imposing presence and by reputation the strongest man in the British army, but Major Mellzing, the 2IC, was nowhere to be found. It was about five o'clock and the Cumberland Hussars had been ordered to counter-attack at the height of the French cavalry attacks, but Hake was having none of it.

Hake told Seymour that 'he had no confidence in his men, that they were volunteers, and the horses were their own property'. They had already taken 60 casualties sitting waiting. Hake thought his men had acquitted themselves sufficiently and enough was enough. 'I was unsuccessful,' stated Seymour at Hake's subsequent court-martial. 'I laid hold of the bridle of the Colonel's horse, and remarked what I thought of his conduct.' All this was to no avail. The rearward movement continued, although some Cumberland officers and troopers, disgusted, rode off to join the other units standing their ground. Thus began the inglorious ride of the Cumberland Hussars to Brussels, an event that, more than any other, perpetuated the myth that foreigners – especially Belgians – were not pulling their weight. The irony of it was that the fleeing Hussars, cantering back towards Brussels, were in fact Germans, 'in whole skins', Cotton sarcastically remarked, as opposed 'to the chance of having them perforated in the field'.[1]

The first part of the Cumberland Hussars' ride to Waterloo was as dangerous as the position they had vacated. 'Shots and shells were falling so thick,' recalled Captain William Verner, with the 7th Hussars on the same road, 'that I considered it next to impossible to reach the village in safety.' Verner had been hit on the right side of his head by a bullet. The disconcerting thwack had attracted the attention of his commanding officer, who said ,'There goes poor Pat Verner.' Surgeons were in short supply, so he was sent off to Brussels. 'My horse kept jumping from side to side as the shells fell and burst close to us,' he recalled. The Brussels road was a virtual 'Via Dolorosa' along its whole length as the mangled wounded made their piteous way through the Forest of Soignes towards the city. 'I can well remember feeling a rather sickening sensation,' recalled staff officer Lieutenant Basil Jackson, on viewing the remains of a Brunswick soldier, 'apparently those of quite a lad', half buried in the mud on the road close to the farm at Mont St Jean. 'A heavy wheel had passed over the head and crushed it flat, leaving the brains scattered about.' What was particularly upsetting was that 'no person thought it worthwhile to pull the body aside, any more than one would think of withdrawing a dead cat or dog from the street'.[2]

Sixteen-year-old Pierre-Jean Tellier, the son of the Waterloo village schoolmaster, watched the dismal flow of traffic from his loft. 'Little by little the number of wounded increased,' he recalled. 'They could not use the paved road as this was congested with ammunition and ambulance wagons', and they had to struggle through the viscous mud and ditches alongside. 'Most of them came to our house, asking for a drink.' His father set him up at the corner with a barrel of beer, increasingly diluted with water, to quench their thirst. Tellier heard 'shouts of *sauve qui peut*' ('every man for himself') – probably the Cumberland Hussars galloping past – which intensified the atmosphere of tension and despair that already permeated the road. Assistant surgeon William Gibney, who was looking on, described the dreadful scene:

> *Nothing could exceed the misery exhibited on this road, which being the high pavé, or I might say the stone causeway leading to Brussels, was crowded to excess with our wounded and French prisoners, shot and shell meanwhile pouring into them. The hardest heart must have recoiled from this scene of horror; wounded men being re-wounded, many of whom had previously received the most frightful injuries.*[3]

Lieutenant George Simmons, wounded earlier at the sand pit with the 1/95th, endured agonising pain, wobbling along on his horse on the same road, 'suffocating with the injury my lungs had sustained'. 'My breast was dreadfully swelled,' he recalled, the surgeon having 'made a deep cut under the right pap and dislodged from the breast bone a musket ball'. As this was happening, stray shots were knocking off dust from the Mont St Jean farmhouse, showering those inside with filth. An agitated wounded dragoon officer had set off a panic, shouting 'It is all up with us!' This sparked off the hasty evacuation of the farmhouse. With French cavalry anticipated at any moment, doctors and wounded were rushed out in an unseemly scramble. 'Many lives might have been saved, that were lost by this false alarm,' Simmons remembered. 'I saw poor fellows who had lost a leg a few moments before, now crawling like crabs out of the place.' He was hoisted up onto a horse next to another wounded fellow officer, Lieutenant Johnson, on another mount. Simmons, dressed only in a shirt and trousers held up by a silk scarf, was seated on the horse of a freshly killed cuirassier. The saddle was still saturated with gore. 'I was a most fearful sight,' he recalled. As they set off on the Brussels road, Johnson was abruptly snatched from the saddle by a bouncing cannon-ball. The road was as assistant surgeon William Gibney described it, filled with walking casualties:

Here a man with an arm suspended only by a single muscle, another with his head horribly mangled by a sabre cut, or one with half his face shot away, received fresh damage.

Simmons recounted that the 'the road was crowded with Belgians running away and our wounded soldiers, I saw several men knocked over'. Down the road came the Cumberland Hussars, 'a whole regiment of Belgians marching away from the field of battle', Simmons claimed.[4]

Riding ahead was 14-year-old Edward Heeley on a mule. He was the son of the assistant quartermaster-general's head groom. Heeley was suddenly confronted by hard riding cavalry, pelting down the road towards him shrieking *'Franceuse! Franceuse!'* ('The French, the French!'). His mule was swept up in the fearful high-speed cavalcade heading for Brussels. 'Such a scene of confusion had now began as baffles all description,' he recalled. The mule, seemingly out of control and at full gallop, was astute enough to turn off the main road when it saw the turning for its stable. The Hanoverians sped on by, accompanied by their women, wives and camp-followers, 'well mounted, riding astride on men's saddles', which added to the surreal picture. Heeley was amazed to see they wore 'boots and trousers like dragoons, and wore a gown over all, with small round bonnets on their heads'. He was unable to discern whether they were Brunswickers or King's German Legion, but they were certainly not British. These women kept up with the lead elements, 'who entered Brussels screaming all the way as they came'. In their wake they left fear and apprehension and the conviction that the battle was lost. 'They rode well,' Heeley observed:

> For their horses feet made the fire fly out of the pavement. I never shall forget them, for they galloped on straight forward and if the Devil had been in the way, they would have went over him.

Slow-moving wounded were barged aside. Simmons characteristically commented, 'I have no doubt if the French had beaten us, the Belgians would have fought better against us than for us.' 'The forest was swarming with soldiers who had left the field,' recalled Lieutenant Basil Jackson, echoing Simmons's chauvinist view of foreign troops in general. 'Whole companies of certain regiments seemed to have marched off,' he observed. He could see arms piled and cooking kettles suspended over blazing fires. There had to be at least 1,000 runaways 'who sought concealment in the forest'.[5]

Captain William Verner was depressed as he made pitifully slow progress along the 'Via Dolorosa' to Brussels. 'The road was in several places completely blocked up,' he remembered, undoing the clearance work the 1/27th Inniskillings had completed early that morning. 'Wagons laden with provisions and forage had been overthrown and the contents strewed all over the road, and even private carriages were upset and plundered.' As the Cumberland Hussars rode by 'it was a regular *sauve qui peut*'. Every man for himself appeared to be the overriding imperative on the 'Via Dolorosa'. Lieutenant Colonel Hill, commanding the Blues, overtook a familiar officer on horseback heading towards the rear. He knew him well and expressed hope that he was not too badly hurt. 'I am not wounded' was the awkward response, followed after a pregnant pause by 'but I have had several very narrow escapes.'

Verner knew of many lucky escapes. One of his regimental officers, Lieutenant Peters, had a lethal grapeshot ball deflected by his sword, which tore away part of his jacket and buttons and lodged in his chest. Painful, but he survived. Another subaltern, Beatty, shot in the cheek, found the musket ball and the three teeth that had arrested its momentum still inside his mouth. Any other deflection would have been fatal. Verner, struck on the head, was fortunate to be alive. His brother in England eventually heard he was wounded, but not in the head. On asking what type of wound, he was told from 'a cannon-ball'. The gentleman with him immediately enquired, somewhat disingenuously, 'if he had heard whether the [cannon] ball had been extracted?'

Verner, quickly ejected during the panic around the Mont St Jean farm, assumed the battle was lost. 'So convinced was I from the appearance of the field when I left it,' he admitted, with 'the French and particularly cavalry, coming on in such force, that I thought nothing would prevent our army having to retreat'. Observing the desperate scenes on the Brussels road had done little to change his mind. A Life Guards trooper, suffering from combat stress, was shooting his carbine in the air as he went along. The gun reports spooked the horses carrying other wounded, adding further to their discomfort. 'I rode up to the fellow and told him if he was so

295

great a coward as to run away himself, he ought to have some feeling for those going to the rear wounded.' The trooper studiously ignored the wild figure in shirtsleeves confronting him and nonchalantly continued to fire away.[6]

In Brussels Major William Frye, who had been caught up in the crisis while on leave, wrote to a friend in England that 'all the townspeople are on the ramparts listening to the sound of cannon'. The battlefield rumours were not good. 'Probably my next letter,' he wrote, 'may be dated from a French prison.' The city, he commented, had 'been in greatest alarm and agitation' since Quatre-Bras, two days before.

François René de Châteaubriand, a well-known author, had been listening attentively at the Brussels Gate since midday. Rumblings 'lasting sometimes a moment, sometimes longer' despite clouds overhead, could not be a storm. The rumblings were followed by 'detonations, which were smaller, less vibrant, less coordinated than those of a thunderstorm', which 'suggested a battle'. In time a southerly wind 'carried the sound of artillery fire more distinctly', denoting a heavy battle. He stopped a courier riding through the city gate and discovered that 'Bonaparte entered Brussels yesterday after a bloody battle'. The depressing news could not be true, of course, because that was the day before. 'It is believed that the Allies have been decisively beaten,' the erroneous report announced, 'and that they have ordered a retreat.'

Whig MP Thomas Creevey recorded a similarly unreal atmosphere inside the city. At 3 pm he had walked out of the Namur Gate towards the army, observing that the Sunday population was behaving as normal:

> Sitting about tables drinking beer and smoking and making merry, as if races or other sports were going on, instead of the great pitched battle which was then fighting.[7]

Sixty minutes later the Cumberland Hussars came galloping ingloriously into the city, accompanied by their shrieking women. 'The French are in the town,' Creevey's stepdaughter Elizabeth Ord announced, and dropped the shutters. Dashing through the Namur Gate, the Hanoverians galloped wildly down the Rue de Namur, raising sparks from the cobblestones as they headed for the Place Royale. They were 'crying out the French were at their heels', recalled Creevey. 'The confusion and mischief occasioned by these fellows on the road was incredible,' the Whig MP remembered, 'but in the town all was quiet again in an instant.'

After the horsemen Creevey did see Frenchmen filing through the Rue de Namur. These were 'a considerable body of French prisoners and one could distinctly recognise one or two eagles'. These were d'Erlon's men, captured during the Union Brigade counter-attack. 'Their number was said to be 1,500,' he remarked. Such appearances formed part of a litany of highs and lows the citizens of Brussels experienced that Sunday. Elizabeth Ord described it as 'the most miserable day I ever spent in my life and one I could never forget if I was to live one hundred years'. 'I then heard fresh shouting,' Creevey remembered, even more prisoners; 'it was said 5,000 in all had arrived'.

Wounded rifleman Edward Costello of the 1/95th Rifles, sitting in the Grand Place, heard an alarm that the French were entering the city:

> In a moment all was in an uproar; the inhabitants running in all directions, closing their doors, and some Belgian troops in the square, in great confusion.

Costello loaded his rifle, but the alarm subsided when 'about 1,700 or 1,800' French prisoners appeared, 'under escort of some of our dragoons'. Young Edward Heeley watched them led off to the Petit-Château barracks a mile northwest of the park. 'The poor fellows cut a sorry figure,' he observed:

> *They must have fought gallantly for scarcely one of them had a hat or cap on, and nearly all of them were more or less wounded, principally sabre wounds. They were drenched to the skin with rain and covered with mud. A few thoughtless people insulted them, with 'Where's Boney now?' and such like, but speaking generally they were more pitied than anything else.*[8]

Despite the arrival of the prisoners, news was generally grim. Tri-coloured cockades to welcome Napoleon were suspended from some houses just in case. Throughout the afternoon Thomas Creevey heard of one disappointment after another. Another MP, Mr Legh, had got back after catching a glimpse of the battlefield. Far from sharing Creevey's optimism regarding the prisoners 'he thought everything looked as bad as possible', to the extent that rather than stable his horses, he kept them at the front door. 'Why sir,' he had been informed in confidence by a Life Guards soldier at the Hôtel Bellevue, 'I don't like the appearance of things at all.' The soldier's view was 'the French are getting on in such a manner that I don't see what's to stop them'.

Later, visiting the Juarenais family, Creevey came across a Foot Guards officer, in excruciating pain while a corporal picked out pieces of his epaulet from an open wound. Apologising for the trouble he was causing the household, he assured them, before he fainted, 'he would not be long with them, as the French would be in that night'. Creevey got the same pessimistic responses from all he asked. Major Hamilton, on Wellington's staff, told him at seven o'clock that 'the Prussians though hanging like a black cloud in sight, never fired a shot when he came away', grimly adding 'he doubted whether Lord Wellington would be able to keep the field'. Elizabeth Ord, Creevey's stepdaughter, took her mother to bed. 'Anne and I laid down, [but] did not take off our clothes' just in case. In the distance the battle could be heard, rumbling and spluttering. It was at least still going on.[9]

The city was becoming overwhelmed with wounded, mostly indifferent to the outcome, their senses dulled with pain. 'The houses were insufficient to contain half,' declared a civilian eyewitness, 'and the churches and public buildings were littered down with straw for their reception.' Those freshly arrived 'appeared to have been dragged for miles through oceans of mud', with torn clothing and often with no boots or shoes. 'The accounts they brought were vague and disheartening.' Hospital assistant John Davy remembered 'the wounded came in immense numbers', the hospitals were overwhelmed and 'they still continued coming'. 'Every place was occupied, so that it became difficult to walk, even in the passages without treading on them.' 'We have had lots of legs and arms to lop off,' wrote Hospital Assistant Isaac James to his brother in England. He was to be up for three nights.[10]

Edward Costello was effusive about 'the humane and indefatigable exertions of the fair ladies of Brussels' in caring for the wounded. 'The most delicately brought up women, and persons of all ranks were occupied in this way,' recalled John Davy. Costello, a hardbitten Peninsula veteran, watched them 'stripping the sufferers of their gory and saturated garments':

Altogether careless of fashion scruples, many of the fairest and wealthiest of the ladies of that city now ventured to assert their preeminence on the occasion.

Medical knowledge was primitive in 1815 and treatment was brutal, even if applied with compassion. Captain Robert Adair, with the 1st Guards, whose thigh had been reduced to shredded flesh and splintered bone by a cannon-ball, made a black joke just as he died at the hands of a surgeon whose knife was blunted by dozens of amputations before him. 'Take your time, Mr Carver,' he bleakly admonished, before expiring with blood loss.[11]

Costello was impressed by the stoic way the British appeared to endure pain compared to other nation's soldiers. He saw one English dragoon veteran hold his arm for the surgeon to amputate below the elbow, animatedly chewing tobacco throughout, 'without displaying the slightest emotion'. Nearby, meanwhile, a Frenchman was 'bellowing lustily' as a surgeon probed his shoulder, seeking to extract a musket ball. This appeared to irritate the dragoon more than anything else, and doubtless as much from the emotional release from pain as anything else, he slapped the Frenchman 'a smart blow across the breech' with his own severed limb. Holding it by the wrist he exclaimed, 'Here, take that, and stuff it down your throat, and stop your damned bellowing!' The sight of some injuries did affect Costello. One young German horse artillery driver had lost both legs from round shot passing through his horse's belly. 'While on the ground in this mangled state, he received a dreadful gash in one of his arms, from a French cuirassier, and a ball in the other.' When the surgeons had finished with him, the young lad, no more than 19, 'lay a branchless trunk'. The horror of it was that, despite others expiring from far lesser wounds, he survived.

Such men, languishing in agony on the straw in the Grand Place, had been brutalised by their medical treatment and were now in need of compassion. 'One lady I noticed particularly,' Costello recalled, because she was young and beautiful, probably no more than 18 years old. She was caring for the wounded with a servant in attendance and came across a tall Highlander, groaning with a severe wound in the thick part of his thigh. Bending down, she gently turned his blood-stained kilt aside and 'commenced washing the wounded part'. The Scottish soldier, clearly embarrassed, 'seemed uneasy at her importunity'. Addressing him in English 'with the sweetest voice imaginable', she insisted, 'Me no shamed of you – indeed, I will not hurt you!' Costello found such empathy inspiring.[12]

Captain Carl Jacobi, one of the few survivors of the Hanoverian Lüneburg Battalion that was cut to pieces by French cavalry outside La Haye Sainte, could consider himself lucky. He had been ordered to march to Brussels with the remaining battalion core and gather together as many of their compatriots as possible. He lost even more men getting beyond the road from Mont St Jean to Waterloo. He found the Brussels road 'blocked everywhere by wagons and carts driven into one another'. 'Even pedestrians were hardly able to pass through,' he remembered. They slowly managed to 'work our way' through the ditches and thick underbrush on the side of the road.

At dusk they reached Brussels. This was fortunate, for Jacobi was only dressed in his short dolman jacket, having lost his coat, and was still wearing his dress boots, after the excruciating cold and wet night the evening before. In Brussels 'I found myself suddenly transferred from the turmoil of the battle and the trampled fields to a quiet, hand-somely appointed room.' He was able to eat and drink, cut his boots from his swollen feet and gain access to a bed. 'Such are the ups and downs of a warrior's life,' he observed; 'last night hungry and stiff from being cold and wet in muck and mud'. His position was likely unique. Eleven miles to the south the battle raged, whereas 'this night' here he was, 'sated and warmed on a dry and comfortable bed'.[13]

'Quiver on the Beam'

Ensign Edmund Wheatley's 5th Line Battalion of the King's German Legion were in position overlooking La Haye Sainte. He had picked up a dead soldier's musket and fired it 'until my shoulder was nearly jellied and my mouth was begrimed with gunpowder to such a degree that I champed the gritty composition unknowingly'. As he stood in square taking a pinch of snuff he looked over a battlefield 'thickened with heaps of bodies and shattered instruments'. It reminded him of an old ballad about Marlborough's former glorious victories his nurse used to recite:

> *Ten thousand slain you say and more?*
> *What did they kill each other for?*
> *Indeed I cannot tell, said she,*
> *But 'twas a famous victory.*

Like many in the lower ranks he was unimpressed by their corps commander. The young and immature Prince of Orange had galloped by 'screaming out' to form line 'like a new born infant', he remembered. The fall of La Haye Sainte had exposed a weakness in the centre of Wellington's line, and Wheatley's brigade commander Baron Christian von Ompteda was ordered to retake it. Ompteda strongly advised against such a rash advance. The Lüneburg Battalion had been annihilated a few hours before attempting the same. The cuirassiers responsible for it were still lurking in the valley. 'I must still repeat my order to attack in line with the bayonet,' the Prince petulantly ordered. 'I will listen to no further arguments.' 'Then I will,' Ompteda responded coolly. He was driven by honour and knew he was leading the 5th Battalion to certain death. 'Try and save my two nephews,' he asked the battalion commander Colonel Linsingen, as they descended the slope.

Wheatley regarded Ompteda as an inspiring commander. '*Charge!*' he heard, and 'we ran forward huzzaing'. The charge was pressed home and he ran past Ompteda, who yelled, 'That's right, Wheatley!' 'No one but a soldier can describe the thrill one instantly feels in such an awful moment,' Wheatley recalled. As hand-to-hand fighting broke out he heard a cry of '*The cavalry! The cavalry!*' and cuirassiers were soon among them. Ompteda astonished the French by galloping calmly ahead and jumping the garden hedge, straight into the assembled French infantry. Captain Charles Berger, attacking with the 5th Battalion, saw that the French officers refused to fire at this very brave and solitary high-ranking officer plunging into their midst, lopping off the tops of shakos with his sword. 'The officers struck the men's barrels up with their swords,' Berger noticed, but it could not last, and soon he saw Ompteda 'sink from his horse and vanish'.

Wheatley was knocked senseless in the cavalry attack and came to, bareheaded and with 'a violent head-ache', in a clay ditch. 'Close by me lay Colonel Ompteda on his back, his head stretched back with his mouth open, and a hole in his throat.' His pockets had been turned out and the singe mark around the hole in his collar indicated he had been shot at point-blank range. Wheatley was pulled out of the ditch by the French and immediately plundered. Colonel Linsingen, the battalion commander, had been pinned to the ground by his wounded horse and had to watch his battalion being wiped out around him. He at least managed to grab Ompteda's two young nephews and hide in a hollow. Less than 20 of his men survived. Not long afterwards the Prince of Orange was wounded and taken off the field – and none too soon was the majority opinion from the British ranks. Even before the battle Private William Wheeler of the 51st had declared 'that boy' was 'not the man for us'.[14]

With the capture of La Haye Sainte, Captain Jonathan Leach, with the 1/95th Rifles on the slope opposite, saw that 'the French instantly filled the house with sharpshooters, whose deadly fire precluded the possibility of holding the knoll' upon which the 27th Inniskillings stood, 'and the ground immediately about it'. Obliged to stand in close order in square, the Inniskillings were hopelessly exposed. Captain Sempronius Stretton, standing with the 40th Regiment behind them, remembers being engaged by 'a double line of *Tirailleurs* sharpshooters, supported by a heavy column of infantry'. They were shooting up at the high ground beyond La Haye Sainte and the sandpit from the prone position and 'appeared to select their objects with great precision'. Most commentators at Waterloo tended to write only about their own battalion's experiences without mentioning any others. For so many of them to mention the Inniskillings was a measure of the extraordinary punishment their square was enduring. Lieutenant-Colonel Sir Andrew Barnard, with the 95th nearby, saw that they 'suffered very much from the enemy's fire', and Major Felix Calvert of the 1/32nd recalled that the 27th had 'nearly lost all its men'.[15]

Man after man went down in the 27th's square as the whup-whup of musket balls swept their obstinate ranks, leaving more men prone than standing. Wounded were dragged inside, the dead thrown out, and the ranks closed again. Gritty physical group cohesion, along with emotional cohesion, held them together. Captain Edward Drewe of the 9th Company had, like Private Alexander Dunlop, lived a charmed life since 1808, but was now hit several times in the left knee and arm. 'I had received my third wound about a quarter before seven o'clock,' Drewe remembered, 'and was then taken from the field.' He was probably surprised on checking his timepiece that he had survived that long. Any ambition of future promotion that Lieutenant William Fortescue had cherished, to support his Catholic wife Honoria and five children, was dashed by musket balls that shattered his chest and arm. He fell to the ground, barely able to draw breath as his lung filled with fluid. Virtually every officer in the 27th was down, 15 in all, and 103 NCOs and men were dead. A further 360 wounded were writhing in agony among the feet of the those left standing in a square that had originally formed up with 698 men.[16]

The fall of La Haye Sainte and the recapture of Plancenoit at 7.30 pm had opened up possibilities for Napoleon. Until now, French attackers had exposed themselves to shot and shell all day, advancing in easily targeted infantry columns, or riding en masse across broken ground, prey to concentrated infantry fire from intact squares. By the end of the day the dead were heaped four deep in places across the Mont St Jean ridge. Now, however, Napoleon had opened a chink in Wellington's centre, while holding the Prussians at bay to his right at Plancenoit. Barely two hours of daylight remained in which to force a decision. Wellington's army was exhausted after nine hours' pounding and he had no infantry reserve, just two brigades of light cavalry. The crisis point had arrived, or as Sergeant Edward Cotton expressed it, 'the fate of the battle seemed to quiver on the beam'.

Napoleon had 11 battalions of elite infantry as yet uncommitted. His cavalry was decimated and his artillery exhausted. He could either use these battalions to cover a withdrawal to fight another day after regrouping with Grouchy, or he could try to snatch victory at the eleventh hour. Withdrawal meant defeat, and the Imperial Guard had never let him down. 'With prudence it might have been possible to avoid a catastrophe,' wrote Kellerman, the commander of the III Cavalry Corps, later. The natural caution of the British suggested withdrawal might work, 'but prudence', Kellerman acknowledged, 'was not a distinctive quality of the commander of the French army'. Napoleon likely gave the dilemma very little thought. 'Whilst a single battalion remained to him, an *écu* to bet, it could not be doubted that he would risk one or the other,' Kellerman perceptively observed. Napoleon was a gambler. He could afford to commit six battalions of the Middle Guard and three of the Old Guard.[17]

The battle had indeed reached its psychological tipping point. 'The *vivida vis animi*, the glow which fires one upon entering into action – had ceased,' reflected Lieutenant Edward Macready, with the 30th Foot, about to receive the Guard onslaught. 'It was now to be seen, which side had most bottom, and would stand the killing longest.' The British had stoically accepted they would endure, but what of their allies? Sergeant Thomas Morris, with the 73rd Regiment, was virtually deaf. 'Continued discharges of the artillery during the battle, had so affected the drums of the ears, that we could scarcely hear anything for two or three days afterwards.' His battalion, which had mustered 29 officers and 550 men, was down to single figures in officers and less than 100 men. The loss of so many familiar faces in such a short time was emotionally crippling. Lieutenant John Kincaid, with the 1/95th Rifles, was 'weary and worn out, less from fatigue than anxiety'. Whenever he moved about 'to get a glimpse of what was going on; nothing met my eye except the mangled remains of men and horses.' He summed up the feelings of many when he observed, 'I had never heard of a battle in which everybody was killed, but this seemed likely to be an exception.' Nobody asked 'who has been hit' now; it was 'who's alive?'[18]

Major-General von Müffling, Wellington's Prussian liaison officer, had been waiting impatiently on the left of Wellington's line for the arrival of von Ziethen's overdue Prussian I Corps. Delays had been caused by misdirection and confusion on the march. Von Bülow's IV Corps was checked outside Plancenoit, and Blücher wanted von Ziethen to change direction to support him. All the indications being received by the approaching vanguard brigade under Karl von Steinmetz was that Wellington's Nassauers were falling back and von Bülow's 15th Brigade had been repelled around Smohain and Frichermont. Von Steinmetz was cautious about advancing into a potential debacle and stopped 1,000 paces away from the French at Ohain.

A series of orders and counter-orders were issued, which culminated in Steinmetz almost turning away, and missing the battle. The dilemma was whether to directly support Wellington's line, visibly crumbling in the centre, or to maintain the pressure deep in the French flank at Plancenoit. Heated exchanges ensued between Lieutenant-Colonel von Reiche, the I Corps chief of staff, convinced by Müffling that Wellington's situation would be dire if they did not intervene, and Captain von Scharnhorst, who vigorously pressed the case that Blücher had ordered support for the failing attack in Plancenoit. Steinmetz's column had already turned about at a crossroads to comply, when von Ziethen returned to the head of his column. A very concerned von Müffling convinced him to support Wellington's left, which would enable him to switch his final cavalry reserve to shore up the crumbling centre.

Steinmetz's leading units came into action shortly after 7.30 pm, at the same time as a fresh Prussian assault towards Plancenoit. This was launched by the newly arrived 5th Brigade, from the third Prussian corps to arrive, von Pirch's II Corps. Nine fresh battalions of over 5,000 men formed the vanguard, supported by the weakened and somewhat exhausted remnants of von Bülow's 14th and 16th Brigades, another 9,000 men. They attacked, together with 10,000 men from the IV Corps, to the north of the village. Within 30 minutes, the two Imperial Old Guard battalions holding Plancenoit were virtually surrounded, amid bitter street fighting.

Prussian soldier Franz Lieber, with the Colburg Regiment, at last arrived on the field. 'It had been again our lot to stand, unengaged for some time,' he recalled. Numerous wounded were carried by as they nervously waited for the call forward. 'Ah, my Colburger,' Blücher announced as he rode up, 'wait, wait a moment, I'll give you presently something to do.' A false alarm resulted when the regiment, called upon to charge a square, was halted again. They could clearly see the battlefield outside Plancenoit. Major von Columb's 8th Hussars waited nearby. Lieber and his comrades were psyched up again to do battle, despite their previous nightmarish fight at Ligny. They could see the action was going well. 'We saw some brilliant charges of our cavalry,' he remembered, 'putting to rout French squares.'

They did not realise it, but they would not be required to fight that day. 'It was heart-rending to halt as we did in the evening,' he recalled, 'on the field of battle after such bloodshed.' As the adrenalin of the wait faded, they began to appreciate how little they had eaten. 'We suffered dreadfully from the cravings of hunger' and more especially thirst. He compared their lot to that of shipwrecked sailors under a scorching sun, describing how it felt 'when for the first time again, he could quaff the delicious crystal liquid'. They had chewed on damp clay during the march to extract some moisture. Lieber would survive this day only to be struck in the neck by a musket ball during the next.[19]

The Imperial Guard had been sitting either side of the Brussels road, just short of the Belle Alliance inn, for upward of six hours. Many of them could see across to the opposite ridge line, but not all. Sergeant Hippoloyte de Mauduit belonged to one of the two senior regiments of Grenadiers, who were behind a small reverse slope and could not. They were 'reduced to stamping around in impatience in the thick mud in which we sank to the ankles'. Only fleeting glimpses of the battle could be seen in any case, through rolling clouds of smoke from cannon and volley fire. The euphoria of expectation that had accompanied their arrival late that morning had long since been dispelled. This was clearly no rearguard action. They scanned the smoke-covered ridge line, spluttering and crackling like the edge of a campfire. It had been traversed several times by lines of infantry and masses of cavalry, but still there was no breakthrough. The flurry of activity to the right had followed the appearance of Prussians, and with the increasing frequency of cannon over-shoots, it began to dawn on the assembled Guard that the battle was not going well.

The Old Guard was especially proud of its distinctive role as Napoleon's shock troops, the ultimate reserve. They were present at every action but were only committed to tip the scales at critical moments. Even so, at Borodino in Russia in 1812 Napoleon refused to commit the Guard when the battle and the outcome of the campaign hung in the balance. 'If there should be another battle tomorrow, where is my army?'

he had asked. The Young Guard was raised to fight and was always the first of the Guard formations to go into action. They had turned the balance against the Prussians at Ligny 72 hours before, and at 6 pm they were committed to Plancenoit.

They were Napoleon's 'children'. He knew hundreds of them by name, remembering their faces when he stopped to speak to them on picket duty, or when they lined up for battle. Napoleon was not addressed as 'Your Majesty' or 'Sire' by the Guard, but simply as '*Mon* Empereur'. Men like Captain Jean-Roch Coignet were completely in his confidence. Coignet had even played Napoleon's wife Marie Louise at billiards. The Empress was 'first rate', he remembered, and 'not afraid to stretch herself out across the billiard table' like the men, to make the stroke, 'with me always on the watch to see what I could'. This could have been quite a lot, bearing in mind the considerable amount of flesh revealed by the fashion of the day. 'She was frequently applauded,' he added, doubtless with a wink.[20]

The Guard lining the muddy Brussels road was not the same quality force that had gained Napoleon's laurels at the height of empire. Most of the half-pay soldiers of the Old Guard were recalled on his return from exile and new regiments created. Not all the discharged veterans turned up. Many who marched to Waterloo were aware that the camaraderie of the traditional Guard, like much of the Armée du Nord, had been diluted by suspected royalist sympathisers in its ranks. Only the 1st Grenadier and 1st Chasseur Regiments had men with 12 years' service, cadred from the faithful Elba battalion. Nevertheless, almost 30 per cent of the men had seen 20 to 25 campaigns, their average age was 35 years, and maybe one third wore bravery awards.

They were battle-hardened veterans, confident to the point of arrogance. Many sported skin tattoos and large golden earrings, giving a piratical appearance. British artist Benjamin Hayden observed them on duty at Fontainebleau the year before and commented:

More dreadful looking fellows than Napoleon's Guard I have never seen. They had the look of thorough bred, veteran disciplined banditti. Depravity, recklessness and blood thirstiness were burned into their faces.[21]

Towering black bearskins accentuated their height, and enormous ragged moustaches added to a ferocious-looking countenance. They had never faced the British.

General Drouhet, their commander, had been acting as an aide to Napoleon. He rode up to Marshal Ney's ADC Levavasseur shouting 'Where is the Guard?' It was approaching 7 pm. The Guard was to finally see action. 'Form square,' Drouhet ordered and the drummer boys began to beat the call.

Veterans can 'smell' the course of a battle and the auguries coming from this one were not good. They sensed the lack of animation around them, and resignation instead of purpose. Nothing had gone right since the Prussians had slipped away in the night two days ago. Having defeated them at Ligny, they had to wonder: what were these black masses on their right doing back? The start of the campaign had confirmed their faith in the Emperor. Clearly he had not lost his operational touch, but they had set off too late after Quatre-Bras to finish off the British. The summer storm appeared to have soaked the momentum out of the Armée du Nord and they meant to restore it. 'It would have been preferable to force him [the enemy] to manoeuvre rather than to leave him to fight on ground of his own choosing,' Sergeant de Mauduit, with the 1st Regiment of Foot Grenadiers of the Imperial Guard, had considered. As veterans they had long learned to do what they were told, however bizarre, and ask no questions. Their 'betters' were in control, and the Emperor would get it right. If there were too few of them to attack, so be it, there had to be a reason, and it was not their concern.[22]

The Guard was unusual in many ways. Each square had a general marching at its head. That day the Guard was to advance in two waves. Five battalions of the Middle Guard numbering 2,850 men would strike Wellington's line first, followed by three battalions of the Old Guard, some 1,700 men, in the second wave. Three further battalions of 1,800 were held in reserve. The Guard, aiming to shatter the centre, would be the vanguard of a general offensive along the whole line. Bachelu's 5th Division was attacking to the left of the Guard with 3,600 men, and Donzelot's 2nd Division was on the right with another 3,000. This was Napoleon's final throw of the dice – 50 per cent smaller than d'Erlon's main effort with 17,000 men that morning, which had failed.

This glorious advance of the Imperial Guard, the emotional highlight of the battle, has long since been shrouded in myth. Once the size of the Guard effort became apparent, Wellington must instinctively have realised he was on the cusp of victory. His reputation was at stake. The Prussians were on the battlefield in strength, and numbers would now count, bearing in mind that the endurance and emotional reserves of both sides had been drawn on equally. All Wellington had to do was to continue to hold the line. There were no infantry reserves; if the line broke, the outcome would be counted a Prussian rescue.

The French advance was directed at the beat of the drum, shouted commands being inaudible above the din of battle, so the drummer played an crucial role. Drummer boys were not as diminutive as might be expected. He might be a stout teenager, old enough, like Louis Canler with the 28th Line, to serve in the ranks. There was no 'boy's size' for the regulation side drum. His role was not that of mascot, he was a functional member of the regiment. Each company had its own drummer, so there might be five or six with every battalion. They were regarded with affection by the soldiers, who tended to adopt and look after the young ones. Their ages are not generally known, but they were not all boys. In British regiments, such as the 23rd opposing, research has revealed there was only one drummer under 18 years old, but two were over 50 and the oldest – drummer John Leeds – was 62. Under half of those researched were less than 18 when they enlisted.[23]

The drummer boy's *raison d'être* was to communicate his commander's intent, alongside the cornet (or bugle). In the Guard, however, squeaky cornets were the objects of derisive amusement rather than martial inspiration. Boys had to master a litany of different drum rolls: the call, assembly, march, prepare to fire, advance and retreat. Because the drum was heavy and ungainly, in the French army also not all drummers were boys. Those that were, needed to be strong, so puny street urchins were often turned down. Skill was required; a beginner had to master light rhythmic taps that did not clatter on the rim of the drum. His survival prospects were better than for the rest of the soldiers because he generally beat the rhythm from behind the company battle line or from within the square. British drummer casualties at Waterloo were surprisingly light: 2 killed and 26 wounded of the 304 committed. Drummers and musicians assisted in the recovery of the wounded and dead.[24]

No man or boy was safe in the face of a contested advance. This was the culminating point of the battle and would provide the ultimate test of the two sides' capacity for endurance. The advance of the Guard made a huge impression on those that saw it. Napoleon had asked the Guard at the presentation of two new eagles at the Ecole Militaire in Paris shortly before the campaign: 'Will you swear to die in their defence?' Words that likely came to mind as they stepped off. 'And you soldiers of the Imperial Guard,' Napoleon had called out, 'do you swear to surpass yourselves in the coming campaign, and die to a man rather than permit foreigners to dictate to the Fatherland?' '*We swear!*' they had roared. '*Vive l'Empereur!*'

'A hundred and fifty bandsmen marched off at the head of the Guard,' recalled Ney's ADC Levavasseur, 'playing the triumphant marches of the Carrousal.'

They began to climb the slope with shouldered arms. There were no skirmishers ahead, possibly because insufficient men would have been left to effectively form imposing squares. Their significant absence exuded an arrogant confidence that they were not needed. Each square was three men deep with a frontage of 45 men. The superb experience and discipline of these greatcoated warriors advancing in perfectly formed squares, outlined by a phalanx of vertically ported bayonets glinting in the sun, was an emotional boost for the whole French army. Here was the Guard at last! Only ever committed with an assured expectation of victory.

As if to emphasise this flush of martial nationalism, the final rays of the sun played on the white cross-belts and bearskin plumes, accentuating the gorgeous spectacle of Napoleon's final fling. When they entered the smoke zone billowing down from the ridge as Wellington's surviving cannon engaged, colours presciently faded. Whole files of men were shaved off square sides by ball and canister. The cannon fire was decidedly weaker. Gaps quickly filled and the squares retained their precise outlines. To Allied and French onlookers alike, the Guard looked irresistible.

It was an unforgettable moment.

'La Garde Recule!' The Collapse

'I could not watch these brave men without pitying them as most marched to their death,' remembered Major Fée, a doctor's assistant watching from the ambulances with Marcognet's division. 'Indeed their renowned bravery made it duty for them to prove they were the best soldiers in the army.' Others observed that the spoiled 'brats' had at last been committed. Nobody had ever withstood an assault by the Old Guard. Passing the Grande Batterie, Lieutenant Pontécoulant, with the Guard artillery, already firing at the British squares, saw that 'Napoleon's face was sombre and very pale; a weak twilight spread a sad light on everything.' There was about 90 minutes of daylight left. He was aware he was observing an epic part of this battle:

> The artillery salvoes succeeded each other slowly, as at an undertakers, the battalions of the Old Guard climbed silently up the slopes of the plateau: everything seemed in unison in this gloomy picture, worthy of a brush of a grand master.

Napoleon, appreciating this was the make or break moment, attempted to bolster spirits with a white lie. He may have been encouraged by the sound of distant gunfire at Wavre, indicating that Grouchy had at last closed with the Prussian rearguard. 'Here is Grouchy!' Napoleon announced to his assembled troops, and Levavasseur was dispatched to gallop along the line shouting *'Vive l'Empereur!'* and announce the same. Grouchy, everybody was told, was coming in from the right; a risky stratagem. 'The excitement of the soldiers was indescribable,' Levavasseur remembered. 'They all cried, *"En avant! En avant! Vive l'Empereur!"'* The ruse had the desired effect. 'A last cry of hope left the ranks,' Napoleon's secretary Fleury de Chamboulon recalled; 'those wounded who were able took a few more steps forward and returned to the fight.' Seventeen-year-old Ensign Edward Macready, with the 30th Foot opposite, had already identified the crucial factor. It was not about tactics now but rather about who had the 'most bottom' for the killing yet to be endured.[25]

It might have been sensible to hit Wellington's line beyond La Haye Sainte, which Ney had already identified as a weak sector and where the French line was nearest. Instead the Guard turned half left and approached the left centre of the Allied line. It was left to Donzelot's division to attack over the more difficult terrain beyond the farm. There is some debate over whether Napoleon, who in retrospect was to admonish Ney, was aiming to attack obliquely or en masse against the centre. In any event he had directed Ney personally, leaving him just short of La Haye Sainte. Ney, suffering from combat stress at the outset of this campaign, had already had five horses shot from under him in this battle. Moderately surprised to find he still lived, he aimed simply to close with Wellington's line. The difficulty of co-ordinating senior generals leading the squares may have had an effect. They may have detected better opportunities to hit the line, as they were on the spot, or perhaps as senior officers they were less used to directing battalion level assaults. Whatever the reason, the outcome was an uncoordinated attack.

The first wave was composed of the Middle Guard fragmented into three assaults, two with two battalions and another one on its own. This sharply inverted the odds against success at the point of impact. The British lines were never hit with more than 1,000 men, and these assaults came at varying intervals. The French attacked an area covered by three British brigades, formed with 10 battalions, some 5,500 men. Advancing uphill, the French were outnumbered on average by five to one, when they should have been advancing with a conventional superiority of three to one. Napoleon's last-gasp effort was literally just that. There were another 4,000 Allied troops in the near vicinity, further inverting odds to an almost derisory ten to one against. The Imperial Guard had only its fearsome reputation and gallantry to compensate for a decisive numerical shortfall.

The courage of the Guard was legendary. It had never been defeated, and every British soldier up to Wellington himself appreciated that its appearance signified Napoleon's final effort. Willpower would decide the outcome. Although the French were totally outnumbered, this was not apparent to Halkett's brigade as they watched the 1/3rd and 4th Grenadier battalions coming into sight just beneath the ridge line. 'As they rose step by step before us, and crossed the ridge,' recalled Ensign Macready of the 30th Foot, 'their red epaulettes and cross-belts put on over their blue greatcoats, gave them a gigantic appearance.' This was accentuated by their high bearskins nodding perceptibly in time to the drumbeat directing them. 'Now for a clawing,' he muttered. The invincible Imperial Guard was looming up and Macready 'looked for nothing but a bayonet in my body', earnestly hoping 'it might not touch my vitals'.[26] Sergeant Thomas Morris, standing in file with the 73rd to his left, thought the approaching mass 'overwhelming in numbers'. The smoke ahead was so thick that many of the British could not see the Guard, but they could hear them. Seventeen-year-old Ensign William

Leeke heard the steady approach of the ominous drumbeats, *'the rumdum, the rumdum, the rummadum, dumadum, dum dum* followed by a hearty cheer of *"Vive l'Empereur!"'*. Then the drums would restart and the whole sequence would be heard again and again.[27]

Marshal Robert Bugeaud had often fought British infantry in the Peninsula. His memories paint a picture of what the Guard may have felt as they climbed the Mont St Jean ridge. Bugeaud remembered the British had a penchant for occupying 'well chosen defensive positions on rising ground where they showed only part of their men'. French failures against such positions often came from insufficiently studying the ground and the best tactical options before taking 'the bull by the horns'. British coolness under pressure, moreover, was intimidating:

> When about 1,000 yards from the English line our soldiers got agitated and exchanged their thoughts; they hurried their march which began to get disorderly. The silent English, with ordered arms, looked in their impassive stillness, like a long red wall – an imposing spectacle, which never failed to impress the young soldiers.

The Guard was steely, but as Bugeaud pointed out, 'more than one of us noted uneasily that the enemy was very slow to fire'. Clearly they were waiting until the last moment. 'This fire, so long withheld, would when it came be very unpleasant,' he remembered thinking, and as a consequence 'our ardor began to abate'.

A British soldier aiming and firing his musket at an enemy over 100 yards away in battle was going to knock him down on average once in every 30 shots. If the range was reduced to between 50 and 70 yards, the hit rate rose dramatically to one in three. Volley fire below 50 yards was normally devastating. Macready recalled:

> *The enemy halted, carried arms about 40 paces from us, and fired a volley. We returned it, and giving our 'Hurrah!' brought down the bayonets.*

Grenadier Franquin, with the 3rd Grenadiers, recalled that 'the English fired a hail of bullets at us'. Standing and firing in extended lines of over a hundred men, two deep, meant that four times the weight of fire was levelled at the French standing in square, offering an average frontage of only 45 men. Franquin and the grenadiers 'replied as best we could to the fire that made large gaps in our ranks'. His battalion commander Guillemin remembered their hopeless predicament. 'We remained in this position for some time,' having barely arrived on the plateau, 'always losing many men.' French horse artillery was with them and also poured in the fire. To French onlookers, like Cuirassier General Baron Jacques Delort watching from below, it looked as though a violent storm had broken out on the contested ridge. Flashes of lightning appeared to flicker from within the rolling clouds of smoke, and the thunderclaps of cannon created a ferocious din.

At this vulnerable moment an additional Dutch-Belgian artillery battery under Captain Krahmer, directed by the 3rd Netherlands Division commander, rolled on to the ridge line. It started to devastate the two French squares already reduced by intense volley fire opposite Halkett's brigade. 'Our surprise was inexpressible,' declared the previously fearful Macready, 'when pushing through the clearing smoke, we saw the back of the Imperial Grenadiers.' The right-hand element of the first wave had broken. 'Some 9 pounders from the rear of our right poured in grape amongst them,' Macready exuberantly observed, 'and the slaughter was dreadful.' As the smoke began to disperse, the British line saw carcasses heaped upon each other. It was just after 7.30 pm.

Halkett's brigade had charged with the bayonet, stopped, and then fallen back, to see what would happen. Although the French Grenadiers had retired, their supporting horse artillery continued to fire into the retiring British and created a confusion that verged on panic. 'An extraordinary number of men and officers of both regiments [the 30th and 73rd] went down in almost no time,' Macready remembered. In the resulting chaos they intermingled with the 33rd and 69th Regiments to their right. 'A friend knocked up against me, seized me by the stock [collar] and almost choked me, screaming, half maddened by his five wounds and the sad scene going on,' he recalled. 'Is it deep, Mac, is it deep?' he desperately shouted. The screams of those cut down by cannon fire intermingled with wails from the wounded, crying out in despair not to be left behind. Panic seized them all until 'someone hurra'd', Macready remembered, and 'we all joined, and every creature halted'. This worrying crisis lasted no more than five minutes. 'I cannot conceive what the enemy were doing about our confusion,' Macready admitted; 'fifty cuirassiers would have annihilated our brigade.'[28]

Some of Wellington's foreign contingents were similarly rocked by the attacks. He had to intervene personally to steady some of the Brunswick squares, which had been ordered forward to check the Imperial Guard. Colonel Olfermann was told by Wellington to advance three Brunswick battalions over the ridge. 'It was on everybody's mind that heavy canister and infantry fire was awaiting us on the other side,' the colonel recalled. He was right, and 'when entire ranks of the battalions were shot down in quick succession' Olfermann thought he should retire, because 'it was impossible to hold out any longer'. Lieutenant-Colonel August von Herzberg explained that the Brunswick infantry were taken aback at the 'unexpected nearness' of the French:

> *The all enveloping dense clouds of powder smoke, the men's exhaustion, the partial disorder of the still incomplete deployment, and, lastly, the powerful thrust of the attack caused several battalions to hesitate at first and fall back a little.*

Resolve was teetering. Kruse's Nassauers drove back Donzelot's men supporting the right flank of the Guard attack, but just as with Halkett's brigade, another panic developed and they retired in confusion. 'Our young men panicked at the moment of their most splendid victory,' admitted General Kruse, blaming the emotional impact of the wounding of the Prince of Orange; 'the battalion fell into disorder and retreated.' For a moment 'the plateau was then held on both sides only by small bodies of brave men'. Napoleon's cavalry was a spent force and did not appear. The panic on the Mont St Jean ridge in the centre bore mute testimony to the failure of the Guard to hit Wellington's line in a compact mass. Kruse admitted how close they had come to breaking. 'Regrettably,' he acknowledged, 'it was well proven here that in critical moments courage alone will not suffice and that unskilled troops will become victims of their inexperience.' Wellington had good cause to be concerned; numbers appeared not to count on the ridge.[29]

Ten minutes later came the second element of the first wave. Two Middle Guard chasseur battalions, despite punishing artillery fire, crested the ridge, steady in square, drums beating and officers shouting encouragement. They were also puzzled, as Robert Bugeaud has illustrated, by the fact that they had not encountered any infantry fire ahead. Maitland's 1st British Foot Guards were lying down, four deep in line, just behind the dirt road on the crest of the Mont St Jean ridge line. Wellington was on horseback with them, and the officers were standing on the road watching the approach of the chasseurs. 'They continued to advance till within fifty or sixty paces of our front,' recalled Captain Harry Weyland Powell. What followed was one of the iconic moments of the battle. 'Now, Maitland! Now's your time!' Wellington urged, with the French just 25 yards away.

Suddenly over 1,400 infantrymen stood up in line four deep, spread over 250 yards and fired a devastating volley. Count Claude Michel, commanding the 3rd Chasseurs, went down in an instant alongside 20 officers and 200 Imperial Guardsmen, like collapsing dominoes. His ADC remembered they had 'arrived on the plateau and half a musket shot from the motionless waiting English' and 'were received by a dreadful discharge'. 'The effect of our fire seemed to force the head of the column bodily back,' recalled Harry Powell.

The British guardsmen pulled out fresh cartridges from their pouches, always a two-fingered move, in case of an accident that might otherwise blow all their fingers off. They bit the top off the paper cartridge and spat it away. Steely self-control was needed to sprinkle just a few grains of gunpowder into the pan. The musket was then rested on the left foot, with the barrel away from the face, as the whole cartridge with ball was rammed down the barrel. Alternatively, during close-range engagements the butt could be swiftly tapped on the ground, to save time with the ramrod. The cocking lever was immediately pulled back and another shot fired off into the mass of dazed French soldiers. 'In less than a minute above 300 were down,' Powell recalled:

They now wavered, and several of the rear divisions began to draw out as if to deploy, whilst some of the men in their rear beginning to fire over the heads of those in front was evident proof of their confusion.

Twenty per cent of the French square had been swept away at the first volley. Harry Powell recalled that Lord Saltoun shouted out: 'Now's the time my boys!' and Maitland's brigade surged forward with the bayonet. 'La Garde turned and gave up little opportunity of trying this steel,' Powell remembered. The 1/3rd and 2/3rd Chasseurs were pulling back from the slope. However, even this triumphant bayonet charge had to be checked when yet another sinister Guard square loomed out of the smoke to their right. The last part of the first wave, the 4th Chasseurs, were steadily toiling up the steep part of the ridge. There was confusion again as the British Guards hurriedly retired back into line.[30]

Off to the right and facing this new French advance was Ensign William Leeke, with the 1/52nd Regiment. Two yards away from him lay 'a dead tortoise-shell kitten', a poignant reminder of life beyond the battlefield. 'It had been frightened out of Hougoumont, which was the nearest house to us.' The pathetic scene caused him 'to think of my friends at home', a world apart from the bizarre sight of horses grazing around, 'notwithstanding that their legs were shot off'. He vividly recalled that 'peculiar smell' that would forever remind him of the climax of this battle: 'a mingling of the smell of the wheat trodden flat down with the smell of gunpowder'.

Leeke belonged to the strongest battalion in the British army. Lieutenant-Colonel Sir John Colborne's 52nd had begun the day with 1,130 men and still numbered short of 900. It formed the centre of three units in Adam's 3rd Brigade line from the 2nd British Division, and was about to play a pivotal role. The appearance of the 4th Chasseur square of the Middle Guard was an uneasy moment for Wellington. He had no more infantry, the Brunswick and Nassau contingents were wavering, and despite repelling much of the first wave, Halkett's and Maitland's British brigades had exhibited some confusion on recovering from their bayonet charges. Now another seemingly perfectly formed Imperial Guard square was striding up the ridge toward his left centre. 'The Duke was very anxious,' observed Charles Lennox, attached to Wellington's staff, and 'his anxiety was to be seen in his countenance'. It was therefore with some relief and surprise that Wellington saw Colborne's 52nd suddenly emerge from the smoke on the left flank of the advancing 4th Chasseurs.

Colborne, 'without having received any orders from the Duke or any other superior officer', Leeke recalled, 'moved forward the 52nd in quick time'. The head of the French square was still 300 yards short of the ridge summit when the 52nd unexpectedly appeared in line off to its flank, perpendicular to the main Allied line and completely on its own. It was a stunning indictment, by its audacious execution, of the fragmented nature of the Imperial Guard attack. French battle cries of '*Vive l'Empereur!*' were answered 'with three tremendous British cheers', Leeke remembered. The countermove was preceded by the 5th Company acting as skirmishers. The deliberate precision of its execution was intimidating. 'When the left of the regiment was in line with the leading company of the Imperial Guard, it began to mark time,' Leeke recalled. The rest of the 52nd closed up to form a parallel line four deep, which turned and began to pour a concentrated fire into the French square opposite. 'The Imperial Guard halted,' he observed, 'then as many files as possible, on the left of each company of their leading column, faced outwards and returned the fire.'

The French stood their ground with admirable discipline. Lieutenant George Gawler, with the 52nd, saw:

> The enemy was pressing on with shouts, which rose above the noise of the firing, and his fire was so intense that, with but half the ordinary length of front [from one side of the square], at least 150 of the 52nd fell in less than four minutes.[31]

Michel Chevalier, a sous-lieutenant in the Imperial Guard, described what it was like to be under such fire. 'It is difficult to say,' he admitted, 'what I felt seeing my comrades, horses and men knocked head over heels.' The initial reaction was dismay at the sight of 'mutilated' and 'dishevelled' wounded, inducing dread and trembling. Senses became dulled until a form of exasperated aggression, at what was happening to them, came to the fore. 'We hurled ourselves at the enemy, and I no longer felt fear.' Rage and obstinacy took over. 'The blood of a Frenchman was coursing through my veins,' Chevalier insisted, but élan and fervour alone did not always suffice. 'I wanted to knock them all down, to avenge my brothers in arms,' he declared, but it was not to be on the slopes of Mont St Jean. The 4th Chasseurs began to fragment.

Despite the punishing incoming fire, the 52nd did not halt to return it, but continued to volley and reload on the move. Their corps commander, Lord Hill, viewing the unconventional development from the ridge, described it after the event as 'one of the most beautiful advances' he had ever seen. 'As we closed,' Leeke recalled, the Guard's 'leading column at first somewhat receded from us, and then broke and fled'. The rear of the square 'also broke and ran'. For the very first time in its illustrious career the Imperial Guard broke. '*La Garde Recule!*' ('The Guard is retreating!') proved to be the emotional tipping point for the whole of the French army as the cry was taken up. At the same time Detmar's Dutch-Belgians wheeled around the left flank of Halkett's brigade and attacked the retreating French. Lieutenant Frederick Pattison, in line with the 33rd Foot, realised:

> *The fire of the enemy, which had been decimating our ranks ... suddenly relaxed and almost in an instant ceased entirely, so that when the smoke had disappeared, not a man was to be seen except those who were retreating in great disorder and consternation.*[32]

Napoleon's white lie about Grouchy backfired when the repulse of the Guard coincided with the strong arrival of von Ziethen's Prussian I Corps. This struck the apex of the French right flank around Papelotte, and the impact on the outnumbered French troops was little short of catastrophic. Captain Chapuis was with the 85th Line, an experienced unit, which was attempting to shore up this flank. 'I believe that we were not lacking,' he recalled 'and that if success did not crown our efforts, it was because of a lack of something other than courage.' It was numbers. They fell back under fire, having done 'everything that it was humanly possible to do'. As von Ziethen's men began to swamp the battlefield, the rout started around Papelotte. Lieutenant Pontécoulant, with the Guard artillery, saw that:

> *The Prussian cavalry hurled itself into this breach and soon flooded the battlefield, sabering isolated soldiers and making it impossible for us to rally. The news, spread by malevolence or fear, that the Guard, the rock of the army, had been obliged to retire and was partly destroyed, augmented the disorder and the precipitation of the retreat.*

The panic that seized the right communicated itself down the French line. La Haye Sainte was abandoned without a fight. Pontécoulant recalled that 'the crowd became terrified; no description can do it justice'. Threatened by the rapid Prussian surge on their right and the British to their front, this sector of the French line dissolved into mayhem. An officer from Halkett's brigade overlooking the scene saw 'a strange hurly-burly on all sides, firing and shouting, and movement, and it lasted several minutes'. He could not quite identify what was going on. 'Our grey great-coated opponents disappeared as if the ground had swallowed them.'[33]

Plancenoit fell to the Prussians some time between 8 and 8.30 pm. Brigadier-General Jean Pelet withdrew along the road between Plancenoit and Le Caillou farm. 'I rallied only a few men,' he recalled, after they had cut their way out. 'One could not see more than four paces' in the smoke and descending gloom. They were surrounded by what they at first perceived to be French lancers, and 'then I realised they were enemies on which we fell with the bayonet'. Constantly skirmishing in the failing light, they shot at everything, 'without considering if it was for better or for worse'. They had to get out.

Remnants of the Middle Guard's first wave were trying to reorganise in the shelter of the valley floor. 'These valiant and unhappy survivors' had fallen back, Sergeant Hippolyte de Mauduit remembered, 'still in good order, but quivering with rage to the foot of the slope'. Of the 2,900 men he had watched ascend the ridge, 'there hardly remained 700 that were fit to fight'. They had lost 2,200 men killed, wounded and missing in less than 20 minutes. 'They had lost their numerical force,' de Mauduit insisted, 'but not their courage!' Long ragged lines of red-coated infantry were beginning to descend the slope after them. Their situation was untenable.

Looking towards the Belle Alliance ridge, they could see the three squares of the second wave, perfectly formed, but motionless. It looked as though the whole of the French army was milling around them as they sought safety further to the rear. With the dramatic change in the situation, Napoleon had ordered them to provide a screen to try and rally his disintegrating army, before total mayhem reigned.

But it was too late.

CHAPTER 10

The Road to Genappe —●

8.30 pm to Midnight

8.30 pm to 9.30 pm

'Merde!'

As the volume of fire diminished, so did the smoke. For the first time since the beginning of the battle, the dying rays of the sun were able to penetrate some chinks in the artificial eco-atmosphere created by the sulfurous gunpowder emissions below. 'I have seen nothing like that moment,' recalled Lieutenant-Colonel Sir Augustus Frazer, commanding Wellington's horse artillery. 'The sky literally darkened with smoke, the sun just going down, and which till then has not for some hours broken through the gloom of a dull day.' Its ghostly glare irradiated a nightmarish scene. One British officer in Picton's division recalled an unforgettable image of Imperial Guardsmen, looking back as they were driven off the ridge:

> *Some lingering rays of the sun falling on their faces through the smoke now cleared away, threw a lurid kind of glare upon their countenances, and gave them a fierce look, particularly when the gleam from the musketry assisted.*

The cheering and English huzzas that accompanied the almost symbolic appearance of the sun was a memorable moment. Victor Hugo contrasted it with the blood-red image of the sun rising over Austerlitz, the zenith of Napoleon's former glory:

The sky had been overcast all day, but at eight o'clock it
cleared to allow the sinister red light of the setting sun to flood
through the elms on the Nivelle road – the same sun that had
risen at Austerlitz.[1]

Wellington had been forward with the 1/52nd, which having
stopped the final push of the Imperial Guard had pushed
on to the Brussels road beyond La Haye Sainte. 'Well done,
Colborne!' said Wellington to their commander. 'Well
done! Go on, don't give them time to rally.' Their initiative
had begun to roll up the French line on its left as it was
being assailed by the Prussians to the right. Pandemonium
broke out in the French ranks. When Wellington raised his
hat three times to order a general advance, cheering rolled
like a wave along the Allied line. Lieutenant John Kincaid
moved forward of the sandpit with the 95th Rifles, their
bayonets reflecting the dying sunlight. Much to his surprise, on emerging from the smoke they realised 'it was a
fine summer's evening, just before sunset', with the French
in full retreat:

> *To people who had been for so many hours enveloped in dark-*
> *ness, in the midst of destruction, and naturally anxious about*
> *the result of the day, the scene which now met the eye conveyed*
> *a feeling of more exquisite gratification than can be conceived.*

The French appeared to be running in a 'confused mass', the
British were moving forward, while the plain to the left was
filling with Prussians.[2]

Much of the Allied army up on the ridge was incredulous
at the sudden turn of events, having been battered bloody by
the pounding all day. Wellington took a calculated risk ordering a general advance; his army was in poor condition to

331

follow up success. Some on his staff urged caution, but the Duke dismissed misgivings with his famous phrase, 'Oh damn it! In for a penny, in for a pound.' In fact this iconic statement was more characteristic of Napoleon. Carl von Müffling, Wellington's Prussian liaison officer, observed the wreckage of the Allied line move off, as 'small masses of only some hundred men at great intervals, were seen everywhere advancing'. Uxbridge, his cavalry commander, warned of the danger, but Wellington thought his advance well supported by his second line of cavalry. It was a poignant moment. 'The position in which the infantry had fought was marked, as far as the eye could reach,' Müffling observed, 'by a red line, caused by the red uniform of the numerous killed and wounded who lay there.' Uxbridge was right to express concern, for at this moment of victory his leg was shot away by French case shot. The staff had edged too far forward. 'I've lost my leg, Egad!' he exclaimed to Wellington, who simply answered, 'Egad, so you have.'

It was not that Wellington was unsympathetic; rather that he was focusing on whether the French were still resisting. Colborne's audacious move forward with the 1/52nd , followed up by the rest of Adam's brigade, had not been at his initiative. Wellington liked to cultivate the image of the successful gentleman 'player', as his remark 'in for a penny' testified. In reality he was the consummate professional, even if, with his civilian attire, he did not dress like one. His soldiers respected him for it; he was shrewd, calculating and took few chances, particularly with their lives. Müffling, an admirer of the Duke, even if it was not reciprocated, had keenly observed how 'his practised eye, perceived that the French army was no longer dangerous'. Not that the Duke's own infantry were really in a fit state to advance:

But if he stood still, and resigned the pursuit to the Prussian army alone it might appear, in the eyes of Europe, as if the English army had defended themselves bravely indeed, but that the Prussians alone decided and won the battle.[3]

The 'Iron Duke' had been feted for his victories in Paris after Napoleon's abdication in 1814, and he had no intention of forfeiting this pedestal at the moment of his greatest victory. The Prussians were late, but after the psychological impasse imposed by the pounding on the ridge, numbers had counted. Wellington, however, would have this day. It would not be called 'La Belle Alliance', as Blücher would later suggest. It was indeed an Alliance victory, but Wellington would call it Waterloo, his practice being to label battles after his headquarter locations.

Wellington's no longer 'infamous' but certainly ragged army began its advance. John Kincaid recalled that his division had been 5,000 strong at the outset, but 'had gradually dwindled down to a solitary line of skirmishers'. Typically British, he had no illusions about who had carried the day. 'If Lord Wellington had been at the head of his old Peninsula army, I am confident that he would have swept his opponents off the face of the earth immediately after their first attack.' Because of the 'heterogeneous' mix of foreigners under command, 'he was obliged to submit to a longer day'.

The relief, however, was indisputable; the French had turned. Sergeant Thomas Morris, whose 71st Regiment was caught up in the drama of repelling the Imperial Guard, conjectured that 'if the Prussians had not arrived, I would say most decidedly, we could have maintained our ground'. Most British soldiers agreed. His Dutch-Belgian counterpart, Sergeant Johann Doring of the 28th Orange Nassau Regiment, thought otherwise. 'The battle now had ended in a victory that was primarily owed to the Prussians,' he assessed, 'because our army could hardly have held on any longer.' His regiment was at the left of the line and under considerable pressure when the Prussians arrived. Morris did concede that the Prussians decided the outcome.

> *But for their prompt arrival, and vigorous pursuit of the enemy, Napoleon would probably have fallen back to join Grouchy.*[4]

The Allied advance soon swamped the far left square of the Imperial Guard's second wave near Hougoumont, trying to cover the rout. They never broke, withdrawing towards La Belle Alliance under Allied infantry and cavalry attacks and swept by canister. Beginning with 580 men, manning a square three deep, they kept moving, shedding human debris the whole way, until they arrived in the vicinity of the inn reduced to a small triangle of two ranks. Sergeant de Mauduit watched as Belcourt their commander re-dressed the ranks 'as each salvo opened a gap, firing at hardly a quarter range', striking down 150 men. After a final defiant volley they were ordered to break up into groups and make their way to Rossomme.

Cambrone's 2/1st Chasseurs did not make it. Reduced to less than 200 men, they were called upon to surrender. '*Merde!*' ('Shit!') was the response from General Count Pierre Cambrone, their roughly spoken commander. The square was reduced with cannon and Cambrone taken prisoner. Coming in from their right was the last of the 1st and 2nd Chasseurs, painfully extricating themselves from Plancenoit. Among them was Captain Lambert de Stuers. 'Everything went badly,' he recalled. 'The march was extremely difficult because of the soaked ground, the trampled corn and a slippery slope.' English cavalry overran his square, 'mistaken in the darkness for French fugitives'.

Just two rocks remained, around which the torrent of panicked fugitives flowed, making no impression. These were the last two Old Guard squares of the 1st and 2nd Grenadiers, 1,200 'old moustaches', each with an average of 20 to 25 campaigns under his belt. They remained immobile, dressed in regulation pattern half-belted overcoats with blue trousers and high bearskins; these were the 'old grumblers' who had shared exile with Napoleon at Elba. The 1st Battalion protected the Regimental Grenadier Eagle, and for a time the Emperor himself. Both squares were bursting with dozens of generals, staff officers, musicians and refugee soldiers; so much so that the sides of the square were packed as many as ten deep. Brigadier Petit, commanding the 1st Grenadiers, ordered his men to fire on the 'torrent of fugitives' and enemy chasing them 'to prevent throwing the squares into disorder'. Overcoming any inhibitions, the Guard volleyed into the approaching masses; as Petit later admitted 'it was a necessary evil to prevent a greater one'.[5]

'Everything was fleeing as fast and as far as possible,' wrote Lieutenant Jacques Martin later. He had survived being ridden down by British cavalry during d'Erlon's early afternoon assault. 'I did the same as everyone else,' he remembered, retreating towards Genappe on the Brussels road, as the French army disintegrated:

> There was nothing more than a confused mass of infantry soldiers, cavalry and guns that rushed, all mixed together, across the plain like an unstoppable torrent.

Darting in and out of this mass, pushed by the hurrahing English infantry behind, were squadrons of Prussian hussars, sabering everyone in sight. Martin glanced across to La Belle Alliance, where several squares of the Guard stood alone, 'immobile as rocks in a raging sea'. He watched as 'crowds of fugitives passed between the squares', until 'soon only the enemy surrounded them'.

Many of the fugitives owed their lives to the steadiness of these squares. Captain Chapuis, with the 85th Line, had been hit several times trying to hold back the Prussians. 'I owed my survival only to the lively fusillade of a battalion of the Imperial Guard,' he recalled, 'that stopped the charge in the middle of which I found myself.' In reality the Allied advance was little better co-ordinated than the French retreat. Major Rigau, with the 2nd Dragoons, argued that some accounts of the disorder were exaggerated. 'The enemy were so surprised by their success,' he later wrote, 'that in their pursuit they only attacked the soldiers in disorder on the plain immediately to the left and right of the road.' Troops boldly marching in between, that aggressively fronted up at the approach of Allied cavalry, bluffed their way through. Captain A Barton, with the 12th Light Dragoons, came across a dense column of Imperial Guard cavalry, who simply ignored their approach, apart from fending them off with a few pistol and carbine shots. Barton and his men were not numerous enough to make an impression and watched as 'they literally walked from the field in a most majestic manner'.[6]

Nevertheless, it was a rash man that underestimated the Guard, who could be lethal even in retreat. Major Frederick Howard attacked an Old Guard square a hundred yards west of La Belle Alliance with the 10th Hussars, unsupported by infantry. The Hussars closed and hacked at the bayonets and made absolutely no headway. Howard was shot through the mouth and toppled from his horse. As soon as he was down, a French Guardsman stepped from the square and unemotionally stoved his head in with a musket butt, then promptly returned to the ranks. Captain Henry Grove, with the 23rd Light Dragoons, had briefly nodded to Howard when they were about to charge, 'within a few minutes of which he was killed'. 'A very fine, handsome fellow he was,' Grove recalled, and left a widow, 'but he evidently looked as if his time was come.' Lieutenant-Colonel Murray, with the 18th Hussars, had a healthy regard for the 'coolness and countenance' of solitary Guardsmen on the retreat. There was 'none of that hurry and confusion that might be imagined when thus suddenly ridden in upon', he remembered. One nearly bayoneted him as he passed.[7]

Falling back from Hougoumont, Lieutenant Puvis of the 93rd Line pushed his men to reach the Brussels road quickly at the point they had left it, with such high expectations, nine hours before. The ranks had started to come apart to get there faster, and he recalled 'there was terrible disorder', but they pressed on, thinking this was only a partial withdrawal on their part of the line. 'We could see over on our right deep masses marching ahead' so were slightly reassured. The Brussels road emerged in the failing light, but 'instead of the security that we expected, we were received by a volley from the Prussian army that had arrived on our rear.' Pandemonium broke out. 'From this moment ranks broke up and we threw ourselves in disorder across the countryside, where we fell into each other in our desperation.'

Sergeant-Major Lerréguy de Civrieux in the same regiment remembers this dispersal of the II Corps on the French left in front of Hougoumont. 'Cries of *"Sauve qui peut! A la trahison!"* were heard.' It was the end; 'all discipline disappeared; the regiments fell into inexpressible disorder,' raked all the while by cannon, which ploughed grisly channels through their massed ranks. Light was fading at eight o'clock, leaving just 55 minutes before sunset. These formations dispersing in the failing light were eerily lit by flashes of cannon fire, amid the increasingly distant stuttering of volley fire from the still intact Imperial Guard squares falling back on Rossomme.[8]

Back at the Hougoumont farm complex, Private Mathew Clay of the 3rd Foot Guards had time to reflect on what had happened. He had spent the afternoon defending a cannon breach overlooking the gateway. 'The shattered fragments of the wall,' he observed, were 'mixed up with the bodies of our dead countrymen.' The shooting had died down and they became aware for the first time that the fires, 'unnoticed by us in the eagerness of the conflict', had totally gutted many of the buildings behind them. As it grew dark he took out the remaining portion of pig's head from his haversack, left over from a hasty breakfast that morning. Taking advantage of 'a clear glowing fire rising from the ruins of a stable', he started to roast it, savouring the smell, before he realised 'the glow of fire arose from the half consumed body of some party who had fallen in the contest'. His unappetising left-overs had 'become much more so', he confessed, 'by its re-dressing'.[9]

All along the Allied line, men who had been measuring life expectancy in minutes, now realised that maybe a whole new future beckoned. 'As the brigade advanced,' remembered Lieutenant Frederick Hope Pattison, with the 33rd Foot, with 'my step so elastic and my heart so joyous' he felt 'as if treading on air'. As the fighting died down he engaged in animated conversation with a small group of officers discussing future prospects. Major Chalmers, who he knew had commanded the 30th for a brief period during the battle, 'was in high spirits', believing 'he would, no doubt, be gazetted Lieutenant Colonel at once'. Everyone was effusive in their congratulations and did not at first notice 'some desultory firing going on in front'. A few musket balls whistled past and Pattison left the group to investigate. French skirmishers were still shooting at the brigade. One shot whizzed closely by his ear, causing him to involuntarily spin round in time to see:

> ... *poor Chalmers leave his friends, advance towards me, put his hand to his breast, lay himself down close to me and immediately expire.*

Chalmers was the last of their officers to be killed at Waterloo, because as Pattison reflected, 'the destroying angel had now stayed his arm and sheathed his sword'.[10]

Promotion prospects had also dramatically changed in the ranks of the 27th Inniskillings. When Lieutenant John Kincaid with the 95th Rifles began his advance from the sandpit next to the Brussels road he turned back to see 'the twenty-seventh regiment were lying literally dead in square, a few yards behind us'. Only a ragged remnant got up at about 8.30 pm to pursue the French beyond La Haye Sainte, leaving 480 of its 698 men lying prone, forming a skeletal scarlet-red square. Sixteen of the 19 officers at Waterloo were killed or wounded, many hit several times. Honour had kept the officers in place, and the men too had stood, rather than accept the loss of face in front of their mates.

That these men were human is proved by the circumstantial evidence provided by the regimental rolls. Three officers were left untouched but never wrote about their traumatic experiences. Major John Hare, the acting commanding officer, got the promotion to lieutenant-colonel he deserved and hoped for at Waterloo. It was confirmed by his formal assumption of regimental command ten years later. One day he would be a general. Captain John Tucker, the third most senior Inniskilling officer, was cashiered weeks after the battle for 'scandalous and infamous conduct'. He was accused of stealing two horses and breaking into the baggage of one of his brother officers killed at Waterloo. Two private soldiers that survived, Mathew Dunnegen and James Brennon, both former labourers, were executed by order of a general court-martial one year later. This was in a camp outside Paris after the war had ended. Neither the crime nor the method of execution is recorded. William Faithful Fortescue, who really needed advancement to support his wife and five children, never got it; he had been shot through the chest and arm and left with a degenerative lung condition. Unable to afford retirement on his lieutenant's half-pay, he stayed on the active list, until succumbing to his old injuries six years later. The 66 per cent casualty figure of the 27th Inniskillings was the worst of any Allied unit that day.[11]

Veteran Major Arthur Rowley Heyland, commanding the 40th Regiment, had written to his wife Mary, the day before the battle, 'I cannot help thinking it almost impossible I should escape wounds or death.' His close shaves during the Peninsula campaign had convinced him of this. The 40th had stood for hours just behind the Inniskillings, enduring punishing fire. According to Sergeant William Lawrence they lost 300 men. When Wellington signalled the general advance, the regiment crossed the Mont St Jean crest line and descended on La Haye Sainte below. 'We gave three cheers and set off full of fresh vigour,' recalled Lawrence, and Heyland strode confidently ahead on foot, hatless and with no sword in hand. He was struck in the neck by a musket ball and immediately killed. He was the same age, thirty-four, as his pregnant wife Mary.[12]

'All I had suffered was a scratch on the face,' Sergeant Lawrence revealed. Some powder, blown from the pan of an over-primed musket fired off next to him, hit him on the face and made him 'dance without a fiddle for a while'. When darkness came, the 40th encamped on the former French positions. 'There never was a more hungry and tired tribe of men than us,' Lawrence remembered.

Fate continued to intervene cruelly, even on the settled battlefield. Private Rouse in Lawrence's company had started to cut wood from a French powder wagon to build a fire on the sodden ground. Sawing through a metal nail created a spark that exploded the powder remaining in the wagon. From some distance away John Kincaid saw this massive explosion propelling 'two poor fellows about 20 or 30 feet up in the air' – a horrible spectacle:

On falling to the ground, though lying on their backs or bellies, some extraordinary effort of nature caused by the agony of the moment, made them spring from that position, five or six times to the height of 8 or 10 feet, just as a fish does when thrown on the ground after being newly caught.

Rouse was still alive and able to speak when Lawrence got to him, although 'everything had been blown from him except one of his shoes'. He was scorched black. 'He said what a fool he was, and cursed his eyes,' Lawrence recalled, 'even though they were both gone.' He staggered off to be transported to Brussels, where 'he died a few days later, raving mad'.[13] The battlefield was crackling and stuttering with occasional reports in the distance, like the dying embers of a wood fire, as the violence abated.

9.30 pm to 10.30 pm

'A Thousand Shall Fall'

Major Harry Smith, with the 95th Rifles, had survived. They had fought over the Lord's Day, a Sunday, when they should all have been at church. Reflecting on the irony, he was reminded of the seventh verse of the 91st Psalm:

> *A thousand shall fall beside thee,*
> *and ten thousand at they right hand,*
> *but it shall not come nigh thee.*

The figures were even worse than in the psalm. As the sounds of cannon and the rattle of muskets receded into the distance, a new and more disturbing noise became apparent. This was the whimpering and groaning of the wounded and dying, punctuated by noises that sounded neither human nor animal. About 180,000 men had crisscrossed this bleak area of three square miles to fight one of the costliest battles in Western Europe, leaving one in four of the men and thousands of dead horses behind. They had fallen at the rate of 90 men per minute since the battle began at 11.30 that morning, carpeting the Mont St Jean ridge and plateau with 54,000 bodies. Sergeant Johann Doring, with the 28th Orange Nassau Regiment, passed the last building in Waterloo village, which was a barn being used as a dressing station. It reminded him of a 'slaughterhouse', an area 'full of amputated arms and legs, some still with parts of uniforms, and the surgeons, with rolled up sleeves like butchers, still busy at work'.

The fallen had been subjected to three types of injury. Heavy blunt macerating or avulsing wounds came from cannon round shot. Low-velocity gunshot wounds were inflicted by musket balls, which frequently deformed or fragmented on impact. Others received cutting and piercing injuries from lance, sword, bayonet and pike. Head and neck wounds were mostly from musket balls and sabre slashes. These caused paralysis, sensory impairment and tissue damage, recognised but little understood. Many torsos had visceral glancing wounds, rib fractures and spinal injuries. Abdominal wounds were generally fatal. Most surgical intervention dealt with limbs, because head and trunk wounds were often mortal or untreatable. Up to 2,000 or 3,000 limbs were amputated after this battle. Doctors reasoned that removal was the only certain cure, because infection was endemic and soon became untreatable. Primary amputations were often 30 per cent fatal, but secondary operations, if infection set in, cost 45 per cent. A good surgeon could take an arm off in a minute and a leg in two. Ten minutes was considered bad and often fatal because speed was essential to offset the shock that came with agonising pain. In all about 9 per cent, or almost one man in ten, died from his wounds.[14]

By modern standards the quality and quantity of nineteenth-century battlefield medical aid was primitive and inadequate. Each British battalion at Waterloo was assigned just one surgeon and two assistant surgeons, responsible for about 800 men. Training was limited and variable. Assistant surgeons might have no qualifications at all. Only a passing acquaintance with medical matters was required when family connections or patronage secured such an appointment. The Inniskillings at Waterloo did not have a surgeon and faced losses of almost seven out of every ten men with just two assistants, who at least had some experience. Surgeons and assistants provided their own instruments. The list of 32 tools required by surgeons included an amputating saw, 24 needles, bullet forceps, six tourniquets, a trephine and 'one strong knippers for bones'. Assistants only had to have 13 different items, such as scissors, needles and probes.[15]

Getting the wounded to the few available surgeons was problematical. It was to take more than a week to clear the battlefield, and no Frenchmen were brought in before the fourth day. Private Thomas Hasker, with the 1st King's Dragoon Guards, was sabered, lanced and bayoneted at two o'clock in the afternoon on the plain beyond the Mont St Jean ridge. 'I lay till night,' he recalled, 'the British army marching, some near me, and some over me, in pursuit of the French.' He was still there the next day when some British soldiers picked him up in a blanket. 'Pray to God, comrade, pray to God, comrade,' they advised on seeing his wounds and appreciating the treatment that would follow.

Lieutenant-Colonel Frederick Ponsonby, who commanded the 12th Light Dragoons, was sabered from his horse, then speared by a passing lancer who indignantly declared, 'You are not dead, knave.' 'The blood gushed into my mouth, a difficulty of breathing came on and I thought all was over,' Ponsonby recalled. He was tugged about and his waistcoat torn open and plundered, but a sympathetic French officer did give him a sip of brandy. He was next used as a makeshift firing platform by a French skirmisher, who gaily chatted with him while shooting until he moved on. Many of the wounded and dead around him were repeatedly struck by near-miss cannonballs, showering him in mud. At dusk two squadrons of Prussian cavalry rode over him, 'in full trot, lifting me from the ground and tumbling me about cruelly', he remembered. 'The clatter of their approach, and the apprehensions it excited, may be easily conceived.' If they had been towing cannon, the wheels 'would have done for me'. As night fell, a soldier from the Royals crawling over his legs in agony caused even more anxiety. 'His weight, convulsive motions, his noises, and the air issuing through a wind in his side, distressed me greatly.' He had a wound like his own, one of seven.

Plunder was the only way a nineteenth-century soldier could make his occupation pay. As a result every wounded man on the battlefield, when approached, would be in fear of a looter's knife. The dead were easy meat, whereas the wounded could be a nuisance, normally settled by a quick slash across the windpipe or thrust with the bayonet. Ponsonby was understandably alarmed when before midnight he was found by a wandering Prussian. Speaking little German, Ponsonby tried to signal that he had already been robbed; 'he did not desist, however, and pulled me about roughly before he left me'.[16]

Not all those scouring the battlefield were predators. Hundreds of anxious wives, friends and children poured onto the muddy field to search for their loved ones. At its densest point, there were 35,000 wounded lying strewn in an area of two and a half square miles. The dead were heaped as many as four high in places. Private Daniel Gale's wife Mary, with the 3/95th Rifles, had already spent a torrid day with her five-year-old daughter Elizabeth, helping the wounded around the Mont St Jean farm, which was being used as a dressing station. Around 6,000 patients were carried or stumbled their way to this site alone. Mary and her daughter passed out water from the well, bandaged, applied slings, adjusted splints and dressings and eased the wounded into more comfortable positions. Later Elizabeth would vividly recall her mother lifting a cloth from a dead soldier's face; the way his vacant eyes stared at nothing terrified her. Thirst was the main problem, despite rain the night before. There were pitifully few wells. Terror and adrenalin had dried their mouths, and biting off gunpowder cartridges had begrimed and parched throats. Dehydration and shock were finishing off many of the sufferers, and the girls were instructed to squeeze water into their parched mouths.

The battlefield was not the place for five-year-old children. Elizabeth had a friend called Barbara, the same age, whose father was also in the regiment.[17] They worriedly searched for their dads. Daniel Gale had enlisted two years before and was in Captain Fullerton's company at Waterloo, deployed behind the château of Hougoumont. Fifty-one men had fallen from this contingent of about 200, and Mary Gale was to discover with some relief that Daniel was not amongst them. He was alive and untouched. Barbara's mother searched on for her husband, sitting atop a wagon that was driven onto the field. He was found mortally wounded, before poignantly passing away with his head in his wife's lap. The future was immediately bleak for Barbara's family; with a surfeit of widows in the regiment, who would look after them now?

The wives likewise scoured the human debris around the ruined 27th Inniskilling square, just off the Brussels road. Captain John Tucker's wife came forward from the regimental baggage just to the rear and found her husband. He had been struck in the leg and was retrieved and taken to a safe place. She then discovered that her brother, Ensign Thomas Smith, also with the regiment, had been severely injured, so back she went again to the ghastly square. Both recovered, and 56 years later Thomas Smith was to attain the rank of lieutenant-general. Tucker, by contrast, was cashiered from the regiment within a few weeks, for stealing from brother officers.[18]

10.30 pm to midnight

On the Road to Genappe

Only 24 hours earlier the French had been chasing the Allies along the Genappe road; now they were streaming back in the gloom, defeated. There were three categories of people on the road that night, moving south: the French fleeing, the Allies and Prussians pursuing, and prisoners of war caught up between. Sergeant Archibald Johnson, with the Scots Greys, described the detritus the traffic left behind:

> All the road along was covered with the slain, bruised in a shocking manner by the wheels of the guns and other warlike vehicles on the retreat of the French army on that road; numbers were actually crushed as flat as a piece of plank and it would have been difficult for any man to distinguish whether they were human or not without a minute inspection; the road was also choked full of guns and ammunition wagons which the enemy left behind them.[19]

The captured Ensign Wheatley with the King's German Legion recalled:

> On reaching the high road I saw a foot soldier in a strange attitude. His head, his hands and knees, bent up to his chest, were forced into the mud and he looked like a frog thrusting itself into the slimy puddle. Shocking!

'Allons! Marche!' he was ordered, and made his way along the Genappe road with crowds of French infantry either side. 'The roads and ditches were crammed with groaning wounded,' he remembered. Mishandled and robbed en route, Wheatley entered Genappe at about 9 pm, and dimly perceived the outline of the small town, 'where the day before I was free as air'. Circumstances had changed; now he was a 'bruised captive, exposed to insults and [the] bravado of thousands of intoxicated insolent enemies'. Alongside him rode a wounded French foot-soldier, ghastly pale, dangling a shattered leg that 'hung down by one single piece of sinew, splashing his horse with gore and marrow'. The man was chewing on dry biscuit to allay his thirst. 'Voilà, un français!'

an officer indicated, 'proud of the fellow's fortitude, not envious of his situation'. Threatened and abused, Wheatley was not permitted to drink, and all around were the wounded, overflowing into the side streets. An injured French infantryman was leaning against a garden wall with his 'head back and both his eyeballs hanging on his cheeks'. A musket ball had passed clean through his head, in one side and out the other:

> *His mouth was open, stiff and clotted, clear blood oozed out of his ears and the purulent matter from his empty sockets emitted a pale stream from the vital heat opposed to the evening cold.*

'So much for honour!' Wheatley reflected and asked himself: 'Will it replace his orbs? No.'

As the ragged column moved out of Genappe, he considered escape. It was getting dark and discipline was evaporating. He sensed this was a defeated army; 'I instantly knew the day was ours by the hurry and tumult visible,' he recalled. Desperate for a drink, he managed to dip his cap into some tubs they passed, which turned out to be brandy. Rendered virtually insensible, he then had his shoes stolen by his captors, who prodded him along barefoot at the point of a bayonet. Before long they passed over a plain strewn with naked bodies, which at least brought some temporary relief to his feet, 'treading on through soft-jellied lumps of inanimate flesh'. This was Ligny, Napoleon's campaign high point two days before. At length, his guards led him off into a field at the side of the road and they all sat down, dejected and exhausted.

Friedrich Lindau, captured at La Haye Sainte when the King's German Legion garrison was overrun, had been held back with a group of prisoners for an hour or so just behind the French line. He too could detect the defeatism in the French rear. 'Even in our sad situation,' he recalled, 'we felt an indescribable joy and communicated it by exchanging glad looks with shining eyes.' He whispered to his companion, 'Were we now a hundred armed men, we could take the whole army prisoner.' When it grew dark the French shut them up in a barn. 'Scarcely were we in there than French infantry, fleeing troops with no discipline or order, burst open the door and began to rob us.' They escaped in the confusion.[20]

At about 9.30 pm, Wellington was riding through the darkness just south of the Belle Alliance inn when he saw a large party of horsemen, surrounded by crowds of Prussian infantry, moving towards the Brussels road. They were coming from the northeast and likely to be Blücher and his staff, so he turned aside to meet them. *'Mein lieber Kamerad, quelle affaire!'* Blücher was allegedly heard to say as he embraced the embarrassed Wellington, unaccustomed to such demonstrations. The Duke was later to joke that these were the only two words of French that the Prussian commander knew. There was a brief conversation, in which Blücher suggested calling the battle La Belle Alliance, 'the fine alliance', after the inn. Wellington remained stony-faced. The pursuit was handed over to the Prussians. Wellington's badly mauled army was in no condition to follow up. Honour for posterity had been maintained by reaching Rossomme before the Prussians. The two leaders shook hands and separated. The meeting lasted just ten minutes. Wellington turned back to plod across the battlefield to his headquarters.

He was deeply depressed and emotionally shocked at the carnage around him. Handing the pursuit over to Blücher had released at a stroke all the tension and weight of responsibility he had endured since leaving the Duchess of Richmond's ball at Brussels three nights before. For the first time he had emotional space for human thoughts and reactions. This has similarly been the experience of coalition leaders in recent times on completing challenging multinational operations. They become introspective and withdrawn, painstakingly considering if they have done the right thing, and enough to maintain professional reputations.[21] Wellington was already mentally preparing the dispatch he would shortly be sending. But as he was obliged to skirt the Brussels road, littered with bodies and wrecked cannon, he was reminded of his own personal losses.

Wellington had remarkably escaped unscathed, despite personally intervening at every crisis point in the battle. His actions had cost his staff dearly. All of his favourites were dead. William de Lancey, who headed his quartermaster's department, and whom he urgently needed now, had been struck in the back by a glancing cannon shot, that had separated his ribs from his backbone. Two of de Lancey's deputies were wounded, leaving only one senior surviving officer in this staff section. Sir Alexander Gordon, Wellington's closest aide-de-camp, was mortally wounded, with already one leg amputated, lying at his headquarters. A whole succession of generals, men with whom he had campaigned for years in the Peninsula, had been carried off the field in a melancholy succession throughout the day. Generals Picton, Ponsonby, Du Plat and van Merlen were dead, as well as Colonel Ompteda. Uxbridge, his cavalry commander, had been hit an hour before, and generals Cooke, Kempt, Pack, Grant, Dornberg, Adam, Bijlandt, Kielmansegge and Colin Halkett were all wounded. Virtually every senior officer of consequence that had mastered a crisis that day was down.

Napoleon, sombre and seemingly impassive, was observing the collapse of his army streaming south along the Genappe road. His mind was racing. The small town of

Genappe, astride the Dyle river, was about two and a half miles behind La Belle Alliance. The single narrow bridge across the river had made it an ideal place to fight a rearguard action the day before, and Napoleon was hoping to achieve the same again, and rally the French behind a rearguard in its narrow streets.

As military commander his options were fast waning. His mind was already probing his political future as head of state. He had to get to Paris. What of Grouchy at Wavre? He was already cut off behind the advance of the Allied armies. 'The loss of time is irreparable in war,' he had written to his brother Joseph nine years before in 1806. 'The reasons that one pleads are always bad since operations do not lack delays.'[22] Opportunities had been missed. Because he had not pursued Blücher's army to the death after Ligny, it was facing him again. Likewise Wellington had stolen a march on him after Quatre-Bras. Time for Napoleon was now fast running out.

Sergeant Hippoloyte de Mauduit remembered approaching Genappe and the rush of fugitives toward their square once the drummers had beat out 'La Grenadière' to gather the troops. So close was the English and Prussian cavalry 'that a great number could not reach us, and were massacred just a few yards from our square!' He was to be haunted by the sounds and images of a 12-pounder battery from the Guard 'sabered without pity by these squadrons', distressing 'because of the impossibility of taking a single step to support them'. They disappeared beneath a welter of barging horses and flashing sabre blades amid cries of 'No quarter! No quarter!'

The Guard continued to maintain discipline and hold itself together throughout the retreat. Moving through fields alongside the road, they had to endure Prussian fire directed from the shadowy hedgerows. Many soldiers were felled, killed and wounded. 'We could not see them,' de Mauduit remembered, 'and we fell without knowing where the blows were coming from.' No eagles were lost. Along the road was the pitiful trail of a 'multitude of wounded'. Many simply lay down, overwhelmed by fatigue and loss of blood. Past memories of English prison hulks, and the certainty of what would transpire if the Prussian Uhlans caught up with them, caused the despairing to blow out their brains by the roadside.

Way ahead of de Mauduit's 1st Grenadier Guard column was Lieutenant Jacques Martin. The 45th Line had long since dispersed when he personally reached the outskirts of Genappe, 'where it was difficult to move forward, such was the disorder and obstacles on the road'. A complete log-jam had developed on the road, insidiously promoting panic and preventing the establishment of the vital rallying point Napoleon sought. Martin witnessed:

> … the mayhem of vehicles of all types, guns and artillery caissons, still mounted cavalry, all attempting to force a passage through the middle of a dense crowd of fugitives and wounded, who were thrown down and crushed in the mud.

Men shouted, swore and lashed out with sabres to get through. 'Even shots were exchanged,' Martin recalled, 'as if a new battle was being fought amongst the unhappy debris of our army.' More and more fleeing troops were backing up and plunging into disorder and chaos, impelled by the merciless Prussians coming up behind.[23]

'Wellington was almost beaten when we arrived, and we decided that great day,' claimed volunteer Henri Nieman, riding with the 6th Prussian Uhlan Regiment. 'At about nine o'clock in the evening the battlefield was almost cleared of the French army,' he remembered:

> It was an evening no pen is able to picture: the surrounding villages yet in flames, the lamentations of the wounded of both armies, the singing for joy; no one is able to describe nor find a name to give to those horrible scenes.

Darkness had fallen. The evening was 'as lovely a one as I ever remember, here and there, a burning homestead', remembered Lieutenant von Reuter, following up with the 6th Artillery Battery, part of von Ziethen's I Corps. They had to watch out for the wounded on the road, who desperately cried out and 'holding up their hands entreated us, some in French and some in English, not to crush their already mangled bodies beneath our wheels'.[24]

The Prussian infantry, inspired by their victory and the desire for revenge, were as exhausted as the French. Their cavalry took up the chase, which resembled a bloodthirsty hunt. Lieutenant Basil Jackson, on Wellington's staff, was swept up in this frenetic vanguard as it cleared La Belle Alliance. He considered himself lucky to be able to pause amid the security of the advancing 1/52nd Regiment, because he 'really thought myself in considerable danger of being shot'. 'As to the unhappy Frenchmen who lay about wounded,' he observed, 'they met with no mercy.' Gneisenau, Blücher's chief of staff, was enjoying 'the finest night of my life'. This was not just revenge for Ligny, but for the whole calamitous course of Prussian fortunes since their disastrous defeat at Jena back in 1806. Gneisenau's remodelled Prussian army was punishing the French with the same relentless fury that the French had shown them throughout the night after Jena.

The Prussian vanguard was hardly numerous. Gneisenau had mounted one of his exhausted infantry drummer boys on a horse, which had kept him up with the head of the pursuing Prussian cavalry. 'It was moonlight, which greatly favoured the pursuit,' he recalled, 'a continuous chase, either in the cornfields or the houses.' Once the French made one of their few desultory stands, this was the cue for the mobile drummer to be brought forward:

> As soon as they heard the beating of our drums, or the sound of the trumpet, they either fled or threw themselves into the houses, where they were cut down or made prisoners.

'Mere detachments pushed before them whole battalions,' recalled Major-General von Pirch, commanding the Prussian II Corps, which had been badly mauled at Ligny. 'Our dead of the battle of 16 June demanded victims.' The Prussian infantry, many of whom had been marching and fighting non-stop for over 20 hours, across 30 miles of ground, began to fall behind. Gneisenau continued to bluff his way with cavalry vanguards. The closer they got to Genappe, the greater the panic and congestion in the narrow streets and at the bottleneck entrance to the bridge.[25]

French Major Lemonnier-Delafosse likened the 'hideous sight' of Genappe to the aftermath of a flood wave that had cascaded through the high street. 'A torrent of water, descending mountains and uprooting every momentary obstacle, is a weak image,' he explained 'of this heap of men, horses and wagons.' Any semblance of discipline had gone completely. Men 'were tumbling over each other, gathering before the slightest obstacle to form a mass to knock over everything on the road it was opening for itself'. If anyone fell in this morass 'he was crushed, lost!'

Napoleon had now completely lost control of his battle. Colonel Octave Levavasseur, Ney's aide-de-camp, was astonished to come across the total block of vehicles clogging the streets, 'to the point where it was impossible to pass them in the roads'. To get past 'the soldiers were obliged to crawl under the wagons to effect a passage'. Retreating cavalry units began to ride around the town.[26] Napoleon abandoned his Goeting Easy Carriage on the road, well before Genappe. This remarkable light carriage, weather-proof, manoeuvrable and highly stable, was used by Napoleon and his chief of staff as a mobile command post. It was admirably equipped for this role, with a lockable cabinet with a leaf, which could be pulled out to make a writing desk, complete with drawers. Napoleon's seat could be converted into a bed and it was replete with all the toiletry necessities, down to a silver chronometer mounted on the wall. Secured inside were the Emperor's diamonds, brought from Paris.

Lieutenant Golz, with the Brandenburg Uhlans, came across a convoy of six carriages jam-packed along the main street of Genappe. Each was harnessed to six or eight good horses. Fleury de Chaboulon, the Emperor's secretary, recalled that 'the treasure was at the head of the convoy and I was in the next carriage'. The Uhlans fell on the vehicles. 'The following five were attacked and the drivers sabered,' de Chaboulon remembered; 'we managed to escape by a miracle'. Most of the French soldiers nearby had discarded their weapons, but for a few canny veterans. 'They were still massacred without pity,' Napoleon's secretary observed.

Golz's Uhlans dismounted to squeeze around the vehicles, 'and no doubt several of the troopers of the squadron took the opportunity to help themselves to some of the contents.' They had to continue the pursuit and 'could not spend long there even though it would have been worth their while.'

Without realising it, they had captured the Imperial baggage train, 'and Napoleon's own carriage, with all his treasures, was among them'.

Following behind was the 15th Fusilier Regiment, which had suffered particularly heavy casualties in Plancenoit. They had more time. Major von Keller, who commanded the battalion, claimed the easy carriage as his prize. When he broke open Napoleon's secured box inside, he discovered a wealth of diamonds. Von Keller was to profit enormously from his prize, making a lot of money by selling the stones to a London dealer. Some were presented to King Frederick William of Prussia, to be incorporated into the crown jewels. The regiment received the King's thanks and Keller was awarded the Pour le Mérite with oak leaves. The next day soldiers were seen crawling on their knees, painstakingly sifting the mud for any diamonds that might have been missed. Von Keller was to exhibit Napoleon's carriage back in his hometown at Düsseldorf. He then sold it on to the British government for the tidy sum of £2,500. It changed hands a number of times before being exhibited at Madame Tussauds of London in 1842, where it remained until accidentally destroyed by fire in 1925.[27]

Any hope that Napoleon might have had of rallying his army behind Genappe was dashed with the approach of midnight. 'The Emperor tried to establish some kind of order among the retreating troops,' remembered Captain Jean-Roch Coignet, with the Imperial Guard, but his efforts were in vain. Frenchmen from all units literally fought their way along the street at Genappe to get out, 'flying before the Prussian cavalry', Coignet remembered, 'which hurrah'd continually in rear of them'. It was over. 'The one thought uppermost in the minds of all was to get across the little bridge,' he explained, 'nothing could stand in the way of them'.

Many veterans seem able to remember where they were and what they were doing at midnight after Waterloo. Sergeant de Mauduit's 1st Grenadier column had begun to move left off the road to bypass Genappe. 'Once you had got into the press,' he observed, 'it would have been impossible to get out and you would have been dragged along despite your efforts.' The column dispersed into groups several hundred strong, which randomly set off down the tracks they judged parallel to the main road, heading for Charleroi. 'Hardly had we covered a mile from the town than we heard midnight sound,' de Mauduit dolefully remembered. Napoleon's army was fragmenting. 'It was midnight and no voice could make itself heard above the tumult,' Coignet recalled. 'The Emperor, recognising his impotence, gave way and let the torrent flow.' He still thought he would be able to stem it next morning.[28]

Blücher was just outside Genappe at midnight, following von Bülow's IV Corps and making certain there was no let-up in hunting down the French. He entered the Auberge du Roi d'Espagne, where Wellington had stayed two nights before, after Quatre-Bras, seemingly a lifetime away. About an hour earlier, Wellington had ridden up to his headquarters at Waterloo, having been in the saddle for over 16 hours without a break. When he uncharacteristically patted his horse Copenhagen on the hindquarters in gratitude, the surprised horse lashed out, nearly kicking him. It was to be his final close shave that day. His considerable intellect was now focused on composing the dispatch that he would have to pass on to his superiors. There had been mistakes before the great day, so the wording would need to be carefully chosen. Supper was a very subdued affair, with virtually no staff left to dine. Wellington anxiously looked up every time the door opened, hoping it might be one of his missing young men.

Nobody came. 'The hand of almighty God has been on me this day,' he confessed to his Spanish liaison officer Alava. By midnight he was asleep.

At the same time Napoleon Bonaparte was riding across the fields, keeping parallel with the road to Charleroi. Captain Fortuné de Brack, with the Guard Lancers, watched him pass by for the final time 'accompanied by two officers wearing greatcoats just like him' ahead of the escort. Napoleon approached and asked about the situation. 'Never, even during the retreat from Moscow, had I seen a more confused and unhappy expression on that majestic face,' he remembered. A shot cracked out down the road and one of his generals hurried him away. De Brack watched him go, and 'our grief knew no bounds', he remembered; it was an indelible image.[29]

Sergeant Thomas Morris, with the 73rd Foot, had managed a little fitful sleep on the battlefield, 'but awoke again at about midnight almost mad, for want of water'. It was difficult to discern who was asleep and who was dead from the light of the moon as he groped about searching for water. Fearfully aware of the scenes around him, he went back to get his brother to accompany him, but was distracted by a man sitting upright leaning against the belly of his horse. 'The hope that I could render him some assistance overcame my terror,' he recalled, but when he placed his hand on his shoulder it 'passed through his body'. Both man and horse had been holed by the same cannon ball.

Fugitive Ensign Edmund Wheatley, on the run from the French, also had 'a parching thirst'. A brief cap full of brandy scooped out of a tub was the only fluid he had tasted since being captured. Spotting a puddle in a ditch, he greedily cupped a handful – only to find it was horse's urine. 'So nauseous and disgusting was the taste it produced an instantaneous nausea.' He began to violently retch into the ditch.

Private Mathew Clay, with the 3rd Foot Guards, was at Hougoumont listening to 'the sound of firing from the Prussians pursuing the retired enemy'. The rattle of musketry and cannon reports 'became fainter, and gradually became inaudible as they distanced us'. He fell into a deep sleep. Meanwhile, near the Genappe road was King's German Legion soldier Friedrich Lindau, who had escaped from the French with fellow Corporal Fastermann. 'It must have been about midnight and was very cold,' he remembered, as they were hiding in a small hollow within a young wood. 'My limbs trembled and my teeth chattered.' To their left they could hear sporadic shooting and continual shouts of *'Vive l'Empereur!'* The cold forced them to move and break cover, and soon they were in open country 'and we could only hear the noise of the surviving French on the retreat in the distance'.[30]

Lamps hovered and moved over the battlefield like so many fireflies. The air was pervaded by the sulfurous smell of low-lying gunpowder smoke, mixed with the aroma of crushed crops and the reek of freshly killed meat. For now it was sanitised by the cold night breeze; decay would come with the sun. Occasional pistol reports rang out as wounded horses and sometimes men were dispatched. Scores of horses were galloping about in the gloom, kicking and plunging, maddened with pain. Wounded men, sensing their approach, cried out in fear to make them go away. Major Harry Smith, with the 95th Rifles, saw heaps of cuirassiers 'literally piled on each other' near La Haye Sainte. Horses were struggling to pull themselves over some of the 'fearfully wounded'. 'The sight was sickening,' he recalled, 'and I had no means or power to assist them.' A pervasive murmuring came from the dark ground, punctuated by the odd shout and flashing report as a life was cut short by a plunderer. One witness described the constant plaintive calls for 'the German Vasser! Vasser!' – mixed with French calls for 'De l'eau! De l'eau!' – rising from the heaped mounds of bodies, a sound 'still sounding in my ears'. There were so many needing help, he recalled overwhelmed, that 'I felt discouraged from attempting to relieve them'.

Private James Anton, with the 42nd Royal Highlanders, saw bodies 'spread promiscuously, heaps of mangled bodies – some without head or arms or legs'. Some faces, he noticed, showed no sign of violent suffering, whereas Lieutenant Frederick Pattison, with the 33rd Foot, 'was struck with the diversity of expression'. Many 'must have had a terrible struggle with the king of terrors; others from the placidity of their expression, seemed as if they had sunk into refreshing slumber'. He was struck by the sheer quantity of the dead, 'scattered over the field like sheaths cut down by the hand of the reaper'.

Beneath the floating lamplights, the compassionate and dispassionate alike sought signs of life. Valuables came in all forms. Teeth were being chipped out of the mouths of the fallen on both sides. They would be shipped by the barrel load to England as the 'teeth of heroes'. An established lucrative trade for the teeth of executed young criminals already existed. A genuine upper row might fetch as much as £30 (£3,000 today) in London during the 1780s. It was of little consequence if the future 'Waterloo smile' was of English, German, Prussian or French origin.[31]

At midnight Captain Alexander Mercer of the horse artillery found himself awake, having dozed since the end of the battle. He was 'chilled and cramped to death from the awkward doubled-up position imposed upon me by my short and narrow bed'. On struggling out from under his cover, he was mortified to realise he had been sleeping across the corpse of one of his own drivers, 'lying mangled and bloody beneath my lair'. Looking up, he could see 'the night was serene and pretty clear'. Only a few clouds scudded across the moon's disc, bathing the battlefield in its reflected light. 'Pale wan faces' were:

> ... *upturned to the moon's cold beams, which caps and breast-plates, and a thousand other things, reflected back in brilliant pencils of light from as many different points.*

Spectacle has always formed part of battle, distracting from the horrors that lurk beneath its epic landscapes.

Mercer could be as sensitive about the suffering of his horses, as he was to the plight of his own men. One way that veterans deal with battlefield carnage is to distance themselves from the dead. It is easier to regard corpses as inanimate objects, no longer capable of human feeling, than as dead comrades. Horses could be just as emotionally troublesome. They were innocent but 40,000 or more had been slaughtered or wounded and were strewn about the field. From Mercer's original gun teams of '200 fine horses with which we had entered the battle', he calculated that 'upwards of 140 lay dead or dying or severely wounded'. Mercer often dwelt on their suffering in his Journal, ascribing almost human feelings to the equine carnage he found all around. 'One poor animal':

> ... *had lost, I believe, both his hind legs; and there he sat the long night through on his tail, looking about, as if in expecta-tion of coming aid, sending forth from time to time, long and protracted melancholy neighing.*

He knew he should shoot the animal, 'but I could not muster courage even to give the order', he insisted. When they moved off, the horse seemed to neigh after them, reproaching them for desertion, but Mercer had seen blood enough.[32]

At midnight, the severely wounded Lieutenant-Colonel Frederick Ponsonby, from the 12th Light Dragoons, was still lying in the open. 'Intervals of perfect silence,' he recalled were 'worse than the noise.' He had been robbed and roughly handled several times by French and Prussian looters, so he was as anxious as he was hopeful at any approach. 'I thought the night would never end,' he remembered, until at last he spotted a soldier in English uniform coming towards him, probably seeking plunder. He turned out to be a soldier from the 40th Foot, who had missed his regiment when it moved off. Ponsonby desperately offered him a reward 'if he would remain by me'. The soldier was unarmed and picked up a discarded sword and stood sentinel over him, 'pacing backwards and forwards'. For the first time since being lanced in the back ten hours before, sabered by cavalry, fought over by French skirmishers, ridden over by Prussian cavalry and successively plundered, Ponsonby thought he might actually live.

He would not only live, he would one day become a major-general and would see the sun rise and set for another 22 years.[33]

Beyond 24 Hours

If Wellington were alive today, he would have been scrutinised by Parliament and the media, invited to account for why he was outmanoeuvred by Napoleon at the outset of the campaign and asked whether such high casualties could have been avoided. Even by the violent standards of the nineteenth century, Waterloo was an extreme event. But the government was grateful to avoid a stalemate and end the crippling costs of the Great European War that had lasted over two decades.

With Napoleon defeated and exiled to St Helena, British industrialisation continued apace during a prevailing peace that was generally to endure in Europe for a century. The Congress of Vienna heralded a more modern period in Europe characterised by negotiated agreements between governments bound together in leagues, pacts and accords. Napoleon's total victories had undermined European power politics. Britain's new ascendency and suzerainty of the seas created the conditions for an empire in the sun, which was to last for another century and a half. Waterloo was the last battle ever fought between England and France.

Wellington had fancied himself as a future statesman during negotiations conducted at Vienna and Paris before Napoleon's return. He had headed an embryonic pan-European military alliance, not unlike NATO, which had achieved decisive victory. Grouchy had broken contact at Wavre on hearing of Waterloo and fell back on Paris. Napoleon was unable to effect a link-up and on 15 July 1815 surrendered to Captain Maitland aboard HMS *Bellerophon* at Rochefort. The Prussians wanted him shot out of hand; Wellington, careful of his gentlemanly image, did not wish to be labelled an executioner. After throwing himself on the mercy of the Prince Regent and providing a brief tourist attraction to crowds at Portsmouth and Plymouth harbour, Napoleon was exiled to the remote island of St Helena. He arrived on 27 October, and died there in 1821.

Nobody took issue with Wellington's account of Waterloo, as precisely articulated in his lucid military dispatch, which was published in *The Times* within four days of the action. It was not to be questioned for a century and a half. His late arrival and lack of support for Blücher at Ligny was explained away by the fact that he was attacked at Quatre-Bras. While diplomatically acknowledging the decisive impact the Prussians had on the battle, Wellington was clear he had won it before they arrived. The advance was under way before the Prussians cleared Plancenoit. 'It has been a damned nice thing – the nearest run thing you ever saw in your life,' Wellington admitted to Whig MP Thomas Creevey, the next morning. And, 'by God! I don't think it would have been done if I had not been there,' he characteristically added.[1]

Nobody questioned this. Only Wellington could have held the army together during the pounding it had received, but there was no credit for initiatives ordered elsewhere. The 1/52nd action that finally turned the Imperial Guard attack received no mention at all in the dispatch, unlike Maitland's Guards. Sir John Colborne received no award. There was also dissatisfaction with the lack of recognition accorded the foreign contingents. They had withstood the same pounding as the British, holding two thirds of the line. Blücher and Napoleon were dead within seven years, and the issue was never raised. When Captain Siborne produced a meticulously researched model of the battlefield 18 years later, depicting 48,000 Prussians making a decisive flank attack, funding from the War Office dried up, even after he offered to remove 40,000 Prussian figures.

Wellington bathed in the reflected glory of Waterloo for years, but would never discuss the detail of the battle. Countless statues and monuments appeared on the battlefield. British towns adopted its name, from Waterlooville north of Portsmouth to Waterloo with Seaforth, as well as scores of English streets, Waterloo railway station and Waterloo Bridge in London. Wellington was loaded with gifts and honours, including Apsley House in London from the grateful nation and nine Field Marshal batons from various states. He was Prime Minister twice and died in 1852, although his political career was never as successful as his military.

Others in the *24 Hours at Waterloo* story benefited or prospered from the battle. Ensign Edmund Wheatley, formerly with the King's German Legion, survived his nightmarish capture and married his beloved Eliza Brookes in February 1820 in London. Her family had come to terms with the reckless young suitor, who used to court her on the Hyde Park turnpike, and were content to be part of the reflected glory of his Waterloo experiences. He was blessed with three daughters.

Sergeant Edward Cotton, with the 7th Hussars, left as a sergeant-major, bought the house opposite the present-day visitors centre, and turned it into an inn and museum. He made a lot of money out of battlefield touring and died in 1849 a rich man. Captain William Verner in the same regiment, was 'reduced to a skeleton' recovering from wounds in Brussels, but survived and retired as a colonel. He went on to serve 36 years as an MP and was made a baronet in 1846 before dying in 1871. Napoleon's Flemish guide, Jean-Baptiste Decoster, cashed in on his experiences and offered his services as a tourist guide. True or not, he regaled his clientele with fascinating anecdotes about Napoleon until he died in 1826.

Captain John Hare, whose 27th Inniskillings lost nearly two thirds of its strength, gained the promotion he sought. He died having reached major-general in 1847. Captain Edward Drewe, commanding his 9th Company, survived his wounds and was granted an annual pension of £70. Private Alexander Dunlop emerged unscathed, took part in the occupation of Paris and remained with the Inniskillings until 1829, when he was pensioned off at 10d a day as 'unfit for service'. Lieutenant William Fortescue, seeking advancement to support a Catholic wife and five children, miraculously survived his chest wound, but was left with a degenerative lung condition. He could not afford to live in retirement on a lieutenant's half-pay of 2s 4d a day and remained on active service until dying of his wounds six years later. He was never promoted.[2]

Jamaican George Rose recovered from his arm wound and transferred to the 42nd Highlanders in 1817. Despite his race, his undoubted experience and Waterloo Medal counted with another regiment that had fought the same battle. In 1829 he was promoted corporal and achieved the lofty rank of sergeant in 1831, an indication of the resourcefulness he had already demonstrated as an escaped slave. His gunshot wound was still bothering him when he was discharged in 1837. In 1849 he was back in Jamaica on missionary service and died at Turnbull Pen near Spanish Town in 1873. George Rose's life had gone through an epic circle. The humble slave was revered as a Waterloo veteran in a local newspaper obituary.[3]

The Waterloo Medal was presented in 1816 to survivors and the families of those who were killed, if they made the necessary application. It was the first ever all-ranks medal and worn with pride. It gave some licence to the wearers to regale sympathetic listeners in taverns throughout the country. The medal, with its two-year pension enhancement, was bitterly resented by men who had fought as long as six years in the Peninsula, and whose regiments were by chance not at Waterloo.

Sergeant William Lawrence, with the 40th Regiment, made a comfortable living as a local innkeeper, treating his customers to campaign stories, until he had them dictated at Studland, Dorset, in 1857. Sergeant Thomas Morris, the Cockney with the 73rd Foot, returned to England after the occupation of Paris, only to see his regiment disbanded, with 'scarcely a man among us who did not shed a tear'. He returned to London after his discharge in 1822, where he 'attained a respectable position in civil society'. Mathew Clay, who had defended Hougoumont with the 3rd Foot Guards, left active service to become a sergeant-major in the Bedford militia. He retired in 1852, on a daily pension of 2s 5d, which had to sustain 12 children. Only three of them survived infancy. On his death in 1873, aged 78, three volleys were fired over his grave in showers of rain. He was never in debt.[4]

Others were less fortunate. Private Thomas Plunkett of the 95th Rifles barely survived his head wound, which forced his return to England and discharge. He married his girl-friend, who had been severely disfigured by the exploding ammunition cart when she accompanied him to Quatre-Bras. In 1851 Plunkett was roaming the country as an impoverished pedlar with his scarred wife, having lost his pension because of bad behaviour. The old soldier had achieved fame with the 'Plunkett' firing position, sniping a French general beyond musket range in the Peninsula. He dropped dead in the streets of Colchester with his wife at his side. Retired Rifles officers came to his widow's aid and paid for his funeral and tombstone.

Hundreds of invalided Waterloo survivors joined the flotsam of twenty years' worth of earlier Revolutionary and Napoleonic campaigns, begging in the streets of cities, towns and villages in England. They might get 6d a day as an out-pensioner from the Chelsea Hospital or given a licence to beg by the local Justices of the Peace. To be down and out in nineteenth-century society was a harsh existence. Former Coldstream Guardsman Sergeant Jackson had lost his leg the year before Waterloo and found the competition for subsistence even more fierce. He sold his scarlet jacket for 30 shillings. Chelsea Hospital was not too sympathetic, commenting: 'Oh, he is a young man, able to get his living.' 'No questions asked of me,' he bitterly recalled, 'but at sight I was knocked off with the pitiful reward of a shilling a day.' A gentleman might stop for a Waterloo Medal, but many injured men sadly reflected whether 6d a day was worth their youth and strength, or an eye, a leg or an arm. One little girl used to ask Sergeant William Lawrence at Dorset during the 1850s, 'Why does your head shake so, Sergeant?' 'Well, Missy, it was like this,' he used to say. 'When I was fighting Boney a cannon-ball took my head off, and when the doctors put it on again, they put it on crooked.'[5]

Many never recovered from their wounds, or the shocking trauma of their handling. 'The silent horror of the greater part of the sufferers was a thing I shall not forget,' remembered an assistant surgeon of the 1st Life Guards. 'The awful sight the men are witness to, knowing that their turn on that blood-soaked operating table is next, seeing the agony of the amputation.' This was something few survivors would ever mentally recover from. 'One realises what our soldiers are made of,' the surgeon commented. French casualties were not picked up until day four, and some lay for as long as two weeks, subsisting on horseflesh. They were like the wounded horses which, unable to move, cropped the grass bald in a circle round about.

Medical after-care was non-existent, unless family or loved ones shouldered the physical and emotional burdens. Trooper Peltier of the 3rd French Lancers was left with a completely distended colon after being slashed across the belly by a sabre. Managing such an injury was socially repugnant. His bowel ends were simply covered with a cloth and changed as required. The inevitable outcome was skin loss after it became sore and infected. He was cared for in a civilian Brussels hospital and what became of him is not recorded. Captain Percival, with the 1st Guards, hit in the face by a musket ball, was an equally distressing case. Guards Ensign Rees Gronow tells us that it 'carried away all his teeth and both his jaws, and left nothing on the mouth but the skin of the cheeks'. Percival recovered sufficiently from his hideous injury to rejoin his regiment in the Tower three years later. Apart from the repugnance his appearance engendered, he could not eat properly. 'He had to be fed with porridge and a few spoonfuls of broth,' Gronow explained. In time his physique deteriorated, 'presenting the appearance of a skeleton', and he died shortly after.[6]

Waterloo was etched on minds as much as it was on bodies. Veterans knew that some men suffered a form of 'tiredness' that could lead to wayward behaviour, but combat stress disorder was not recognised as a medical condition. Men might allude to this emotional state among themselves, but it was neither openly discussed nor was anything done about it. They lived in an exceedingly violent age and were often stoic, even apparently immune to sights of suffering.

'Shedding blood had deadened their sensibilities,' was how Private Thomas Playford with the 2nd Life Guards described behavioural change after battle. 'It required time for them to regain their former principles and tenderness.'

Playford, who had ridden through d'Erlon's infantry corps without once crossing swords with anyone, was afflicted by combat stress disorder himself. 'The occurrences of the 18th June have a place in my memory like a dreadful dream,' he later recalled, 'like some fearful vision of the night when gloomy horrors brood on the mind.' He had bad dreams. 'Scenes of frightful destructions flit before my mind as shadows and yet I know that they represent awful realities.' He was not the only sufferer. Thomas, a soldier with the 71st Foot, was similarly 'harassed by dreams', in which 'I was fighting and charging, re-acting the scenes of the day which were strangely jumbled with the scenes I had been in before.' Lieutenant Colonel Wyndham, with the Coldstream Guards, could never bear to close a door for the rest of his life after assisting in closing the gates at Hougoumont. Everybody knew the reason for his eccentric behaviour, which continued until he died aged 70, but no medical conclusions were ever drawn from it. Wyndham simply had to exist with his personal demons.[7]

The children on the Waterloo battlefield lived to ripe old ages. Daniel Gale, with the 3/95th Rifles, whose daughter Elizabeth searched for him with his wife Mary, lived on to 96, dying in 1875. Elizabeth herself went on to have ten children, dying in 1904. Barbara [Moon], who found her father in the same regiment, mortally wounded, died in 1903. Madame van Cutsem, the five-year-old daughter of the gardener at Hougoumont, who was treated kindly by British soldiers, was still alive in 1877. 'Hale and hearty', according to the 3 March edition of the *Evening Post*, she was 'visiting England for the first time in her life'.

Less is known about the French survivors of the battle. The politically naive Marshal Ney was conveniently blamed in Napoleon's whitewash account of the campaign. He was executed by a royalist firing squad in the Jardin du Luxembourg in Paris. His death brought more opprobrium to the discredited Bourbon family, restored by force of Allied arms, than any other event. Universally regarded as the 'bravest of the brave', the 'Red Lion' refused a blindfold at his death and gave the command to the soldiers to 'fire straight at my heart'. He lived the legend. 'I have fought a hundred battles for France, and not against her,' he defiantly roared at the firing squad, 'Soldiers, fire!' His death deeply divided the French public.

Lieutenant Jacques Martin, who had survived d'Erlon's infantry attack with the 45th Line and being ridden down by British heavy cavalry, escaped the log-jam at Genappe. A letter he wrote to his mother on 1 August formed the basis for his subsequent published account. Captain Pierre Duthilt, who had survived the Revolutionary and Napoleonic wars and now Waterloo, lived on until 1852. His son was already dead by then, killed in May 1840 at Abd el Kader, fighting with the French army in Algeria. Captain Jean-Roch Coignet, one of Napoleon's favoured officers in the Imperial Guard, ran a tobacconist's shop. He learned to read and write after Waterloo, writing his memoirs in 1848 before dying in 1865. Former drummer boy Corporal Louis Canler escaped the rout and joined the police after the war, where after a long career he was appointed the Chef du Service de Süreté, dying the same year as Coignet.

King's German Legion soldier Friedrich Lindau, who was captured at La Haye Sainte, recovered from his head wound, but it was to affect him for the rest of his life. He was not reunited with his brother Georg, who was in the same battalion, until the occupation of Paris. Georg had been convinced he had already buried him on the battlefield. His second brother Christian, with the Legion artillery, also claimed he had shovelled over his corpse elsewhere on the battlefield, so he was twice resurrected. Lindau remained illiterate, but told his story to the local rector of his hometown at Hamelin on return to Hanover, where it was published in 1846. He returned to shoemaking and became a master, marrying twice with at least nine children, before passing away in 1865.

Prussian soldier Franz Lieber survived Ligny and marched the whole day to Waterloo without firing a shot. He was hit in the neck by a musket ball, during the pursuit the following day, and lay untended for 24 hours before being recovered for a long period of recuperation at Liège. When he returned to Berlin, the peace had been signed and his family had thought him long dead. Six years later he fought in the Greek War of Independence. His political sympathies caused him to flee Prussia for the United States and settle in South Carolina, where he became a professor at South Carolina College (now the University of South Carolina) and later a professor at Columbia College, New York. Franz developed the 'Lieber Code' during the American Civil War, which was to form the basis for one of the first laws on war. He died in 1872.

Many of Wellington's foreign officers never changed their opinion about the shabby treatment they received during the campaign and the scant recognition after it. Captain Carl Jacobi, with the Hanoverian Lüneburg Field Battalion, barely survived a sabering outside La Haye Sainte, but was one of the few Waterloo veterans to spend that night in a comfortable bed in Brussels. He was still complaining about the British during the occupation of Paris, where there were no tents, the food was 'inedible' meat and biscuits instead of bread, and dysentery broke out when the 'dirty' Seine was offered up as their primary source of drinking water. 'If they take time at all to listen to our grievances,' he complained, 'they will forget them the next moment they spend time again in the arms of a French woman or in a wine tavern.' Although the foreign troops had stood bravely in the line with their British allies and endured the same vicious pounding and casualties, British officers and men continued to maintain the same low opinion of 'rid Jarmins' that they had before the battle. As these provided two of every three men in the line, the battle would not have been won without them.[8]

The Dutch-Belgians got their own back when they built the Butte du Lion, or Lion Mound monument, ten years later, commemorating the spot where the Prince of Orange was wounded. It was also the iconic place where the Imperial Guard recoiled from British infantry firepower. It took three years of work to excavate the ten million cubic feet of earth required to create the 130 ft mound, which is crowned at the pinnacle by a statue of a lion. It transformed the outline of the Mont St Jean ridge into its present shape. Today the battlefield can be viewed in its entirety from the top of its 226 steps. 'They have ruined my battlefield,' Wellington complained.

For a bereaved wife back home, the loss of a gentleman husband was as much an economic disaster as it was an emotional catastrophe. Honoria had married Lieutenant William Fortescue of the 27th Inniskillings in 1798, the year of bloody Rebellion that polarised the Catholic/Protestant divide. William, a Protestant gentleman, had had the temerity to marry a Catholic, so when he succumbed to his wounds in 1821, his pension was strangely delayed. With five children to support, an increasingly desperate Honoria appealed to her husband's former comrades for assistance. Despite testimonials from many Inniskilling officers, including their Waterloo commander, John Hare, testifying to Fortescue's sacrifice in the square, Dublin Castle was unsympathetic. It insisted that his marriage, 'once a felony, is still highly penal'. It took eight months' pressure from Army Horse Guards in London to reverse the decision not to authorise a pension. By that time Honoria had died, not knowing whether her children would be cared for or not.[9]

Major Arthur Rowley Heyland, the 40th Regiment commander killed in the dying moments of the battle, had comfortably provided for his large family of two daughters and four sons. He had even suggested which arms of the service his sons should apply for in his last letter. The tragedy continued when his wife Mary, pregnant with Herbert at the time of Waterloo, lost him shortly before the first anniversary of Arthur's death. The eldest son, John, was to distinguish himself with the 35th Foot in the Crimea 39 years later, and the youngest son lost an arm at the battle of the Alma. It is not known whether Mary was still alive then, but the nation was still exacting a price from the Heyland family.

Two hundred years on, these events covered in *24 Hours at Waterloo* have lost some of their immediacy. Recent excavation of a plot of land in front of the Lion Mound monument, overlooking the area where the Imperial Guard was repelled, unearthed a complete skeleton. It was uncovered by a mechanical digger during the excavation of a car park for the 200th anniversary of Waterloo. The bucket unfortunately shattered the skull. 'We realised it was something exceptional,' commented Dominique Bosquet from the archaeological department of Belgium's Walloon region. 'It's a soldier found probably at the site of his death.' He had been interred in a shallow grave, covered with only 15 inches of soil. Abrasion grooves on the skull's molars suggest he had torn cartridge tubes open with his teeth. An intact musket ball was found lodged in his chest, the likely cause of death. 'One possibility was that he crept away wounded from the front', because the British line was nearby, 'and settled down to die here.' Alternatively, Bosquet suggested, 'he was carried here by his comrades'.

The skeleton is one of the best preserved dating from the battle, although it is missing a foot and some small hand bones. Early analysis points to a man aged 20 who was only about 5 ft 1 in tall. His body had not been plundered, because 20 coins remained in his possession, among them an 1811 half-franc coin. Bosquet suspects 'he could have been buried by a comrade or simply missed when the bodies were gathered up after the battle for burial'. Finds like this infuse life into contemporary narratives of the action. A small block of wood with the letters 'CB' etched on it could be the remains of a decayed musket butt. The coins were found where his pocket ought to have been, together with a rifle flint and a piece of material, perhaps from the pocket or a purse. An iron spoon covered in soil may yet provide crucial evidence if it is found to be embossed with a regimental insignia.[10]

This soldier may well be one of the many thousands of Wellington's 'Infamous Army', unknown and uncelebrated. Wellington, characteristically parsimonious with his praise, did pay one soldierly tribute to his unknown men:

> *When other Generals commit any error, their army is lost by it, and they are sure to be beaten; when I get into a scrape, my army get me out of it.*[11]

Most of them were quickly forgotten. Three years after Waterloo, 'Tom', a veteran with the 71st Highland Light Infantry, wrote to his friend John:

> *These three months I can find nothing to do. I am a burden on Jeanie and her husband, I wish I was a soldier again. I cannot even get labouring work.*

'I will go to South America,' he decided, 'and be a burden to no one.' He left behind a manuscript of his Waterloo experiences with his friend John, writing, 'It is yours: do with it as you think proper.' The journal was published in Edinburgh in 1819, and again in 1822, 1828 and 1835. Tom wrote that if he succeeded in the south, 'I will return and lay my bones besides my parents: if not, I will never come back.'

Like many of those who witnessed these 24 Hours at Waterloo, he probably never did and disappeared into obscurity.[12]

Acknowledgements

The spark for the idea of doing this book came from an impossible task I set myself to track figurines represented in a Waterloo chess set across the battlefield on the day of the battle. Gareth Glover's *Waterloo Archive*, a plethora of unseen contemporary accounts and letters about the battle, was the spark to proceed, for which I would like to offer heartfelt thanks. He has since completed five volumes, with the series due to culminate in time for the bi-centenary celebration. Anybody seeking to visit the battlefield should consult Mark Aidkin's masterly *Waterloo Companion*, whose maps, panoramic photographs and encyclopaedic nuggets proved an indispensable tool for my own project.

Andrew Orgill and the staff at the Royal Military Academy Sandhurst library were crucial in patiently making many nineteenth-century and lesser-known accounts available. My thanks also to Brigadier (retd) Vere Hayes, who assisted at the Royal Green Jackets Museum at Winchester, and Julian Farrance at the National Army Museum in London. My agent Charlie Viney and Kate Moore and Elen Jones at Random House provided the infectious enthusiasm necessary to keep the *24 Hours* clock ticking on until midnight.

Endnotes

Introduction

1 *Le Moniteur Universel*, headlines, 9-22 Mar. 1815.

2 Aidkin, *The Waterloo Companion*, pp. 120-1, 123-4.

Chapter 1. Summer Storm

00.10 am. Night and Driving Rain

1 Cotton, *A Voice from Waterloo*, pp. 34. Mercer, *Journal of the Waterloo Campaign*, pp. 147-8.

2 Morris: Selby, ed., *Thomas Morris*, pp. 72-3. Lewis: Glover, ed., *The Waterloo Archive*, Vol. I, p. 160.

3 Weather and conditions: Neumann, 'Meteorological Aspects of the Battle of Waterloo', and Wheeler and Demarée, 'The Weather of the Waterloo Campaign'.

4 Wheeler, *The Letters of Private Wheeler 1809-1828*, 19 Jun. 1815, p. 170. Morris, p. 73. Hay, *Reminiscences 1808-1815 Under Wellington*, p. 173.

5 Kincaid, *Adventures in the Rifle Brigade and Random Shots*, pp. 154-5 and 162. Costello: Brett-James, ed., *Edward Costello: Peninsular and Waterloo Campaigns*, p. 150. Turner: letter, 3 Jul. 1815, in Glover, Vol. I, p. 96. Frazer: Sabine, ed., *Letters of Sir Augustus Simon Frazer*, Letter XXI, 17 Jun. 1815, Longman 1859, p. 542.

6 Staff officer, *Recollections of Waterloo by a Staff Officer*, *United Services Magazine*, Part 3, 1847, p. 5. Dehnel: Glover, Vol. II, p. 28. Eaton: Crumplin and Leaper, *Ladies of Waterloo*, p. 119. Whale: Glover, Vol. IV, pp. 33-4. Smith: Brett-James, *The Hundred Days*, pp. 95-6.

7   Jeremiah: Glover, Vol. IV, p. 185. Playford, ibid., p. 37.

8   Eyre: Glover, Vol. III, pp. 114-15. Knight and Harris: Caldwell and Cooper, *Rifle Green at Waterloo*, pp. 128, 130. Wedgewood, letter to father, Paris 15 Jul. 1815, in Glover, Vol. I, p. 149. Simmons: ibid., Vol. IV, p. 216.

1 am. 'Foreigners' and Bad Memories

9   Gagern and Doring: Glover, *Waterloo Archive*, Vol. II, pp. 192-4, 165-6.

10 Jacobi and von Scriba: Glover, Vol. II, pp. 103,131-2.

11 Wheeler, *Letters*, No. 73, 19 Jun. 1815, p. 170. Morris, *Thomas Morris*, pp. 69, 74. Biedermann: Glover, Vol. V, p. 40.

12 Morris, pp. 68-9, 71-3. Pigot: Siborne, *The Waterloo Letters*, No. 143, p. 327.

13 Clay, *A Narrative of the Battles of Quatre-Bras and Waterloo*, p. 10. Finlayson: Glover, Vol. III, p. 220.

14 Anton: Fitchett, ed. *Wellington's Men*, p. 298.

15 Verner: 'Reminiscences of William Verner 7th Hussars', *Society for Army Historical Research*, Special Issue No. 8, 1965, pp. 42-3. Hodge: 'Correspondence concerning the death of Major Hodge, 7th Hussars, at Genappe 17 Jun. 1815', 15 letters, Jun.-Sep. 1815, *Army Historical Research*, Vol. 43, 1965, pp. 80-91. Cotton, *A Voice from Waterloo*, p. 35.

16 Playford: Glover, Vol. IV, p. 36. O'Grady: Siborne, *Letters*, No. 65, p. 136. Kincaid, *Adventures*, p. 161.

17 Wheeler, p. 170.

1.50 am. 'Blind Man's Bluff': The French and Prussians

18 French Officer, Anon., *Journal of the Three Days of the Battle of Waterloo*, p. 40.

19 Martin: Uffindell and Corum, *On the Fields of Glory*, p. 30. Guillot: trans. P. Wisken, 'The Death of the Eagle', *Weapons and Militaria* magazine 1980. De Mauduit: Brett-James, *The Hundred Days*, pp. 93-4.

20 Mameluke Ali, Uffindell and Corum, p. 31.

21 Donezelot, according to General Noguès: Field, *Waterloo: The French Perspective*, p. 35. Labedyère and Napoleon: ibid., pp. 36, 33-4.

22 De Mauduit: Brett-James, pp. 93-4. Duthilt: Field, p. 36.

23 Martin: Field, p. 38. Duthilt: ibid., p. 37. De Vatry, ibid., pp. 38-9.

24 Canler and de Civrieux: Field, p. 37. De Mauduit: Uffindell and Corum, p. 26.

25 Mercer, *Reminiscences*, p. 158.

26 Cotton, p. 117. Saxon revolt: Blumberg, 'To Hell With the Prussians', *MHQ*, Autumn 2002, Vol. 15, No. 1, p. 6.

27 Gneisenau: Longford, *Wellington. The Years of the Sword*, p. 513. Müffling, *The Memoirs of Baron von Müffling*, p. 240.

28 Prussian captain: Brett-James, p. 86.

29 Staff officer and von Reiche, ibid., p. 82.

30 Lieber, *The Miscellaneous Writings*, Vol. 1: *Personal Reminiscences. The Battle of Waterloo*, pp. 158-9.

31 13th Brigade log: Hofschröer, *1815: The Waterloo Campaign*, p. 40.

Chapter 2. Twilight to Morning

2 am. Dark and more Rain

1 Deacon: Morris, *Thomas Morris*, pp. 69-70. Costello: *Edward Costello*, p. 153. Elizabeth Gale: Crumplin, M., and Leaper, J., *The Angels of Waterloo*, article, Rifles Museum, Winchester.

2 Regulations and Macready: Divall, *Inside the Regiment*, pp. 197-8.

3 Wellington: Brett-James, *Wellington at War*, p. 164. Skiddy: Divall, p. 200. Senior Officer: ibid., p. 197. Clay, *Narrative*, p. 7.

4 Wheeler, *Letters*, p. 188. Clay, p. 7. Plunkett, *Braintree and Witham Times* article, 17 Nov. 2010. Parsons: *Thomas Morris*, pp. 83-4.

5 Blücher's message: Hofschröer, *1815: The Waterloo Campaign*, pp. 30-1.

6 Inniskillings story: Bois, *Men, Cohesion and Battle: The Inniskilling Regiment at Waterloo*, pp. 163-4, 173-4, and Dalton, *The Waterloo Roll Call*, pp. 132-4.

7 Napoleon (Somerset de Chair, ed.), *The Waterloo Campaign*, p. 105. French Officer, Anon., *Journal of the Three Days of Waterloo*, 15 Jun., pp. 30-1.

8 Napoleon: ibid., p. 105.

5 am. The Reluctant Reveille

9 Cotton, *A Voice from Waterloo*, pp. 40-1. Morris: *Thomas Morris*, p. 74.

10 Verner, 'Reminiscences', p. 43; Cotton, *Voice*, p. 56.

11 Dickson: Llewellyn, *Waterloo Recollections*, pp. 190-1. Robertson, ibid., p. 83. 'Tom', *A Soldier of the 71st*. Thomas Morris, p. 75.

12 Clay, *Narrative*, pp. 15-16.

13 Doring: Glover, *Waterloo Archive*, Vol. II, pp. 166-7. Von Scriba: ibid., p. 104. Jacobi: ibid., pp. 132-4.

14 Soldier: 'Tom', *A Soldier of the 71st*, p. 106. Wheatley, *The Wheatley Diary*, p. 63. Mercer, *Journal of the Waterloo Campaign*, p. 160.

15 Martin, *Souvenirs de Guerre du Lieutenant Martin 1812-1815*, Henckens: Uffindell and Corum, *On the Fields of Glory*, p. 151.

16 Trefçon, *Carnet de Campagne du Colonel Trefçon 1793-1815*, Paris, 1914, p. 185. French Officer, Anon., *Journal*, p. 30.

17 Decoster: Charlotte Eaton's description, Crumplin and Leaper, *Ladies of Waterloo*, p. 135, and Sir Walter Scott, quoted in Brett-James, *The Hundred Days*, p. 101.

18 Martin, *Souvenirs de Guerre*, Canler: Uffindell and Corum, pp. 151-2.

19 Napoleon: Field, *French Perspective*, p. 49. De Mauduit: ibid., Introduction.

20 Napoleon, *The Waterloo Campaign*, p. 107.

21 Wellington: Aidkin, *Waterloo Companion*, p. 93. Gronow: Foulkes, *Dancing Into Battle*, p. 177.

Sunrise to 10 am. The Prize: Brussels

22 Eaton: Uffindell and Corum, *On the Fields of Glory*, p. 250. Creevey, *The Creevey Papers*, p. 145.

23 Eyewitness, *United Service Journal*, 1829, Part 1, pp. 87-8. D'Hooghvorst: Uffindell and Corum, p. 251.

24 Eyewitness, ibid., p. 89. Costello, *Edward Costello*, p. 154. Capel: Brett-James, *The Hundred Days*, p. 123. Davy: Glover, *Waterloo Archive*, Vol. I, p. 218.

25 Eaton and Wylie: Crumplin and Leaper, *The Ladies of Waterloo*, pp. 47, 52. Eyewitness, pp. 87-8. Davy: Glover, Vol. I, p. 218.

26 Frye: Llewellyn, ed., *Waterloo Recollections*, p. 23. Burney: Uffindell and Corum, p. 254.

27 Creevey's step-daughter: Glover, Vol. I, p. 227, Davy, ibid., p. 219.

Chapter 3. The Men

10.00 am. The Multi-Coloured Line: Wellington's Army

1 Officer: Uffindell and Corum, *On the Fields of Glory*, p. 60. James: Vansittart, J., ed., *The Journal of Surgeon James*, 1964, p. 31.

2 Wheatley, *Diary*, pp. 63-4.

3 Hardinge and Wellington: Brett-James, *The Hundred Days*, p. 20.

4 Wellington: Longford, *Wellington: The Years of the Sword*, pp. 484-5. Creevey, *Creevey Papers*, p. 142.

5 Staff officer, *United Services Magazine*, 1847. Kincaid, *Adventures*, p. 171. Mackenzie: Glover, *Waterloo Archive*, Vol. I, p. 185.

6 Frye: Llewellyn, *Waterloo Recollections*, p. 19. Ath commander: Longford, p. 486. Saltoun: Brett-James, p. 26.

7 Jacobi: Glover, Vol II, pp. 122-3.

8 Wheeler, *Letters*, p. 160. Wellington: Foulkes, *Dancing Into Battle*, p. 21.

9 Lindau, *A Waterloo Hero*, p. 38. Lehman: Divall, *Napoleonic Lives*, p. 81.

10 Wheatley, *Diary*, pp. ix-xi, 64.

11   Gunn: Glover, Vol. I, p. 194.

12   Rose, Discharge papers, Nat. Archive WO 97/581/52 dated 29 Jul. 1837. Affleck, ibid., WO 97/12. Wilson, WO 97/146.7. Ellis, J.D., *George Rose – An Examplary Soldier 73rd and 42nd Foot*, Scottish Military History Website, and *Black Soldiers in the British Army*.

13   Research figures from Bois, *Men, Cohesion and Battle*.

14   Verner, 'Reminiscences', p. 66.

15   Pay comparison figures, Bois, pp. 70-1. Poster, A.F. Scott, *Everyone a Witness*, p. 384. Recruiting: Divall, *Inside the Regiment*, p. 67. 'Crimps': Neuburg, *Gone For a Soldier*, p. 22.

16   Lawrence, *A Dorset Soldier*, pp. 17-18. Morris, *Thomas Morris*, pp. 2-4. Hopkins: Holmes, *Redcoat*, p. 56. Soldier sizes: James, C., *The Regimental Companion*, Vol. I, 1800, p. 413.

17   Flogging figures: Bois, p. 111. Colborne: Divall, *Napoleonic Lives*, p. 17.

18   Kincaid, *Adventures*, p. 273. Anton: Bois, p. 102.

10.30 am. *The French in Review*

19   Verner, 'Reminiscences', p. 49.

20   Cotton, *Voice*, p. 57. Napoleon, *The Waterloo Campaign*, pp. 108-9. Belgian appeal: Franklin, ed., *Waterloo: Netherlands Correspondence*, p. 16. Robertson: Llewellyn, ed., *Waterloo Recollections*, p. 82.

21   French Officer, Anon., *Journal of the Three days of the Battle of Waterloo*, p. 44. Fée: Field, *The French Perspective*, p. 59. Coignet, *Captain Coignet*, p. 271.

22   Trefçon and Canler: Field, p. 55.

23   Coignet, pp. 261-2. French Officer, Anon., *Journal*, p. 20.

24   Martin: Field, pp. 13, 18.

25   Asses: Aidkin, *Waterloo Companion*, p. 197. French Officer, Anon., *Journal*, p. 25.

26   Coignet, p. 266, Martin: Field, p. 56. Pétiet: Brett-James, *The Hundred Days*, p. 102.

11.30 am. The Prussians: Wavre to St Lambert.

27 Diedrichs: Hofschröer, *1815: The Waterloo Campaign*, p. 54.

28 Lieber, *Reminiscences*, pp. 151-4, 157.

29 Von Reiche: Parkinson, *Hussar General*, p. 235. Westphalian officer: Brett-James, *The Hundred Days*, p. 80. Lieber: ibid., p. 75.

30 Westphalian officer: Brett-James, p. 86. Blücher and von Nostitz: Parkinson, p. 235, and Weller, *Wellington at Waterloo*, p. 130.

31 Elsner: Hofschröer, p. 55.

32 Lieber, pp. 154, 156.

Chapter 4. The First Shots

11.30 am to 1.15 pm. The Wooded Château: Hougoumont

1 Büsgen: Glover, *Waterloo Archive*, Vol. II, pp. 156-8. Leonhard: ibid., p. 158.

2 Wheatley, *Diary*, p. 64. Gawler and Lane: Siborne, *Letters*, No. 124, p. 280 and No. 69, p. 144. Home: Glover, Vol. I , p. 142 and Leonhard, Vol. II, p. 159.

3 Levavasseur: Field, *French Perspective*, p. 67. Foy: Uffindell and M. Corum, *On the Fields of Glory*, p. 157. Büsgen and Wellington: Glover, Vol. II, p. 155-7.

4 Jolyet: Field, p. 64. De Civrieux and Lemonnier-Delafosse: ibid., p. 65.

5 Cotton, *A Voice from Waterloo*, p. 63. Casualties, 1st Line and Baird: Crumplin, M., *The Price of Hougoumont*, Article 20, Nov. 2011, www.waterloo200.org. Clay, *Narrative*, p. 18.

6 Clay, ibid., pp. 19, 26.

7 Macdonell: Llewellyn, *Waterloo Recollections*, p. 41. Clay, pp. 18-19, 26. Wyndham: Aidkin, *Waterloo Companion*, p. 330.

8 De Lorraine: Crumplin and Starling, *A Surgical Artist at War*; the watercolour and medical history are at pp. 46-7.

1 pm to 1.30 pm. The Objective: The Mont St Jean Ridge

9 Desalles: Field, *French Perspective*, p. 75. Jacobi: Glover, *Waterloo Archive*, Vol. II, pp. 134-5. Kincaid, *Adventures*, pp. 164-5.

10 Lindau, *A Waterloo Hero*, p. 163. Lehman: Divall, *Napoleonic Lives,* p. 79. Biedermann: Glover, Vol. V, pp. 41-2.

11 Wheatley, *Diary*, p. 65.

12 Albrecht, evidence from medical watercolour by Surgeon Charles Bell: Crumplin and Starling, *A Surgical Artist at War*, p. 66.

13 Lawrence: Llewellyn, *Waterloo Recollections*, pp. 96-7.

14 Napoleon's comment: Field, p. 71. Tuittmeyer, evidence from Bell watercolour: Crumplin and Starling, p. 82.

15 Martin, *Souvenirs de Guerre*, pp. 279, 283.

16 Canler: Field, p. 99.

1.35 pm. The Prussians: Chapelle St Lambert

17 Napoleon, *The Waterloo Campaign*, pp. 116-19.

Chapter 5. The Muddy Slope

1.50 pm. Advance: The Intermediate Valley before Mont St Jean

1 Duthilt: Brett-James, *The Hundred Days*, pp. 114-15. Guillot: P. Wisken, trans., 'The Death of the Eagle', *Weapons and Militaria* magazine, 1980. Noguès: Field, *French Perspective*, p. 98.

2 Gronow, *Waterloo Recollections*, p. 114. Kincaid, *Adventures*, p. 166.

3 Martin: Field, p. 99.

4 Finlayson: Glover, *Waterloo Archive*, Vol. III, p. 217.

5 Duthilt: Field, p. 99. Dallas, letter, 25 Jun. 1815, Glover, Vol. I, p. 179. Canler, Field, p. 100. French conscript: Aidkin, *Waterloo Companion*, p. 346.

6 Martin: Howarth, *A Near Run Thing*, p. 89.

2 pm. The Breakwater: La Haye Sainte

7 Kincaid, *Adventures*, p. 166.

8 Baring and Lindau: Lindau, *A Waterloo Hero*, pp. 167-8, 187. Biedermann: Glover, *Waterloo Archive*, Vol. V, p. 42.

9 Jacobi: Glover, Vol. II, p. 135. Baring: Lindau, pp. 187-8. Ordner: Field, *French Perspective*, p. 94.

10 Biedermann: Glover, Vol. V, pp. 42-3. Ordner: Field, p. 96. Jacobi: Glover, Vol. II, p. 135.

2.15 pm. The Crest of the Mont St Jean Ridge

11 Mackenzie, Memorandum extract, Glover, *Waterloo Archive*, Vol. I, p. 185. Gerard, Journal, in Glover, Vol. I, pp. 190-1.

12 Bijlandt: Franklin, ed., *Waterloo: Netherlands Correspondence*, p. 67.

13 Dickinson: Llewellyn, ed., *Waterloo Recollections*, p. 192. Hope: Glover, Siborne, *Letters*, No. 186 , p. 283.

14 Schelten: Brett-James, *The Hundred Days*, p. 114. Bijlandt: Franklin, *Netherlands Correspondence*, p. 64.

15 Picton: Uffindell and Corum, *On the Fields of Glory*, p. 78.

16 Duthilt: Brett-James, p. 115. Martin, *Souvenirs de Guerre*, and Field, *French Perspective*, p. 103.

Chapter 6. A Cascade of Cavalry

2 pm. Behind the Mont St Jean Ridge

1 Verner, 'Reminiscences', pp. 43-4.

2 Veteran: Costello, *Edward Costello*, p. 152.

3 Dickinson: Llewellyn, *Waterloo Recollections*, p. 194. Robertson: ibid., p. 83. Ross: Siborne, *Letters*, pp. 276-7.

4 Kinchant: Glover, *Waterloo Archive*, Vol. II, pp. 28-30. Lord, letters to wife and parents, 3 Jul./8 Aug. 1815: Glover, Vol. I, p. 16. Clarke, letter to parents, 8 Jul. 1815: ibid., pp. 28-9. Hasker, letter, 18 Jun. 1815: ibid., p. 18. Sergeant, letter, 25 Jun. 1815: ibid., p. 31. Verner, pp. 44-5.

5 Stanley, letter, 15 May 1815, Price, *If You're Reading This...*, pp. 17-18.

6 Shaw: Llewellyn, *Waterloo Recollections*, pp. 176-7. Morris, *Thomas Morris*, p. 76. Hodgeson, Haydon account: Glover, Vol. I, p. 232.

7 Playford: Glover, Vol. IV, pp. 38-9.

8 Dickinson: Llewellyn, p. 193-5. Robertson, ibid., p. 84. Johnston, Journal, in Glover, Vol. I, p. 51.

9 Alexander: ibid., Bell watercolour, pp. 62-3. Clark Kennedy: Siborne, No. 34, p. 77.

10 Lord brothers, letter, 3 Jul. 1815, Glover, Vol. I, pp. 14-15. Playford: Glover, Vol. IV, p. 39.

2.30 pm. The Other Side of the Hill: Grande Batterie Ridge

11 Ewart: Glover, *Waterloo Archive*, Vol. II, pp. 32-3.

12 Duthilt: Brett-James, p. 115. Conscript: Aidkin, *Waterloo Companion*, p. 346. De Lacy Evans: Siborne, *Letters*, No. 31, p. 68. Noguès: Field, *French Perspective*, p. 111.

13 Martin, *Souvenirs de Guerre*, Canler: Uffindell and Corum, *On the Fields of Glory*, p. 168. Duthilt: Brett-James, *The Hundred Days*, pp. 115-16. Tomkinson: Siborne, *Letters*, No. 59, p. 118. Wyndham: ibid., No. 40, p. 85. Ewart, letter, 16 Aug. 1815: Brett-James, pp. 119-20, and Glover, Vol. II, p. 32. Kennedy-Clark, ibid., p. 120.

14 Johnston, Journal, in Glover, Vol. I, p. 51. Dickinson and Napoleon: Llewellyn, ed., *Waterloo Recollections*, pp. 197, 198. De Lacy Evans: Siborne, No. 31, pp. 68-9.

15 Playford: Glover, Vol. IV, pp. 45-6. Johnston, Journal, in Glover, Vol. I, p. 51. Mounsteven: Siborne, No. 151, p. 339.

16 De Commerès: Aidkin, p. 355. Duratte: Field, *French Perspective*, p. 116.

17 Hasker, letters, 18 Jun. 1815 and 13 Dec. 1841, in Glover, Vol. I, pp. 18-21.

18 Bell, *A Surgical Artist at War*, pp. 42-4.

19 De Brack, Aidkin, p. 224. Playford: Glover, Vol. IV, pp. 41-2. Hodgeson: Haydon account in Glover, Vol. I, p. 232. Sergeant, letter, 25 Jun. 1815, ibid., pp. 32-3.

20 Shaw accounts: Waymouth and witnesses, Siborne, No. 23, p. 57. Morris, *Thomas Morris*, p. 76. B. Low, Llewellyn, *Waterloo Recollections*, pp. 184-5. Haydon on Shaw: Glover, Vol. I, p. 232.

21 Canler: Field, *French Perspective*, p. 119. Martin, *Souvenirs de Guerre*.

22 Canler: Uffindell and Corum, p. 168, and Field, *French Perspective*, pp. 119-20. Duthilt, Dupuy and Desalles: Field, pp. 120-1.

23 Playford: Glover, Vol. IV, p. 38.

Chapter 7. *'En Avant!'* The Cavalry Charges

3 pm to 4 pm. Twin Breakwaters: Hougoumont and La Haye Sainte

1 Wheeler, *Letters*, p. 172.

2 De Civrieux, Standen and Puvis: Field, *French Perspective*, pp. 124-5. Büsgen: Glover, *Waterloo Archive*, Vol. II, p. 157.

3 De Mauduit and Saltoun: Field, pp. 126, 127. Büsgen, Glover, Vol II, pp. 157-8.

4 Facsimile of Wellington's message, Wellington Museum, Apsley House, London.

5 Leonhard: Glover, Vol. II, p. 159. Clay, *Narrative*, p. 26

6 Wheeler, *Letters*, p. 174. Clay, p. 27. Büsgen: Glover, Vol. II, p. 158. Seymour, Siborne, *Letters*, No. 9, p. 30.

7 Home: Glover, Vol. I, p. 144. Van Cutsem, *Evening Post*, Vol. XV, Issue 52, 3 Mar. 1877, front page.

8 Müller: *Ludwig von Wissel's Glorious Feats*, Glover, Vol. V, p. 197.

9 Lindau, *Waterloo Hero*, pp. 168-9. Kincaid, *Adventures*, pp. 166-8.

10 Levavasseur: Field, *French Perspective*, pp. 131-2. Lindau, *Waterloo Hero*, p. 170.

11 Simmons: Glover, Vol. IV, pp. 217-18.

12 Lindau, *Waterloo Hero*, pp. 171-2. Baring: ibid., p. 189.

3 pm to 4.15 pm. Charge à la Sauvage

13 Heyland: Price, *If You're Reading This…*, pp. 17-20.

14 Drewe: Siborne, *Letters*, No. 174, pp. 378-9. Crowe: Bois, *Men, Cohesion and Battle*, p. 160.

15 Bijou, according to de Mauduit: Field, *French Perspective*, p. 287. Melet and Cadet: Meistrich, 'En Avant!', p. 53.

16 Schacht: letter, 25 Aug. 1815, in Glover, *Waterloo Archive*, Vol. V, p. 66-7. Von Gagern: Glover, Vol. II, p. 195.

17 Delort: Uffindell and Corum, *On the Fields of Glory*, pp. 175-6. Lasalle: Meistrich, p. 48. Heymès: Field, p. 139.

18 De Brack: Roberts, *Waterloo*, pp. 76-7; 1835 letter at 126-8. Napoleon: Meistrich, p. 49.

19 Gronow: Brett-James, *The Hundred Days*, p. 134. Mercer, *Journal*, pp. 168, 174. Wheatley, *Diary*, p. 65.

20 Eyre: Glover, Vol. III, p. 115. Morris, *Thomas Morris*, p. 77.

21 Mercer, *Journal*, pp. 174-5. Rudyard: Brett-James, p. 138. French officer: quoted in Mercer, p. 172.

22 Napoleon: Houssaye, H., *1815 Waterloo*, p. 211.

4 pm to 4.30 pm. Chequer-Board Battle

23 Gronow: Brett-James, *The Hundred Days*, p. 134. Morris, *Thomas Morris*, pp. 78-9.

24 Napoleon: Meistrich. 'En Avant!', p. 48. British witness and Létang: Field, *French Perspective*, pp. 142, 148.

25 Macready: Divall, *Redcoats Against Napoleon*, p. 170. De Brack: Roberts, *Waterloo*, pp. 127-8. Uxbridge: Siborne, *Letters*, No. 6, pp. 21-2.

26 Weiz: Glover, *Waterloo Archive*, Vol. II, pp. 183-5. Morris, pp. 77-8.

27 Von Scriba: Glover, Vol. II, pp. 105-7.

28 Guyot: Field, pp. 149-50.

29 Verner, 'Reminiscences', pp. 45-6. Wheeler, *Letters*, pp. 173-4.

30 Trefçon: Field, p. 140. Delafosse, ibid., pp. 142-3, and Uffindell and Corum, p. 180.

Chapter 8. Death of a Regiment

4.30 pm to 6.30 pm. 'A Mere Pounder After All.' The Ridge

1 Stretton: Siborne, *Letters,* No. 177, pp. 282-3. Lawrence, *A Dorset Soldier,* p. 110. Browne: Siborne, No. 172, pp. 376-7.

2 Rosters: UK War Office *1/27th Regiment Rosters 1815-1816.* Bois, *Men, Cohesion and Battle,* pp. 169-70. Grattan: ibid., p. 121. Hunger: ibid., p. 117.

3 Leeke: Brett-James, *The Hundred Days,* p. 132.

4 Mill: Bois, p. 33. Lawrence, p. 110. Ordner: Field, *French Perspective,* p. 147. Wellington: Longford, *Wellington: The Years of the Sword,* p. 564.

5 Napoleon, *The Waterloo Campaign,* pp. 120-1, 125-6.

6 Decoster, according to interview 15 Jul. 1815, Eaton, De Lancey and Smith, *Ladies of Waterloo,* p. 135. Also Hibbert, *Waterloo,* p. 194.

7 Mercer, *Journal,* p. 169. Weather: Neumann, 'Meteorological Aspects of the Battle of Waterloo', and Wheeler and Demarée, 'The Weather of the Waterloo Campaign'.

8 Mercer, pp. 167, 172-3.

9 Kellerman: Field, *French Perspective,* p. 149. Laussat, pp. 150-1. 71st Soldier: 'Tom', *A Soldier of the 71st,* p. 108. Morris, *Thomas Morris,* p. 79. De Brack: Field, p. 152. Gronow: Brett-James, *The Hundred Days,* pp. 135-6. Rigau: Field, p. 153.

10 Kellerman and de Brack: Field, p. 158. De Mauduit: ibid., p. 287. Melet: Meistrich, 'En Avant!', p. 49.

11 Gronow: Brett-James, p. 135. Lewis: ibid., pp. 136-7.

12 Morris, *Thomas Morris,* pp. 78-9. Dallas: Brett-James, pp. 180-1. 'Tom', *A Soldier of the 71st,* pp. 106-7.

13 Keppel and Fraser: Glover, *Waterloo Archive,* Vol. I, pp. 172-3, and Brett-James, p. 147.

14 'Tom', *A Soldier of the 71st,* p. 108. Soldier 1/30th: Keegan, *The Face of Battle,* p. 140. Macready: Divall, *Redcoats Against Napoleon,* pp. 172-3. Wheeler, *Letters,* p. 173.

4.30 pm to 7.30 pm. 'Night or the Prussians Must Come.' Plancenoit

15 Wellington: Parkinson, *The Hussar General*, p. 236. Lieber, *Reminiscences*, p. 159.

16 Marchand, Canler and Duuring: Field, *French Perspective*, p. 166-7.

17 De Mauduit: Field, p. 286.

18 Dyneley: Uffindell and Corum, *On the Fields of Glory*, p. 213.

19 Hiller: ibid., pp. 219-20. Verdurel: the service book is in a private collection; photograph in Bernard and Lachaux, *Waterloo Relics*, p. 99.

20 Pelet and Golzio: Field, p. 178.

21 Pelet, ibid., p. 180.

4.30 pm to 7 pm. 'Rid Jarmins and the Like'

22 Lindau, *A Waterloo Hero*, pp. 192-4.

23 Graeme: Siborne, *Letters*, Nos. 179 and 190, pp. 387-90. Baring: Lindau, *A Waterloo Hero*, Appendix 1.

24 Lindau, p. 174.

25 Weiz: Glover, *Waterloo Archive*, Vol. II, pp. 188-9. Henninger: ibid., Vol. V, p. 139.

26 Von Scriba: Glover, Vol. II, pp. 107-9. Dehnel: Glover, Vol. V, p. 32.

27 Mercer: Siborne, *Letters*, No. 89, p. 216, and Mercer, *Journal*, pp. 170-2. Gronow: Llewellyn, *Waterloo Recollections*, p. 119. Schutte: Glover, Vol. II, p. 208.

28 Craddock, Manley and Smith: Dalton, *The Waterloo Roll Call*, pp. 132-3. Mill: Bois, *Men, Cohesion and Battle*, p. 33.

29 Stretton, Siborne, *Letters*, No. 177, p. 383. Mill: Bois, p. 33.

Chapter 9. The Crisis

Late afternoon to dusk. The 'Via Dolorosa' to Brussels

1 Cumberland Hussars: Seymour: Siborne, *Letters*, No. 9, p. 29. Cotton, *Voice from Waterloo*, p. 107, and Aidkin, *Waterloo Companion*, pp. 218, 223.

2 Verner, 'Reminiscences', p. 46. Jackson: *United Services Magazine*, Part 3, Nov. 1847, p. 356.

3 Tellier: Brett-James, *The Hundred Days*, pp. 196-7. Gibney: Uffindell and Corum, *On the Fields of Glory*, p. 55.

4 Simmons: Brett-James, p. 199, and Glover, *Waterloo Archive*, Vol. IV, pp. 219-20.

5 Heeley: Foulkes, *Dancing Into Battle*, p. 183. Simmons: Glover, Vol. IV, p. 220. Jackson: *United Services Magazine*, Part 3, 1847, p. 185.

6 Verner, 'Reminiscences', pp. 47-8.

7 Frye: Llewellyn, *Waterloo Recollections*, pp. 22-3. Châteaubriand: Brett-James, p. 124. Creevey, *Creevey Papers*, p. 146.

8 Ord: Glover, Vol. I, p. 228. Costello, *Edward Costello*, pp. 154-5. Heeley: Uffindell and Corum, p. 255.

9 Creevey, pp. 147-9. Ord: Glover, Vol. I, p. 228.

10 Civilian witness, Anon., *Waterloo, the Day After the Battle*, *United Service Journal*, 1829, Part 1, pp. 89-90. Davy: Glover, Vol. I, p. 219. James, ibid., p. 223.

11 Costello, p. 155. Davy: Glover, Vol. I, p. 219. Adair: from Gronow, in Llewellyn, *Waterloo Recollections*, pp. 128-9.

12 Costello, *Edward Costello*, pp. 155-6.

13 Jacobi: Glover, Vol. II, pp. 136-7.

7 pm to 7.30 pm. 'Quiver on the Beam'

14 Wheatley and Ompteda: *The Wheatley Diary*, pp. 67-71. Wheeler, *Letters*, p. 160.

15 Leach: Siborne, *Letters*, No. 160, p. 352. Stretton: ibid., No. 177, p. 382. Barnard: ibid., No. 158, p. 349. Calvert: ibid., No. 152, p. 341.

16 Drewe and note on casualties: Siborne, No. 174, pp. 378-9.

17 Cotton, *A Voice from Waterloo*, p. 135. Kellerman: Field, *French Perspective*, p. 184.

18 Macready: Brett-James, *The Hundred Days*, p. 154. Morris, *Thomas Morris*, pp. 80-2. Kincaid: Fitchett, *Wellington's Men*, pp. 134-5, 137.

19 Lieber, *Reminiscences*, pp. 159-60.

20 Coignet, *Captain Coignet*, p. 191.

21 Hayden: Aidkin, *Waterloo Companion*, p. 199.

22 De Mauduit: Field, *French Perspective*, Introduction.

23 23rd Regiment: Holmes, *Redcoat*, p. 125.

24 Drummers, Lord Hill Napoleonic Discussion Message Board, *The Myth of the Drummer Boy*, Internet, 17 Jan. 2009.

7.30 pm to 7.50 pm. 'La Garde Recule!' The Collapse

25 Pontécoulant: Field, *French Perspective*, pp. 188-9. Levavasseur and de Chamboulon: ibid., pp. 186-8.

26 Macready: Brett-James, *The Hundred Days*, pp. 154-5. Morris, *Thomas Morris*, p. 80. Leeke: Uffindell and Corum, *On the Fields of Glory*, p. 133.

27 Delort: Uffindell and Corum, p. 188. Franquin and Guillemin: Field, pp. 196-7. Macready: Brett-James, pp. 155-6.

28 Olfermann: Glover, *Waterloo Archive*, Vol. II, p. 200. Herzberg: Glover, Vol. V, p. 160.

29 Wellington and Maitland: Aidkin, *Waterloo Companion*, p. 397. Powell: Siborne, *Letters*, No. 109, p. 249.

30 Leeke: Aidkin, p. 395, and Sale, *Wellington's Waterloo Secret*, p. 13. Lennox: ibid., p. 35. Gawler: Siborne, *Letters*, No. 124, p. 285.

31 Chevalier: Forrest, *Napoleon's Men*, pp. 113-14. Hill and Leeke: Sale, pp. 14, 25.

32 Pontécoulant and British officer: Field, p. 206. Chapuis: ibid., p. 205.

33 Pelet and De Mauduit: Field, pp. 206, 214.

Chapter 10. The Road to Genappe

8.30 pm to 9.30 pm. 'Merde!'

1 Frazer and British officer: Uffindell and Corum, *On the Fields of Glory*, p. 137. Hugo, *Les Misérables*, quoted ibid., pp. 195-6.

2 Wellington, according to Leeke: Sale, *Wellington's Waterloo Secret*, p. 15. Kincaid, *Adventures*, p. 171.

3 Müffling, *Memoirs*, p. 250. Wellington: Sale, p. 17.

4 Kincaid, *Adventures*, pp. 170, 172. Morris, p. 85. Doring: Glover, *Waterloo Archive*, Vol. II, p. 168.

5 De Mauduit: Field, *French Perspective*, p. 208. De Stuers, ibid., p. 210. Petit, ibid., p. 225

6 Martin: Field, p. 216. Chapuis: ibid., p. 223. Rigau: ibid., p. 222. Barton: Siborne, *Letters*, No. 50, p. 117.

7 Grove: Uffindell and Corum, *On the Fields of Glory*, p. 139. Murray: Siborne, No. 76, p. 181.

8 Purvis and de Civrieux: Field, pp. 220-2.

9 Clay, *Narrative*, pp. 27-8.

10 Pattison: Webb-Carter, 'A Line Regiment at Waterloo', *Army Historical Research*, 43, (1965), p. 66.

11 Inniskillings: Bois, *Men, Cohesion and Battle*, pp. 173-4, and Dalton, *Waterloo Roll Call*, pp. 132-3. Wellington saved Tucker from being cashiered on reviewing his sentence, and Tucker transferred to the 18th Foot in May 1816. The two enlisted men were executed on 2 Aug. 1816.

12 Heyland letter: Glover, Vol. III, p. 140.

13 Kincaid, *Adventures*, p. 173. Lawrence, *A Dorset Soldier*, p. 112.

9.30 pm to 10.30 pm. 'A Thousand Shall Fall'

14 Medical figures: Aidkin, *Waterloo Companion*, p. 315.

15 Inniskillings medical assistance: Bois, *Men, Cohesion and Battle*, pp. 148-51.

16 Hasker: Glover, Vol. I, p. 21. Ponsonby: Glover, Vol. IV, pp. 57-9.

17 Elizabeth Gale: Crumplin, M., and Leaper, J., article, 'The Angels of Waterloo', Rifles Museum, Winchester.

18 Mrs Tucker: Bois, pp. 115, 151-2, and Dalton, *Waterloo Roll Call*, p. 134.

10.30 pm to midnight. On the Road to Genappe

19 Johnston: Glover, *Waterloo Archive*, Vol. I, p. 56.

20 Wheatley, *Diary*, pp. 72-6. Lindau, *A Waterloo Hero*, p. 175.

21 This has been the author's experience viewing Coalition commanders after the First Gulf War in Kuwait and Iraq in 1991 and the later NATO intervention in Bosnia in 1996.

22 Napoleon: Lachouque, *Waterloo*, p. 199.

23 De Mauduit: Field, *French Perspective*, pp. 226, 229, 234. Martin: ibid., p. 234.

24 Nieman: Glover, Vol. V, p. 170. Von Reuter: Glover, Vol. II, p. 214.

25 Jackson: Uffindell and Corum, *On the Fields of Glory*, p. 235. Von Pirch: ibid., p. 236. Gneisenau: ibid., p. 238.

26 Lemonnier-Delafosse: Uffindell and Corum, p. 237. Levavasseur: Field, p. 235.

27 Golz: Aidkin, *Waterloo Companion*, p. 404. De Chaboulon: Field, p. 236.

28 Coignet, *Captain Coignet*, p. 273. De Mauduit: Field, p. 237.

29 Wellington: Longford, *Wellington: The Years of the Sword*, p. 583. De Brack: Field, pp. 237-8.

30 Morris, *Thomas Morris*, p. 82. Wheatley, *Diary*, p. 76. Clay, *Narrative*, p. 29. Lindau, *Waterloo Hero*, p. 176.

31 Smith: Uffindell and Corum, p. 43. Civilian witness, Anon., *Waterloo, the Day After the Battle, United Service Journal*, 1829, Part 1, p. 90-1. Anton: Fitchett, *Wellington's Men*, pp. 304-5. Pattison: Uffindell and Corum, pp. 42-3. Teeth: Pollard, J., *Charge! The Interesting Bits of Military History*, p. 147.

32 Mercer, *Journal*, pp. 181-3.

33 Ponsonby: Glover, Vol. IV, p. 59.

Beyond 24 Hours

1 Creevey, *Creevey Papers*, pp. 150-1.

2 Drewe and Dunlop: Regimental Records and Description Book, Dalton, *Waterloo Roll Call*, pp. 132-4, and Bois, *Men, Cohesion and Battle*, pp. 132-4. Fortescue: ibid., pp. 173-4

3 National Archive Discharge Papers WO 97/581/52 dated 29 Jul. 1837. Ellis, J.D., *George Rose – An Examplary Soldier 73rd and 42nd Foot 1809-1837*, Scottish Military History website, Napoleonic War 1803-1815.

4 Morris, *Thomas Morris*, p. xi

5 Jackson: Lewis-Stempel, J., *The Autobiography of the British Soldier*, p. 163. Lawrence, *A Dorset Soldier*, p. 142.

6 Peltier: Crumplin and Starling, *A Surgical Artist at War*, pp. 68-70. Gronow: Llewellyn, *Waterloo Recollections*, pp. 129-30.

7 Playford: Glover, Vol. IV, pp. 38, 47. 'Tom', *A Soldier of the 71ˢᵗ*, p. 109.

8 Jacobi: Glover, Vol. II, p. 140

9 Fortescue affair: Bois, pp. 174-5.

10 Soldier's remains: *ABC News*, 16 June 2012.

11 Wellington: Sale, *Wellington's Waterloo Secret*, p. 42.

12 'Tom': letter, Edinburgh, May 1818; Lewis-Stempel, J., *The Autobiography of the British Soldier*, p. 163; also 'Tom', *A Soldier of the 71ˢᵗ*, Introduction.

Some of the Voices from Waterloo

Field-Marshal Gebhard von Blücher was the slightly addled 73-year-old commander of the Prussian army. He had survived a mutiny in his army barely weeks before and was undismayed despite the mauling administered by Napoleon at Ligny 48 hours before. He was no strategist, leaving that to 'The Brain', his chief of staff Count von Gneisenau, but Blücher had an instinctive feel for the battlefield and an exalted concept of honour. He would support his respected ally Wellington, come what may, and to do so was completing an epic forced march across inhospitable and difficult terrain with the bulk of his army from Wavre. Nobody realised it would take so long.

Captain Fortuné de Brack was an impulsive young lancer with the 2nd Chevau-Légers. He subscribed like many of his companions to the famous cavalry maxim 'Any Hussar not dead at thirty is a malingerer!'

Napoleon Bonaparte: Emperor of France and Commander of the French armies. Having thrashed the Prussians at Ligny he was confident that he would finish off Wellington's Allied army on the day and be in Brussels by nightfall. Although overweight he was still driven by steely self-ambition. He expected to win.

Corporal Louis Canler was an 18-year-old former drummer boy with the French 28th Line Regiment, who had made good. This was going to be his first big battle and he didn't really know what to expect. He observed the Mont St Jean ridge ahead with mixed feelings. He would advance with d'Erlon's I Corps.

Private Mathew Clay was in the Hougoumont farm complex with the 3rd Foot Guards. The horrors of the battle at Quatre-Bras and an extremely close shave 'not to be forgotten in haste' still bothered him. He was concerned that his musket was not working properly and he would not get a new one until soldiers around him began to die.

Captain Jean-Roch Coignet was a trusted member of Napoleon's Imperial Guard. He had even played the Empress at billiards, more concerned to observe her revealing cleavage than win. Coignet had already seen and confided to Napoleon that much of the British army was skulking out of sight in dead ground.

Rifleman Edward Costello of the 95th Rifles had been wounded at Quatre-Bras and was with the other evacuated wounded in the Grand Place in Brussels on the day of the battle, surrounded by horribly disfigured casualties.

Sergeant Edward Cotton was an astute observer of the battle, positioned with the 7th Hussars to the right of the line above Hougoumont. He would one day make a living relating his experiences and escorting tourists around the iconic battlefield.

Mrs Martha Deacon, the wife of the wounded Ensign Thomas Deacon of the 73rd Regiment, spent the night preceding and the morning of Waterloo plodding along the rain-swept Brussels road in the last stages of pregnancy with her three children in tow. She was still looking for her wounded husband.

Jean-Baptiste Decoster, the reluctant civilian Flemish guide forced to advise Napoleon, spent the day attached by his saddle bow to one of the Emperor's cuirassier escorts, nervously twitching at each gun report. He simply wanted to go home. His information was useless and his story unverified, but it was to contribute to a future living as a battlefield guide.

Sergeant Johann Doring, with the 28th Nassau Regiment on the left wing of Wellington's army, had spent a wet and miserable night enduring frequent false alarms about French attacks. His unit was edgy and jumpy. Better to fight than wait.

The 45-year-old **Captain Pierre Duthilt,** with the French 45th Line Regiment, was an experienced 20-year veteran of both the French Revolutionary and Napoleonic wars. He thought d'Erlon's attack formation against the Mont St Jean ridge was all wrong and made them very vulnerable to cavalry attack.

Pierre Guillot was the eagle-bearer of the French 45th Line Regiment. He had already been wounded three times on the Spanish Peninsula and then incarcerated on a British prison hulk. He had returned the year before and sought revenge.

Private Thomas Hasker, lined up with the 2nd Dragoon Guards across the Brussels road, had no idea why he was fighting or what for.

Lieutenant William Fortescue in the Irish 27th Inniskillings Regiment was a Protestant gentleman married to a Catholic wife with five children to support. His only hope of advancement was to survive his brother officers.

Second Lieutenant Heinrich von Gagern, with the 1st Nassau Light Infantry Regiment to the left centre of Wellington's line, had found his baptism of fire at Quatre-Bras 'scary'. It was moreover his first night ever in the open, and the retreat to Waterloo had been the first time he had marched on foot all day in his life. He was to experience worse this day.

Elizabeth Gale was the five-year-old daughter of Private Daniel Gale, with the 3/95th Rifles. She was in the Forest of Soignes behind the Mont St Jean farm assisting her mother Mary cutting and scraping lint dressings for the coming battle.

Captain John Hare, the acting commanding officer of the 27th Inniskilling Regiment in the centre of the Allied line, realised that with the absence of his commanding officer, this battle might transform his fortunes.

Captain Carl Jacobi, with the Hanoverian Lüneburg Battalion, reciprocated the obvious British disdain for foreigners and was still bridling over a lost staff appointment, when his unit alongside many others was reorganised under overall British command. He was no veteran and had been separated from his coat throughout the wet night because he had given it to a servant to carry. He longed for daylight and to get this battle over.

Captain John Kincaid, defending with the 95th Rifles in the sandpit next to La Haye Sainte alongside the Brussels road, was a perceptive observer of the battle's highlights, having already fought in Portugal and the Spanish Peninsula. He knew what he was doing.

Cornet Francis Kinchant, with the Scots Greys, having enjoyed the bordellos of Brussels and a privileged life, was looking forward with anticipation to the promotions that always followed such a large battle.

Sergeant William Lawrence from Dorset, a grizzled veteran of the Peninsula and North America, was serving with the 1/40th Foot in the centre of Wellington's line next to the 1/27th Inniskillings above La Haye Sainte. He was well aware of the risks but still taken aback by the bloody violence and intensity of this battle.

Franz Lieber, barely 16 years old, was a Landwehr volunteer with the Prussian Colburg Regiment. He had to bring his own musket and cast his own musket balls. He had killed his first man 48 hours before at Ligny, a disturbing experience, and been on the march retreating through rain ever since. He was now slithering across muddy tracks from Wavre to get to Waterloo. He and his companions wanted to avenge their comrades lost at Ligny.

Private Friedrich Lindau, in the 2nd King's German Legion Light Infantry Battalion, was a hardbitten Peninsula veteran who had allegedly killed a man in a bar brawl the year before. He was one of the defenders of La Haye Sainte, a sure marksman with a sharp eye for potential loot.

Private Joseph Lord, with the 2nd Life Guards lined up for a cavalry charge behind Picton's division by the Brussels road, was looking out for his brother in the same regiment. He hoped they would both survive the coming battle.

Lieutenant Jacques Martin, with the 45th French Line Regiment, was still bitter at the lack of shelter and the preferential treatment afforded senior officers during the miserable wet night before the battle. He was patriotic and anxious to prove himself after the pointless marching to and fro, which resulted in his I Corps missing the French victory at Ligny. It was a slow start to the day and he was impatient for the advance to begin, so they could finish off this British rearguard and enjoy the delights of Brussels by nightfall.

Sergeant Hippolyte de Mauduit, with the 1st Grenadier Regiment of the Imperial Guard, was waiting in reserve. An astute observer, he wondered why Napoleon was letting the British defend on ground of their own choosing, when the French were so much better at manoeuvre.

Captain Alexander Mercer commanded a Royal Horse Artillery battery and had no idea what was going to happen next, having arrived late the previous night after fighting the rearguard retreat to Waterloo during the summer storm. Were they going to fight or retire? No orders had been given.

Sergeant Thomas Morris, a Cockney with the 73rd Regiment, was to the right of the line in the same regiment as escaped Jamaican slave George Rose. He had already seen a British square slashed to pieces by French cavalry the day before at Quatre-Bras. They themselves had barely escaped the same fate under their inept Captain Robertson and had considerable misgivings about the approaching battle, serving under the same leader.

Marshal Michel Ney was known as 'Redhead' and the 'Red Lion' by French troops, who loved and respected him. Ironically he was suffering combat stress from the failed Russian campaign. Courage was no compensation for tactical failings. He commanded Napoleon's left wing during the advance towards Brussels and had missed the opportunity to follow closely behind Wellington's army when it slipped away after Quatre-Bras. Napoleon was incensed.

Private Thomas Playford, with the 2nd Life Guards cavalry, was about to charge through a French corps without once crossing swords with anyone.

Private George Rose, with the 2/73rd Regiment, was a resourceful man, an escaped slave from Jamaica, who had joined in 1809 and seen action in the Low Countries and at Quatre-Bras. Despite his race, if he could demonstrate proficient active service and read and write, he might be promoted, if he survived this coming battle.

Trooper John Shaw, with the 2nd Life Guards, was a renowned pugilist and champion prizefighter, who was the hero of the London mob. The Life Guards had adopted him as a sort of exotic recruiting mascot. Having been dispatched to pick up the unit's allocation of 'Hollands' gin before the battle, he was already drunk. He therefore viewed the coming battle with a degree of intoxicated equanimity. He loved a scrap.

Lieutenant George Simmons, with the 95th Rifles, had spent the previous night with a fellow soldier beneath a blanket smeared with mud to keep the rain out and had fried his breakfast inside a dead French cuirassier's armoured breast plate. His watch would stop when he was hit at four o'clock in the afternoon.

Captain William Verner, with the 7th Hussars, had already lost close friends the night before in the cavalry rearguard action at Genappe, fighting to protect the army's retreat to Waterloo during the violent summer storm. His preparation for this day had been standing a pointless picket in a soaking wheat field all night. He and his men willed the onset of daylight and a start to the battle.

Captain Friedrich Weiz was a company commander with the 1st Nassau Regiment in the left centre of Wellington's line. He was uneasy about how his raw recruits might respond to inevitable French cavalry attacks and nervous that his inexperienced battalion commander was totally unfamiliar with commanding his unit in battle.

Arthur Wellesley, the Duke of Wellington, was the gentleman 'player' commander of the Allied army. While he dressed the relaxed role, in reality he was the consummate professional. He was wary of Napoleon, having been out-generalled thus far in the campaign, and couldn't afford any more mistakes. Two thirds of his force were unproven foreigners and he was reliant upon yet another foreign contingent, the Prussians, to come to his aid. He was concerned.

Ensign Edmund Wheatley was with the King's German Legion in the centre of the Allied line. It was a Sunday and he was aware his beloved Eliza Brookes, whom he had courted in London, would be in church. He was disdainful of his own German officers and wondered why he had to kill the French opposite. He was taken aback at the horrific injuries that cannon fire inflicted on the first casualties.

Sergeant William Wheeler, like many of the Peninsula veterans with the 51st Regiment to the right of Wellington's line, thought the rain from the summer storm was a good omen. It had been the precursor to several of Wellington's victories in Spain. He was an astute professional observer and always on the lookout for loot.

Bibliography

General Published Sources

Aidkin, M., *The Waterloo Companion* (Aurum, 2001)

Bernard, G., and Lachaux, G., *Waterloo Relics* (Histoire & Collections, 2005)

Boulger, D.C., *The Belgians at Waterloo* (Naval & Military Press, 1900)

Brett-James, E., *The Hundred Days* (Macmillan, 1964)

Busk, H., *The Rifle and How to Use It* (Routledge, 1860)

Caldwell, G., and Cooper, R., *Rifle Green at Waterloo* (Bugle Horn, 1990)

Crumplin, M.K.H., and Starling, P., *A Surgical Artist at War* (Royal College of Surgeons, Edinburgh, 2005)

Divall, C., *Redcoats Against Napoleon* (Pen & Sword, 2009)

—— *Inside the Regiment* (Pen & Sword, 2011)

—— *Napoleonic Lives* (Pen & Sword, 2012)

Field, A.W., *Waterloo: The French Perspective* (Pen & Sword, 2012)

Forrest, A., *Napoleon's Men* (Hambledon & London, 2002)

Foulkes, N., *Dancing Into Battle* (Weidenfeld & Nicolson, 2006)

Gale, I., *Four Days in June* (historical novel, HarperCollins, 2006)

Hibbert, C., *Waterloo* (Cooper Square Press, 2003)

Hofschröer, P., *1815: The Waterloo Campaign – The German Victory* (Greenhill, 1999)

—— *Wellington's Smallest Victory* (Faber & Faber, 2004)

Holmes, R., *Redcoat* (HarperCollins, 2002)

Lachouque, *Waterloo* (Arms & Armour Press, 1972)

Longford, E., *Wellington: The Years of the Sword* (Panther, 1971)

Neuburg, V., *Gone For a Soldier* (Cassell, 1989)

Parkinson, R., *The Hussar General* (Wordsworth, 2001)

Paget, J., and Saunders, D., *Hougoumont* (Pen & Sword, 2001)

Price, S., *If You're Reading This...* (Frontline Books, 2011)

Roberts, A., *Napoleon and Wellington* (Phoenix Press, 2002)

Rogers, H.C.B., *Napoleon's Army* (Purnell Books, 1974)

Sale, N., *Wellington's Waterloo Secret* (private pub., 2005)

Scott, A.F., *Every One A Witness. The Georgian Age* (Martins, 1970)

Uffindell, A., and Corum, M., *On the Fields of Glory* (Greenhill, 1996)

Wason, D., *Battlefield Detectives* (Granada, 2003)

Weller, J., *Wellington at Waterloo* (Greenhill, 1992)

Windrow, M., and Hook, R., *The Footsoldier* (Oxford, 1982)

Nineteenth-Century Published Memoirs and Personal Accounts

Clay, M. (Glover, G., ed.), *A Narrative of the Battles of Quatre-Bras and Waterloo; with the Defence of Hougoumont* (Ken Trotman, 2006)

Coignet, J.-R., *Captain Coignet* (Leonaur, 2007)

Costello, E. (Brett-James, E., ed.), *Edward Costello* (Longmans, 1967)

Cotton, E., *A Voice from Waterloo* (Leonaur, 2007)

Creevey, T. (Gore J., ed.), *The Creevey Papers* (Folio Society, 1970)

Eaton, C.A., De Lancey, M., and Smith, J., *Ladies of Waterloo* (Leonaur, 2009)

Fitchett, W.H., ed., *Wellington's Men* (Smith, Elder, 1900)

French eyewitness, Anon., *Journal of the Three Days of the Battle of Waterloo* (Leonaur, 2010)

Hay, W., *Reminiscences 1808–1815 Under Wellington* (Simpkin, Marshall, Hamilton, Kent, 1901)

Kincaid, J., *Adventures in the Rifle Brigade and Random Shots from a Rifleman* (Richard Drew, 1981)

Lawrence, W., (Hathaway, E., ed.), *A Dorset Soldier* (Spellmount, 1993)

Leach, J., *Rough Sketches of the Life of an Old Soldier* (London, 1831)

Lieber, F., *Reminiscences, Addresses and Essays*, Vol. 1 of *Miscellaneous Writings, The Battle of Waterloo* (Philadephia, 1881)

Lindau, F., *A Waterloo Hero* (Frontline Books, 2009)

Llewellyn, F., ed., *Waterloo Recollections* (Leonaur, 2007)

Marbot, J.-B., *The Exploits of Baron de Marbot* (Constable, 2000)

Mercer, A., *Journal of the Waterloo Campaign* (Greenhill, 1985)

Morris, T. (Selby, J., ed.), *Thomas Morris* (Longmans, 1967)

Müffling, C. (Hofschröer, P., ed.), *The Memoirs of Baron von Müffling* (Greenhill Books, 1997)

Tom (Hibbert, C., ed.), *A Soldier of the 71st* (Leo Cooper, 1975)

Wheatley, E. (Hibbert, C., ed.), *The Wheatley Diary* (Longmans, 1964)

Wheeler, W. (Liddle Hart, B.H., ed.), *The Letters of Private Wheeler* (Michael Joseph, 1951)

Archive Sources

Published

Dalton, C., *The Waterloo Roll Call* (Arms & Armour Press, 1971)

Frazer, S. (Sabine, E., ed), *Letters of Sir Augustus Simon Frazer* (Longman, 1859)

Franklin, J., ed., *Waterloo: Netherlands Correspondence* (1815 Ltd, 2010)

Glover, G., ed., *The Waterloo Archive* (Frontline Books): Vol. I *British Sources* (2010); Vol. II *German Sources* (2010); Vol. III *British Sources* (2011); Vol. IV *British Sources* (2012); Vol. V *German Sources* (2013)

Siborne, H.L., *The Waterloo Letters* (Leonaur, 2009)

Unpublished

Bois, M., *Men, Cohesion and Battle: The Inniskilling Regiment at Waterloo* (MA Thesis, University of Louisville, 2006)

Evening Post, Vol. XV, Issue 52, 3 March 1877. Facsimile

Regimental rolls and discharge papers as annotated in the notes

Periodicals

Anon. Eyewitness, 'Waterloo, the Day After the Battle', *United Service Journal*, Part 1 (1829)

Blumberg, A., 'To Hell with the Prussians', *MHQ*, 15, No. 1 (Autumn 2002)

Hodge, F.R., and Marquis of Anglesey, 'Correspondence Concerning the Death of Major Hodge, 7th Hussars, at Genappe 17 Jun 1815', *Army Historical Research*, 43 (1965)

Hunter, R., 'Lambert's Brigade', *War Monthly* (1974)

McGuffie, T., 'The British Soldier at Waterloo', *History Today*, 15 (1965)

Meistrich, I., 'En Avant!', *MHQ*, Vol. 1, No. 3 (Spring 1989)

Neumann, J., 'Great Historical Events That Were Significantly Affected By The Weather. Part 11: Meteorological Aspects of the Battle of Waterloo', *Bulletin of the American Meteorological Society* (1993)

Staff Officer, 'Recollections of Waterloo', *Colburn's United Services Magazine*, Part 3 (1847)

Verner, W., 'Reminiscences of William Verner 7th Hussars', Society for Army Historical Research, Special Pub. No. 8 (1965)

Webb-Carter, B.W., 'A Line Regiment at Waterloo', *Army Historical Research*, 43 (1965)

Wheeler, D., and Demarée, G., 'The Weather of the Waterloo Campaign 16 to 18 June 1815: Did it change the course of history?', Royal Meterological Society pub. *Weather*, 60, No. 6 (June 2005)

Film and TV

Holmes, R., Granada BBC Wales, *Wellington: The Iron Duke* (2009)

Granada TV, *Battlefield Detectives* (2003)

Line of Fire Animated History Series, *Waterloo* (2003)

Pen & Sword Military Series, *The Waterloo Collection*. Saunders, T., Cooper, G., Peters, M., Duff, A., Toogood, F., and Dormer, T.

—— *Ligny and Quatre-Bras*

—— *Hougoumont and D'Erlon's Attack*

—— *Cavalry Charge: La Haie Sainte and Plancenoit*

—— *Victory and Pursuit*

Index

Entries in *italics* indicate illustrations, photographs and maps.

Also available in the 24 Hours series:

24 Hours at Agincourt by Michael Jones
SEPTEMBER 2015

24 Hours at the Somme by Robert Kershaw
MAY 2016